WHITE EAGLES

The Aircraft, Men and Operations of the Polish Air Force 1918-1939

Bartołomiej Belcarz & Robert Pęczkowski

HIKOKI PUBLICATIONS

First published in Great Britain in 2001 by
Hikoki Publications Ltd
Ashtree House, Station Road, Ottringham, East Yorkshire, HU12 0BJ
Tel: 01964 624223 Fax: 01964 624666
E-mail: hikoki@dircon.co.uk
Website: http://www.hikokiwarplanes.com

ISBN 1 902109 73 2

Edited by Martin Derry & Sue Bushell
Translation by Wojtek Matusiak
Artwork by Artur Juszczak & Jon Field
Design by Sue Bushell
Printed in Great Britain by
Ian Allan Printing, Hersham

Distribution & Marketing
in UK & Europe by
Midland Publishing
(a part of the Ian Allan Group)
4 Watling Drive, Sketchley Lane Industrial Estate,
Hinckley, Leics, LE10 3EY
Tel: 01455 233747 Fax: 01455 233737
E-mail: midlandbooks@compuserve.com

Distribution & Marketing
in USA & Canada by
Howell Press Inc
1713-2D Allied Lane, Charlottesville,
Virginia 22903-5336, USA
Tel: (001) 804 977 4006 Fax: (001) 804 971 7204
E-mail: HowellPres@aol.com

Caption to photograph on title page: *PWS-26 aircraft were painted olive-green or silver. This photograph shows silver aircraft of the Szkoła Lotnicza at Dęblin. (Kopański)*

DEDICATION

Naszym najbliższym

– To our families

ACKNOWLEDGEMENTS

For this book you should blame Barry Ketley, as he is really the 'father' of it. Thanks to his ideas and our naivety we started this project. Full of enthusiasm, over two years ago we started our work, but it was more difficult than we expected.

During this project we were lucky enough to meet many very interesting and helpful people, who using their knowledge and experience gave us a lot of help. Without their help our book could not have been finished.

We would like to express our thanks to: Tomasz Kopański for his help in providing photos and much information; Andrzej Olejko for his help in our work regarding Polish Navy Aviation; Andrzej Glass for the first ideas of how this book should be, and his experience; Jan Hafmann and Krzysztof Radwan from the Muzeum Lotnictwa Polskiego in Krakow for many interesting photos; Roger Wallsgrove for many things, but most of all for his patience, and the hospitality offered over the years by him and his wife Di — your friendship is inestimable; and Artur Juszczak, our best friend for many years, author of the colour profiles in this book. (We hope that our text is good enough to match your drawings)

Also we would like to thank many more who helped with our work: Wiesław Bączkowski; Mariusz Konarski; Jan Koniarek; Wojtek Matusiak and Jerzy Pawlak.

CONTENTS

POLISH MILITARY TERMS - TRANSLATIONS

The following list gives English translations of the Polish unit names and official titles used in the book. Those not directly related to aviation matters are given in Italics. Where several similar names appear in the text, differing only by number identifiers, the main body of the name is given here, with the numbers omitted.

A Polish Eskadra is approximately equivalent to a British WWII **Squadron** (6–12 aircraft).

A Polish Dywizjon (Dyon) is approximately equivalent to a British WWII **Wing** (2–3 squadrons).

A Polish Pułk Lotniczy is an Air Regiment.

Polish names of Polish air units are used throughout the text.

Polish name	English translations
Armia	*Army*
Awiacja I Korpusu Polskiego	Aviation of the I Polish Corps
Awiacyjny Oddział Wojsk Polskich	Aviation Unit of the Polish Forces
Batalion Uzupełnień	Replacement Battalion
Baza Lotnictwa Morskiego	Naval Aviation Base
Baza Lotnicza	Air Base
Centralne Składy Lotnicze	Central Aircraft Depot
Centralne Warsztaty Lotnicze	Central Aircraft Works
Centralne Warsztaty Wojskowe	Central Military Works
Centrum Wyszkolenia Lotnictwa	Aviation Training Centre
Czechosłowacka Eskadra Rozpoznawcza	Czechoslovak Reconnaissance Squadron
Ćwiczebna Eskadra Pilotażu	Flying Training Squadron
Department Aeronautyki Ministerstwa Spraw Wojskowych	Aeronautics Department of the Ministry of Military Affairs
Department Spraw Morskich Ministerstwa Spraw Wojskowych	Naval Affairs Department of the Ministry of Military Affairs
Detaszowany Dywizjon Lotniczo-Zwiadowczy	Detached Air-Scouting Wing
Detaszowany Dywizjon Lotniczy	Detached Air Wing
Dowódca Lotnictwa	Aviation Commander
Dowódca Wojsk Lotniczych	Army Air Forces Commander
Dowódca Wybrzeża Morskiego	Sea Coast Commander
Dowództwo Armii Wielkopolskiej	Wielkopolska Front HQ
Dowództwo Floty i Służb Nabrzeżnych	Fleet and Coastal Services HQ
Dowództwo Frontu Wielkopolskiego	Wielkopolska Front HQ
Dowództwo Lotnictwa	Aviation HQ
Dowództwo Lotnictwa Ministerstwa Spray Wojskowych	Aviation HQ of the Ministry of Mililtary Affairs
Dowództwo Okręgu Korpusu Nr 1	No 1 Corps District HQ
Dowództwo Wojsk Aeronautycznych	Aeronautical Forces HQ
Dowództwo Wybrzeża Morskiego	Sea Coast HQ
Dywizja Strzelców Polskich	*Division of Polish Fusiliers*
Dywizjon Bombowy	Bomber Wing
Dywizjon Bombowy Lekki	Light Bomber Wing
Dywizjon Krakowski	Krakow Wing
Dywizjon Liniowy	Line Wing
Dywizjon Lotniczy (Dyon Lotniczy)	Air Wing
Dywizjon Myśliwski	Fighter Wing
Dywizjon Niszczycielski	Destroyer Wing
Dywizjon Rozpoznawczy	Reconnaissance Wing

Polish name	English translations
Dywizjon Szkolny	Training Wing
Dywizjon Towarzyszący	Accompanying Wing
Dywizjon Warszawski	Warsaw Wing
Dywizjon Zapasowy	Replacement Wing
Eskadra Bojowa	Combat Squadron
Eskadra Bombowa	Bomber Squadron
Eskadra Bombowa Lekka	Light Bomber Squadron
Eskadra Breguetów (Escadrille Breguet)	Breguet Squadron
Eskadra Ćwiczebna Obserwatorów SPL Dęblin	Observers' Training Squadron of PSL Dęblin
Eskadra Ćwiczebna Pilotażu SPL Dęblin	Flying Training Squadron of SPL Dęblin
Eskadra Korpusu Obrony Pogranicza	Border Defence Corps Squadron
Eskadra Liniowa	Line Squadron
Eskadra Lotnicza	Air Squadron
Eskadra Lotnicza 4 Dywizji	Air Squadron of the 4th Division
Eskadra Łącznikowa	Liaison Squadron
Eskadra Łącznikowa Dowództwa Obrony Lwowa	Liaison Squadron of Lwów Defence HQ
Eskadra Myśliwska	Fighter Squadron
Eskadra Myśliwska im. 'Tadeusza Kościuszki'	Fighter Squadron 'Tadeusz Kosciuszko'
Eskadra Myśliwska Nocna	Night Fighter Squadron
Eskadra Niszczycielska	Destroyer (Bomber) Squadron
Eskadra Niszczycielska Nocna	Night Destroyer Squadron
Eskadra Obserwacyjna	Spotting Squadron
Eskadra Rozpoznawcza	Reconnaissance Squadron
Eskadra Salmsonów (Escadrille Salmson)	Salmson Squadron
Eskadra Spadów (Escadrille Spad)	Spad Squadron
Eskadra Szkolna	Elementary Training Squadron
Eskadra Szkolno-Treningowa	Elementary/Advanced Training Squadron
Eskadra Toruńska	Toruń Squadron
Eskadra Towarzysząca	Accompanying Squadron
Eskadra Treningowa	Advanced Training Squadron
Eskadra Warszawska	Warsaw Squadron
Eskadra Wywiadowcza	Reconnaissance Squadron
Francuska Szkoła Pilotów	French Pilots' School
Generalny Inspektor Sił Zbrojnych	General Inspector of the Armed Forces
Główna Kadra Lotnicza	Main Air Cadre
Główny Inspektorat Sił Zbrojnych	Chief Inspectorate of the Armed Forces
Grupa Aeronautyczna	Aeronautical Group
Grupa Lotnicza	Air Group
Grupa Operacyjna	Operational Group
Inspektor Obrony Powietrznej Panstwa	State Air Defence Inspector
Inspektor Wojsk Lotniczych	Army Air Forces Inspector
Inspektorat Obrony Powietrznej Panstwa	State Air Defence Inspectorate
Inspektorat Wojsk Lotniczych	Air Forces Inspectorate
Instytut Badań Technicznych Lotnictwa	Aviation Technical Research Institute
Kierownictwo Marynarki Wojennej	Navy Direction
Komendant Obrony Powietrznej Warsawy	Warsaw Air Defence Commandant
Komisja Wojskowa	Military Commission
Komitet do Spraw Uzbrojenia i Sprzętu	Armament and Equipment Committee
Kompania Balonowa	Balloon Company

Polish name	English translations
Kompania Balonów Obserwacyjnych	Spotting Balloon Company
Kompania Balonów Zaporowych	Barrage Balloon Company
Kompania Szkolna	Training Company
Korpus Ochrony Pogranicza	*Border Defence Corps*
Korpus Polski	*Polish Corps*
Lotnictwo Armii 'Pomorze' ('Poznań', etc.)	'Pomorze' ('Poznań', etc.) Army Aviation
Lotnictwo Armijne	Army Aviation
Lotnictwo Dyspozycyjne	Discretionary Aviation
Lotnictwo Morskie	Naval Aviation
Lotnictwo Batalion Uzupełnień	Air Replacement Battalion
Lubelska Wytwórnia Samolotów	Lublin Aircraft Factory
Lwowska Grupa Lotnicza	Lwów Air Group
'Mazowiecka' Brygada Kawalerii	'Mazowsze' Cavalry Brigade
Ministerstwo Spraw Wojskowych	Ministry of Military Affairs
Morska Eskadra Obserwacyjna	Naval Spotting Squadron
Morska Eskadra Wielosilnikowa	Naval Multi-engine Squadron
Morska Szkoła Pilotów	Naval Pilots' School
Morski Dywizjon Lotniczy	Naval Air Division
Naczelna Komenda Obrony Lwowa	High Command of Lwów Defence
Naczelne Dowództwo	Supreme HQ
Naczelny Dowódca Lotnictwa	Supreme Aviation Commander
Niższa Szkoła Pilotażu w Warszawie	Elementary Flying School in Warsaw
Niższa Szkoła Pilotów	Elementary Pilots' School
Niższa Szkoła Pilotów w Krakowie	Elementary Pilots' School in Krakow
'Nowogródzka' Brygada Kawalerii	'Nowogródek' Cavalry Brigade
Obóz Warowny	Entrenched Camp
Oddział Lotnictwa Myśliwskiego Bazy Nr 3	Fighter Aviation Outfit of Base no. 3
Oddział Lotniczy w Lublinie	Air Outfit in Lublin
Oddział Obrony Ladowej	Land Defence Outfit
Oddział Portowy	Port Outfit
Oddział Wojsk Polskich na Kubaniu	*Polish Forces Outfit at Kuban*
Oficerska Szkoła Aeronautyczna	Officer Aeronautical School
Państwowe Zakłady Lotnicze	State Aircraft Works
Park Lotniczy	Aircraft Park
Park Ruchomy	Mobile Park
Pluton Lotniczy	Air Platoon
Pluton Lotniczy Warszawskiej Brygady Pancerno-Motorowej	Air Platoon of the 'Warsaw' Armoured-Motorised Brigade
Pluton Łącznikowy	Liaison Platoon
Pluton Łącznikowy Dowódcy Ladowej Obrony Wybrzeża	Liaison Platoon of the Land Coastal Defence Commander
Pluton Łącznikowy Naczelnego Dowódcy Lotnictwa	Liaison Platoon of the Supreme Aviation Commander
Pluton Łącznikowy Prezydium Rady Ministrów	Liaison Platoon of the Cabinet
Pluton Rozpoznawczy Lotniczy	Air Reconnaissance Platoon
Pluton Rzeczny Wodnopłatowców	River Hydroplane Platoon
Pluton Samolotów Towarzyszących	Accompanying Aircraft Platoon
Podlaska Wytwórnia Samolotów	Podlasie Aircraft Factory
Polska Organizacja Wojskowa	*Polish Military Organisation*
Polska Korpus Interwencyjny	*Polish Intervention Corps*
Polski Obóz Lotniczy	Polish Air Camp
Polski Oddział Awiacyjny	Polish Aviation Unit

Polish name	English translations
Polski Oddział Awiacyjny Bojowy	Polish Combat Aviation Unit
Polskie Zakłady Skoda	Polish Skoda Works
Pomorska Brygada Kawalerii	'Pomerania' Cavalry Brigade
Pułk Bombowy	Bomber Regiment
Pułk Liniowy	Line Regiment
Pułk Lotniczy	Air Regiment
Pułk Myśliwski	Fighter Regiment
Pułkowa Szkoła Pilotażu	Regimental Flying School
PZL Wytwórnia Platowców Nr 1 (Nr 2)	PZL Airframe Factory no.1 (no. 2)
PZL Wytwórnia Silników Nr 1 (Nr 2)	PZL Engine Factory no. 1 (no. 2)
Rada Obrony Państwa	State Defence Council
Rada Regencyjna	*Regency Council*
Referat Lotnictwa Morskiego Departamentu Spraw Morskich	Naval Aviation Section of the Naval Affairs Department
Rezerwowa Eskadra Rozpoznawcza SPL Dęblin	Reserve Reconnaissance Squadron of SPL Dęblin
Ruchomy Park Lotniczy	Mobile Aircraft Park
Rzeczna Eskadra Lotnicza	River Air Squadron
Rzeczny Pluton Lotniczy	River Air Platoon
Samodzielna Eskadra Bombowa	Independent Bomber Squadron
Samodzielna Grupa Operacyjna	*Independent Operational Group*
Sekcja Ćwiczeń	Exercise Section
Sekcja Foto	Photo Section
Sekcja Radiolotnicza	Air/radio Section
Seckcja Żeglugi Napowietrznej	Aerial Navigation Section
Seckcja Żeglugi Napowietrznej Departamentu Technicznego Ministerstwa Spraw Wojskowych	Aerial Navigation Section of the Technical Department of the Ministry of Military Affairs
Służba Techniczna Wojsk Polskich	Technical Service of the Polish Armed Forces
Szef Departamentu Aeronautyki Ministerstwa Spraw Wojskowych	Head of the Aeronautics Department of the Ministry of Military Affairs
Szef Departamentu IV Żeglugi Powietrznej Ministerstwa Spraw Wojskowych	Head of the Aerial Navigation Department IV of the Ministry of Military Affairs
Szef Departamentu Lotnictwa Ministerstwa Spraw Wojskowych	Head of the Aeronautics Department of the Ministry of Military Affairs
Szef Departamentu Żeglugi Powietrznej Ministerstwa Spraw Wojskowych	Head of the Aerial Navigation Department of the Ministry of Military Affairs
Szef Kierownictwa Marynarki Wojennej	Head of the Navy Direction
Szef Lotnictwa Polowego	Head of the Field Aviation
Szef Sekcji Żeglugi Napowietrznej Ministerstwa Spraw Wojskowych	Head of the Aerial Navigation Section of the Ministry of Military Affairs
Szef Stacji Lotniczej Ławica	Head of Ławica Air Station
Szef Sztabu Generalnego	Chief of the General Staff
Szefostwo Lotnictwa przy Naczelnym Dowództwie WP	Aviation HQ at the Supreme HQ of the Polish Army
Szkolma Eskadra Szkoły Obserwatorów Lotniczych	Air Observers' School Training Squadron
Szkoła Lotnicza	Flying School
Szkoła Obserwatorów Lotniczych	Air Observers' School
Szkoła Obsługi Lotniczej	Air Servicing School
Szkoła Oficerska Aeronautów-Obserwatorów	Officer School of Aeronauts-Observers
Szkoła Pilotażu	Flying School
Szkoła Pilotów	Pilots' School
Szkoła Podchorążych Lotnictwa – Dęblin	Aviation Cadet Officers' School – Dęblin
Sztab Główny	Main Staff
Sztab Lotniczy przy Sztabie Głównym	Air Staff at the Main Staff
Tymczasowy Komitet Rewolucyjny Polski	*Temporary Polish Revolutionary Committee*
Tymczasowy Naczelnik Panstwa	*Temporary Head of the State*
Warsztaty Naprawcze	Repair Workshops
Wielkopolska Eskadra Bojowa	Wielkopolska Combat Squadron

Polish name	English translations
Wielkopolska Eskadra Lotnicza	Wielkopolska Air Squadron
Wielkopolska Eskadra Polna	Wielkopolska Field Squadron
Wielkopolska Grupa Lotnicza	Wielkopolska Air Group
Wojska Lotnicze	Army Air Forces
Wojsko Polskie	Polish Army
Wojskowa Szkoła Lotnicza	Military Air School
'Wolyńska' Brygada Kawalerii	'Wolyn' Cavalry Brigade
Wódz Naczelny	Supreme Commander
Wydzielony Dywizjon Towarzyszący	Separate Accompanying Wing
Wydzielony Oddział Lotniczy	Separate Air Unit
Wyższa Szkoła Lotników	Advanced School of Airmen
Wyższa Szkoła Pilotażu	Advanced Flying School
Wyższa Szkoła Pilotażu Grudziądz-Ułęż	Advanced Flying School
Zespół Lotniczy Dowództwa Obrony Warszawy	Warsaw Defence HQ Air Team
Zgrupowanie Balonów Zaporowych	Barrage Balloon Groupement
Zgrupowanie Bombowe	Bomber Groupement
Zgrupowanie Myśliwskie	Fighter Groupement
Zjednoczone Grupy Lotnicze	United Air Groups
Związek Lotników	Airmen Association

Polish Air Force ranks

Polish Air Force ranks were identical to ranks in the army. Flying personnel were identified by adding the word pilot (*pil.*) or obserwator (*obs.* – English observer/navigator).

Polish rank	Polish abbreviation	direct translation	RAF equivalent
Szeregowy	szer.	private	aircraftsman
Starszy szeregowy	st. szer.	senior private	leading aircraftsman
Kapral	krp.	corporal	senior aircraftsman
Plutonowy	plut.	platoon commander	corporal
Sierżant	sierż.	sergeant	sergeant
Starszy sierżant	st. sierż.	senior sergeant	flight sergeant
Chorąży	chor.	warrant officer	warrant officer
Podporucznik	ppor.	sub-lieutenant	pilot officer
Porucznik	por.	lieutenant	flying officer
Kapitan	kpt.	captain	flight lieutenant
Major	mjr	major	squadron leader
Podpułkownik	ppłk.	sub-colonel	wing commander
Pułkownik	płk.	colonel	group captain
Generał brygady	gen. bryg.	brigadier general	air commodore
Generał dywizji	gen. dyw.	divisional general	air vice marshal
General lotnictwa	gen. lotn.	air force general	air marshal
Generał armii	Gen. armii	army general	Air Chief Marshal

INTRODUCTION

Poland – a Central European state whose history has always been determined by its geographical position. In 1795 the Polish people lost territorial and political independence to its neighbours: Germany, Russia and Austria. This situation continued for 123 years, until the end of World War I. At the end of 1918 Poland regained independence. This was the time of the creation of the Polish Air Force, simultaneously with the creation of the modern Polish state. The young state would face many problems, one of which was the struggle to establish its borders. In December 1918 Polish authorities controlled the lands of two previously occupied zones: those belonging to Russia and Austria. Wielkopolska was engulfed by an anti-German uprising which resulted in this province being incorporated into Poland in February 1919. Eventually, the shape of Poland would be decided at the Paris Conference (German border) and in combat (Russian border). The Polish delegation presented its requests on 29 January 1919 at the assembly of the Supreme Council during the Paris Conference. As a result of the work of a special commission headed by the Frenchman J. Cambon it was decided that Gdańsk (Danzig) would become a so called Free City, under the management of the League of Nations, while the status of Warmia and Mazury would be voted in plebiscites.

1: Karaś *aircraft of 22 and 21 Eskadra Liniowa (Rozpoznawcza) photographed from the roof of a hangar at Aleksandrowice airfield near Bielsko in October 1938 (Kopański)*

The situation in the East was much more difficult. Initially it was the German-Russian front line that formed the border. When the Germans started evacuation of their units, their positions were taken over by Polish troops which resulted in encounters with Bolshevik units. 17 February 1919 saw the first, victorious, skirmish at Maniewicze, which marked the beginning of the Polish-Russian war that would continue until the end of 1920.

The turn of 1918 was also difficult for the emerging armed forces. In November 1918 these comprised nine thousand soldiers, in February 1919 – 150,000, in September 1919 – 600,000 soldiers.

Apart from the border issue and the difficulties related to forming the foundations of an army, there was one more important question – establishment of strong and uniform state authorities. Suffice it to say that at the very beginning there were four different administrations aspiring to the role of the political centre. Eventually Józef Piłsudski took the principal position in the country, assuming the title of Tymczasowy Naczelnik Panstwa (Polish unit names, ranks, and official titles are explained in preface). Poland was differentiated in economical, social and political terms. The republican system of the new state suffered from political confrontation between the smaller and bigger parties. This resulted in the assassination of the first democratically elected president, Gabriel Narutowicz (16 August 1922). Political struggle continued for several years more, until it was stopped by the coup d'etat by Piłsudski on 12-14 May 1926. Three days of fighting cost 379 dead, and 900 wounded. This started the authoritarian rule of Piłsudski which lasted until his death in 1935.

The international situation of Poland in the first half of the 1920s was similar to that of Hungary, Finland, Estonia, Latvia, Lithuania, and other countries established after World War I. Polish policy remained under the strong influence of France which wanted to see Poland as the guarantor and representative of its own interests in Central Europe. This way the French, unlike the British, wanted to weaken the position of Germany. The Versailles system was supposed to guarantee a lasting peace in Europe. However, as soon as April 1922 (the Rapallo Treaty) the first defect appeared on the new European map. The future would prove that the German-Russian treaty signed there would have a tragic impact on the fate of Poland. Isolated on the international scene, Germany and Russia tried to overcome this, and the unstable situation in Europe was an advantage for them. The attempt to drag Germany away from that alliance by France and Britain resulted in the signing of the Rhine Pact at Locarno (1925). This recognised Germany as a partner in talks. France, Britain and Belgium received confirmation of the inviolability of Western borders of Germany, while Poland and Czechoslovakia, also participating in the talks, failed to obtain that. At the same time the German Foreign Minister, G. Stressemann, explained this fact by stating that the Eastern border of Germany had to be revised, and both Danzig and the 'corridor' that linked Poland with the Baltic Sea had to return to Germany. In 1926 Germany became a member of the League of Nations, and their position in Europe was getting stronger. Piłsudski based Polish foreign policy on the assumption that no major changes would take place in Europe. He believed that the most important factor for Poland was the position of France towards Germany, as the alliance between Poland and France was based on this.

In 1934 Poland signed with Germany a mutual non-aggression declaration for 10 years. Also the Polish-Soviet non-aggression treaty from 1932 was prolonged in the same year for a similar period. In 1935 Piłsudski died. Although apparently this fact had little impact on the international scene, it would have its effect on Poland's relations with its neighbours.

It was at that time that German demands towards neighbouring countries started to grow. Occupation of Czechoslovakia led to the change of the liberal policies of France and Britain towards Hitler, as set by the Munich treaty of 1938. This fact forced Poland's allies, France and Britain, to sign alliance pacts. The allies tried also to include the USSR, conducting talks with Stalin between April and August 1939. At the same time Stalin negotiated with the Germans, considering the interest of Western powers a trump card with Hitler. Eventually a few days before the talks with the Western allies were broken off, on 23 August the Ribbentrop-Molotov pact was signed, including its secret protocol. This document sanctioned another partition of Poland, this time between the Third Reich and the USSR.

2: *Albatros B IIa no. 4 with an old emblem of Oficerska Szkoła Obserwatorów Lotnictwa (an eye) and Polish Navy flag applied on the Polish national markings. In the cockpit are, left to right,* por. mar. *W. Doński and* kpt. mar. pil. *B. Filanowicz. Puck 20 July 1921 (Konarski)*

THE POLISH AIR FORCE 1918-1921

The first Polish air units were created before the Polish state was reborn. In the summer of 1917, after the fall of the Tsar, the I Corps of *gen.* Józef Dowbór-Muśnicki started forming I Polski Oddział Awiacyjny (Polish Aviation Unit) at Mińsk in Byelorussia. Command of the outfit was given to *kpt. pil.* Zygmunt Studziński. Initially the unit had one aircraft, a training Nieuport. Later on, at Bobruysk, a train was captured which carried aircraft equipment. This, and continuous training of pilots, in March 1918 allowed the unit to expand into the Awiacja I Korpusu Polskiego (Aviation of the I Polish Corps) under command of *ppłk pil.* Piotr Abakanowicz. Thanks to the captured equipment of the disintegrating Russian Army, by the spring of 1918 the unit was at full strength. On 2 April 1918 ceremonial consecration of the aircraft took place in the presence of the Corps Commander, *gen.* Dowbór-Muśnicki. Unfortunately, the Corps was demobilised and disarmed by the Germans, and the aircraft were destroyed by Polish pilots to prevent them from falling into German hands. The Corps' last orders were issued on 20 June 1920. Demobilised pilots went to Kuban, where another air unit was formed, while some of them arrived in Warsaw.

The next air unit was formed within II Korpus Polski at Kamieniec Podolski. This took the name of I Polski Oddział Awiacyjny Bojowy, and was commanded by *rtm.*[1] *pil.* Tadeusz Grochowalski. The unit had 4 aircraft. At first it included some 12 airmen. This unit, too, was disarmed by the Germans, at Kaniów on the night of 10 May 1918.

3: *Assembly of captured aircraft at Poznan-Ławica airfield workshops. Summer 1919 (MLP – Kraków)*

In December 1917 II Polski Oddział Awiacyjny was formed at Jassy in Bukowina. In May 1918 this unit was encircled by German cavalry and disarmed. Most airmen were interned, only a few managed to evade capture. On 23 October Polski Oddział Awiacyjny was formed in Odessa. Polish airmen from all over Russia started to arrive in this unit. In April 1918 it had over a dozen airmen. Some 9 aircraft had been captured by that time, as well as over a dozen vehicles. The capture of Odessa by Austrian troops marked the end of the unit's operations. On 18 April the unit's commander, *rtm.* Łupiński, transferred the entire equipment to the Odessa local authority, and the airmen dispersed.

In October 1918 Polski Oddział Awiacyjny commanded by *por. pil.* Waldemar Narkiewicz was formed at the Oddział Wojsk Polskich na Kubaniu (Polish Forces Outfit at Kuban). The air unit was formed at Stanica Paszkowska. When the Oddział Wojsk Polskich na Kubaniu was transformed into 4 Dywizja Strzelców Polskich (Division of Polish Fusiliers) the air unit was renamed I Awiacyjny Oddział Wojsk Polskich (Aviation Unit of the Polish Air Force). It was not until the 4 Dywizja moved to Odessa that the air unit received 8 used aircraft. In spite of the extensive wear of the aircraft, in March 1918 Polish pilots commenced flying reconnaissance missions on behalf of the French HQ. In order to evade internment the I Awiacyjny Oddział Wojsk Polskich, also mentioned in other sources as Eskadra Lotnicza 4 Dywizji, was evacuated to Rumania. At Cernautsi (Chernovtsy) the Eskadra was replenished and its personnel brought back to full numbers. In June it moved to Stanisławów, and at the end of July 1918 it arrived at Brześć on Bug (Brest Litovsk), renamed 10 Eskadra Lotnicza.

Aviation of the Polish Army in France

On 5 June 1917 the President of the French Republic formed an autonomous Polish Army in France for the duration of the war. Even though on 18 June 1918 President Poincaré handed over the colours of the air arm, initially no formation of such units was planned. Since, however, strong initiative was shown by lower ranks, as many Polish airmen came to France, it was decided to establish such units.

In July 1918 the first group of airmen and prospective airmen was sent to the flying school at Dijon. Upon completion of the elementary training, pilots were moved to the advanced flying school at Pau. No air unit was officially formed by that time, however. It took the C-in-C of the Polish Army in France, *gen.* Haller, to intervene with the French Minister, to establish in March 1919 the Polski Obóz Lotniczy (Polish Air Camp) at Pau. This unit was commanded by *kpt. pil.* Jerzy Kossowski. At that time the camp had 88 pilots and student-pilots, 3 observers, 2 engineering officers, and some 110 ground crew and apprentices. While preparing for a return to Poland, *gen.* Haller tried to obtain as much equipment as possible, especially as the air force at home suffered from shortages in this respect. French authorities decided to put 7 Escadrilles with full equipment, and an air park, at Haller's disposal. Due to shortages of skilled personnel, mostly French airmen volunteers manned the units. They would be replaced by the Poles as training went on. That is why Haller's Army included two fully equipped flying schools, one advanced and the other elementary, with French equipment and instructors. Haller obtained 39 and 59 Escadrille, equipped with Breguet XIV A2s; 66 Escadrille equipped with Breguet XIV B2s; 580, 581 and 582 Escadrille with Salmsons, and 162 Escadrille with Spad fighters. All these units had a full complement of 12-15 aircraft, 8-10 vehicles and a few reserve aircraft. They moved to Poland in two groups. The first arrived in Warsaw at the beginning of May 1919, and later moved to Lublin. Some units took part in fighting against the Ukrainians, but due to political reasons France banned its soldiers from participation in front line fighting.

Military Airfields during the Wars 1918-1920

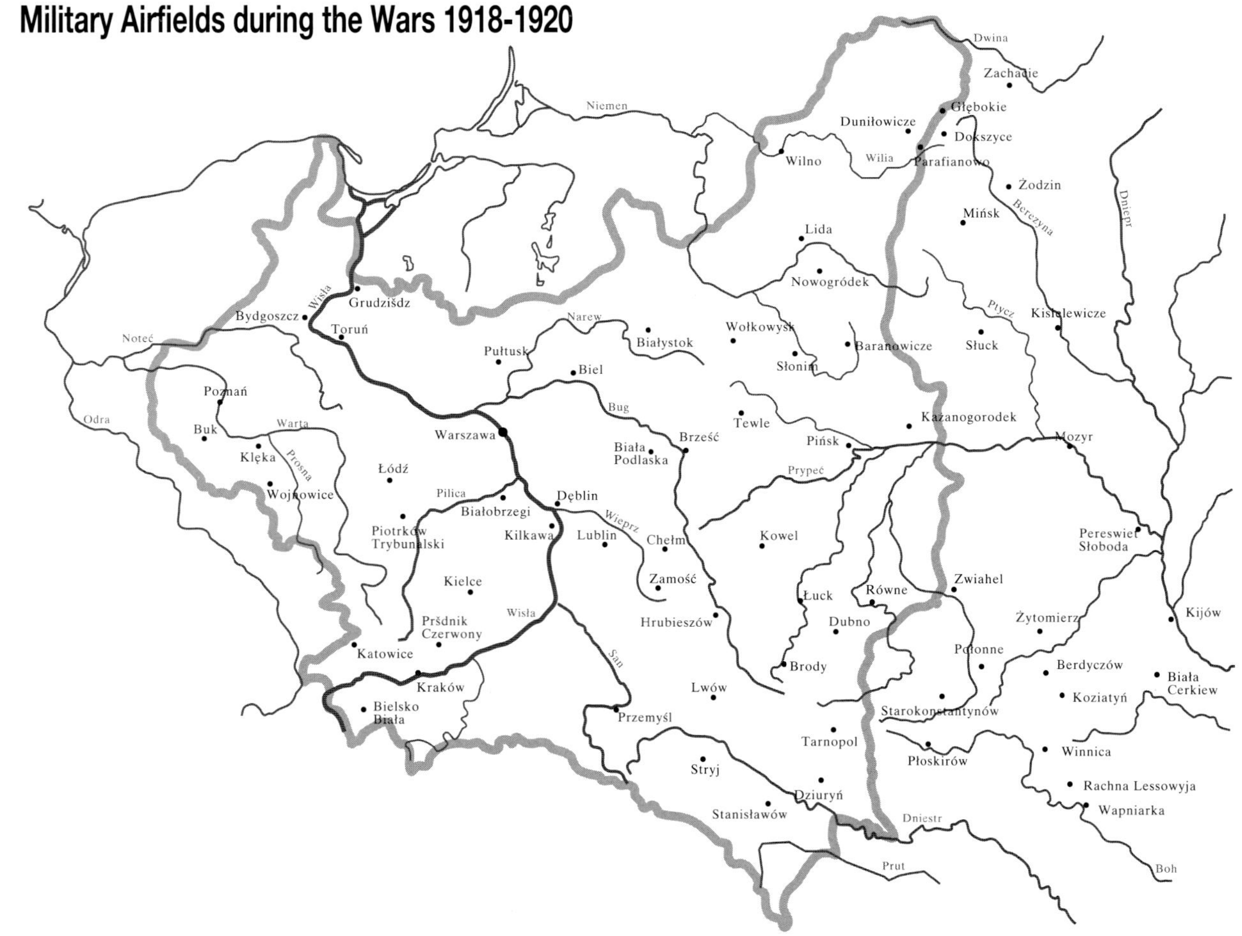

4: *An Oeffag C II series 52 reconnaissance aircraft. One of 15 aircraft of the type used in the Polish Air Force, all war prizes. The photo, taken at Lwów during winter 1918-1919 shows, starting from the aircraft tail:* por. *Roland,* por. *Toruń,* kpt. *Bastyr (MLP – Kraków)*

5: *The wing assembly hall at Poznan-Ławica airfield, 1919 (MLP – Kraków)*

6: *Personnel of 6 Reconnaissance Squadron at Lwów airfield. The Brandenburg C I no. 27.76 bears the early type of Polish markings without outlines. The photo was taken during summer 1919 (Kopański)*

7: *DFW C-Vs were manufactured from 1916 at the Deutsche Flugzeug Werke in Leipzig. The Polish Air Force used more than 60 aircraft of the type. The photo shows example no. 7.10 in the painting scheme from the first half of the 1920s (St. Kopa)*

8: *One of the aircraft types most widely represented in the Polish Air Force was the Albatros B II trainer. Some examples survived until 1935 (MLP – Kraków)*

9: *An Albatros C I reconnaissance aircraft after a landing mishap at Ławica airfield in 1921. Note the clearly visible arrangement of markings on the upper wing (MLP – Kraków)*

10: *Another Albatros B IIa in a rare colour scheme from the first half of the 1920s (MLP – Kraków)*

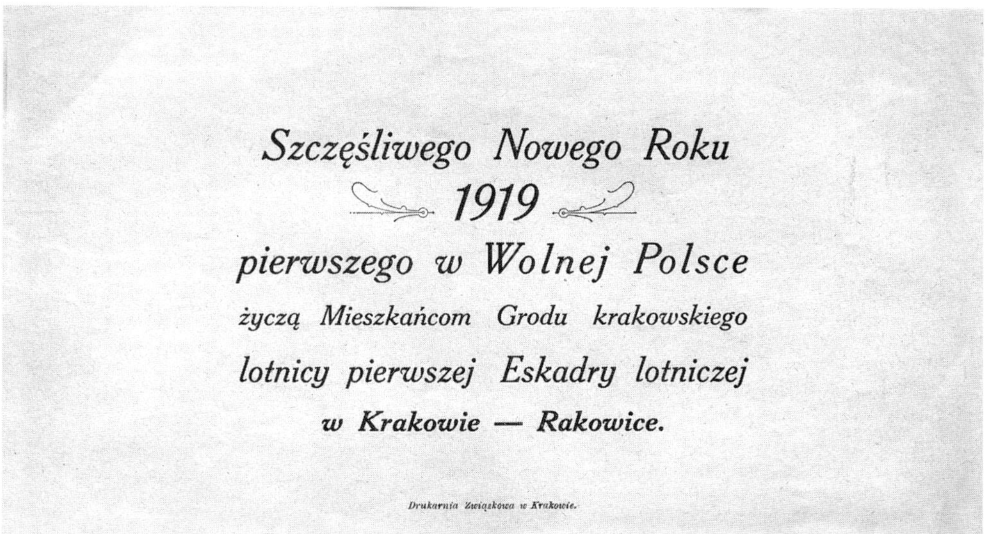

Szczęśliwego Nowego Roku

1919

pierwszego w Wolnej Polsce

życzą Mieszkańcom Grodu krakowskiego

lotnicy pierwszej Eskadry lotniczej

w Krakowie — Rakowice.

Drukarnia Związkowa w Krakowie.

11: *New Year postcard issued by the personnel of I Air Squadron in Kraków at the turn of 1918 (Belcarz – Pęczkowski)*

12: *An Albatros D III fighter captured at Poznan-Ławica airfield. Note the early type markings on the wings. They had no outlines and covered the entire wing chord, extending between the leading and trailing edges (MLP – Kraków)*

13: *An Albatros B IIa manufactured in 1917 (factory no. 1302/17), powered by a 150hp Benz III engine. It was used for training in Poznan and Bydgoszcz (MLP – Kraków)*

14: *Railway shipment of an Albatros B II from 17 Reconnaissance Squadron. The photograph was taken in August 1920 (MLP – Kraków)*

15: *After the end of hostilities Poland undertook to build her own aircraft, copied from existing designs. Such efforts were undertaken at Lwów and Kraków, with Brandenburg as the pattern. The photograph shows a Kraków-built example of a Brandenburg, which has been equipped with a radio-set for artillery spotting (MLP – Kraków)*

French units were moved to the rear in anticipation of Polish personnel replacing them.

After the partitioning powers fell in the autumn 1918 the State of Poland started to be re-established. Polish troops were hastily formed to take over the installations of the withdrawing occupational forces. Polska Organizacja Wojskowa (POW; Polish Military Organisation) was formed for this very aim, as well as the cadre for a regular army. Units of the occupying powers were in disarray, so it was rare for them to deliberately destroy the equipment they were forced to leave. POW took special care of those towns with airfields and aircraft workshops. POW units were often assisted by Poles impressed into occupants' armies, who served at these premises.

The first airfield to be captured by the Poles was Rakowice at Krakow. On 31 October 1918 a handful of Polish airmen serving at this airfield in the Austrian forces, with assistance from civilians, captured the airfield, preventing destruction of the aircraft or their escape to Austria. This 'revolt' was led by *kpt. pil.* Roman Florer. Several days later the airfield was used to form the first Polish air unit in the Polish homeland. The first to enter combat, however, was the unit based at Lwów (Lvov). That unit took the name of '1 Eskadra Bojowa' (1st Combat Squadron), and it was organised by *rtm. pil.* Stanisław Jasiński, who was also its first commander. At the beginning of January 1919 the unit moved to Przemyśl, to take part in fighting. Its entire strength at that time consisted of 7 aircraft. In the autumn 1918 '3 Eskadra Bojowa' was also formed at Krakow. That unit was organised by *kpt. obs.* Karol Stelmach who took command of it.

Lwów was the second Polish city where an airfield was captured. Polish airmen at Lwów, led by *por. obs.* Janusz de Beaurain, formed a POW outfit and prepared a plan to capture the airfield. On the night of 31 October 1918 the Ukrainians unexpectedly captured a major part of Lwów. On 2 November the POW outfit started negotiations with the airfield commandant. The Austrian commander of the airfield was pro-Ukrainian and did his best for them to capture the airfield. He used trucks to bring Ukrainian troops to the airfield, but a group of Polish airmen made a surprise attack and forced them to withdraw. The Austrian commander thus surrendered the airfield on 3 November to Polish troops. The Poles found in the hangars over a dozen Brandenburgs that could be used after an overhaul. On 4 and 5 November the small Polish force resisted Ukrainian attacks, and managed to keep the airfield. Already by 4 November two Brandenburgs had been made serviceable, and this was immediately reported to the Naczelna Komenda Obrony Lwowa (High Command of Lwów Defence). Persenkówka railway station was selected to be the first target, as newly arriving Ukrainian troops were unloading there. In the morning of 5 November the two overhauled aircraft were to be test flown. In one of them the engine caught fire during the run-up, the aircraft becoming unserviceable. By the afternoon of 5 November the first Polish crew consisting of *por. pil.* Stefan Bastyr and *por. obs.* Janusz de Beaurain took off for the first combat mission against Ukrainian troops. Three 15kg bombs were carried. The railway station was attacked with bombs, and then strafed using the only serviceable machine gun of the unit. The same day one more combat mission was flown. This time the aircraft carried the first Polish markings: white and red stripes at the wing tips. No stock of suitable paint had been available prior to the earlier mission. This day would later become the Polish Air Force Day. On 6 November two more pilots managed to get through to the airfield, until then there was only *por. pil.* S. Bastyr. With *por.* Stec and *por.* Roland it was now possible to fly missions with three aircraft. On 7 November all 3 aircraft attacked Ukrainian positions at Lwów. Upon return from the mission the crew of *por.* Bastyr and *por.* de Beaurain was ordered by the Naczelna Komenda Obrony Lwowa to fly to Krakow, to report on the situation and ask for reinforcements.

Lwów airmen flew several missions a day, and thanks to the arrival of pilots and observers from Krakow the intensity of flying could grow further. On 13 November *por.* Stec left with a report to Warsaw. He stopped over at Krakow, picking up *por.* Stanisław Nazarkiewicz who

16: *A Brandenburg B-I, one of 34 aircraft of the type captured in Kraków. The side radiator is clearly visible, and immediately behind it is the so-called 'Kraków marking' a red 'Z' in a white square (MLP – Kraków)*

carried a report from *gen.* Roja, and on 15 November they left for Warsaw. Both airmen were met by Piłsudski. Stec returned to Lwów on 16 November. It can be assumed that the reports brought by Stec prompted Piłsudski to issue orders that accelerated preparations to relieve Lwów. Due to the units of *płk* Michał Karaszewicz-Tokarzewski that arrived from Przemyśl on 20 November, Ukrainian troops withdrew from Lwów between 21 and 23 November. During the defence of Lwów some 69 missions were flown, some 250 bombs were dropped and enemy positions, trains, and convoys were strafed. Seven passenger and 12 liaison flights were also made.

Individual pilots flew the following numbers of combat missions:[2]

Pilot	number of combat missions
por. Stefan Bastyr	28
por. Stefan Stec	19
por. Eugeniusz Roland	15
por. Stefan Bogusz	5
sierż. Józef Cagasek	2

Przemyśl

The situation at Hureczko airfield at Przemyśl was even more difficult. In the first days of November the Austrian crews, upon learning what was going on in Russia at the front, and in Austria, were preparing to fly back home. The Poles, led by *por.* Wiktor Robotycki, demanded that the airfield commandant hand over the field, together with the equipment. Upon capture of the airfield the Poles were not able to defend it from the approaching Ukrainian troops, so they decided to evacuate the aircraft to Krakow. On 3 November, faced by the approaching Ukrainians, 12 *ad hoc* crews took off. During take-off the aircraft fell under enemy fire. Two were shot down. Two more, probably due to damage inflicted by the ground fire, suffered engine malfunction and crashed. Two force-landed at Bochnia, and upon following repairs to slight damage made it to Krakow, joining there the other six.

Lublin

Lublin had a perfectly organised POW unit. On 5 November it secured without problem the hangar with large quantities of fuel, lubricants and spare parts. They also managed to capture 5 Lloyd aircraft. In late November an air unit was established in Lublin, later renamed 2 Eskadra Lotnicza. *Mjr pil.* Jerzy Syrokomla-Syrokomski became the unit's commander.

Warsaw

Mokotów airfield in Warsaw was home to a German observers' school and repair workshops (Aircraft park). In the autumn of 1918 Polish airmen in German units attempted to conspire to capture the airfield during the anticipated fall of Germany. To this end they established contacts with civil workers of the airfield, in order to obtain data as to the equipment, location of hangars, etc. The organisation was named Związek Lotników (Airmen Association), and was headed by *ppłk pil.* Hipolit Łossowski. After preparations, on 9 November he ordered a mobilisation of the organisation with the aim of capturing the airfield. On 11 November a Polish delegation went to the airfield and demanded that the Germans hand over the equipment and facilities. After 4 days of negotiations the Germans, threatened by a Polish attack, gave up the airfield. The Poles took over the complete equipment of the observers' school: aircraft, stores, spare parts. All this was priceless for the emerging Polish units. The first Polish aircraft flew over Warsaw on 20 November 1918. According to contemporary newspapers, the crew consisted of *ppor. pil.* Stanisław Jakubowski and one of the participants of the capture of the airfield, Witold Ehrenpreis, a student.

Aviation in the former Prussian zone

Poznań

Ławica airfield in Poznań was the base of the German no. 4 Replacement Air Unit with some 200 soldiers. Large quantities of aircraft, auxiliary equipment, spare parts and materials were stored there. The outbreak of the revolution in Germany in November 1918 weakened the morale of German soldiers in Poznań. Units stationed in the city were easily disarmed by Polish organisations. It took a well planned action of Polish troops on the night of 5 January 1919 to capture Frankfurt am Oder. By the end of December the entire Poznań garrison was disarmed. The airfield crew, though, continued to resist and attempted to evacuate the serviceable aircraft, equipment and various materials the airfield. Some 70 aircraft were captured including 26 ready for service. A Zeppelin Hangar, which had been turned into a *Sierz* store, housed 200 aircraft of various types, most of them crated. Large quantities of food, fuel, and a lot of equipment were also captured.

As early as 7 January 1919 6 aircraft took off from the airfield, performing a flypast over Poznań, which raised enormous enthusiasm amongst the Polish population. *pil.* Wiktor Pniewski became the Szef Stacji Lotniczej Ławica (Head of Ławica Air Station).

On 15 January *gen.* Dowbór-Musnicki took command in Poznań, appointing *płk* Macewicz the head of the Polish Army air service in the former Prussian zone of partition. At that time fighting to establish the border with Germany continued against German police units, and at times even against regular German army units. However, knowing the serious situation of the air units in the East (fighting at Lwów and in the Eastern Frontiers), Macewicz decided to send to Warsaw 32 serviceable

17: *One example of the reconnaissance Albatros C X was converted in Poznan workshops during the 1920s. Initially it had an additional fuel tank, and in 1924 it was modified to carry stretchers. An opening fuselage side with three windows was fitted to that end (MLP – Kraków)*

18: *The reconnaissance Lloyd C IV, manufactured in Hungary from 1916, was a rare aircraft in Poland. Only 7 aircraft of the type were captured from the occupying powers at Kraków, Lublin, and Przemyśl. The photo shows example no. 44.41 used at the Kraków Pilots School in 1919 (Kopański)*

19: *This Oeffag C II series 52 was captured at Rakowice airfield in Kraków. Note the Polish markings on the rudder, painted on top of the Austro-Hungarian emblems. Parts of the black cross are discernible on white fields of the chequerboard (MLP – Kraków)*

20: *Another example of a Polish-built Brandenburg, this time from Lwów production. This was the first aircraft assembled by the workshops of the III Ruchomy Park Lotniczy, initially designated 'P 1' (as the photo shows), and subsequently '27.III.1' ('27' – denoted the Austrian series used as the pattern for the manufactured aircraft, 'III' – the number of Lwów Air Group, and '1' was the number of the manufactured airframe) (MLP – Kraków)*

21: *Fokker E-V (D-VIII) no. 00.1 (187/18) belonging to 7 Eskadra Lotnicza. This aircraft was the personal mount of* por. *Stefan Stec who is believed to be the author of the Polish national insignia. On the fuselage in front of the marking national insignia is the pilot's emblem – a horizontal 'S' with superimposed four-arm star in white and red (Kopański)*

22: *A view of the assembly hall of captured aircraft at Stacja Lotnicza Ławica. In the foreground is a reconnaissance Halberstadt CL-II Bay no. 208/18. It was used by the Szkoła Pilotów Ławica and subsequently by 10 Eskadra Rozpoznawcza, and was struck off charge in April 1921 (MLP – Kraków)*

23: *Fokker E-V no. 00.2 (193/18) captured at Poznań-Ławica airfield. The photo shows the aircraft as crashed by* por. *Ludwik Idzikowski at Lewandówka airfield in Lwów. During 1928/29 Idzikowski would undertake two attempts to fly westwards across the Northern Atlantic in an Amiot 143, and was killed on 13 July 1929 in a forced landing at Graziosa island (Azores) – his colleague* mjr. *K. Kubala survived the accident (Kopański)*

24: *Another shot of the Fokker E-V no. 00.1 during a photographic session at Lewandówka airfield in Lwów. In the cockpit of the aircraft is* por. *Stefan Stec (Kopański)*

25: *This Gotha G-IV bomber was one of five aircraft of the type in Poland (MLP – Kraków)*

26: *Fokker D VII in flight over Poznań. The photo was taken on 11 May 1921 by* por. *Korcz (MLP – Kraków)*

27: *This photo, taken on 3 May 1919 at Poznan-Ławica airfield, shows Albatros fighters. The three on the left were D III types, while the last one was a D V. The first Albatros D III on the left, bearing number 1835/17, belonged (like the rest) to the Advanced Flying School and crashed on 7 November of the same year (Kopański)*

28: *DFW C-V no. 220/17 and 2019/1700 crashed on 7 September 1919 at Ławica airfield. (MLP – Kraków)*

29: *Gotha G-IV no. 100/17 bomber aircraft after landing without its undercarriage at Lewandówka airfield in Lwów – 31 August 1920 (Kopański)*

aircraft and 12 airframes, and later on to add more as the equipment was being re-assembled from captured stocks (compare state of aircraft and aircraft supply during 1918-1920). With the substantial amount of captured equipment, it was decided that five eskadra units would be formed in Wielkopolska province: four reconnaissance and one destroyer (bomber). There was no question of fighter units for one reason: lack of suitable equipment. Plans were also at hand to establish balloon forces. Lack of skilled personnel was a major handicap. Dowództwo Wojsk Aeronautycznych (Aeronautical Forces HQ) was established and would continue to operate as an independent unit for the former Prussian Zone for some 8 months.

The following units and organisations were formed:

Inspektorat Wojsk Lotniczych

1 Wielkopolska Grupa Lotnicza at the Dowództwo Frontu Wielkopolskiego, consisting of:
- 1 Wielkopolska Eskadra Lotnicza
- 2 Wielkopolska Eskadra Lotnicza
- 3 Wielkopolska Eskadra Lotnicza
- 4 Wielkopolska Eskadra Lotnicza

Stacja Lotnicza Ławica, which included:
- flying school, workshop school, aircraft workshops, air stores.

As mentioned above, the air forces in Wielkopolska suffered from shortages of personnel. In Germany the Poles had had virtually no chance of promotion, so there was a lack of aviation officers. Dowództwo Armii Wielkopolskiej decided thus to quickly promote airmen from the Prussian Zone, which allowed them to rapidly build up the core of the air force.

A decree also established the Szkoła Lotnicza. By 1 August 1919 it had trained 24 pilots, and by the end of the year, the (by then) Wyższa Szkoła Lotników provided 25 more pilots.

Thanks to the operations aimed at obtaining air personnel, and the equipment captured at Ławica, the standard strength of the Eskadra units in Wielkopolska province was higher than in other parts of the country.

The Wielkopolska standard was 6 pilots, 4 observers, 2 air gunners. At first the units were mixed, with 5 reconnaissance, 3 combat and 2 reserve aircraft. It was also precisely stipulated that an Eskadra should have 10 aircraft guns, 200 bombs of 10kg and 20kg size each, 2 cameras etc.

On 12 February the 1 Wielkopolska Eskadra Lotnicza was formed, under command of *ppor.* Pniewski. Already in March it was sent to the front line at Przemyśl.

On 14 February 2 Eskadra commenced forming, commanded by *rtm.* Grochowalski. In April the unit, with 5 pilots, 6 observers and 8 aircraft, operated over the Wielkopolska Front, performing reconnaissance for the Polish forces.

On 6 March the third Eskadra started to be formed. This too was organised by *rtm. pil.* T. Grochowalski. Upon achieving operational readiness, the unit was taken over by *ppłk* Krzyczkowski. Initially this Eskadra also operated over the Wielkopolska Front, losing one aircraft and its crew which were taken prisoner.

The fourth Eskadra was formed in June 1919 by *ppor.* Dziembowski. The personnel of this unit went to Warsaw, to collect new Spads purchased in France.

In September 1919 Wielkopolska Aviation was united with the 'national' air force, and that of *gen.* Haller's army, thus ending the 8 months of independent operations.

At the end of January 1920 the airfields at Toruń, Bydgoszcz and Grudziądz were also captured. However, the Germans, drawing experience from the Poznań events, evacuated all their equipment and damaged the facilities.

First air authorities and the organisation of the air force until 1921

In parallel with establishing Polish state institutions the air administration was also created. Initially the authorities covered the former Russian and Austrian partition zones.

On 27 October 1918 the Rada Regencyjna (Regency Council) decided to establish a 'regular national army'. At that time the Military Commission had no air section. It was not until November 1918 that an informal group of airmen assembled. They worked in the technical section of the newly established Ministerstwo Spraw Wojskowych (Ministry of Military Affairs). On 14 November the first formal air organisation commenced activity, the Sekcja Żeglugi Napowietrznej Departamentu Technicznego Ministerstwa Spraw Wojskowych (Aerial Navigation Section of the Technical Department of the Ministry of Military Affairs). *Ppłk* Hipolit Łossowski was appointed the Head of the Sekcja.

The first decree of the air authorities was the order of the Minister Spraw Wojskowych that set the initial status of the Mokotów Airfield:

Szef Sztabu Generalnego, Warsaw, 21 November 1918
Orders of the Sztab Generalny L. 23
for the Organisation of the Służba Techniczna Wojsk Polskich
To establish
...
Główna Kadra Lotnicza units

. . .
Two Główna Kadra Lotnicza units, the 1st at Mokotów Barracks in Warsaw under command of płk *Studziński, the 2nd in Krakow under temporary command of kpt. Florer, forming according to the orders.*
. . .
Szef Sztabu Generalnego
Szeptycki, generał dywizji.[3]

Upon taking the position of the Wódz Naczelny by Józef Piłsudski, his authority included the Sztab Generalny which took care of organisation, training and combat use of the emerging forces, and the Ministerstwo Spraw Wojskowych responsible for the supplies. The Sekcja Żeglugi Napowietrznej covered the whole of the air force matters, and thus fell under both these institutions. Such a solution made the Section's work difficult, but the tense situation made changes impossible, as with the imminent threat from the East combat units had to be quickly formed.

In December the Sekcja issued orders which defined the detailed organisation of the Air Force, including military authorities at all levels.

The orders said that the Dowódca Wojsk Lotniczych in Warsaw was to report directly to the Szef Sztabu Generalnego of the Wojsko Polskie (WP), while in turn all Wojska Lotnicze units reported to him.

HQs of the two Grupa Lotnicza units, based in Warsaw and in Krakow, were also established.

The orders also detailed the structure of eskadra units. These would consist of 6 aircraft, with the aims of communication, reconnaissance and artillery spotting, as well as destroying enemy aircraft and combat co-operation.

The following units were listed as being formed:
1 Eskadra in Warsaw
2 Eskadra in Lublin
5 Eskadra in Krakow
6 Eskadra in Przemyśl
7 Eskadra in Lwów. [4]

Also mobile aircraft parks were established for aircraft servicing: 1 Ruchomy Park Lotniczy in Warsaw and 2 RPL in Krakow.

The Wojskowa Szkoła Lotnicza was also established in Warsaw.

According to plans, the first units would achieve operational status in January 1919. However, the spontaneously formed units had entered combat in November 1918. The air unit formed at Lwów participated in the defence of the city, as mentioned earlier. The unit was initially called 2 Eskadra Bojowa. On 25 November 3 Eskadra Bojowa from Krakow arrived at Lwów. Both these units formed Lwowska Grupa Lotnicza under *por.* Stefan Bastyr. In December 1918 both eskadras units were used to support ground troops. Lwów was still facing Ukrainian troops on three sides. The only link with the rest of the country, through Przemyśl, was under constant threat. The units flew reconnaissance missions, in spite of the lack of suitable equipment. In December both eskadras flew a total of some 30 combat missions.

At that time 1 Eskadra Bojowa from Krakow operated at the airfield in Bielsko Biała, monitoring the Czech troops' activities from the air. The unit was reporting to *gen.* Latinik, the commander of Polish troops in śląsk Cieszyński region. Apart from reconnaissance sorties many propaganda missions were flown.

Unit naming was standardised in December 1918. The Orders of 21 December established two units: 1 Eskadra in Warsaw, under *rtm.* Grochowalski, and 2 Eskadra in Lublin, under *mjr* Syrokomla-Syrokomski. The units created spontaneously in Małopolska region were re-named: 1 Eskadra Bojowa from Krakow was named 5 Eskadra, 2 Eskadra Bojowa at Lwów – 6 Eskadra, and 3 Eskadra at Lwów (from Krakow) – 7 Eskadra. A week later *ppłk* Łossowski ordered the formation of 3 Eskadra in Warsaw.

On 9 January subsequent units were established: 4 Eskadra in Warsaw, 9 Eskadra in Krakow, and then on 16 January 1 Eskadra Łącznikowa in Warsaw, 11 Eskadra in Warsaw and 12 Eskadra in Krakow.

Most of the newly established units existed on paper only, and those already in action demanded reinforcement, as during front line operations their equipment numbers dropped rapidly.

Strength of the units on 13 March 1919 was as follows:

Eskadra	Number of aircraft	number of pilots	number of observers	number of ground crew	number of enlisted men
1 Eskadra in Warsaw	6	5	2	-	62
2 Eskadra (at the front line)	3	4	2	3	114
3 Eskadra (at the front line)	3	4	4	15	91
4 Eskadra in Warsaw	-	5	3	-	71
5 Eskadra (at the front line)	5	5	3	8	97
6 Eskadra (at the front line)	4	8	3	17	111
7 Eskadra (at the front line)	4	7	2	9	74
9 Eskadra (at the front line)	6	5	5	16	150
11 Eskadra in Warsaw	-	1	2	-	32
12 Eskadra in Krakow	-	3	3	25	104
1 Eskadra Łączinkowa	1	3	3	12	14

On 19 March 1919 the structure of the air force HQ was expanded. A new organisation of the air forces was introduced:

30: *Nieuport 24bis fighters at the airfield of 5 Eskadra Lotnicza in Przemyśl. Both Nieuports, with serials 9252 and 4301, were captured from the Russians. Behind them is a Brandenburg and Bristol Fighters. The photo was taken in the spring of 1921 (MLP – Kraków)*

31: *Nieuport 24bis no. 5086 'Diana' of* por. *Juliusz Gilewicz from 5 Eskadra Lotnicza. The aircraft gives an example of non-standard shape and positioning of national insignia. The checkerboard on the rudder is outlined, as opposed to the one without outlines applied on the lower wing surfaces. Painting horizontal tail undersurfaces in white and red provides a further unusual recognition marking (Kopański)*

32: *LVG C-V no. 9.2 assembled at Ławica, served subsequently in: 2 Eskadra Rozpoznawcza, 17 Eskadra Rozpoznawcza and 6 Eskadra Rozpoznawcza. It was struck off charge in 1921 (MLP – Kraków)*

33: *Halberstadt CL-II Bay no. 202/18 used by the Stacja Lotnicza and Szkoła Pilotów at Ławica. Aircraft of the type enjoyed good reputation among Polish pilots. The restored fuselage of the aircraft is now displayed at the Aviation Museum in Kraków, being one of the most precious exhibits (MLP – Kraków)*

34: *Another shot of the same Halberstadt CL-II Bay. The 'Bay' designation indicates that the aircraft was licence-manufactured at Bayerische Flugzeug Werke AG (MLP – Kraków)*

35: *Oeffag C II no. 52.11 from the first batch powered by 160 hp Austro Daimler engines. The second batch had 185 hp engines. The example shown here had a radio-set of the type FU-3. It was shot down by the Russians in late June 1920 – the crew survived (Kopański)*

- Inspektorat Wojsk Lotniczych (Air Forces Inspectorate) reporting to the Ministerstwo Spraw Wojskowych
- Szefostwo Lotnictwa przy Naczelnym Dowództwie WP (Aviation HQ at the Supreme HQ of the Polish Army)
- Sekcja Żeglugi Napowietrznej (Aerial Navigation Section).

In June 1919 most units still suffered from substantial shortages of personnel and equipment. Air support was necessary for the imminent offensive. Therefore, it was decided to send all units to the front, regardless of their status, with the assumption that reinforcements would be provided whilst at the front line. I Grupa Lotnicza (1 and 4 Eskadra plus 8 Eskadra re-formed from 1 Łącznikowa Eskadra) was in the most difficult position. 12 and 9 Eskadra would form II Grupa Lotnicza. The Group CO, realising the shortages, united both Eskadras into a single 9 Eskadra Lotnicza, under *por.* Matula. 2 and 3 Eskadra formed IV Grupa Lotnicza at the front line near Kowel.

In May 1919 7 French Escadrilles arrived in Poland with *gen.* Haller's army. Two of these, nos. 39 and 59, were grouped together, while the rest would operate individually. Initially, when *gen.* Haller's troops took part in the offensive against the Ukrainians, the French 39 Escadrille successfully supported these actions. Since its personnel consisted mainly of French airmen, and France was not at war with Bolshevik Russia, all French units were withdrawn to the rear, where they awaited Polish personnel. This state of affairs continued until the autumn, when some units received Polish personnel, and some were disbanded.

At the same time *gen.* Żeligowski's division came from Odessa, bringing the Eskadra 4 Dywizji Strzelców (mentioned earlier), albeit without aircraft. The unit was re-named 10 Eskadra and moved to Brześć for replenishment.

In the summer 7 Eskadra was reformed into a fighter unit, upon receiving new aircraft and fighter pilots from other units. *Por.* Stec took command of the eskadra.

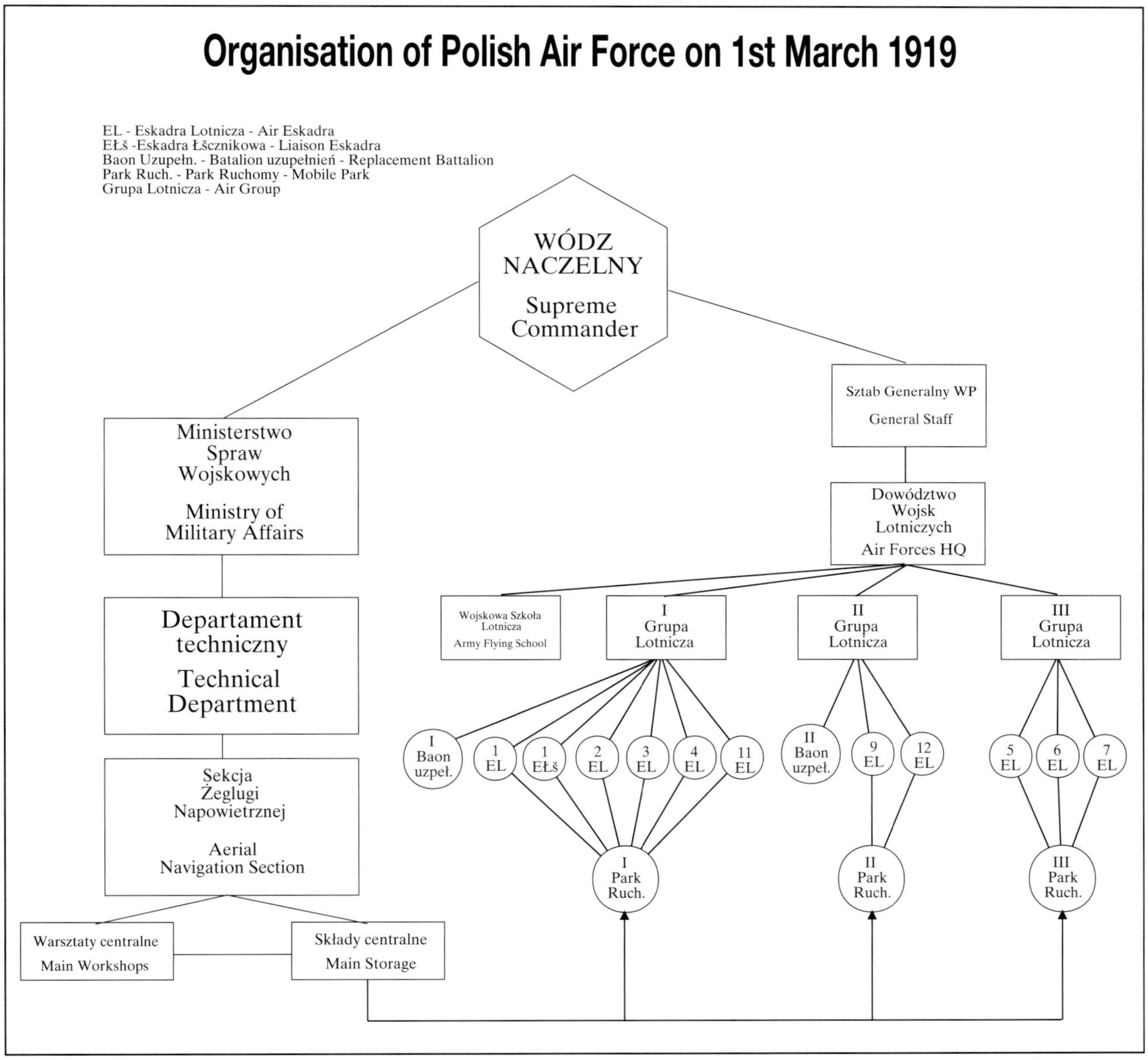

At that time the strength of the national units (not counting the Wielkopolska and French units) was as follows:[5]

Eskadra	pilots	observers	ground crew	aircraft
1 Eskadra	3	2	22	2
2 Eskadra	5	3	8	1
3 Eskadra	3	3	9	2
4 Eskadra	4	4	23	4
5 Eskadra	6	6	15	4
6 Eskadra	4	6	22	3
7 Eskadra	5	-	11	4
8 Eskadra	3	2	16	4
9 Eskadra	5	3	5	3
11 Eskadra	3	3	12	1

The report does not mention 10 Eskadra which, although in existence, had no aircraft.

At that time there were a total of 11 home eskadras of doubtful combat value, and 4 Wielkopolska units of a higher level of usefulness.

On 25 September 1919, when the new commander, *gen.* Macewicz, took the post of Inspektor Wojsk Lotniczych (Army Air Forces Inspector) he had 11 national eskadras, 4 Wielkopolska and 7 French ones. He ordered unification of all these units under one command. This posed no problems in the case of the Wielkopolska units, while it was not as simple with French ones.

On 26 September the French Military Mission transferred the following units to Polish command:

Eskadra Name	Initial strength
39 Eskadra Bregeutów (39 Escadrille Breguet)	10 + 2 Breguet 14 A1
59 Eskadra Bregeutów (59 Escadrille Breguet)	10 + 2 Breguet 14 A1
66 Eskadra Bregeutów (66 Escadrille Breguet)	14 + 3 Breguet 14 A1
580 Eskadra Salmsonów (580 Escadrille Salmson)	10 + 2 Salmson 2 A2
581 Eskadra Salmsonów (581 Escadrille Salmson)	10 + 2 Salmson 2 A2
582 Eskadra Salmsonów (582 Escadrille Salmson)	10 + 2 Salmson 2 A2
162 Eskadra Spadów (162 Escadrille Spad)	10 Spad 7C1

Since many aircraft had already been damaged by French airmen, and there were not enough skilled personnel, only 4 Polish eskadras were formed.

By the orders of the Sztab Generalny HQ no. L.2173/I of 13 April 1920 Grupa Lotnicza units were renamed Dyon (Dywizjon) Lotniczy.[6] Names of eskadras were also changed. As of that time the name indicated the role of the unit, for example: 1 Eskadra Wywiadowcza (reconnaissance), 7 Eskadra Myśliwska (fighter), 21 Eskadra Niszczycielska (destroyer) etc. Wielkopolska and French units received numbers in the general range.

1 Eskadra Wielkopolska – 12 Eskadra Wywiadowcza
2 Eskadra Wielkopolska – 13 Eskadra Myśliwska
3 Eskadra Wielkopolska – 14 Eskadra Wywiadowcza
4 Eskadra Wielkopolska Bojowa – 15 Eskadra Myśliwska
39 Eskadra Breguetów (39 Escadrille Breguet) – 16 Eskadra Wywiadowcza

Organisation of Polish Air Force, 15 February 1921

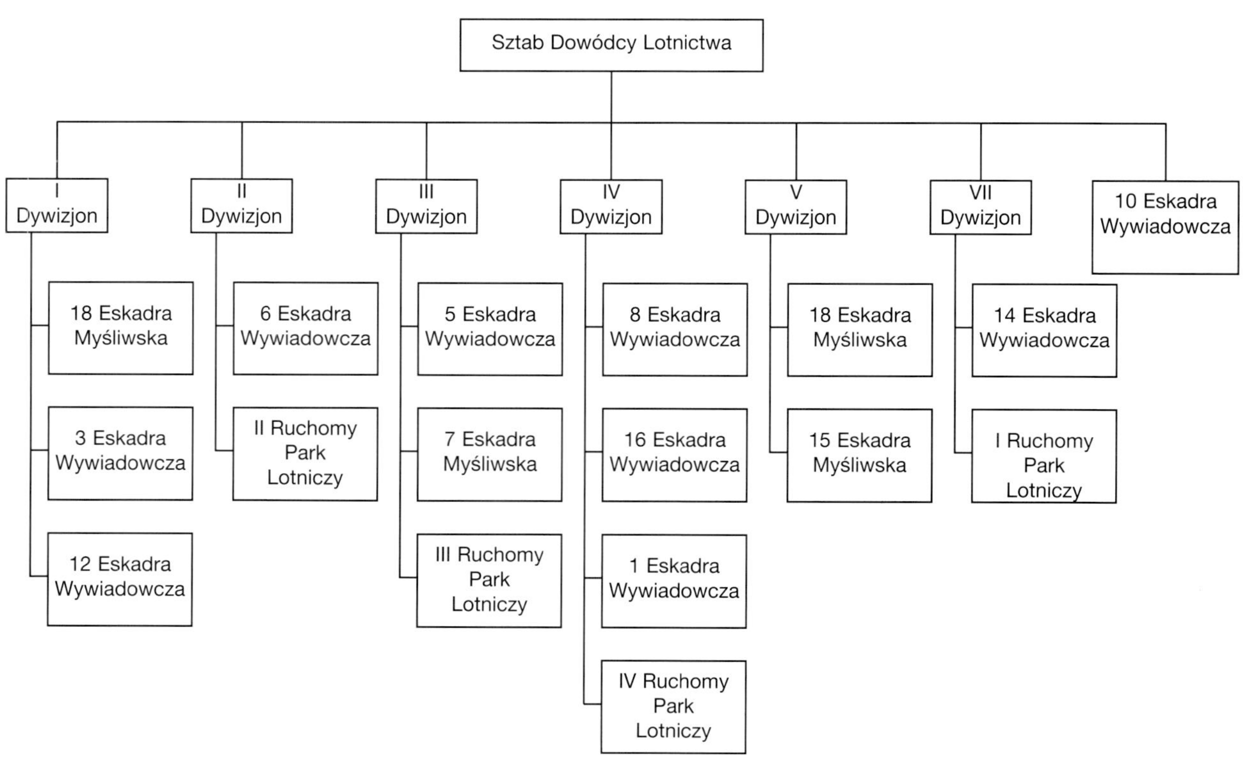

36: *A Rumpler C-I reconnaissance aircraft (MLP – Kraków)*

37: *Hannover Roland CL II no. 218/18 photographed at Ławica airfield (MLP – Kraków)*

38: *Railway shipment of an LVG C-V aircraft fitted with Austro Daimler engine (MLP – Kraków)*

39: *Aircraft at Przemyśl airfield. The photo was taken in May 1919. Right to left: an Albatros D-III, three Hannover CL-IIs and two DFW C-Vs (MLP – Kraków)*

40: *Rumpler C-I no. 5410/16 from Szkoła Pilotów at Ławica, damaged during landing (MLP – Kraków)*

41: *An LVG C-VI reconnaissance aircraft captured from the Ukrainians. German markings show through the Ukrainian tridents (MLP – Kraków)*

42: *There is no doubt that Fokker D-VII was one of the best German fighters during WWI. After the cessation of hostilities some 50 aircraft of the type, mostly purchased, were used in Poland. The exact number of Fokkers is difficult to ascertain, as four different numbering systems were used on the type (MLP – Kraków)*

43: *A Brandenburg B-I training aircraft (MLP – Kraków)*

44: *A reconnaissance Albatros C-XII. Note the streamlined shape – its fuselage followed the pattern of the Albatros D-V fighter (Kopański)*

45: *A Fokker E-V at Lewandówka airfield in Lwów.* Por. *Stec is standing in front of the aircraft (Kopański)*

46: *Oeffag D-III, or licence-built version of the German Albatros D-III. The aircraft in the photo is shown in the markings of the elite 7 Eskadra Myśliwska. The photo was taken in 1921 when the airframe no. 253.234 was overhauled in the workshops at Kraków (MLP – Kraków)*

47: *Oeffag C-II no. 52.27 captured at Kraków-Rakowice airfield. The photo was taken in 1919, when the aircraft was used by 5 Eskadra Lotnicza. (MLP – Kraków)*

48: *Interesting photograph of a Fokker D-VII manufactured by Albatros Werke, factory no.1075/18 (Polish serial 502/18). The aircraft, in the markings of 15 Eskadra Myśliwska, has two underwing racks for 12.5kg bombs and cassettes for 'mice' (small 1kg anti-personnel bombs) (MLP – Kraków)*

Organisation of Polish Air Force, January 1922

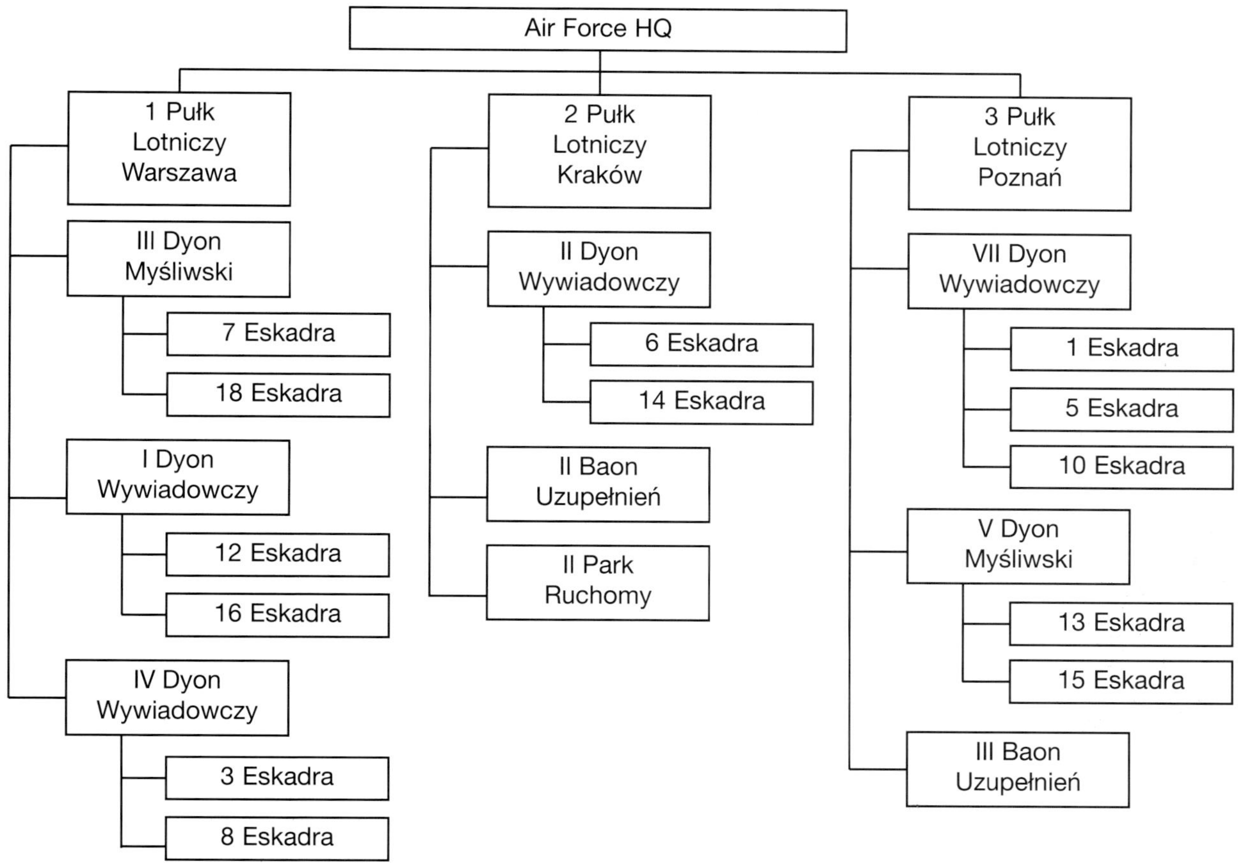

59 Eskadra Breguetów (59 Escadrille Breguet) – 17 Eskadra Wywiadowcza
580 Eskadra Salmsonów (580 Escadrille Salmson) – 18 Eskadra Wywiadowcza
162 Eskadra Spadów (162 Escadrille Spad) – 19 Eskadra Myśliwska

1 Dywizjon Lotniczy, under *mjr* Narkiewicz was formed from I Grupa Lotnicza
2 Dywizjon Lotniczy, under *kpt.* Perini, was formed from II Grupa Lotnicza
3 Dywizjon Lotniczy, under *kpt.* Bastyr, was formed from III Grupa Lotnicza
4 Dywizjon Lotniczy, under *por.* Jurkiewicz was formed from IV Grupa Lotnicza
5 Dywizjon Lotniczy, under *mjr* Kossowski, was formed from V Grupa Lotnicza
7 Dywizjon Lotniczy, under *rtm.* Buckiewicz was formed from I Grupa Lotnicza Wielkopolska

The following eskadras formed part of each dywizjon *(early June 1920)*

1 Dywizjon	2 Dywizjon	3 Dywizjon	4 Dywizjon	5 Dywizjon	7 Dywizjon
1 Eskadra	2 Eskadra	5 Eskadra	11 Eskadra	3 Eskadra	10 Eskadra
2 Eskadra	9 Eskadra	6 Eskadra	18 Eskadra	16 Eskadra	12 Eskadra
8 Eskadra	7 Eskadra	15 Eskadra			13 Eskadra
		17 Eskadra			14 Eskadra
		21 Eskadra			19 Eskadra

49 Below: *Engine nacelle of the Friedrichshafen G-IIIanr 511/17. The 260 hp Mercedes D Iva engine is perfectly visible. Polish Air Force used only 3 examples of the aircraft (two of G-III and a single of G-IIIa version). One of these, no. 511/17, took part in fighting against the Bolshevik Russia. (Kopański)*

Later on the allocation of eskadras to dywizjons would change depending on operational requirements and eskadra roles at the front line.

This number of eskadras remained until the end of the war and the cease-fire. When the armistice was signed and the armed forces changed to peace-time conditions, Dowództwo Lotnictwa (Aviation HQ) decided to temporarily reduce the number of units, as the inventories of most of them left much to be desired and virtually made independent existence impossible.

By the orders of the Supreme HQ no. L. Dz. 120/Lot. T. J. 18. 01. 1921 by combining the existing units only 13 eskadras were to be retained.

- 1 and 2 Eskadra were combined under the name 1 Eskadra Wywiadowcza, and based in Białystok
- 3 Eskadra Wywiadowcza remained as such in Warsaw
- 5 Eskadra Wywiadowcza remained as such in Przemyśl.
- 6 and 17 Eskadra were combined as 6 Eskadra Wywiadowcza in Łuck.
- 7 Eskadra Myśliwska remained as such in Lwów
- 8 and 11 were combined as 8 Eskadra Wywiadowcza in Lida
- 9 and 10 were combined as 10 Eskadra Wywiadowcza in Krakow.
- 12 Eskadra Wywiadowcza remained as such in Wilanów
- 13 Eskadra Wywiadowcza remained as such in Bydgoszcz
- 14 and 21 were combined as 14 Eskadra Wywiadowcza in Grudziądz
- 15 Eskadra Wywiadowcza in Ostrów Wielkopolski
- 16 Eskadra Wywiadowcza in Wilno
- 18 and 19 were combined as 18 Eskadra Myśliwska in Dęblin.

State of aircraft and aircraft supply during 1918-1920

When taking over airfields, the POW and other underground organisations aimed at capturing as many serviceable aircraft as possible. Also the Sekcja Żeglugi Napowietrznej during the initial period of its activities outlined its most urgent priorities as follows:

1. inventory of the captured equipment
2. foreign purchases
3. setting up of repair workshops
4. establishing an indigenous aircraft industry and foundation of air research and development organisations.

The first inventory of the equipment captured in the Russian and Austrian zones is listed in the tables below and on page 41. The report said that there were only 12 aircraft suitable for immediate use.

Aircraft captured in the former Russian and Austrian zones of Poland according to the report of 12 May 1919

Aircraft

Type	Origin	Number
Brandenburg BI	Austrian	15
Brandenburg CI	Austrian	33
Oeffag	Austrian	8
Uffag	Austrian	1
Lloyd CIV and CV	Austrian	10
Albatros CI	German	9
Albatros CII	German	1
Albatros CIII	German	7
Albatros CVII	German	2
Albatros CX	German	15
Albatros CXII	German	4
Albatros BII	German	14
Albatros DIII	German	10
Rumpler CI	German	21
Rumpler CIV	German	10
Rumpler CV	German	1
Rumpler CVI	German	1
Rumpler CVII	German	2
DFW CV	German	1
LVG CII	German	3
LVG CV	German	7
LVG CVI	German	1
Roland CLII	German	15
BF CXII	German	3
AEG CI	German	1
AEG CIV	German	6
Fokker EV	German	2
Nieuport (unknown version)	French	1
Bleriot (unknown version)	French	2
SPAD (unknown version)	French	1
Total		217

Engines

Type	Number
Mercedes 100 hp	19
Mercedes 160 hp	29
Mercedes 260 hp	18
Benz 160 hp	23
Benz 220 hp	9
Hiero 85 hp	6
Hiero 240 hp	2
Daimler 100 hp	3
Daimler 160 hp	63
Daimler 180 hp	4
Opel 180	9
Stoever 180 hp	3
Argus 180 hp	37
Oberrusel (rotary engine)	7
Total	232

50: *Hungarian reconnaissance aircraft Lloyd C-V no. 46.36 used in the second half of 1919 by the Szkoła Pilotów at Kraków (MLP – Kraków)*

51: *Friedrichshafen G-IIIa no. 511/17, after a forced landing at Uhrynkowce in October 1919 (Kopański)*

52: *Spad VII of the Szkoła Pilotów at Bydgoszcz, around 1921 (MLP – Kraków)*

53: *Air display at Ławica airfield – 3 May 1919. A Rumpler Ru C I is in the foreground (Kopański)*

54: *Ansaldo A-300-4 24517, A demonstrator example from the Gio Ansaldo company. The photo was taken at the turn of September 1923 in Kraków (MLP – Kraków)*

55: *Unique photo of a Halberstadt C-V, one of a dozen of these captured aircraft used by the Polish Air Force. The aircraft carries the markings of II Eskadra Wielkopolska – 1919 (Kopański)*

56: *A crashed Breguet XIV, still wearing French camouflage (Kopański)*

57: *Nieuport 17 C1 no. 11.01 captured at the southern front. Crashed at Toruń airfield in the hands of* por. *Jan Matecki on 26 February 1920 (Kopański)*

58: *The Szkoła Pilotów – Ławica. Albatros JI 217/18 is in the foreground (Kopański)*

59: *Friedrichshafen G-IIIa landing at Lwów airfield in 1920 (Kopański)*

60: *Fire in III RPL at Lewandówka airfield in Lwów (Kopański)*

61: *Anatra Anasal no. 815 captured on 19 April in Wilno by Polish troops. The aircraft was allocated to 1 Eskadra Lotnicza within 1 Grupa Lotnicza based at Porubanek airfield (Kopański)*

Later inventory of equipment prepared by Inspektorat Wojsk Lotniczych

Aircraft role	Number
fighter	9
spotting	100
training	70
withdrawn from use	21
Total	200

Even worse was the situation with on-board instrumentation and equipment, as there was virtually none. Serious shortages affected everything from cameras down to flying controls and instruments.

The first combat eskadras were in fact combat units only on paper, as there were no machine guns, bomb racks, or cameras. For example, the first reconnaissance photographs during the defence of Lwów in 1918 were taken with the observer's private camera.

There were also problems with fuel. Sufficient stores were only available in Krakow, Lwów and Przemyśl. Warsaw and Poznań suffered shortages.

The materiel situation could only be cured at that time by foreign purchase. Individual units undertook efforts to that end. Officers were sent, mostly to Vienna where, using contacts from the old Austrian forces, they would buy equipment, often illegally. After a centralised administration of aviation supplies was formed in Warsaw, such purchases were made in a more organised way, by special military missions or the military attaché in Vienna. Already at the end of November 1918 he had contacted Oeffag, Phoenix, and WKF factories, as these had finished aircraft in storage. After the former Prussian zone territory was incorporated into Poland, the Germans were contacted, and these proved eager to sell aircraft and equipment. The aircraft would be ferried by German pilots to Polish private companies. This went on unofficially, but with Polish government consent. German pilots would simply 'lose their bearings' and land on Polish territory. After a short inspection of the aircraft they would get their payment and go back for another aircraft. At that time it was virtually the only way to obtain aircraft for the Polish Air Force.

In 1919 agreements with the Italian and British governments regarding aircraft deliveries were signed. At the beginning of 1920 special commissions went to these countries in order to select the most suitable equipment. First deliveries were scheduled to arrive in Poland in March 1920. Unfortunately, the deliveries were delayed due to problems with crossing the Czech and German borders, as well as to public feelings in Italy, where leftist activists prevented shipment of equipment for a country at war with Bolshevik Russia. The whole of Europe was at that time to some degree captivated by the idea of the Bolshevik revolution.

Foreign aircraft purchases

Type	Number
From France	
Breguet XIV A2	70
Spad XIII	40
Spad VII	15
Nieuport (training)	16
Caudron (training)	20
Renault 300 hp engines	50
Hispano Suiza 220 hp engines	30
aircraft bombs	4000
From Britain	
DH.9	20*
Sopwith Dolphin	10*
Sopwith Camel	1#
Bristol Fighter	105
Hispano Suiza 300 hp engines	20
Le Rhone 80 hp engines	60
From Italy	
Balilla (fighter, with SPA 220 hp engine)	35
SVA (spotting, with SPA 220 hp engine)	80
From Austria and Germany	
Albatros and Oeffag DIII with Daimler 220 hp engine	38
Fokker DVII with Daimler 330 hp engine	30
Miscellaneous	30
Austro-Daimler 185 hp and 225 hp engines	82
Mercedes 100 hp engines	32

* A gift from King George V

Private aircraft of Lt. Murray, later re-sold to the Polish Air Force

62 Below: *The engine manufacturing company Salmson designed an aircraft around their own Canton Unné engine. This proved to be one of the best reconnaissance aircraft of World War I. A total of 3200 examples were manufactured (Kopański)*

Only some of the aircraft purchased in Britain arrived before the offensive of August 1920.

Wielkopolska proved a rich source of equipment, as some 400 engineless fuselages (at Ławica airfield and in Winiary Zeppelin hall, near Poznań) were captured there. Even though many airframes were worn and not fit for use (some 100), for some time these aircraft were the main source of reinforcement for combat units at the front line.

The following tables indicate numbers of captured and assembled aircraft:

Serviceable aircraft captured at Ławica airfield on 6 January 1919:

Type	Number
AEG CIV	1
Albatros CIB	3
Albatros CIII	2
Albatros CVII	3
Albatros CX	1
Albatros JI	1
Fokker DVII	1
Halberstad CLII	1
LVG CV	3
Rumpler CI	10
Total	26

Aircraft and airframes despatched to Warsaw as reinforcements on 14 January 1919:

Type	Number of aircraft	Number of airframes without engines
AEG CIV	2	6
Albatros CI	6	
Albatros CIII	1	
Fokker EV	7	
Halb CLII	1	
Halb CV	2	
LVG CII	5	1
LVG CV		2
Rumpler CI	3	
Rumpler CIV	5	3
Total	32	12

Aircraft handed over to combat units (February, March, May 1919)

Type	Number of aircraft	Number of airframes without engines
AEG CIV	1	
Albatros BII	2	1
Rumpler CI	1	
Rumpler CIV	4	
Total	*8*	*1*

Between January and December 1919 the following numbers of aircraft were assembled from parts captured at Ławica airfield:

Type	Number
AEG CIV	20
Albatros BII	17
Albatros CIA	6
Albatros CIB	8
Albatros CIII	3
Albatros CVII	10
Albatros CX	1
Albatros DII	1
Albatros DIII	7
Albatros DVa	2
Aviatik CIII	3
DFW CV	14
Fokker DVII	3
Fokker EV	1
Gotha GIV	1
Halberstadt CLII	10
Halberstadt CV	11
LVG BIII	1
LVG CII	5
LVG CV	32
Pfalz DXII	2
Rumpler CI	26
Rumpler CIV	4
Rumpler CVII	6
Sablatnik CI	1
Total	*195*

Inventory of aircraft captured in the former Austrian and Russian zones of partition:

Type	Number
Oeffag CI	2
Oeffag CII	11
Brandenburg CI	33
Brandenburg BI	15
Lloyd CIV	7
Lloyd CV	4

In 1919 the workshops of III Ruchomy Park Lotniczy at Lwów undertook production of Brandenburg aircraft copied from the Austrian series 27. By April one aircraft was assembled from the parts left by the Austrians. In June 1919 the first airframes copied from the series 67 were completed. These aircraft had a modified fuselage structure. They received serial numbers in 67III . . . range. A total of 9 aircraft were made, numbered 67III1 to 67III9.

More aircraft of the series 27 pattern were also built (27III1 to 27III4). Thus the Lwów workshops turned out 14 Brandenburgs. Unfortunately, the air authorities decided that workshop production would not meet the demand and foreign purchases were necessary, so the workshops were not assigned funds and production was halted.

In 1920, after a fire, a part of the workshops was moved to Krakow, where Brandenburg production recommenced. By 1923 between a dozen and 30 aircraft were built there, powered by 200 hp Austro-Daimler engines. The aircraft built in Krakow were designated KW-2. They were mostly used by the Eskadra Szkolna of 2PL in Krakow.

63: *Aircraft of the Szkoła Pilotów – Ławica. Nearest the camera is an Albatros C-X (Kopański)*

64: *A clear view of Albatros C.X no. 4.9 wearing an unusual soft-edged camouflage pattern*

65: *The dis-assembled Nieuport 24bis 'Diana' no. 5086 in which* por. *Juliusz Gilewicz defected to the Polish side on 7 July 1919. From 7 January 1920 Gilewicz took command of 5 Eskadra Lotnicza, to which he brought his aircraft. The naked form of 'Diana the huntress' can just be made out on the fuselage. This aircraft is also shown in photo 31 (Kopański)*

66: *This French-manufactured Sopwith 1 1/2-Strutter was acquired by the Polish Air Force as a war prize captured from the Bolsheviks. The photo of the aircraft was taken in May 1919 at Lewandówka airfield in Lwów. It flew from there to Rumania with Rumanian (!) markings as a liaison machine (MLP – Kraków)*

67: *Spad VII C1 no. 11616 purchased in 1919 by the Polish Military Purchasing Mission in Paris. Upon delivery to Poland it was found that the aircraft were extensively worn. A specially established Polish-French commission evaluated their value at 24% of that of new aircraft (MLP – Kraków)*

68: *Spad XIII C1 no. 24.13 (French no. 8752) from the first batch of 18 aircraft delivered to Poland in early September 1920. The aircraft entered service with 19 Eskadra Myśliwska (MLP – Kraków)*

Aircraft captured during the 1918-1920 war

During hostilities between 1918 and 1920 Polish forces captured substantial numbers of aircraft. Many were captured with railway trains, some aircraft were brought in by defectors from Ukrainian or Bolshevik units, and some erroneous or forced landings occurred. Some aircraft shot down in combat were also repaired.

Of the total number of some 50 captured machines, the following aircraft were used in combat:

5-6 Nieuports of various versions
2 Sopwith 1½ Strutters
1 Anatra Anasal
1 LVG CVI
2 Friedrichshafen G III
1 Gotha GIV

The rest were used as training or liaison aircraft, or often they were not overhauled, but struck off charge after an initial inspection.

Warsztaty Naprawcze (Repair Workshops) organised by the air authorities played an important part in supplying equipment to Polish units. The first such workshops were established at Lwów. Subsequently Centralne Warsztaty Lotnicze were established in Warsaw. Ruchomy Park Lotniczy units were also established, to handle on-going repairs in the front line area. A total of 5 Aircraft Parks were formed, of these nos. I, II and III operated at the front line, while nos. IV and V handled the acceptance of aircraft purchased abroad.

On 21 December 1918 Centralne Składy Lotnicze was formed in Warsaw. This took care of supplying spare parts and aircraft to units.

Flying training centres

Next to the shortage of aircraft, the lack of suitably trained flying personnel was the most important problem of the emerging Polish Air Force. It was therefore necessary to quickly set up training units for both flying and ground personnel.

The airfields in Warsaw, Krakow and Poznań were the main centres of training in 1918-1920. Later on flying schools at Bydgoszcz, Toruń and Dęblin were established.

In December 1918 it was decided to start training at the Mokotów airfield in Warsaw. On 20 December 1919 the unit was officially named Wojskowa Szkoła Lotnicza. In May 1919, within the re-organisation of the training system this unit was renamed II Szkoła Pilotów. The school existed until autumn 1919, when most of its aircraft were destroyed by fire, and the authorities decided to move it to Krakow, where it was incorporated into I Szkoła Pilotów. The new unit was named Niższa Szkoła Pilotów w Krakowie (Elementary Pilots' School in Krakow).

In spite of its modest equipment, as the school only had 9 obsolete training aircraft, during the 8 months of its existence 43 pilots were trained, with 3 fatal accidents.

I Niższa Szkoła Pilotów was formed on 11 April 1919 at Rakowice airfield in Krakow. The school was based on foundations left behind by the Austrian air force. The school was responsible for elementary flying training, and upon the merger with the Warsaw school it provided elementary and conversion flying training. Upon completion of training at this school its graduates were posted to Wyższa Szkoła Pilotażu. At the end of 1919, when Austrian equipment was phased out from air units and replaced by the new French and Italian aircraft, the school was moved to Bydgoszcz and then in October 1920 it was merged with the French flying school which moved to Bydgoszcz from Dęblin. During its independent existence, the Krakow school trained 84 pilots, with 4 fatal accidents.

Limited pilot training capabilities forced Polish air authorities to apply to France for providing a fully-equipped flying school with instructors. Negotiations were concluded successfully and on 12 May 1919 Francuska Szkoła Pilotów started operation at Mokotów airfield in Warsaw. Initially the entire staff and equipment (some 50 Caudron and Nieuport aircraft) of the school was French. Subsequently the school staff positions were doubled by Polish personnel. This allowed renaming of the school on 15 February 1920 as the Niższa Szkoła Pilotażu w Warszawie. In the spring of 1920 the school moved to Dęblin. The subsequent Bolshevik offensive forced the school to withdraw to Bydgoszcz. In July 1920, upon completion of the contract, the entire French personnel left the school, and on 1 December 1920 the school was merged with Niższa Szkoła Pilotów in Krakow. Francuska Szkoła Pilotów had trained 43 pilots, with 3 fatal accidents.

Complete training of a combat pilot requires training in combat aircraft. That was the purpose of the Wyższa Szkoła Pilotażu at Ławica airfield in Poznań, formed during winter 1919/20. Upon completion of the school a pilot would receive his pilot's diploma, while the pilot's wings were only granted after 10 combat missions were flown. The school had excellent equipment given the general Polish situation at that time, as well as a crack instructor's team. During 1920 115 combat pilots were trained; 3 student pilots were killed in accidents.

Air operations of the period required a relevant number of observers. The number of observers in the early period of Poland's aviation was even smaller than that of pilots, so the Szkoła Obserwatorów Lotniczych was formed. It was opened on 1 August 1919 at Mokotów airfield in Warsaw. Subsequently, during spring 1920, the school moved to Toruń airfield, where it operated until June 1920. Then the school personnel formed the Eskadra Torunska, which in June1920 left for the front line. The school trained a total of 65 observers in 3 courses.

There were three more air schools: Szkoła Oficerska Aeronautów-Obserwatorów in Toruń, Szkoła Obslugi Lotniczej in Warsaw, and a similar one in Poznań.

Polish combat operations 1918-1920

On 11 November 1918 Ukrainian troops from the former Austro-Hungarian Army captured Lwów, surprising the Poles. This led to protracted conflict with the West Ukrainian People's Republic. In spite of the surprise attack and lack of military forces in this area, the Poles spontaneously formed armed troops and put up resistance in the city. Ukrainian forces reached as far as Przemyśl and river San, temporarily cutting Lwów off from the rest of Poland. The first relief operation started from Przemyśl, under *płk.* Karaszewicz-Tokarzewski, on 19 November 1918. These forces drove the Ukrainians out of Lwów. In March the Ukrainians launched an offensive which again interrupted the connection between Lwów and Przemyśl, and it was the second relief operation under *gen.* Iwaszkiewicz that forced the enemy to retreat to the east.

Withdrawal of German forces (Ober-Ost) from the Ukraine changed the situation in this area. The Ukrainian People's Republic was created in the territory left by the Germans. This emerging country's forces reached for Wołyń and Chełm regions.

May 1919 brought the decisive offensive by Polish forces. West Ukrainian forces, attacked by the Poles from one side and by the Bolsheviks from the other, signed an armistice with Poland on 1 September 1919, and later even joined the Polish forces against the Red Army.

Withdrawal of the German army to East Prussia resulted in a rapid Bolshevik advance westwards. On 5 January 1919 the Red Army captured Wilno, and on 14 February the Polish troops which entered the territory left by the German army had its first encounters with Bolshevik troops. The Polish-Bolshevik front line in Lithuania and Byelorussia was formed. The Polish army aimed at stopping the westward drive of the Red troops, in order to prevent the Bolshevik plans to incorporate Poland into the Soviet Union. The first combat, victorious for the Poles, took place on 17 February at Maniewicze.

Marshal Józef Piłsudski started offensive operations in March, and in April 1919 Wilno, Baranowicze and Lida were captured. By mid-July the front line was stabilised. After the fiasco of peace talks held in June and in August, the Poles undertook an offensive, capturing Mińsk on 8 August and Bobruysk on 29 August.

In the Ukraine, fighting with the Red Army commenced in July 1919, after the cessation of hostilities between the Polish and Ukrainian forces.

In September Poland signed an agreement with Semen Petlura, the leader of the Ukrainian People's Republic, declaring war against the Red Army. Unfortunately, attempts to achieve an agreement with the White Russian leader Denikin failed, as he aimed at re-creating the pre-WWI Russia, which meant denouncement of Poland's independence. Thus Piłsudski ordered combat operations to halt so as not to support the anti-Polish Denikin.

In October negotiations with the Bolsheviks commenced. These negotiations lasted until December 1919 in Moscow and in the Polesie region. Lack of actions by the Polish forces allowed the Red Army to destroy Denikin's and Petlura's forces.

In January 1920, at the request of the Latvian government, *gen.* Rydz-Śmigły led 1 and 3 Divisions to Dyneburg (Daugavpils) in Latvia and forced the Red Army out of that area. The city was then handed over to the Latvians.

On 29 January 1920 the Bolshevik government offered an armistice to Poland, simultaneously preparing an offensive which was soon launched from the north. It was, however, quickly stopped by the Polish troops.

On 25 April the Polish offensive commenced. Polish troops under *gen.* Rydz-Śmigły, with support from the Ukrainian troops under Petlura, reached Kiev at the beginning of May, capturing the city on 8 May.

Meanwhile the Bolsheviks withdrew east, and started a concentration of troops preparing for a major counter-offensive. On 26 May the Russians, led by Tukhachevsky, launched the counter-offensive and soon broke through the Polish defence lines, driving Polish forces westwards. The hastily formed reserve army under *gen.* Sosnkowski temporarily forced Tukhachevsky's army to retreat.

After Denikin's defeat the Budenny horse army arrived at the Polish front and at the end of May launched another offensive against the Poles. Budenny managed to break the front line at Samohorodek and make a deep penetration towards Żytomierz and Berdyczów. Polish forces, threatened with encirclement, were forced to retreat rapidly, and Budenny's army reached as far as Lwów and Zamość. On 4 July Tukhachevsky's army launched another offensive in the north. In spite of heroic defence the Polish army retreated westwards. The Polish HQ attempted to arrange a defence line along the old German trenches on Szczara and Niemen rivers, but the Bolsheviks soon got to the Narew and Bug rivers. This line fell, too, and Tukhachevsky's forces found themselves on the Vistula river in the heart of Poland.

With the capital city facing surrender the Government of Poland resigned and on 1 July full

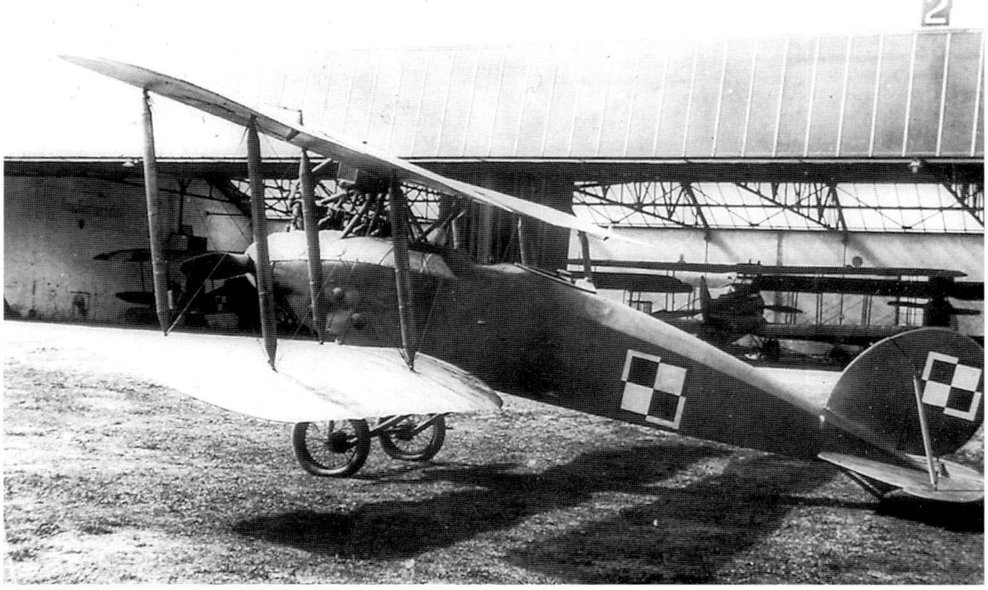

69: *The multi-role Albatros XV had been developed at the end of the war and few examples took part in the fighting. 15 aircraft of the type were used in Poland, purchased between August and November 1920 (MLP – Kraków)*

70: *A Brandenburg B I used by the Szkoła Pilotów, based at Bydgoszcz (MLP – Kraków)*

71: *Rumpler C-I no. 104/17, manufactured by Markische Flugzeug Werke, used by the Szkoła Pilotów at Ławica in Poznań (MLP – Kraków)*

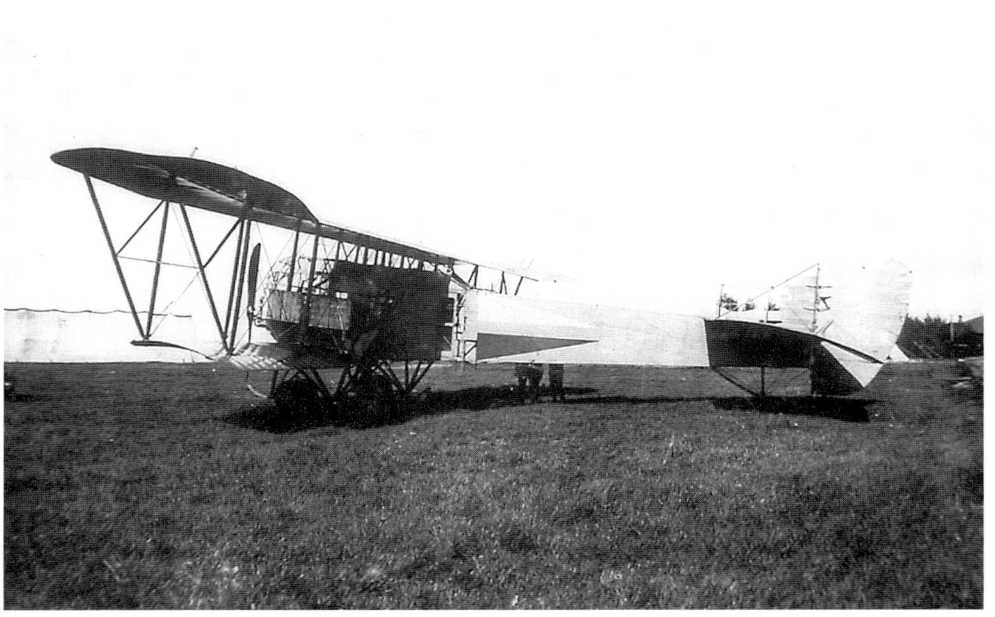

72: *An Ilya Muromets version D destroyer aircraft. Aircraft of the type were used by Polish pilots serving in the Tsar's army. One of these went to I Polish Corps at Bobruysk (MLP – Kraków)*

73: *Hannover CL-II no. 8.2 (13253/17) was taken over by the Poles in Warsaw. It crashed on 4 February 1920, killing the commander of 6 Eskadra Lotnicza,* por. *Kazimierz Swoszowski (Kopański)*

74: *The CWL series 18 was the first Polish-manufactured aircraft and was a copy of the Hannover CL-II. The prototype, no. 18.01, crashed on 23 August 1919 during a public display in presence of Marshal Piłsudski, Polish C-in-C. The aircraft was informally called 'Słowik' (literally 'nightingale') because that was the last name of the manager of the Centralne Warsztaty Lotnicze plant where it was built. The manager inspired the construction and was killed in the crash (MLP – Kraków)*

75: *An LVG C-VI reconnaissance aircraft used in the officers' Szkoła Obserwatorów Lotniczych in Toruń. In the foreground is no. 550/18, with no. 1505/18 behind. Note the man on the left with a bandaged head (MLP – Kraków)*

76: *Hannover CL-II no. 681/18 (later Polish serial 8.15) during overhaul in Lwów in June 1919. The machine was assigned to the commander of II Grupa Lotnicza,* kpt. *Camillo Perni (Kopański)*

77: *Reconnaissance AEG C-IV no. 7123/17 (Polish serial 5.3) in the markings of 9 Eskadra Rozpoznawcza at Rakowice airfield in Kraków (MLP – Kraków)*

78: *An Albatros C-XII at the Lwów airfield.* Por. *Stefan Stec, the author of the Polish aircraft national marking, is standing in front of the machine (Kopański)*

79: *Halberstadt CL-II no. 223/18, manufactured by Bayerische Flugzeug Werke, during overhaul in the workshops at Poznań-Ławica (MLP – Kraków)*

80: *Spad XIII C1 no. 24.25 used in 1 Pułk Lotniczy in Warsaw (MLP – Kraków)*

authority was taken over by the Rada Obrony Państwa headed by *marsz.* Józef Piłsudski.

After the failure of attempted negotiations by Entente governments, which met with no response from the Bolshevik leader, the Poles were left alone to fight with all the forces they could muster. Unfortunately, deliveries of Western equipment were delayed. On 28 July the Bolsheviks established at Białystok a puppet communist government of Poland, the Tymczasowy Komitet Rewolucyjny Polski. In August the decisive Bolshevik offensive was started. Preparations for the counter-attack were prepared according to plans of *marsz.* Józef Piłsudski. On 13 August the Russians commenced an all-out attack against Warsaw. After heavy fighting on 14-15 August Tukhachevsky's army was stopped. On 16 August an attack was launched against Bolshevik positions. A special strike group counter-attacked from the Wieprz river towards the rears of Tukhachevsky's army. The counter-offensive cut Tukhachevsky's forces off from the rest of the Bolshevik armies, preventing their retreat. Tens of thousands of Red Army troops were captured. The rest of Tukhachevsky's forces withdrew to Lithuania via Prussia. On 20 August another Polish offensive was launched against Budenny's horse army. After heavy fighting at Zamość, Budenny's army was forced to retreat and the Poles captured Kowel and Równe.

Bolshevik forces tried to organise their defence along the Niemen river. After re-grouping their forces, the Polish army undertook further offensive actions and another major battle was fought on the Niemen. On 20 September a Polish attack commenced. 2 Army under *gen.* Rydz-Śmigły managed to break the Bolshevik defence and capture Grodno and Lida.

On 12 November a preliminary truce was signed, as the Polish army had achieved its goals and the newly born country needed peace. On 18 October at 24.00 hours all hostilities were halted at the Russian front line.

81: *Friedrichshafen G-IIIa no. 511/17 with a Polish marking in a non-standard position – on the nose (MLP – Kraków)*

82: *Fokker D-VII fighter no. 22.04, fitted with a 160 hp Mercedes D-III engine. The aircraft had Polish markings applied, but retained the German lozenge fabric finish (MLP – Kraków)*

At that time Wilno (Vilnius), a city with a large proportion of Polish people, was under Lithuanian control according to a Lithuanian-Bolshevik agreement. On 7 October a group of troops under *gen.* Żeligowski, following secret orders from *marsz.* Piłsudski 'revolted' and attacked Wilno. The city was captured on 9 October. In subsequent days the control was expanded to neighbouring territory, creating the so-called Litwa Środkowa (Central Lithuania) which was subsequently incorporated into Poland.

A peace agreement with Bolshevik Russia was signed on 18 March 1921 in Riga, Latvia. The treaty marked the official end of the war and defined Poland's eastern borders.

1 *Rtm. – rotmistrz*, a rank in Polish cavalry, commander.
2 according to a listing by Tomasz Kopański.
3 According to "Ku czci poległych lotników . . ."
4 At the time it was issued the order was already outdated by the events, as units were formed spontaneously in other locations: 1 and 3 Eskadra Bojowa in Krakow, 2 Eskadra Bojowa in Lwów.
5 According to the report of the Head of the French Military Mission, *Gen.* Henrys.
6 The abbreviated form Dyon was commonly used in official reports and records, as well as by historians in parallel with the full name of Dywizjon.

83 Right: *Rumpler C-I no. 1121/17 at Ławica airfield (MLP – Kraków)*

84 Below: *Reconnaissance aircraft LVG C-V no. 9.5. In the cockpit is the crew: pilot* sierż. sztab. *Katarzyński and observer* pchor. *Szczepański from 12 Eskadra Rozpoznawcza. Katarzyński was a pilot who flew some 50 sorties in the Polish-Bolshevik war. He was killed in another LVG C-V in September 1920. The lizard motif was applied only on the port side of the aircraft (Kopański)*

85: *A Rumpler C-IV photographic reconnaissance version. In Poland this version was given a suffix Rubild. This was short for the German name Rumpler Bildflugzeug. The photo shows airframe no. 4099/18, seen at Kraków-Rakowice airfield (MLP – Kraków)*

86: *Nieuport 17 no. 4233 used by the HQ of I Dywizjon Lotniczy from mid-1920. The aircraft was unarmed (MLP – Kraków)*

87: *LVG C-VI no. 22465 crashed on 10 February 1919 in the hands of* por. *Prauss. The LVG with a white code number '22' belonged to 3 Eskadra Lotnicza (MLP – Kraków)*

ESKADRA HISTORIES

From 1918 to the 1921 Polish-Bolshevik Armistice

1 Eskadra Wywiadowcza

The Eskadra was formed by the orders of the Aviation Commander of 21 December 1918. *Rtm. pil.* Tadeusz Grochowalski undertook to establish the unit at Mokotów airfield in Warsaw. Unfortunately, lack of trained personnel and, above all, lack of aircraft prevented the eskadra from attaining combat operational status until February 1919, under the command of *por.* pil Henryk Skoczdopole.

On 20 March the Eskadra, with incomplete equipment (5 Albatros CIIIs and 1 Albatros CX), was assigned to the Lithuanian-Byelorussian Division and moved to Dojlidy airfield near Białystok. The Eskadra flew reconnaissance and bombing missions. Due to extensive action, by April the unit was not fit for operations as only two unserviceable aircraft were left. Operations were resumed when aircraft of 11 Eskadra were transferred.

At the end of May the unit moved to Porubanek airfield at Wilno. From June the Eskadra had 6 aircraft: 3 Albatros C-Xs, 1 Roland CL-II and a captured Anatra Anasal plus an Albatros C-II undergoing repair.

In July only 3 serviceable aircraft were left, but still, 16 combat missions were flown. From mid-July *por. pil.* Wiktor Willman took command of the unit. Lack of observers was the main problem during this period, which often resulted in ground personnel performing the role of observers. In August the Eskadra still operated from Porubanek airfield.

At the end of September 582 Eskadra Salmsonów was incorporated into 1 Eskadra, which increased its strength to 5 aircraft. *Por.* Bogusz was appointed the new commander. From the moment of the merger of 582 Eskadra, 1 Eskadra remained as the reserve of the Supreme HQ Wojsko Polskie. During autumn 1919 the Eskadra rested as the front line stabilised for a while. In the winter the unit was reinforced by foreign volunteers: three Englishmen, Capt. Sterling, Capt. Tanquwray and Lt. Woodhouse. (Later on, in September 1920 a Belgian, Lt. Robert Vanderauvera arrived.) The intensity of flying increased in January 1920. A good example here is the flight of a mixed crew which attacked Lithuanian positions. During the attack the observer was wounded, upon return the pilot, with another observer, took off for another attack against enemy units. In February an attempt was made to unify unit equipment, and 1 Eskadra was to be equipped with Salmson aircraft, but this went on slowly due to troubles with obtaining

88: *LVG C-V from I Eskadra Wielkopolska, 1919. The names presumably relate to the wives or girlfriends of the crew (Kopański)*

suitable numbers of aircraft. Similar shortages also applied to personnel, particularly with the lack of observers. At the beginning of March 1 Eskadra had 7 aircraft and 9 pilots, but only 4 observers.

In April, before the Kiev offensive, the unit was made part of IV Grupa Lotnicza and moved to Zahacie airfield. The Eskadras again incorporated aircraft, this time from 11 Eskadra, along with a proportion of its personnel. From Zahacie airfield Eskadra crews flew mainly reconnaissance missions in search of Red Army concentration areas. These missions were often connected with bombing. During the retreat in the summer 1920 the Eskadra evacuated airfields no less than 7 times. Evacuation of Zahacie airfield was the most difficult one, when airmen were left without protection from enemy ground troops. The unit took off at dawn, during a thunderstorm, but there was no time to wait as Red Army units approached. In August the Eskadra reached Warsaw with just one Nieuport aircraft . . . on a railcar. Fortunately in Warsaw the unit was replenished, receiving new Bristol Fighters. *Por.* Domes took command of the unit. Combat operations were resumed on 15 August, when they carried out reconnaissance duties east of Warsaw, on behalf of the 5th Army. By 22 August crews had flown 22 combat missions, plus a few liaison flights. From the following day the unit was assigned to the 2nd Army HQ. When the Battle of Niemen started the Eskadra was based at Dojlidy airfield near Białystok, where it flew mostly close reconnaissance missions. From mid-September 1 Eskadra aircraft reconnoitred Bolshevik fords across the Niemen river. The reconnaissance operation ended on 19 September, allowing Polish units to start their decisive attack. On 21 September the Battle of Niemen started, and the aircraft supported their own infantry in the attack, which earned the Eskadra special commendation from the Army commander. By the end of September the Eskadra flew in support of ground troops attacking eastwards. On 2 October it moved to Lida airfield, and the intensity of fighting decreased significantly, due to the slow down of the Polish offensive. The Eskadra was still at that airfield at the time of the armistice.

During the hostilities a total of 203 combat missions were flown in a total time of 474 hours. 2 airmen were lost.

2 Eskadra Wywiadowcza

The Eskadra was formed on 5 November at Lublin airfield as the Oddział Lotniczy w Lublinie, also known as 2 Eskadra Bojowa. It was organised and first commanded by *mjr pil.* Jerzy Syrokomla-Syrokomski. From the beginning the Eskadra had difficulty in obtaining both equipment and personnel. In early February it was renamed 2 Eskadra Lotnicza, and then 2 Eskadra Wywiadowcza. In March the Eskadra was assigned to the group of *gen.* Babiański, operating at Kowel. Due to logistics problems, the whole unit could not move at once, so a part of the unit was moved to Włodzimierz Wołyński airfield, while the rest was loaded on railcars and waited at Lublin. It was with the unit in such shape that the command was taken over in April by *por.* Wiktor Robotycki. Unfortunately, at the end of April fire destroyed nearly all the unit equipment whilst on railcars. Only 3 serviceable aircraft were left: 2 Albatros CIs and a Rumpler.

In this condition the Eskadra, or its remnants, was assigned to the staff of the Commander of the Ukrainian Front, and was based at Równe. At that airfield, in terrible conditions, the Eskadra remained until spring 1920. In the spring of 1920 it participated in the offensive against Kiev, while based at Koziatyń. Due to the loss of aircraft, within a few days it was transferred to Równe, and subsequently to Łuck. During the fighting in Ukraine one of Eskadra 2's pilots was captured, but when the Polish troops captured Żytomierz he took advantage of the panic among the Bolsheviks and escaped. At the railway station he forced a Bolshevik soldier-driver to give up a car, and returned in it to his Eskadra. In July the personnel and equipment of 9 Eskadra was incorporated into 2 Eskadra. After that the unit operated extensively against the advancing Budenny offensive. During the retreat the unit withdrew to Lublin airfield, where it remained as the reserve of the HQ of the Front commanded by *gen.* Rydz-Śmigły, and subsequently, in a few days, it was withdrawn to Dęblin for replenishment of equipment and personnel.

During the Polish counter-offensive the Eskadra operated from Dęblin airfield until the armistice. Combat operations of the unit amount to 193 sorties in a total time of 434 hours. By the orders of the Supreme HQ of 18 January 1921 the Eskadra was incorporated into 1 Eskadra Wywiadowcza.

3 Eskadra Wywiadowcza

The Eskadra was established as the 'Eskadra Warszawska' in December 1918. *Kpt. pil.* Julian Słoniewski was its first commander. The Eskadra was organised rather quickly, and on 24 January 1919 it left by rail for the front line at Lublin. It commenced combat operations in February, reporting to the commander of the group at Włodzimierz Wołyński. Subsequently the Eskadra operated from Kowel airfield as part of IV Grupa Lotnicza. The Eskadra's initial equipment included a DFW C of an unspecified version, an Albatros CI, 2 Albatros CXs, an Albatros DIII, an LVG CV and an LVG CVI, and just three crews. Operations consisted mainly of reconnaissance missions, but also bombing, principally using captured Russian bombs. In June 1919 the Eskadra, by then commanded by *kpt. pil.* Donat Makijonek, was moved to Ciechanów and became the reserve of the new Front Mazowiecki. In October it

89: *Lloyd C-V no. 46. 37 crashed in Kraków in July 1919 (MLP – Kraków)*

90: *Albatros D-III in flight (MLP – Kraków)*

91: *An Italian SVA-10 reconnaissance aircraft, one of 90 examples obtained by Poland during 1920-21 (MLP – Kraków)*

92: *LVG C-V no. 224/17 used initially in Szkoła Pilotów at Poznań-Ławica, and later by 6 and 17 Eskadra Rozpoznawcza (MLP – Kraków)*

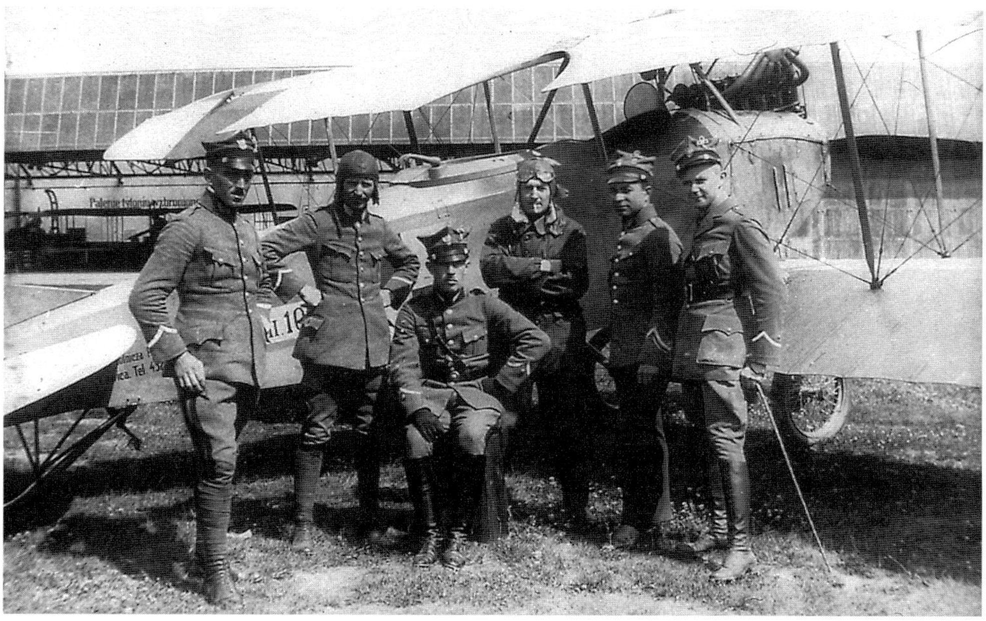

93: *An Albatros C-III. Fifteen aircraft of the type were used in Poland for training, of which ten had been captured in Warsaw (MLP – Kraków)*

94: *All Albatros C-X aircraft in Polish hands were war prizes. Most had been captured in Warsaw. They formed the equipment of most reconnaissance units in early 1920. The photo taken in May 1919 shows an Albatros C X of 3 Eskadra Lotnicza (MLP – Kraków)*

95: *LVG C-V no. 1099/18 damaged at the beginning of 1920 (MLP – Kraków)*

96: *Oeffag D-III no. 253.237 from the last delivery. The photo was taken soon after purchase (MLP – Kraków)*

97: *Albatros C-X no. 4.14 at Lwów airfield. The aircraft has a white eagle – the Polish coat of arms – painted on the fuselage aft of the national marking (MLP – Kraków)*

98: *The second in the batch of Lwów Brandenburgs, no. 67.III.1, during shipment of the fuselage (MLP – Kraków)*

99: *Ansaldo A-300-3 no. B-5 during an air display on the Regimental Day at 2 Pułk Lotniczy, 15 May 1922, Kraków (MLP – Kraków)*

100: *Ansaldo A-1 Balilla fighter no. BAL.117 built in Poland under licence. Production of Balillas in Poland was undertaken by the Plage and Laśkiewicz company in Lublin. The photo was taken at Poznań in 1926 (St. Kopa)*

moved to Krakow, where it was replenished with new Breguet XIVs and new personnel. It stayed in Krakow until April 1920 training on the new equipment. It was during that month that, together with 39 Eskadra Breguetów renamed 16 Eskadra Wywiadowcza, it formed part of the new 5 Dywizjon Lotniczy and was despatched to the front line at Kiev, where it arrived on 13 April 1920. Its main task was aerial reconnaissance for the Wódz Naczelny. At that time the Eskadra operated from Starokonstantynów airfield. In April 3 Eskadra flew a total of 19 combat missions.

As the Polish offensive advanced, the Eskadra moved to subsequent airfields: at Zwiahel, Stawiszcze, Żytomierz, and eventually at Kiev. Based at Post Wołynski airfield at Kiev the Eskadra co-operated with ground troops, attacking the Dneper fords, for example. Also river shipping was attacked, and on 30 May an enemy vessel was sunk.

On 3 June the unit commenced attacks against Bolshevik troops which formed a bridgehead north of Kiev. At that time the Eskadra had just 4 serviceable aircraft. During the retreat the Eskadra was mainly used for assault duties, attacking Budenny's cavalry. It was based in turn at the following airfields: Szepietówka, Łuck and Lublin, being replenished with new equipment at the latter. It was then moved to the Chełm region. In that area its crews attacked the enemy, displaying courage and bravery. From August the Eskadra was based at Dęblin airfield and worked for the Wódz Naczelny. With only four serviceable aircraft, during the critical days of 15-19 August it flew many reconnaissance and attack sorties. Subsequently the Eskadra operated from Mińsk Mazowiecki airfield, but due to the destruction of all its aircraft it was soon moved to Warsaw to receive new equipment. Upon replenishment the Eskadra moved to the Niemen Front. It went to Białystok airfield, where it arrived on 22 September. Reconnaissance missions in the 2nd Army area of operations were mainly flown from that airfield. As the offensive advanced, the unit operated from Wołkowysk, Słonim, and then Baranowicze airfields. It was at the latter when the armistice was signed.

During the war the Eskadra flew a total of 469 combat missions in 1265 flying hours, with no losses.

4 Eskadra Wywiadowcza

This Eskadra was formed as the second air unit in Warsaw, on 5 January 1919, *rtm. pil.* Aleksander Serednicki becoming its first commander. A large proportion of the new unit's personnel consisted of graduates of the Wojskowa Szkoła Lotnicza.

Even though the Eskadra had only 4 aircraft (2 Albatros CIIIs and 2 Hannover CL IIs) and 2 trained crews, it was sent in April to Białystok, assigned to the Lithuanian-Byelorussian Division. At the same time *por. pil.* Artur Jurkiewicz was appointed the new commander. Nominally the Eskadra was part of I Grupa Lotnicza. Operating from Dojlidy airfield near Białystok the Eskadra participated in fighting in the Wilno area. After capture of the city it moved to the nearby Porubanek airfield. Operations from that airfield continued until 24 May 1919. On that day 4 Eskadra moved to Lida with the HQ of I Grupa Lotnicza. June was a period of intensive air operations, including the bombing of Mińsk railway station. According to reports in mid-June 4 Eskadra had 3 aircraft: a Nieuport[1], an Albatros CX and a Hannover CLII, the latter undergoing repair. In July aircraft of the unit performed mainly reconnaissance missions for the front HQ. Unfortunately, in the next month the Eskadra virtually ceased to operate due to extensive wear of its equipment. In September *kpt.* Iwaszkiewicz was appointed the new commander of the Eskadra, having at his disposal only two serviceable aircraft, both extensively worn.

By the end of October the Eskadra flew over a dozen combat missions, and subsequently a part of the personnel was posted to Szkoła Obserwatorów in Warsaw, while the rest, with their aircraft, moved for a winter rest at Wilno. Fortunately, at the end of December 1919 the French 66 Eskadra, equipped with the excellent Breguet XIV B2s, was incorporated into the unit. Unfortunately, in spite of this replenishment, the Eskadra suffered from shortage of personnel, particularly observers. In March 1920 the inventory included: 5 aircraft, 10 pilots, 2 observers (!) and 21 fitters.

In April the personnel of 4 Eskadra was supplemented with men from 11 Eskadra, and the unit was assigned to IV Dywizjon (meanwhile the unit names were changed from Grupa to Dywizjon). The commander was also changed, *por. pil.* Bolesław Narkowicz taking over this post. At that time the principal task consisted of reconnaissance missions, flown very extensively. Since the Eskadra operated during a retreat, it was forced to change airfields very frequently, which made its work difficult, and increased wear of the equipment. In July the Eskadra found itself at Lida with one serviceable aircraft, after having changed airfields seven times, and *por.* Antoni Sielicki was appointed the new commander of what was left of the unit. This led to the decision that a part of the unit, with the new commander, would be sent to Bydgoszcz, and then to Toruń for replenishment.

The part of Eskadra that had been sent in the autumn 1919 to Warszawska Szkoła Obserwatorów, was evacuated to Toruń in June1920, facing the rapidly advancing front. Heavy fighting and the difficult situation at the front line led the school commandant, *por. obs.* Wiktor Szandrowski, to re-establish 4 Eskadra 'Toruńska' (4 'Toruń' Eskadra) from the school personnel. The Eskadra left for the front, commanded by *kpt. pil.* Stanisław Rybka. The Eskadra was based at Hrubieszów airfield. After a month of fighting the Eskadra was withdrawn to Poznań due to heavy losses, in order to replenish both personnel and equipment. Upon replenishment it quickly returned to the front line, under command of *ppor. pil.* Józef Szyfter, operating from Białystok airfield, and then from Slonim and Baranowicze.

After the end of hostilities 4 Eskadra 'Toruńska' returned in 1921 to Toruń as the Szkolna Eskadra Szkoły Obserwatorów Lotniczych. 4 Eskadra flew a total of 95 combat missions in 217 flying hours, losing 5 airmen.

5 Eskadra Wywiadowcza

This Eskadra was formed on 7 November 1918 in Krakow as the 'I Eskadra Bojowa'. *Por. pil.* Stanisław Jasinski was its first commander. Even before it reached full operational capability, in December 1918 several crews operated at the Czech front line in the Cieszyn area, flying reconnaissance and propaganda missions. In January 1919 the Eskadra was renamed 5 Eskadra Wywiadowcza, and with its 4 aircraft moved to Hureczko airfield near Przemyśl. It was included in the III Grupa Lotnicza. Aircraft of the Eskadra operated mainly along the railway line between Lwów and Przemyśl, protecting it from being severed by the advancing Ukrainian units.

In February the Eskadra had 3 aircraft; a Brandenburg, an Oeffag CII and an Albatros DIII. In spite of such modest equipment the Eskadra continued combat operations with great heart. In May it was moved to II Grupa Lotnicza and undertook offensive operations. It subsequently operated from Stryj, Łuka and Buczacz airfields. In July its organisational assignment was changed once again, when it returned to III Grupa Lotnicza.

Relative quiet at the front line meant that the autumn of 1919 was spent by the Eskadra at Dżuryń airfield near Buczacz, training its pilots and observers. In February the Eskadra's employment in combat operations grew, and during that month the Eskadra's aircraft flew a total of 47 combat missions. In the following month the Eskadra was assigned to 12th Infantry Division with which it would co-operate during the imminent Kiev offensive. During that month it had 6 aircraft, 7 pilots, 6 observers and 13 fitters. Also in March 1920 *por. pil.* Julian Gilewicz was appointed 5 Eskadra's new commander, while *por. pil.* Jasiński was transferred to Warsaw. March was not too difficult, as only 6 combat missions were flown. During the offensive the Eskadra operated from Rachny Lessowyja airfield.

May and June (due to Budenny's counter-offensive) was a very busy period for 5 Eskadra crews. By 6 June some 100 combat missions had been flown, and over 3,500 kg of bombs dropped. Unfortunately, two airmen were lost, and 3 suffered serious wounds. 5 Eskadra pilots were among the first to spot large concentrations of Budenny's cavalry, which later forced the Polish troops to retreat. During the retreat the Eskadra moved to Płoskirowo, and subsequently to Tarnopol where it received its new aircraft, de Havilland DH 9s, which significantly increased its combat capability. From 18 until 22 June, in co-operation with 21 Eskadra Niszczycielska, the unit attacked enemy armoured trains, damaging one of them. Once again the Bolshevik offensive forced the Eskadra to withdraw to Lewandówka airfield at Lwów, with a few *ad hoc* airfields en route. Operating from the Lwów airfield, in August 1920 5 Eskadra crews prevented the capture of the city, forcing Budenny's cavalry to pass the city by. The crews flew almost without rest, several times a day, bombing and strafing the attacking cavalry.

At the end of August, after such extensive fighting, 5 Eskadra had only 1 serviceable aircraft left, plus 5 in repair, so at the beginning of September the Eskadra was withdrawn to Przemyśl. It was the end of combat operations for 5 Eskadra. It was still at Przemyśl at the time of the armistice. Eskadra pilots flew a total of 362 combat mission in 676 flying hours. 7 airmen were killed.

6 Eskadra Wywiadowcza

As mentioned previously, 6 Eskadra entered operations under the name of 2 Eskadra Bojowa on 5 November 1918 at Lwów. *Kpt.* Bastyr was its first commander. By 22 November, when Ukrainian troops were forced out of Lwów, the Eskadra was continuously engaged in fighting. During that time some 69 combat mission were flown, some 250 bombs dropped, and numerous positions, trains, and convoys strafed. Seven passenger and 12 liaison flights were made.

On 25 November 2 Eskadra Bojowa together with 3 Eskadra Bojowa, which arrived from Krakow, formed part of the Lwów Grupa Lotnicza.[2] Until about mid-December, when weather conditions deteriorated, the Eskadra within the Lwów Grupa Lotnicza flew ground support missions in the Lwów area. In December the Eskadra was renamed 6 Eskadra Lotnicza.

In January 1919 the Eskadra had five Brandenburg aircraft, three Oeffags, and an Albatros CXII. It was commanded by *por.* Józef Schmidt, and then from January by *por.* Eugeniusz Roland.

The hard winter did not favour air operations, but in February, when Ukrainian troops attacked, the Eskadra was sent into action immediately. Airmen of 6 Eskadra claimed the first aerial kill of the Polish Air Force. On 24 February 1919, during air reconnaissance over Lwów, the crew of *sierż. pil.* Józef Cagasek and observer *pchor. obs.* Stanisław Pietruski, flying an Albatros C-XII with code no. 7 was attacked by a Ukrainian Nieuport. In a short combat *pchor.* Pietruski managed to hit the fuel tank of the Nieuport and the Ukrainian pilot was forced to land.

101: *A Polish-built Ansaldo A-1 Balilla in the factory's paint scheme (MLP – Kraków)*

102: *Breguet XIV A2 no. 7057 used by 39 Eskadra Breguetów in the Polish-Ukrainian campaign in the second half of May 1919 (Kopański)*

103: *Breguet XIV from 66 Eskadra Breguetów in 1919, with a non-standard six-field checkerboard on the rudder (Kopański)*

104: *One of three examples of the Italian SVA-5 single-seat reconnaissance aircraft. The machine shown in the photo, no. 12211, was tested in 1920 by 7 Eskadra Myśliwska at Lwów (MLP – Kraków)*

105: *A training Nieuport 83 E1 of the Francuska Szkoła Pilotów, used for third level flying training (single-seat, single set of controls) – May 1919 (MLP – Kraków)*

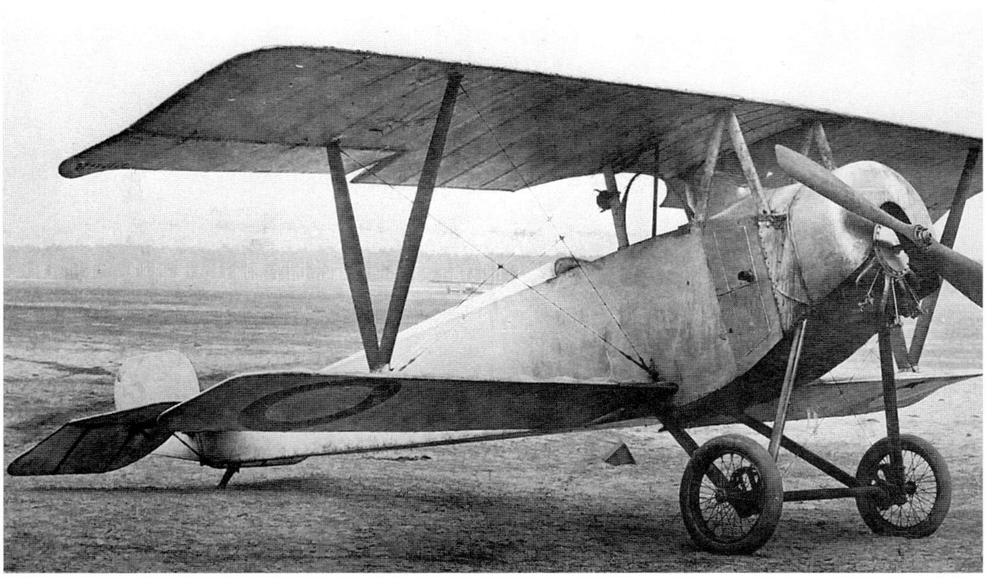

106: *A Nieuport 81 D2 (two-seat, dual controls) for the first level of flying training at the Szkoła Pilotów in Bydgoszcz – 25 February 1921 (MLP – Kraków)*

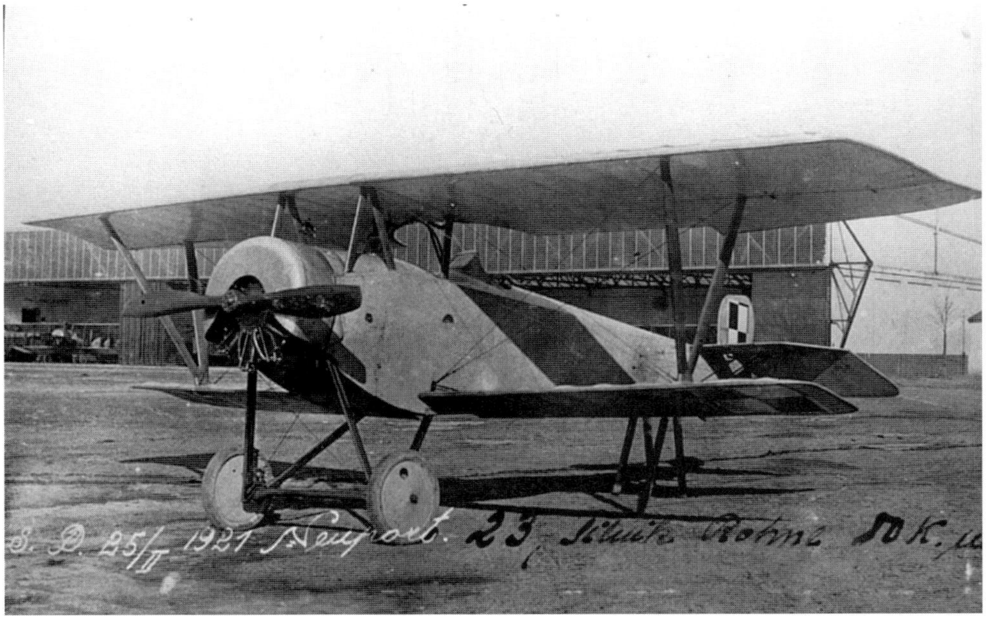

107: *Allegedly a Rumanian Nieuport 11 at Lwów airfield (Kopański)*

108: *The Francuska Szkoła Pilotów in Bydgoszcz. In the first two rows are Caudron G-III training aircraft (MLP – Kraków)*

109: *This training Caudron G-III ended by landing on its nose. The Caudron is in a dark-green paint scheme; first examples were unpainted (MLP – Kraków)*

110: *The personal Spad XIII C1 of* por. *Ludomił Rayski (crescent and star on an oval background were his personal emblems) who would later become the commander of the Polish Air Force (Glass)*

111: *SVA-10 no. S.V.A. 30 of the Wyższa Szkoła Pilotażu at Grudzi1dz. The school's emblem consisted of the letters 'W' and 'S' painted under the cockpit (Olejko)*

112: *21 examples of the training Morane Saulnier MS 30 E1 were acquired by Poland. The aircraft is still in French markings. Morane MS 30s remained in service until the mid-1920s, when they were replaced by more modern Morane Saulnier MS 35s (MLP – Kraków)*

The Eskadra was assigned to co-operation with the army group of *gen.* Leśniewski. March 1919 was particularly difficult, when the Ukrainian attack broke the front and the railway line from Przemyśl to Lwów was captured by the enemy. At the end of March Grupa Lotnicza's structure was rearranged, and 6 Eskadra together with 7 Eskadra formed part of III Grupa Lotnicza under *kpt.* S. Bastyr.

After the Polish offensive commenced in April, II and III Grupa Lotnicza were amalgamated into Zjednoczone Grupy Lotnicze under command of *kpt.* Perini. In total the Eskadras of II and III Grupa flew some 200 combat missions in 180 flying hours. A total of 3,700 kg of bombs were dropped.

Prior to the planned offensive 6 Eskadra had the following equipment: 4 Brandenburgs, 2 Roland CL IIs, 2 Oeffags, and an Albatros C XII.

In May the Eskadra, still within III Grupa, was heavily committed, attacking ground targets, performing reconnaissance, and aerial combats were also fought. The Eskadra performed bravely at Kulików, where it fiercely and effectively attacked Ukrainian positions.

In June the intensity of fighting diminished. In July 6 Eskadra flew only a dozen or so combat missions, and was moved to Tarnopol. *Por.* Kazimierz Swoszowski was appointed the new commander.

By the time the fighting with the Ukrainians was over (a neutrality agreement was signed with the Ukraine on 1 September) the Eskadra had flown 322 combat missions in a total time of 463 flying hours.

The autumn and the winter of 1919 was a period of relative rest and replenishment for the Eskadra. In October 18 reconnaissance missions were flown, for example, while in November only 12 missions.

In February 1920 the commander, *por.* K. Swoszowski, was killed in flight. *Por.* Peter became the acting commander of the unit. The Eskadra flew 43 combat missions. March brought another change of the Eskadra's top brass. *Por.* Adolf Wiesiołowski was appointed the new commander, and would lead the unit until the end of the war. In March the unit had 10 aircraft, 6 vehicles, 6 pilots, 4 observers and 19 fitters.

In April the Eskadra was ordered to move to Płoskirów. This was due to the planned offensive against Red Army troops at Kiev.

During the retreat before the advancing Budenny army, the Eskadra was transferred to Berezowica at Tarnopol, unfortunately by that time all the aircraft had been lost in fighting.

In June the Eskadra received 3 new aircraft, de Havilland DH 9s, so that it could resume combat operations. However, by July 1920, when the Eskadra was moved to Lwów, it had only 1 serviceable aircraft. This, unfortunately, crashed on landing at the airfield at Krasne. In August several overhauled aircraft were obtained at Lwów and the Eskadra took part in the defence of Lwów. It gave particularly meritorious service on 15-18 August. On 18 August, due to direct threat to the airfield at Lewandówka, the Eskadra moved to an airfield at Przemyśl. On 25 August the Eskadra was in lamentable shape, with only 3 serviceable aircraft, plus two more under repair.

During the retreat of Budenny's Army the Eskadra took part in pursuit of the Red Army units, and was subsequently based at Lewandówka airfield at Lwów. The Eskadra's last combat mission was flown on 1 October 1920.

Operations totalled 670 combat missions in 1265 flying hours, with 5 pilots and observers lost.

In January 1921, during the general re-organisation, it was amalgamated with 17 Eskadra, forming 6 Eskadra Wywiadowcza.

7 Eskadra Myśliwska

On 7 November 1918 at Rakowice airfield in Krakow, III Eskadra Lotnicza Bojowa started to be formed. Lack of both aircraft and pilots allowed only the establishment of the basic cadre of the Eskadra. Although *kpt. obs.* Karol Stelmach was appointed commander, it was *kpt. pil.* Camillo Perini who actually commanded the unit. It was organised on the principle of voluntary service. The dramatic military situation at Lwów led to the decision to send the still not fully organised unit to the front. At the end of November the Eskadra moved by rail to Lwów area, and combat operations were started using two Oeffag 51 and one Oeffag 52 aircraft. On 21 December the Eskadra was named 7 Eskadra Lotnicza, and *por.* pil Jerzy Borejsza was appointed commander. At the same time it entered the structure of II Grupa Lotnicza. The crews were havily committed in the Lwów area, performing mainly attack and reconnaissance duties.

In March a reorganisation followed and 7 Eskadra was made part of III Grupa Lotnicza, together with 6 Eskadra. In April, after an accident to *por.* Borejsza, *por. pil.* Stefan Stec became the new commander. In May the Eskadra had 7 aircraft: 3 Fokker E-V/D-VIIIs, 3 Brandenburgs and an LVG CVI. The Eskadra was reinforced before the planned Polish offensive. In May the Eskadra operations became more intensive. On 14 May aircraft of III Grupa Lotnicza attacked Ukrainian troops, thus supporting the Polish infantry. Fierce attacks by the airmen resulted in heavy losses, so that both

Eskadras lost a total of 2 aircraft. Additionally, one was seriously damaged, while the rest all had numerous bullet holes. This was the price paid for flying 18 sorties and dropping some 600 kg of bombs. In June the activity of the Eskadra was much weaker (although one pilot was killed in an accident), and it virtually ceased to exist due to lack of equipment. It was then that the Eskadra commander, *por.* Stec, applied to the HQ with a proposal to reform the 7 Eskadra as the first fighter eskadra. This initiative was met favourably, and in August the Eskadra received 12 new Oeffag D III (Albatros) fighters (purchased in Austria). It was also reinforced with pilots from other Eskadras and at the same time transferred to the command of the Wódz Naczelny which enabled it to train pilots on the new aircraft. In October command of the Eskadra was taken over by *por. pil.* Ludomił Rayski, thus ending the first stage of its activity. Up until that moment the Eskadra had flown 197 combat missions in a total time of 225 flying hours.

At that time American volunteers were posted to the Eskadra. The idea of organising a group of American airmen to fight the Bolsheviks was first brought up during the visit of Cooper[3] to Lwów in the spring of 1919, where they were with Hoover's food missions. Using his connections he talked demobilised American pilots into coming to Poland. The idea was not popular with the Poles, but due to the serious lack of pilots it was decided to accept foreign pilots in the unit. In October the first group of volunteers, consisting of 7 pilots, arrived. They were posted to 7 Eskadra which in December was officially named '7 Eskadra Myśliwska im. Tadeusza Kościuszki'[4] *Maj.* Cedric Fauntleroy took command of the Eskadra. Throughout the winter the Eskadra was at the disposal of the Supreme HQ and was based at Lwów. American airmen were eager to fight and the Eskadra commander, *Maj.* Fauntleroy petitioned frequently for the unit to be sent to the front line. In March 1920 the Eskadra had: 12 aircraft, 12 pilots, 3 observers and 19 fitters. Eventually in April 1920 the Eskadra was moved to Połonne airfield and commenced combat operations. It formed part of 2 Dywizjon Lotniczy. The first combat mission was flown on 10 April, flying reconnaissance sorties for the 2nd Army HQ. In spite of its fighter name, 7 Eskadra Myśliwska pilots performed mainly reconnaissance missions due to lack of Bolshevik opposition in the air. This role was fulfilled with excellence, gaining them ever increasing confidence from staff officers. In April Eskadra aircraft attacked Bolshevik troops during their retreat from Żytomierz. They also attacked enemy columns in the Beryczów area. American pilots twice returned wounded in damaged machines. In May the unit moved to Beryczów and Biała Cerkiew airfields. It also received new aircraft, Ansaldo A-1 Ballilas. These aircraft were mainly used for attack missions against Budenny's cavalry, which had just opened a counter-offensive. It was the airmen of 7 Eskadra who were one of the first to spot concentrations of troops and report that fact to their own HQ. During May enemy troops were attacked constantly, without loss to 7 Eskadra. As recalled by Kenneth Malcolm Murray in his book *Wings over Poland*, during Budenny's offensive the pilots of 7 Eskadra effectively delayed the advance of the Bolshevik cavalry. An interesting mission was carried out by Fauntleroy. He noticed a Cossack outfit planting mines on a railway track on which a Polish train was coming. The pilot decided to warn the train driver and force the train to stop. In co-operation with the American pilot Polish troops from the train defeated the Cossack unit.

In May the Eskadra flew 147 combat mission, the pilots spending a total of 201 hours and 45 minutes in the air. 360 pounds of bombs were dropped and 7,295 rounds of ammunition fired. The next airfield of 7 Eskadra was located at Koziatyń. At the end of May a small unit was extracted from the Eskadra, and this operated from Kiev under *Col.* Cooper, in co-operation with 3 and 16 Eskadra Wywiadowcza. During the retreat aircraft moved to Beryczów and Zwiahel airfields. Large numbers of combat missions in June led to losses of both aircraft and men (4 pilots wounded) and the Eskadra was send back to Lwów for replenishment. By 13 July the Eskadra was back at the front line. Hołoby was the new airfield. While operating from that airfield, two airmen were taken prisoners, and one was killed when flying as an observer in a 21 Eskadra aircraft. Later on the Eskadra moved to Uscilug airfield, and subsequently to Korczów. Eventually the Eskadra found itself at Lwów again. Throughout August crews of 7 Eskadra participated in the defence of Lwów from Budenny's forces. At that time the Eskadra commander was posted to take command of III Dywizjon, replacing *kpt.* Stefan Bastyr after the latter's tragic death, and command of 7 Eskadra was given to *Capt.* George Crawford. The last loss of the Eskadra was the death of *Capt.* T. V. MacCallum on 31 August at Lwów. At the time of the armistice the Eskadra was based in that city.

The Eskadra flew a total of 402 combat mission in 682 flying hours.

The following American pilots served in 7 Eskadra:
pilot *Col.* Cedric E. Fauntleroy VM[5]
pilot *Lt. Col.* Merian Cooper VM
pilot *Maj.* George M. Crawford VM
pilot *Capt.* Edward Corsi VM
pilot *Capt.* T. V. MacCallum – killed in a training flight
pilot *Capt.* Carl Clark VM
pilot *Capt.* Harmon Rorison VM
observer *Capt.* Arthur Kelly VM (killed in a combat mission)
pilot *Lt.* Kenneth Shrewsbury VM
pilot *Lt.* Elliot Chess VM
pilot *Lt.* Kenneth Murray VM
pilot *Lt.* Earl F. Evans
pilot *Lt.* Inglis Maitland
pilot *Lt.* John Speaks
pilot *Lt.* Thomas H. Garlick
pilot Edmund Graves – killed in a training flight

113: *The Ansaldo A-1 Balilla did not enjoy a good reputation among Polish fighter pilots. This was no doubt due to a number of crashes of these aircraft. In the background is a Spad XIII C1 damaged in collision with the Balilla (MLP – Kraków)*

114: *Breguet no. 7490 of 39 Eskadra Breguetów at Kraków airfield in mid-1919. Note the rare example of painting Polish markings on top of French rudder stripes (MLP – Kraków)*

115: *Training Caudron G-III E2 no. 7025 of the Szkoła Lotnicza based at Bydgoszcz (MLP – Kraków)*

116: Col. *Fauntleroy (third from right) and* gen. *Haller (sixth from right), in the company of pilots from 7 Eskadra Myśliwska (MLP – Kraków)*

117: *SVA-5 no. 12090 during a review at the Rakowice airfield in Kraków in February 1920 (Kopański)*

118: *Salmson 2A2 no. 12.16 in the markings of 6 Eskadra Lotnicza. The photo was taken on 15 October 1920 in Lwów (Kopański)*

119: *A Salmson 2A2 with the individual name 'Winiuś', seen after a crash on the Lithuanian-Byelorussian front (Kopański)*

120: *Hanriot HD-28 no. 30.2 converted to a med-evac aircraft (MLP – Kraków)*

121: *Ansaldo A.300.4 at Mokotów airfield, Warsaw. Aircraft of the type were used by 8 and 14 Eskadra Rozpoznawcza in 1924 (MLP – Kraków)*

122: *Nieuport 80E2 no. 11000 at Bydgoszcz airfield (MLP – Kraków)*

123: *Ansaldo A-1 Balilla.* Mjr. *Stanisław Ratmański is standing in front of the aircraft (MLP – Kraków)*

124: *An Oeffag D-III. The landing ended in the loss of the undercarriage (MLP – Kraków)*

125: Lt. Col. *Merian C. Cooper. Lwów, May 1921 (Kopański)*

By special orders of Szef Lotnictwa Polowego all these airmen received special thanks for participation in the fighting. They were also decorated with the Krzyż Walecznych (Cross of Valour), and most received also the Cross of Virtuti Militari (VM) – the highest Polish military decoration.

8 Eskadra Wywiadowcza

The Eskadra was formed as I Eskadra Łącznikowa on 16 January 1919. Establishment of such an Eskadra followed from the need to provide a liaison service for the emerging Polish Air Force. Formation of the unit was entrusted to *ppor. pil.* Zygmunt Herget. The Eskadra received 4 aircraft: 2 Albatros C-XIIs, 1 Albatros C-II and 1 Rumpler C-I. On 8 March 1919 the Eskadra was renamed 8 Eskadra Wywiadowcza. In April it was sent to the front line at Brześć on Bug (Brest Litovsk), initially assigned to IV Grupa Lotnicza, and subsequently to I Grupa Lotnicza, flying reconnaissance missions for the group of *gen.* Listowski. In June it moved to Brodnica airfield near Pińsk. At that time the Eskadra had 4 aircraft including one undergoing repair. In early July an 8 Eskadra crew performed an extremely successful operation, bombing a Bolshevik HQ at Luniec and a railway engine overhaul facility. The attack caused a rapid retreat of Bolshevik forces from that town, which was then easily captured by Polish units. Also in July *ppor.* Karol Chlupka became the new commander of the Eskadra. In August combat missions were halted due to lack of equipment. At the end of the month the unit moved to Kozanogródek airfield near Łuniniec. Unfortunately, at that time the Eskadra had no serviceable aircraft. In spite of that it moved to Porubanek airfield in Wilno, and *rtm. pil.* Piotr Niżewski was appointed the new commander. At Porubanek the Eskadra was reinforced with 3 aircraft. It was at that airfield that the unit spent the winter of 1919. In January 1920 combat operations re-commenced. It flew mainly reconnaissance sorties for the front commander. Intensive operations resulted in a situation where, during an inspection in March, it was found that after the February unification of equipment it had 9 aircraft, but only 3 observers, which reduced its combat capability significantly. During the Polish offensive the Eskadra continued to operate from Porubanek airfield, flying mainly reconnaissance sorties.

By June its inventory had shrunk to 4 serviceable aircraft. In July, due to the progress of the enemy offensive, the Eskadra moved to Szepietowo airfield, whence it continued combat operations. At the end of July the Eskadra had no aircraft capable of operational flying, so it was withdrawn to Warsaw for replenishment. On 12 August, upon receipt of 2 aircraft, the Eskadra joined in the fighting. It attacked ground targets at Pułtusk and Wyszków. Subsequently the Eskadra participated in pursuit of the defeated Bolshevik troops after the Battle of Warsaw. Again due to wear it was withdrawn from the front line for replenishment. Two Halberstadt aircraft were allocated. Upon replenishment the Eskadra was assigned to 2 Dywizjon Lotniczy and operated from airfields in the Chełm and Lublin area. The Eskadra's principal task was to combat Budenny's retreating troops. Following the rapidly moving front line the Eskadra moved in October to Korzec. On 8 October three aircraft of 8 Eskadra forced an armoured train to retreat. At the time of the armistice 8 Eskadra was based at Korzec airfield. The combat effort of 8 Eskadra amounted to 171 sorties in 401 flying hours, with 3 airmen lost.

9 Eskadra Wywiadowcza

This Eskadra started forming in early January 1919 at Rakowice airfield. Already by this time two crews had flown combat mission from Bielsko Biała airfield over Śląsk Cieszyński.

In April 1919 the unit moved to Przemyśl (Radymno) in order to support Polish units fighting against the Ukrainians in the Lwów area. At that time the Eskadra formed part of II Grupa Lotnicza. After the Ukrainian troops were forced out of the city, it moved to Lewandówka airfield at Lwów. In June the newly formed 12 Eskadra was merged with 9 Eskadra. *Por. pil.* Władysław Matula was appointed the commander of the amalgamated Eskadras. The Eskadra followed the front line in its eastward advance, being subsequently based at Kniazie and Brody airfields. From September until the spring 1920 it was based at Dubna. It took until the spring before it re-entered combat again, operating from Płonne airfield where, together with 7 Eskadra, it supported troops in the capture of Beryczów. Subsequently some crews moved to Koziatyń, where they co-operated with *gen.* Jan Romer's cavalry. The high intensity of operations by the Eskadra led to a rapid reduction in airworthy equipment. In June, by the orders of the Aviation Commander, the Eskadra was withdrawn from the front line, arriving at Dubna and subsequently Lublin airfields. It was there that a large proportion of the personnel was posted to 2 Eskadra, while the remaining airmen were posted to Warsaw, placed at the disposal of the Head of Aviation of the Supreme HQ.

In July 1920 *kpt. pil.* Julian Słoniewski was charged with forming an Eskadra for photographic survey duties. The unit was formed from the personnel of the former 9 Eskadra. The new unit received new Bristol F2B Fighter aircraft and the old title of 9 Eskadra Wywiadowcza. *Kpt.* Słoniewski was appointed its first commander. After initial problems, pilots mastered the new aircraft's flying characteristics and found these to be much better than the previous German and Austrian types. During fighting at Warsaw the Eskadra was assigned to the Northern Front HQ. The unit distinguished itself during fighting at Radzymin. Subsequently the Eskadra moved to Lublin airfield and then, as the Polish counter-offensive advanced, it was based at Chełm and Łuck. On 25 September *kpt.* Słoniewski, the unit commander, was killed when returning from a combat mission, and *por. pil.* Bolesław Narkowicz replaced him. At the time of the armistice the Eskadra was based at Łuck.

During the war the Eskadra flew a total of 171 combat mission in 293 flying hours, losing 9 airmen. In January 1921 it was merged into 10 Eskadra Wywiadowcza.

10 Eskadra Wywiadowcza

The Eskadra was formed as early as October 1918 in Kubań, as part of the 4th Fusiliers Division under *gen.* Lucjan Żeligowski. On 10 June 1919 *por. pil.* Ludomił Rayski, the commander of the Eskadra arrived at Lwów. He flew in using the sole Eskadra aircraft, a Breguet XIV A2. The rest of the Eskadra arrived at the front line several days later. With this one aircraft the Eskadra entered combat, flying reconnaissance and liaison missions. Unfortunately, the aircraft's technical condition deteriorated rapidly and the commander was forced to 'borrow' an Albatros D-III from 5 Eskadra. He used this aircraft until mid-July, when he was wounded. Deprived both of its aircraft and commander, the Eskadra moved to Brześć n. Bug under temporary command of *por. obs.* Bolesław Kopyciński. At Brześć *ppłk. pil.* Jan Kiezuń took command. At that time the Eskadra underwent reorganisation and was renamed as 10 Eskadra Wywiadowcza. In October it moved to Ławica airfield at Poznań in order to convert to Breguet XIV A2 aircraft. In the autumn and winter of 1919/1920 the Eskadra underwent conversion training on these new aircraft. At the same time, being in reserve for the Wódz Naczelny, the Eskadra flew propaganda and reconnaissance missions over Pomorze, as Poland prepared to take it over. After Pomorze was incorporated into Poland, the Eskadra moved to Bydgoszcz airfield. At the end of April the Eskadra was moved by rail to the Eastern front, to Kozienki airfield near Mozyrz, assigned 9 Inf. Div. as a part of 7 Dywizjon Lotniczy.

At that time the Eskadra had 7 aircraft, of which only 4 were serviceable. The first mission was flown by Eskadra aircraft on 2 May 1920. Initial sorties were restricted to reconnaissance only, due to a lack of bombs. Only after bombs were delivered on 5 May were several bombing missions flown. At the end of May the aircraft moved to Rzeczyca airfield, and subsequently to Pereświt-Słoboda village. The area of operations reached as far as Homel. Both enemy ground troops and river shipping were attacked, as were spotting balloons. At the end of May the Eskadra carried out extensive operations against the Bolshevik counter-offensive. In mid-June it was forced to withdraw to Kozienko. During the two weeks of June, by the time of withdrawal, the Eskadra flew 20 combat missions, dropping over 100 kg of bombs. The unit's subsequent airfield was located at Kazanogródek, used for only a few days. At the beginning of July the Eskadra reported to Woroniec airfield near Biała Podlaska, but on 11 July it was transferred again to Brześć. When based at that airfield it managed to overhaul 2 Breguets, so that the Eskadra had a total of 3 serviceable machines. Withdrawing before an oncoming offensive, the Eskadra found itself on 5 August in Warsaw where it received new Bristol F2B Fighters (10 aircraft). Subsequently it flew reconnaissance and assault missions in the vicinity of Warsaw. As part of the preparations for the Polish offensive, the Eskadra flew reconnaissance and assault sorties, initially from Mokotów airfield in Warsaw, and from 15 August from Kilkawy airfield near Puławy, in co-operation with the 4th Army of *gen.* Skierski. In pursuit of the enemy, 10 Eskadra moved to Mińsk Mazowiecki, and subsequently to Biel airfield near Małkinia. At the beginning of September the Eskadra was in Brześć. Still operating within the 4th Army, as the only unit of combat value it flew over 30 reconnaissance sorties in just 10 days. From 21 September, after the Battle of Niemen started, Eskadra aircraft attacked the retreating enemy troops. At the beginning of October the Eskadra moved closer to the front line, to Piaski airfield near Słonim. In October combat activity of the Eskadra decreased markedly, and mainly reconnaissance and liaison missions were flown. The last combat mission of the Eskadra was flown on 15 October.

During the hostilities aircraft of 10 Eskadra flew 167 combat missions in a total time of 438 flying hours. Personnel losses amounted to 3 men.

11 Eskadra Wywiadowcza

The Eskadra was formed on 9 January 1919 as the last of the Eskadras formed in Warsaw, and therefore it had the greatest difficulty in obtaining equipment as well as skilled personnel. In the initial period it was organised by *rtm. pil.*Piotr Niżewski.

On 7 April 1919, under its new commander, *rtm. pil.* Antoni Buckiewicz, it moved to Dojlidy airfield near

126: *Breguet XIVs of 66 Eskadra Breguetów at an unprepared airfield. Note the non-standard marking on the tail of the aircraft on the right (MLP – Kraków)*

127: *Hanriot HD 28 no. 30.266 of a training unit. There appears to be a personal name (Marysieńka) under the cockpit (MLP – Kraków)*

128: *Hannover CL-II no. 8.4 (13154/17) – spring 1920 (MLP – Kraków)*

129: *Accident to a Bristol Fighter on 2 September 1923. The crew consisted of* por. *Flaszyński and* por. *Bajan (MLP – Kraków)*

130: *Hanriot HD 28 trainers of one of the flying training schools waiting for take-off (MLP – Kraków)*

131: *Ansaldo A-1 Balilla. American volunteers who fought in the Polish-Russian war of 1920 are standing in front of the aircraft together with Poles. The photo was taken at the turn of October 1920 (MLP – Kraków)*

132: *Ansaldo A-300-3 no. B.2 (MLP – Kraków)*

Białystok, albeit without aircraft. It was there that the unit received one DFW CV which, unfortunately, was unserviceable! Subsequently the Eskadra had two more aircraft assigned, this time serviceable ones. After the Eskadra entered the structure of I Grupa Lotnicza, the group commander ordered these aircraft transferred to the battle-proven and more experienced pilots of the other units in I Grupa (1 and 4 Eskadra).

In July 11 Eskadra was extracted from I Grupa Lotnicza and assigned to the 1 Lithuanian-Byelorussian Division of *gen.* Mokrzycki. With one serviceable aircraft (DFW CV) plus a Roland CL II under assembly, it was based for a while at Slonim airfield. During the ferry flight to Baranowicze the sole aircraft was damaged. Fortunately, the serviceable engine from the Roland was fitted to it, and on 31 August the Eskadra reached operational capability. The first combat mission, a reconnaissance sortie, was flown on 1 August.

The Polish offensive moved the front line eastwards which resulted in a new threat from the north (East Prussia, and the possibility of a German attack). In the autumn 1919 the new Front Mazowiecki was established and 11 Eskadra went back to Białystok, operating over this front during the autumn and winter. On 23 January, after incorporation of Pomorze, the Eskadra was moved to Toruń, where *por. obs.* Tytus Karpiński took command. In April, under a new commander, *ppor. pil.* Wacław Makowski, the Eskadra moved to Zahacie on the Northern Front. At that time the Eskadra had only two crews. In May the Eskadra was divided among 1, 4 and 18 Eskadras, mostly entering 1 Eskadra. Thus 11 Eskadra ceased to exist as an independent unit for a while.

At the end of September, after the victorious Battle of Warsaw, 11 Eskadra was reformed in Toruń. Crews came from 4 Eskadra. *Por. pil.* Antoni Sielecki was appointed the new commander. Upon delivery of aircraft the unit went to Lida where it would form part of 4 Dywizjon. It failed to participate in combat operations, however, due to the armistice.

The Eskadra flew a total of 16 combat missions in a combined time of 41 flying hours, without losses in personnel. On 18 January 1921 the Eskadra was merged with 8 Eskadra, under the name of 8 Eskadra Wywiadowcza.

12 Eskadra Wywiadowcza

The Eskadra was established on 13 February 1919(?) at Ławica airfield in Poznań as 1 Wielkopolska Eskadra Lotnicza Polna. It was organised by *ppor. pil.* Wiktor Pniewski. The Eskadra was equipped with aircraft captured at Ławica airfield during January 1919. At the beginning of March the Eskadra was despatched to the Ukrainian front with substantial equipment (7 aircraft). The Eskadra formed part of II Grupa Lotnicza under *kpt.* Perini and on 17 March started combat operations, flying from Hureczko airfield near Przemyśl. During the offensive against Ukrainian troops in April 1919, 12 Eskadra (at that time still known as 1 Eskadra Lotnicza Wielkopolska) was charged with attacking Ukrainian troops in the Glinniki and Pustomyty area. In June, after the offensive ended, the Eskadra was withdrawn to Poznań, significantly weakening the Polish Air Force at the Ukrainian front. In September 1919 the Eskadra returned to the Eastern Front and was sent to Bobrujsk airfield. The late autumn weather rarely permitted flying, and when it did it mainly consisted of bombing operations. In spite of the adverse weather, Eskadra crews flew 50 combat missions during October, dropping over 2,000 kg bombs. On the other hand only a dozen or so reconnaissance sorties were flown in November and December. The Eskadra entered the New Year with a new commander, *por. obs.* Maksymilian Kowalewski. During January and February extensive flying was not possible and the Eskadra flew few combat missions. In February an attempt to unify equipment within the Polish Air Force was undertaken. In March 1920 the Eskadra had 8 aircraft, 9 pilots, 5 observers and 26 fitters on strength. During the same month more extensive operations commenced, with *kpt. pil.* Władysław Jurgenson taking command of the Eskadra, which was renamed 12 Eskadra Wywiadowcza. Together with other Wielkopolska Eskadras, the unit operated at that time within the Wielkopolski Dywizjon Lotniczy, soon renamed 7 Dywizjon Lotniczy. With the opening of the offensive, a busy time began for the Eskadra. Just between 6 and 15 April 31 combat missions were flown, dropping some 1,000 kg of bombs on Bolshevik positions. Later on the activity of the Eskadra was reduced a little, although on 17 April Eskadra aircraft performed a successful group attack against Bolshevik river vessels and artillery at Berezyna. During this raid the crews dropped some 600 kg of bombs. At the end of April the Eskadra had 12 aircraft, only half of which were serviceable. In May operations increased, thus increasing losses, mainly due to aircraft wear. Particularly painful was the loss of the commander, who was shot down in combat and taken prisoner, and who was later shot dead. Retreat meant frequent airfield changes and co-operation with the 14th Infantry Division. During this fighting the Eskadra fought whilst divided into three groups which facilitated frequent airfield changes. Passing via Białystok (among others) the Eskadra ended up in Warsaw, where it operated with the 3rd Army under *gen.* Sikorski. During the counter-offensive the Eskadra followed the front, operating with the 2nd Army HQ. Subsequent airfields included: Białystok, Grodno and Lida. In September the last loss was reported, when on 22 September a crew was lost during one of the last combat missions. After the armistice in November the Eskadra moved near Warsaw.

The Eskadra flew a total of 515 combat mission in 756 flying hours. Losses of the unit amounted to 8 aircrew.

13 Eskadra Wywiadowcza

The Eskadra was formed as the second one in Poznań. It received the name 2 Wielkopolska Eskadra Lotnicza Polna. Its beginnings date back to 14 February 1919, when *rtm. pil.* Tadeusz Grochowalski started forming the Eskadra. Like most units formed in Poznań, it did not suffer from a lack of equipment. The Eskadra was equipped with Halberstadt CL-II and C-V aircraft as well as Albatros D-III fighters. On 2 April the Eskadra under *ppor. pil.* Edmund Norwid-Kudla went to the Wielkopolska front. Based at Klenka airfield near Nowe Miasto the Eskadra flew numerous patrols to monitor the German Grenzschutz moves. Propaganda missions were also flown, dropping leaflets. During one such mission the Eskadra suffered its first loss. From mid-June 1919 Eskadra aircraft operated from an airfield at Kruszwica, providing reconnaissance during the take over of Pomorze.

On 4 August the Eskadra received orders to move to the Eastern Front, to Chorzewo airfield near Mołodeczno, where it would co-operate with the 4th Army of *gen.* Stanisław Szeptycki. The Eskadra formed part of I Grupa Lotnicza and on 6 August started combat operations. It first combat mission was extremely successful when 5 aircraft bombed the railway station at Mińsk, destroying two steam engines, damaging an armoured train, and breaking the rails in a few places. After the capture of Mińsk a few days later, large quantities of military equipment were captured as the air raid had prevented it from being evacuated. Soon after that the Eskadra moved to an airfield close to Mińsk, whence it could operate over Bobrujsk, contributing largely to the capture of this town. Throughout September Eskadra crews continued an exhausting cycle of combat operations, flying both reconnaissance and bombing missions. This, obviously, reduced the unit's combat capability, and at the end of September the Eskadra had only 4 serviceable aircraft left. In October the intensity of fighting dropped and the Eskadra flew only a dozen or so reconnaissance sorties. By the end of the year air operations in this sector of the front line virtually ceased. From January more intensive combat flying recommenced and 2 Eskadra Wielkopolska flew 14 missions during that month. In February, within the equipment unification, the Eskadra transferred all its aircraft to other units, receiving Oeffag D III fighters and the new name of Eskadra Myśliwska. In April it was renamed 13 Eskadra Myśliwska and formed part of Wielkopolski Dywizjon Lotniczy, later renamed 7 Dywizjon Lotniczy. From mid-April the Eskadra flew mainly reconnaissance missions. Between 30 April and 5 May two aircraft of 13 Eskadra, operating from Żodzin airfield, escorted the missions of 12 and 14 Eskadra, often attacked by Bolshevik aircraft. However, in spite of many interception scrambles, no air combats ensued. In May the Eskadra operated in the Bobrujsk area, detecting (among others) a Bolshevik ford over the river Berezyna which allowed the preparation of a counter-attack. After heavy fighting in mid-May there was a relatively quite period until 28 June, and the Eskadra flew mainly reconnaissance missions. In the last days of June the enemy attacked with overwhelmingly superior numbers which forced Polish troops to withdraw. During the retreat the Eskadra was based at Baranowicze, Hajnówka, and Siedlce. Its aircraft flew reconnaissance, and also attack and bombing missions. In August it moved to Siekierki airfield near Warsaw and was assigned to the 5th Army of *gen.* Władysław Sikorski. After the counter-offensive following the Battle of Warsaw it was mainly used to attack ground troops, and distinguished itself several times. After the end of the counter-offensive the front command structure was reorganised, and air unit assignments changed accordingly. All Eskadras, including no. 13, moved to airfields in the Białystok area. During the relative stabilisation of the front line 13 Eskadra aircraft were used for local reconnaissance and supported their own troops in local skirmishes. When the Niemen offensive started, 13 Eskadra was fighting enemy troops at the crossing of Swislocza river. At the time hostilities ended the Eskadra was based at Lida.

Combat effort of the Eskadra amounted to 647 missions in 793 flying hours, for the loss of 4 aircrew.

14 Eskadra Wywiadowcza

Similar to the other Wielkopolska Eskadras this Eskadra was established at Ławica airfield. On 6 March 1919 *rtm. pil.* Tadeusz Grochowalski started forming the unit, named 3 Wielkopolska Eskadra Lotnicza Polna As it was the third unit to be formed there it did not boast as good equipment as nos. 1 and 2 Eskadra Wielkopolska. On 4 April command of the fully formed unit was taken over by *ppłk. pil.* Marek Krzyczkowski, and subsequently it moved to Góra airfield near Jarocin. It formed part of the Wielkopolski Front that fought against German troops. The Eskadra was mainly equipped with LVG C-V and Halberstad CL II aircraft. Its crews flew mostly reconnaissance and propaganda missions, dropping leaflets. During these missions the Eskadra lost 2 aircraft with one crew taken prisoner.

In mid-June 1919 the Eskadra moved to Lwów, where it would replace 1 Eskadra Wielkopolska which had been exhausted in the fighting. At Lwów command of the Eskadra was taken over by *ppor. pil.* Józef Mańczak. The Eskadra failed to undertake combat operations in the Lwów area, as after a few days it was moved to an airfield near Brzezany, and did not commence operations until July.

Subsequently it was sent to Żodzin airfield near Borysów, moving there in October 1919. Thus the Eskadra was made part of I Grupa Lotnicza. By the end of the year all was quiet at the front line and aerial activity did not increase before January. In February 3

133: *Bristol F.2B Fighter no. 20.7 of a 3 Pułk Lotniczy unit based at Poznań. The Fighters were used in Poland from 1920 until early 1930s (MLP – Kraków)*

134: *The only Sopwith F.1 Camel (no. 5234) used in Poland. It was owned by an American volunteer,* Lt. *Kenneth M. Murray (MLP – Kraków)*

135: *Bristol F.2B Fighter in the colour scheme it received during an overhaul. The dark olive-green aircraft has the new type designation on the fuselage. First Fighters had only the type number (i. e. 20) and individual aircraft number applied. Later on letters 'BR' were added forward of the type number (MLP – Kraków)*

136: *Hanriot HD 28 of the Szkoła Lotnicza based at Bydgoszcz (MLP – Kraków)*

137: *Lewandówka airfield in Lwów. Aircraft of 7 Eskadra Myśliwska: Ansaldo A-1 Balilla, Sopwith F.1 Camel and Oeffag D-III. The photo was taken in late spring or early summer 1921 (MLP – Kraków)*

138: *In the spring of 1921* Lt. *Murray sold his Camel to Polish authorities (he was returning to the USA). Unfortunately, the Camel did not last long in the Polish Air Force – it was damaged in July 1921 by* ppłk. *Ludomił Rayski, who visited 7 Eskadra Myśliwska in Lwów in his capacity of the head of Sekcja Techniczna Departamentu III řeglugi Powietrznej (MLP – Kraków)*

Eskadra Wielkopolska suffered seriously, losing 2 crews which significantly reduced its combat capabilities. In March the Eskadra had 8 aircraft, 7 pilots and 8 observers. At the end of March, within the renumbering process, 3 Eskadra Wielkopolska was renamed 14 Eskadra Wywiadowcza and entered the Wielkopolski Dywizjon Lotniczy, later renamed 7 Dywizjon Lotniczy. The Eskadra was heavily engaged in the offensive that commenced in April, flying many successful operations, including one on 14 April, when during an attack against an enemy airfield at Sławnoje the crew of *ppor.* Ziembiński and *kpr.* Dzierzgowski managed to shoot down a Bolshevik Nieuport. On 18 April an armoured train was successfully attacked, and seriously damaged. On 30 April another air combat took place, but was inconclusive. In April the Eskadra had 10 aircraft, with only 4 serviceable. May brought a large number of combat missions, air combats also occurred, albeit without victories. On 1 May a 14 Eskadra crew was attacked by 3 Bolshevik fighters, but managed to evade them and return to its own airfield, although the aircraft was so badly shot up that it had to undergo a major repair, and that was the last serviceable aircraft at that time. New aircraft only arrived some days later, on 5 May. They were put to good use the same day, when three aircraft attacked a railway station at Prijamno. The poor equipment situation of the Eskadra led the commander to personally go to Poznań in order to accelerate deliveries of equipment. Due to a lack of equipment some pilots were granted leave, and some were even released from service; in mid-May 14 Eskadra had only 2 pilots. At that time Eskadra crews often spotted suspicious activity by Bolshevik units, but this was not associated with preparations for an offensive. The last flight of 14 Eskadra in this area was made on 6 June. By 28 June the Eskadra virtually ceased combat operations, due to the low activity of enemy troops, as well as its own modest forces. The Bolshevik offensive forced the Eskadra to change airfields. It moved to Serebrianka airfield near Mińsk and subsequently to Baranowicze. The Eskadra had at that time only two serviceable machines. During the first days of July several reconnaissance sorties were flown, and subsequently it was decided to withdraw the Eskadra from the front line. It was sent back to Poznań for replenishment, arriving there on 1 August. On 23 August it returned to the front line, equipped with new aircraft. Its first airfield upon return was located at Lublin, and subsequently at Chełm and Łuck.

From Chełm the unit attacked Budenny's retreating units. On 22 September Eskadra crews became very activty, performing reconnaissance duties over a wide sector of the front, and also strafing Budenny's cavalry troops.

Combat effort of the Eskadra amounted to 191 combat mission in a total time of 353 flying hours, and the loss of 3 airmen.

15 Eskadra Myśliwska

On 25 May 1919 *por. pil.* Jerzy Dziembiński started forming the last air unit in Wielkopolska, 4 Wielkopolska Eskadra Lotnicza Polna (also knows as 4 Wielkopolska Eskadra Bojowa). While forming the unit, equipment difficulties were encountered. For training the Eskadra received three fighter aircraft: a Fokker D-VII, a Fokker E-V and an Albatros D III. Plans called for the Eskadra to be equipped with Spads purchased in France. When the Eskadra received these it became a true combat unit, but remained in reserve as a unit at the disposal of the Wódz Naczelny. At that time the personnel underwent intensive training, particularly in formation flying and air combat. In the spring the Eskadra converted to Fokker D VIIs and on 16 May it arrived at Wapiarka airfield in the Podole region, forming part of 3 Dywizjon Lotniczy. The Eskadra, together with other Eskadras of 3 Dywizjon, immediately undertook extensive combat operations. The most successful actions of 3 Dywizjon in this period included an attack which destroyed artillery posts at Zielonka having been carried out by 5 aircraft of 15 Eskadra on 24 May, and joint attacks by 5, 15 and 21 Eskadra aircraft on 27 and 28 May against Malewannaja railway station, where armoured trains and military transports were attacked. Mass raids were carried out by groups of at least 11 machines. During two days a total of 2,350 kg of bombs were dropped. As a result of this action the 12 Inf. Div. captured two armoured trains, and two more were damaged.

In spite of the fierce defence by Polish units, the Red Army advanced which forced the Eskadra to evacuate to Płoskirów airfield. By 23 June the Eskadra remained at that airfield flying no combat missions. From 25 June it was based at Deraznia airfield, whence it recommenced operations, but it flew from that airfield for just 2 days before it returned to Płoskirów, and subsequently moved to Tarnopol, arriving there on 1 July. At that airfield the Eskadra remained until 13 July, flying just 1 combat mission in that time. On 14 July it arrived at Lwów, where it was reinforced with several Fokker D VIIs, a Fokker E-V and an Albatros BII. Combat operations were undertaken again on 21 July. During the first part of August the Eskadra flew only a dozen or so combat missions, these being mostly attack sorties. At Lublin the Eskadra remained until 15 October.

Combat effort of the Eskadra amounted to 277 combat missions in 346 flying hours, with the loss of 1 pilot. For its combat operations the Eskadra received special commendation from the Aviation Commander.

16 Eskadra Wywiadowcza

This Eskadra was 'purchased' by the Polish government in 1919, and still as Escadrille BR 39, under *Cne* de Drouas, equipped with 10 Breguet XIV aircraft, was sent by rail to Poland on 18 April 1919. The unit arrived in Warsaw on 26 April and was sent to the Polish-Ukrainian front as part of *gen.* Haller's army. By the time it was withdrawn from the front line four aircraft of the Eskadra (with just one Polish pilot) had flown 12 combat missions in the Lwów area.

Since the French government refused consent for their soldiers to fight against Bolshevik Russia, in June the unit was withdrawn to Krakow, where it remained until April 1920. Official take-over of the unit by Polish personnel took place on 26 September 1919. The Eskadra had at that time 5 Breguets, of which only 2 were airworthy. All the unit's equipment was in very poor condition. *Kpt. pil.* Jerzy Rudlicki was appointed the first Polish commander.

In March 1920(?) the Eskadra was assigned to V Grupa Lotnicza and commenced preparations for participation in the Kiev offensive. On 11 April the unit left for the front, and 2 days later official orders renamed it 16 Eskadra Wywiadowcza. On 16 April the unit arrived at its operational airfield near Starokonstatynów. The first combat mission for the 13th Infantry Division was flown on 19 April by *sierż.* Tołuściak and *ppor.* Moszczyński. Due to difficulties in supplies the Eskadra failed to receive any bombs, which obviously prevented full operational use. The deputy commander of the unit attempted to solve the problem and *ad hoc* production of bombs was started by adding wooden fins to artillery shells. These makeshift bombs proved their worth in combat operations. They were first used on 20 April during bombing of Bolshevik lines near Czudów. Seven bombs were dropped, destroying 3 railway cars and damaging a platform and a steam locomotive. After the offensive started on 25 April, the number of combat mission increased. During that day only the Eskadra flew 3 combat missions. Following the rapidly moving front line the Eskadra moved on 9 May to an airfield at Koziatyń. From that airfield sorties were flown in support of the 2nd Army operating in the Kiev area. After the capture of Kiev, under its new commander, *por.* Komorowski the unit moved on 23-24 May to Kiev. Aircraft of 16 Eskadra, together with other Eskadras of 5 Dywizjon fought Bolshevik shipping on the Dneper. This was intended to hinder ferrying of Bolshevik units. The Bolsheviks tried to secure a bridgehead in the Rzyszew area south of Kiev and the Okunin area north of Kiev. On 5 June Budenny's 5th Horse Army broke through Polish lines and on 9 June the commander of the 3rd Army, *gen.* Rydz-Śmigły gave orders to leave Kiev. The next day aircraft of 16 Eskadra flew some sorties out of Kiev and subsequently flew to Zwiahel airfield near Nowogród Wołyński. At that airfield the airworthy aircraft of 16 Eskadra were taken over by 3 Eskadra, while the personnel went to Łuck for new equipment. At Łuck command of the unit was taken over by *por. pil.* Władysław Gliński. Unfortunately, the unit failed to obtain its equipment there and, withdrawing with the rest of Polish troops in front of the advancing Bolsheviks, via Lublin and Siedlce it arrived in Warsaw on 5 August. There it was based at Mokotów airfield. *Por. pil.* Franciszek Rudnicki was appointed the new commander. At that airfield the Eskadra received aircraft from the central repair works. These aircraft were of different types and in varying condition. Immediately after replenishment combat operations recommenced. During the Battle of Warsaw the unit was heavily employed. Unfortunately, lack of suitable numbers of aircraft led to a situation where 16 Eskadra airmen often flew equipment from other Eskadras. By 17 August Eskadra airmen had flown 45 combat missions, including 14 in aircraft of other Eskadras. Losses during that time amounted to 4 killed and one severely wounded.

At the end of August the unit received reinforcement in the form of several Breguets, and moved to an airfield at Białystok. It formed part of the 2nd Army of *gen.* Rydz-Śmigły and required to participate in the Battle of Niemen. The Eskadra arrived at Białystok airfield on 3 September. Its first combat mission from that airfield took place on 16 September, being a reconnaissance sortie over the Niemen river area. Eskadra aircraft operated from that airfield until 2 October, combating enemy ground units and flying reconnaissance sorties. On 2 October the Eskadra moved to Grodno. On 5 October aircraft of the Eskadra attacked a Bolshevik armoured train, destroying one of the cars, and on 10 October the unit changed airfields again, moving to Lida. On 14 October the last combat mission against Bolshevik units was flown.

When the free state of Poland was re-established in 1918 it was assumed that it would also include the Wilno (Vilnius) area, inhabited mostly by Poles. Wilno was lost on July 1920 during Tukhachevsky's offensive, and on 26 July Wilno was taken over by the Lithuanians following an agreement with the Bolsheviks. Successes of the Wojsko Polskie in the Battles of Warsaw and of Niemen river led the Polish HQ to opt for a forced solution of the Wilno question. The unfavourable attitude of the Entente and the League of Nations meant that the take over of Wilno could not be carried out as an official operation of the Wojsko Polskie. Therefore Piłsudski decided that Wilno would be captured by a separate formation. This was formed as a 'spontaneous movement' of people anxious about their homeland, so all soldiers participating in this operations signed declarations saying that they came from the Wilno region. The staged 'revolt' included some units of the 3rd Army under *gen.* Żeligowski. These units would later also include 16 Eskadra. On 8 October *gen.* Żeligowski's units, i.e. 1 Lithuanian-Byelorussian Inf. Div., 201 Inf. Rgt, Cavalry Squadron and two batteries of 216 Field Art. Rgt headed for Wilno. Easily pushing back weak Lithuanian forces, they captured Wilno the following day. During subsequent days all the territory lost in July 1920 was re-captured. A separate state of Central Lithuania was

139: *De Havilland DH-9 no. 26.17 when used by the Oficerska Szkoła Obserwatorów Lotniczych in Toruń (MLP – Kraków)*

140: *One of the first DH-9s in Poland. They were delivered to Lwów crated, and at the turn of May 1920 they were assembled there. The aircraft in the photo has the early national markings (Kopański)*

141: *Another DH-9 (British serial H4315) assembled in Lwów. The photo probably shows an accident to an aircraft of 6 Eskadra Rozpoznawcza on 16 September 1920 (MLP – Kraków)*

142: *Hanriot HD-19 training aircraft (MLP – Kraków)*

143: *Poland purchased in 1920 a single example of the Martinsyde F-4 Buzzard. By the end of 1924 it was little used. After an overhaul at the beginning of 1925 it was painted in white and red stripes which earned it the nickname of 'mattress'. It was the personal aircraft of* gen. *Włodzimierz Zagórski, the PAF commander (until March 1926) (Glass)*

144: *Two examples of the SE-5a reached Poland at the beginning of 1920. The first crashed in February 1920, and the second, no. 19.01 (British serial F9135) was delivered to the front line, to 7 Eskadra Myśliwska. Flown by* kpt. *Stefan Ciecierski it was shot down during its first combat mission. The photo was taken on 14 or 15 July 1920 at the 7 EM airfield in Hołoby (Glass)*

145: *Fighters of 5 Eskadra Lotnicza in Przemyśl – 1921. First two on the left are 20.39 (H1278) and 20.44 (H1274) (MLP – Kraków)*

146: *Bristol Fighter no. 20.48 (H1279) of 1 Eskadra Rozpoznawcza. The airmen are Skorobohaty and Gwizdalski. The photo was taken during the Polish-Russian war (Kopański)*

147: *In September 1920 an Avro 504K (no. F or H 2326) was captured from the Russians. It was not overhauled until 1923 and subsequently served in Sekcja Doświadczalna of Wojskowa Centrala Badań Lotniczych based at Warsaw (Kopański)*

established there. Initially the Central Lithuanian troops included no air units. It was soon found, however, that such a unit was necessary, and therefore 16 Eskadra was selected to be transferred there, as at that time it was based nearby in Lida. On 28 October 5 aircraft of 16 Eskadra landed at Porubanek airfield in Wilno. Even before they were dispersed at the airfield, a Lithuanian LVG arrived overhead, and its crew managed to drop a single bomb. The airmen considered this a challenge. Needless to say, before their arrival the entire personnel of the Eskadra volunteered to join the Central Lithuanian Army, and everybody signed the declaration saying that they came from this region. All aircraft received new markings. Polish markings were overpainted, and new markings consisted of an amaranth (bright red) square with white outline on one wing, and a white one with amaranth outline on the other. Elevators and rudders were painted in white-and-red stripes. On 31 October a pilot from 12 Eskadra in an Albatros CXV no. 23.3 arrived as a reinforcement. He was officially on leave.

The first combat mission of the Central Lithuanian Air Force was flown the same afternoon. One Breguet crew bombed Lithuanian troops. The Lithuanians immediately filed a protest to the League of Nations, stating that the civilian population had been bombed, killing 11 people and injuring many more. Whilst operating within the Central Lithuanian Air Force, 16 Eskadra flew some 30 combat missions. These were mostly reconnaissance and bombing sorties. The last combat mission was flown on 25 November 1920. Four days later an official armistice was signed between Lithuania and Central Lithuania. After combat operations were suspended the aircraft of 16 Eskadra flew a dozen or so reconnaissance sorties dropping leaflets. These missions were flown until January 1921. On 3 March 1921 the Eskadra was sent back to Krakow for reorganisation.

Eventually on 10 September 1921 the Eskadra went to Warsaw, where it formed part of 1 Pułk Lotniczy. During hostilities the Eskadra flew 177 combat mission in a total time of 275 flying hours, without losses.

17 Eskadra Wywiadowcza

The Eskadra arrived from France in May 1919 with *gen.* Haller's Army as the French Escadrille BR 59. It was first based at Krakow. In September 1919 it was taken over by the Polish authorities, and *kpt. pil.* Jan Strwiąż-Smolnicki was appointed as commander. During the autumn and the winter of 1920 training of Polish personnel took place. At the end of March 59 Eskadra (renamed 17 Eskadra in April) was despatched to Tarnopol where it became part of 3 Dywizjon Lotniczy of *kpt.* Bastyr. The Eskadra immediately commenced combat operations from Ploskirów airfield. Unfortunately, on 18 April the commander was killed together with a fitter when taking off to test fly a Breguet XIVA2. *Por. pil.* Tadeusz Wereszczyński took command. The main task of the Eskadra at that time consisted of long range aerial reconnaissance. The Eskadra moved along with the advancing Polish offensive. It operated from Rachna Lessowyja airfield some 130 km south of Płoskirów. In June and July the Eskadra operated in very difficult conditions, often changing airfields due to the rapid advance of Budenny's army. By orders of the commander of the Front aviation, three crews were extracted from the Eskadra for service on Kowel airfield. During the ferry flight two crews forced landed due to engine failure, so eventually only one operated with the Front HQ. By mid-July the rest of the Eskadra ceased combat flying due to lack of equipment. The Eskadra was thus despatched to Krakow for replenishment. Unfortunately, whilst there the Eskadra only received old aircraft from the Krakow Pilots' School, and was sent to Warsaw, assigned to the 2nd Army. It arrived in Warsaw in early August and from the moment it arrived the Eskadra operated actively for the 2nd Army, flying reconnaissance missions. During the heavy fighting at Radzymin on 14 and 15 August 17 Eskadra aircraft supported ground troops. In the first days of the Polish counter-offensive the Eskadra resumed reconnaissance duties over principal sectors of the front. After the success of the counter-attack, air units were re-grouped and 17 Eskadra was assigned to the HQ of the 4th Army and moved to Pułtusk airfield. From that airfield their aircraft flew mainly reconnaissance missions along the East Prussian border. At the end of August the Eskadra was sent to Warsaw for replenishment. In mid-September the Eskadra was sent to Brześć on the Bug where it operated for the 4th Army. *Por. pil.* Władysław Kalkus was appointed the new commander. The Eskadra had only 3 old aircraft, more fit for an overhaul than combat. At the time of the armistice the unit was moved to Przemyś where, by the orders issued on 18 January 1921, 17 Eskadra was merged into 6 Eskadra Wywiadowcza.

During the war the Eskadra flew 58 combat missions, totalling 132 flying hours, with the loss of 2 airmen.

18 Eskadra Wywiadowcza

The future 18 Eskadra arrived in Poland in June 1919 together with *gen.* Haller's Army as the Escadrille SAL 580, with entirely French personnel. It was based at Piotrków Trybunalski airfield, as the French airmen were not allowed to participate in combat operations against the Bolshevik army. It was not until the end of September 1919 that the Eskadra was taken over by Polish crews, and command was given to *kpt. pil.* Władysław Krawiec-Iwanowski. Preparations for incorporation of Pomorze led to inclusion of the Eskadra into IV Grupa Lotnicza, which entailed a move to Toruń airfield at the beginning of February 1920. The difficult situation at the Eastern

Front forced the HQ to transfer the unit to Zahacie airfield near Polock and commencement of operations for the commander of the Byelorussian-Lithuanian Front. Using the range of the aircraft many long-distance reconnaissance sorties were flown as far as Psków and Witebsk. In May the few well-equipped crews were reinforced with airmen from 1 and 11 Eskadras. Also in May *por. pil.* Stanisław Gogoliński was appointed the new commander. Unfortunately, he was soon killed (on 24 June 1920) during a ferry flight to Duniłowicze airfield. *Kpt. obs.* Edward Karaś succeeded him as the commander. During the retreat the unit was based at airfields in Mołodeczno, Duniłowicze, Królewszczyzna, Parafianów, and Dokszyce. Frequent airfield changes resulted in increased equipment wear, and only 1 serviceable aircraft reached Lida. Such events forced the HQ to send the unit back to Bydgoszcz for replenishment. From Bydgoszcz it moved to Toruń where, together with 4 Eskadra, it formed IV Dywizjon Zapasowy. At that time *por. pil.* Juliusz Gilewicz was the unit's commander.

Lack of reconnaissance aircraft, as well as the usefulness of fighter units, resulted in the decision to convert the Eskadra into a fighter unit. In order to achieve thisthe Eskadra moved to Warsaw and subsequently to Grudziądz. Whilst there awaiting new aircraft the armistice was signed.

The short period at the front line resulted in 38 combat missions flown in a total time of 86 flying hours, with the unfortunate loss of 2 aircrew.

19 Eskadra Wywiadowcza

The Eskadra arrived in Poland with the Army of *gen.* J. Haller, as the French Escadrille SPA 162. Upon arrival it was located at Mokotów airfield in Warsaw. Polish authorities took the unit over in September 1919, and *kpt. pil.* Stefan Ciecierski was appointed the Polish commander. From December *por. pil.* Kazimierz Tomaszewicz took over command of the unit. Training of Polish pilots lasted until April 1920, when the unit, led by *por. pil.* Antoni Mroczkowski, went to the front. It was at that time renamed 19 Eskadra Myśliwska. Its full complement at that time consisted of 6 Spad aircraft and just 3 fighter pilots. Zodzin at the Lithuanian-Byelorussian Front was the first airfield on which the Eskadra was based. Eskadra aircraft arrived at that airfield on 1 May and the unit became part of 7 Dywizjon Lotniczy. From the first days of May the three Eskadra pilots flew extensively (52 combat sorties in May alone) facing enemy fighter aircraft, numerous at this sector of the front. Air combats, rare during the Polish-Bolshevik war, were thus frequent there. On 6 May the unit's first victory was achieved by *por.* Mroczkowski, and several days later *ppor.* Pawlikowski shot down an observation balloon. On 16 May *por.* Mroczkowski again forced a Bolshevik fighter to land, while on 21 May *ppor.* Pawlikowski shot down another balloon. There were also numerous attempts to intercept attacking enemy bombers, but Polish fighter were usually warned too late. On 23 May the Eskadra moved to the vicinity of Borysów and operated from there until 6 June. Later in Mińsk the unit personnel was increased by one pilot. By the end of June it was relatively quiet at that sector of the front, it was not until the end of the month that the Bolshevik offensive started. 19 Eskadra moved to the Mińsk area, flying reconnaissance sorties from there. On 8 July, with just 2 serviceable aircraft, it withdrew to Baranowicze, and in mid-July to Brześć. Soon after that the Eskadra was withdrawn to Warsaw, where it would be employed for air defence of the capital city. In Warsaw the Eskadra was equipped with some new Sopwith Dolphins. A pilot who had just arrived in the Eskadra as a reinforcement was killed during a training flight in a captured Sopwith $1^1/_2$ Strutter. The Eskadra commander was appointed Komendant Obrony Powietrznej Warszawy (Warsaw Air Defence Commandant), and the Eskadra was employed for air reconnaissance in the immediate vicinity of the city.

By the end of September 1920 19 Eskadra was based in Warsaw. At that time it converted to SPAD XIII aircraft and received a few pilots as reinforcements. From October the Eskadra resumed combat operations within the 4th Army. The Eskadra operated from Piaski airfield near Slonim. Its participation in the war was ended on 13 October by a formation flypast over the recently liberated Mińsk Litewski. The Eskadra flew a total of 121 combat mission in combined time of 253 flying hours, with the loss of 2 pilots.

The largest number of combat missions, 32, was flown by the unit commander, *por.* Mroczkowski, followed by 27 of *ppor.* Pawlikowski.

21 Eskadra Niszczycielska

While expanding the Wielkopolska air force it was decided to form an Eskadra Niszczycielska (literally 'destroyer', i.e. bomber unit). Once Gotha and Friedrichshafen bomber aircraft were captured, formation of such a unit became realistic. Formation started on 15 April 1920 in Poznań. The unit was named 21 Eskadra Niszczycielska. It was organised and first commanded by *por. pil.* Ludomił Rayski. Initially the unit had 7 aircraft: six AEG C IVs and a Gotha.

Soon after forming, the Eskadra moved to Rachny Lessowyja airfield, where it was part of III Dywizjon Lotniczy, co-operating with the 6th Army. The Eskadra was based at that airfield until 15 May 1920. The same day the Eskadra suffered its first losses when one of the crews was forced to land in enemy territory due to engine failure. During May Eskadra crews flew reconnaissance and bombing missions, and distinguished themselves during the raid of 27 and 28 May against Malewannaja railway station (mentioned earlier). The sole Gotha bomber proved particularly useful. While withdrawing before the advancing enemy in the first days of June, the Eskadra moved back to Płoskirów. During the retreat in June many successful attacks were carried out, in co-operation with aircraft of 5 Eskadra, against Bolshevik armoured trains as well as against the charging cavalry of Budenny. On 3 July Płoskirów airfield was left and the Eskadra moved to Hołoby airfield near Kowel. Assault attacks were made against Budenny's cavalry from that airfield, in concert with 7 Eskadra. Due to lack of personnel, 21 Eskadra aircraft were also often flown by the American airmen of 7 Eskadra. During one such mission a mixed crew of *ppor. pil.* Stanisław Skarżyński[6] and *Capt. obs.* Artur H. Kelly was shot down and killed. On 27 July both units were forced to leave the site and went to Uścilug airfield. High losses resulted in the unit significantly reducing flying operations. At the end of July L. Rayski left the unit, as he was posted to Italy to collect new aircraft. He was replaced by *por. pil.* Franciszek Wiedeń. The unit's subsequent airfield was located at Korczów near Sokalem, and from there the Eskadra flew its last combat missions as early as August. Due to the wear of the aircraft the unit was withdrawn to Dęblin and remained as the reserve of the Wódz Naczelny. Upon replenishment of the equipment the Eskadra returned to the front on 4 October 1920, to Tarnopol airfield, becoming part of 2 Dywizjon which operated for the group of *gen.* Lamezan. The Eskadra co-operated mainly with the Polish cavalry in its raids against the enemy rear. These operations were carried out extensively until the end of hostilities on 18 October 1920. By that time *por.* Rayski had resumed command of the unit.

During its wartime operations aircraft of the Eskadra flew 117 combat mission in a total time of 270 flying hours, losing 3 airmen.

1 Captured aircraft.
2 Later renamed III Grupa Lotnicza
3 He was a member of American Hoover's food mission and later became a pilot of the Eskadra.
4 Kosciuszko was a famous Polish General in the late 18th century. He was fighting for Polish independence, and later he had to leave Poland and he went to America and took part in America's fight for independence.
5 Cross of Virtuti Militari (VM) – the highest Polish military decoration.
6 Stanisław Skarżyński made the first solo flight over the Atlantic from West to East in a small Polish aircraft, a RWD-5bis.

148: *Bristol Fighter – the photo was taken at Dęblin (MLP – Kraków)*

149 Below: *Gotha G-IV photographed in 1919 at Poznań airfield (Kopański)*

INTER-WAR PERIOD 1921-1939

As already mentioned, on 18 January 1921 the Polish Air Force reduced the number of eskadras to 13 (9 reconnaissance and 4 fighter eskadras). In spite of this reduction the numbers of aircraft in each eskadra was still below the stipulated level. Eskadras had only 4-5 combat aircraft each, which totalled some 60 serviceable aircraft. In mid-February 1921 a reorganisation of the air force was implemented by forming 6 Dywizjons. This was only a transitional reorganisation, and at the end of the year and during 1922 eskadras were assembled into 3 Pułk Lotniczy units: in Warsaw, Krakow, and Poznań. At that time the principle aircraft in the Polish Air Force inventory consisted of the following types: Breguet XIV A2, Ansaldo Balilla, Spad XIII, SVA 10, and Ansaldo A.300, as well as the Bristol F.2B Fighter. Fokker D.VII and Albatros D.III fighters were in also in use. The head of the air force at that time, *gen.* Gustaw Macewicz who on taking the post of the Szef Departamentu Żeglugi Powietrznej Ministerstwa Spraw Wojskowych on 22 July 1922, set as his principal task the need to increase the number of personnel, as this was insufficient, even when operating such a small number of aircraft. The equipment was mainly obtained by foreign purchase. From mid-1921 the E. Plage and T. Laśkiewicz factory at Lublin started to manufacture equipment, building Ansaldo A.300-2 and Ansaldo Balilla aircraft under Italian licence. The Polish government ordered 200 A.300 aircraft and 100 Balillas from that plant. Unfortunately, the factory lacked skilled labour and production was very slow. The quality of the aircraft also left much to be desired. When production of these aircraft was terminated, only some 50 Balillas and 70 A.300s had been completed. Another factory, 'Francopol', was opened within the framework of Polish-French co-operation. The plant was given a 10-year order for production of 300 airframes and 600 engines. Unfortunately, the factory never started production.

150 Above: *Breguet XIX of 42 Eskadra Liniowa of 4 Pułk Lotniczy at Toruń (Kopański)*

In January 1923 a French *Gen.* Francois-Leon Leveque was appointed the head of the Polish Air Force, after *gen.* Macewicz resigned due to health problems. The new commander presented a comprehensive expansion plan for the Polish Air Force. He proposed to establish a new branch of the so-called line aviation. The plans of the new commander called for the formation of 5 dywizjon liniowy units ('line' wings), 5 dywizjon myśliwski units (fighter wings) and a reserve of the Wódz Naczelny consisting of 3 dywizjon myśliwski, 3 dywizjon liniowy and 2 eskadra bombowa (bomber squadrons) by 1927.

The planned equipment was as follows:
- Dywizjon liniowy – 4 eskadras, 10 aircraft each
- Dywizjon myśliwski – 2 eskadras, 15 aircraft each
- Eskadra bombowa – 6 aircraft

A total of 572 aircraft would be available in first line units. In order to achieve this ambitious plan a quarter of the French armament loan would be spent, which amounted to approximately 400 million French francs. The following numbers of aircraft and equipment were ordered in France: 150 Potez XVs, 70 Hanriot HD 14s, 4 flying boats, plus 1,500 295 kW Lorraine engines and 750 552 kW Lorraine engines. Moreover, licences for Hanriot and Potez aircraft were purchased. The Hanriots would be manufactured by 'Samolot' in Poznań, while Podlaska Wytwórnia Samolotów (PWS) at Biała Podlaska would turn out Potez aircraft. The 'Samolot' factory received an order for 25 Hanriots, and PWS for 150 Potez. It was not until 1925 that the first aircraft from these plants started to be delivered to units, whilst those ordered in France started arriving in mid-1924. In 1924 a new, 4 Pułk was formed in Toruń by disbanding the Observer School there. Initially the Pułk consisted of a dywizjon with three eskadras. Disbandment of the school in Toruń was due to a change of concept in aircrew training. A centre was established at Dęblin for pilot training. In June 1924 *Gen.* Leveque left his post. During his rule the average number of aircraft in eskadra rose to 8. Unfortunately, it was found that an ambitious plan to greatly increase the number of Eskadras by 1926 was unrealistic. During this short time *Gen.* Leveque introduced the French air force doctrine, according to which aviation was an auxiliary weapon co-operating closely with the army.

Płk. Włodzimierz Ostoja-Zagórski became the new head of the air force on 1 July 1924. He was appointed by the new Minister Spraw Wojskowych, *gen.* Władysław Sikorski, whose concept of the air force was different from those of his predecessors. With *gen.* Sikorski's support, *gen. bryg.* W. Zagórski presented a new plan for air force expansion. This was a long-term plan covering 12 years. It called for an establishment of 200 eskadras with 2,306 aircraft by 1938. At the same time the entire Polish Armed Forces would grow to 60 infantry divisions. *Gen.* Zagórski soon commenced implementation of this ambitious plan, incorporating some lessons from his predecessor. He ordered and purchased 300 Spad 51 and Spad 61 fighters, 250 Breguet XIX B2 light bombers, and 32 Farman Goliath bombers from France. He also purchased 101 training and maritime aircraft. Additionally he purchased 150 59 kW Le Rhone engines, as well as licences for production of Potez XXVII and Spad 61 aircraft.

Gen. Zagórski did not forget the Polish industry. He ordered 405 more aircraft there and commenced reorganisation of Centralne Zaklady Lotnicze, where Hanriot production was located. He also brought the 'Francopol' company back to grace, ordering 150 of the licence-produced Spad 61s and 150 50 kM Lorraine Dietrich engines, paying for this with a promotion. This decision would later have its effect on his career. Among *gen.* Zagórski's merits was also announcement of the first competition for a project for a Polish-designed combat aircraft. This competition resulted in Władysław Zalewski's WZ-X reconnaissance-fighter aircraft project and its construction being authorised. This was the first Polish combat aircraft built in independent Poland. Production of this aircraft would be handled by the C.W.L. plant.

In February 1925 forming of 6 Pułk Lotniczy started at Lwów. It consisted of two dywizjons, each with two eskadras. The remaining pulks were expanded to two dywizjons each.

It was at that time that the concept of single-role pułks with one type of aircraft was put forward. Formation of five pułk liniowy, one pułk myśliwski and one pułk bombowy was planned. Each pułk would have 2-3 eskadras with 6 to 10 aircraft, depending on its role.

The first pułk to be established according to this concept was the two-eskadra 11 Pułk Myśliwski. It was planned to form a bomber pułk with Goliath aircraft, while 6 Pułk organised at that time was going to be a line unit.

Organisational changes in the air force in 1925 shaped the operational concept of the Polish Air Force, divided into the following roles:

- line aviation: an original idea of Polish military theory. The primary tasks of this type of aviation included reconnaissance behind enemy lines (strategic reconnaissance), day bombing, battlefield co-operation with first line units, and assault operations. A standard eskadra would have 10 aircraft;
- fighter aviation: its aim was to combat enemy aircraft in the air, and perform assault operations. Eskadra standard was 6-10 machines;
- destroyer (bomber) aviation: night bombing behind enemy lines. Standard eskadra was to have 8 aircraft;
- light (accompanying) aviation was at the design stage at that time: its task would include co-operation with infantry, cavalry and artillery, maintaining communication at the battle field, battlefield observation, and tactical reconnaissance. The name 'accompanying' denoted that this type of aviation would be closely connected with large ground units and accompany them at the battlefield. A pluton with 3 to 6 machines would be the basic combat unit. Plutons were organised in eskadras with 3 plutons each.

Auxiliary air formations included the following types of units:

- training,
- transport,
- medical.

The reorganisation of the air force led to a renumbering of eskadras and changing their names. The eskadra numbers of the Polish-Russian war vintage disappeared. Eskadras were numbered in connection with their pulks. The first digit in the Eskadra number was the pułk number. Fighter eskadras received 3-digit numbers, whilst 2-digit numbers were used for other units.

Organisation of Polish Air Force, April 1925

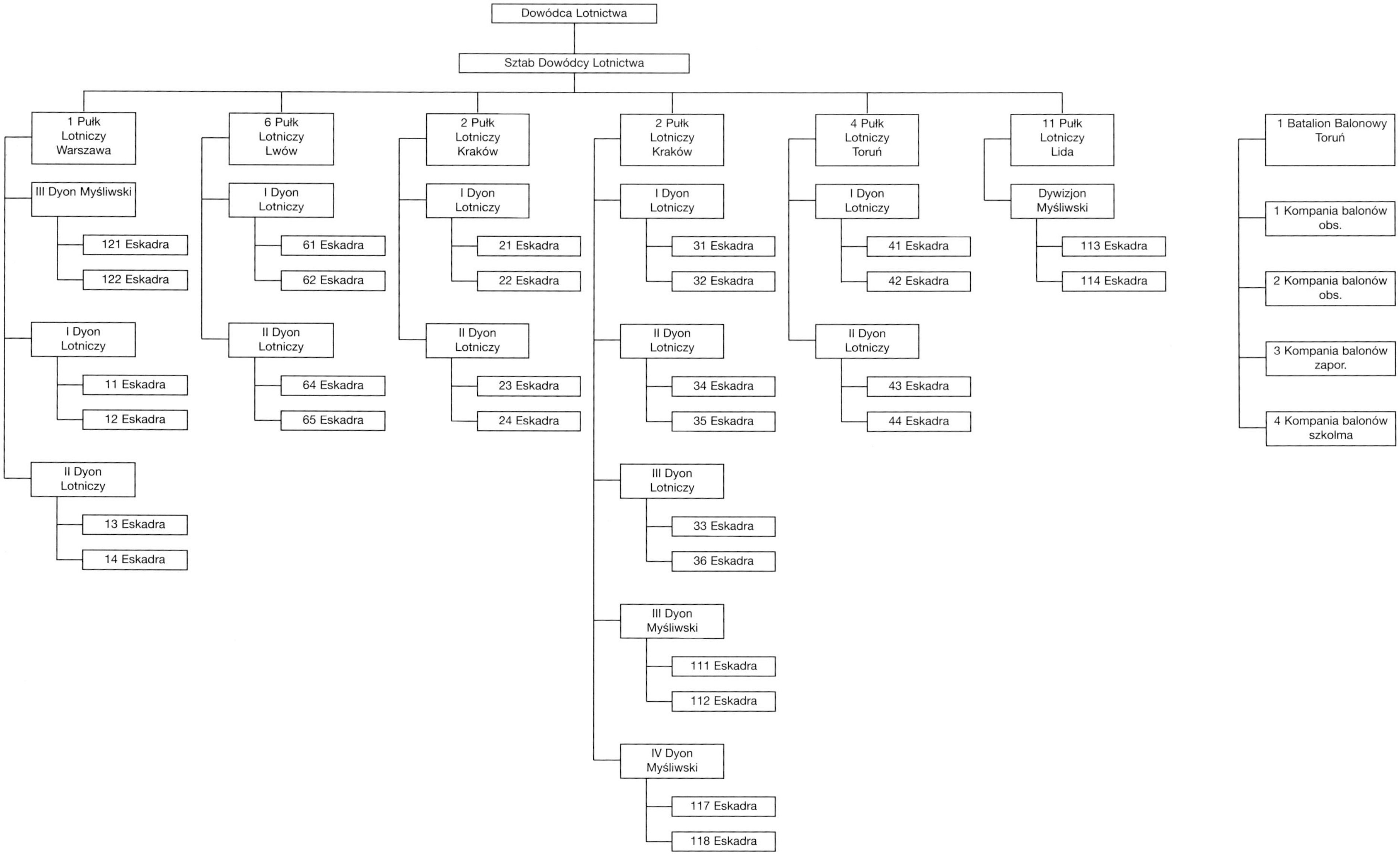

151: *Breguet XIX of 64 Eskadra Liniowa. The emblem was used from 1932 (Kopański)*

152: *Breguet XIX B-2 no. 1240 of* por. *Bolesław Orliński, in which he flew from Warsaw to Tokyo and back to Warsaw in 1926. Note the damaged and clipped left wing of the aircraft (Kopański)*

153: *Overhaul of a Breguet XIX, note the wing of the aircraft less its fabric covering in the foreground (MLP – Kraków)*

154: *A Breguet unit of one of the regiments during a review by a Rumanian delegation (MLP – Kraków)*

155: *Breguet XIX under the canvas of a field hangar at Stanisławów (Sikorski via Belcarz)*

156: *An experimental colour scheme on a Breguet A2 no. 1322, tested in 1928-30, which consisted in covering the upper surfaces of the aircraft with a pattern of rectangular fields in various bright colours. The photo was taken at Powursk airfield in 1930. In front of the aircraft is the crew of* ppor. *Olgierd Cumft and* kpr. *Tadeusz Nowierski (Kopański)*

157: *Spad 61 C1s from 121 Eskadra Myśliwska of 2 Pułk Lotniczy in Kraków (Koniarek)*

158: *Breguet XIXs of 11 Eskadra Liniowa (white cross on a red square) of 1 Pułk Lotniczy in Warsaw. Geometric unit markings were used between 1927 and 1932 (Kopański)*

159: *A paratrooper leaves the wing of a Farman Goliath (Belcarz)*

160: *Farman F. 68 Goliath no. P 31 was one of 32 aircraft of the type in the Polish Air Force. They remained in first-line use during 1929-30 (MLP – Kraków)*

161: *Farman F. 68 Goliath no. P 22 was used in 1 Pułk Lotniczy in Warsaw around 1930 (MLP – Kraków)*

162: *Farman F.68 Goliath no. P 3 (MLP – Kraków)*

The reorganisation also affected flying training. Aviation schools at Grudziądz, Poznań and Bydgoszcz were all expanded.

Gen. Zagórski was dismissed on 18 March 1926, but he stayed on duty till May. He left 26 eskadras with a total of 265 aircraft in the first line. *Gen.* Zagórski left in an atmosphere of scandal. He was accused of misuse of the French loan, and above all of connections with the 'Francopol' company which failed to manufacture a single aircraft or engine on order.

1926 brought a change in the political situation in Poland, when Piłsudski formally resumed power after the coup d'etat in May. This resulted in a changed attitude towards development of the armed forces and the air force. The latter was reduced again to the status of an auxiliary formation for the ground forces.

Zagórski was succeeded by *płk* Ludomił Rayski, who took the post of the Head of the Aeronautics Department in May 1926. By August *płk* Rayski presented his plan for aviation development, calling for 30 eskadras in 1928 and 52 eskadras in 1935. This meant a great reduction when compared to the *gen.* Zagórski plan, especially in the fighter force as the fighter eskadra standard was reduced to 6 aircraft. Even this modest plan was rejected by the authorities. At the same time guidelines for the organisation and use of aviation were approved. One paragraph that would have a profound effect on the future value of the Polish Air Force was the one which defined the use of aviation during war. It read as follows: *"In wartime aviation must above all operate to provide reconnaissance and communication"*. It can be stated that these guidelines reduced the combat value of the air force and had a decisive effect on its structure, eventually affecting the value of the air force in 1939.

One result of accepting such a concept was abandoning the plans to form specialised fighter and bomber pulks, which led to disbandment, in 1928, of 11 Pułk Myśliwski that had been established by *gen.* Zagórski. 1927 brought guidelines for the aviation organisation which stated that the expansion of existing roles should be halted at the present level of 28 eskadras, and the new light accompanying aviation should be introduced for the benefit of infantry and cavalry divisions. The guidelines also suggested shifting the stress to fighter aviation, and reduction of the number of line aircraft by selling them abroad. In order to reduce spending, Rayski decided to obtain equipment from Polish factories. This led to a rapid development of Polish aircraft engineering and industry. By 1926 Rayski had ordered 100 Potez XXVs each from the PWS and Lublin factories. In 1928 and 1929 the PWS company received an additional order for 50 Potez XXV aircraft. In 1929 the same company obtained an order for a project of the PWS 1 two-seater reconnaissance aircraft which, however, never entered production. Lublin works commenced production of the Lublin R-VII aircraft designed by Jerzy Rudlicki. The plant received a contract for production of 5 of these machines.

The 'Francopol' factory which had received a large contract from Zagórski, turned out only two incomplete Spad 61s and not a single engine during 1926. Rayski transferred the production of Spads to C.W.L., where some 30 were manufactured, and had a contract signed between the Polish government and the Czech Skoda company to undertake production of Skoda aircraft engines in Poland. Polskie Zakłady Skoda started production in 1927, and 'Francopol' was finally liquidated in 1927. In November 1927 the Polish government signed a licence contract with the Bristol company of Britain for production of Jupiter engines (later also Mercury and Pegasus) in the Skoda-Polska works. Also in 1927 the Centralne Warsztaty Wojskowe were transformed into the Państwowe Zakłady Lotnicze. The works began its official existence on 1 January 1928, and manufactured, as mentioned earlier, Spad 61 aircraft.

The main task of the Polish industry at that time was to replace the faulty Spads with other aircraft.

Since there was no ready project for a Polish aircraft, it was decided that a licence would be purchased for the Czech Avia BH-33, to be built as the PWS-A, and for the French all-metal Wilbault. Production of the Avias was started at the PWS plant, whilst that of the Wilbault began at PZL.

A group of young aircraft engineers, educated after the war, started extensive design work at the PZL plant. Work was carried out on 5 types of aircraft: P.1 fighter, Ł.2 spotting aircraft, PZL 3 bomber, PZL 4 passenger transport, and PZL 5 trainer. A competition for an observation-liaison aircraft was announced in 1927, and three designs participated: PZL Ł.2, PWS-5 and Lublin R-X. All three were ordered for the Polish Air Force: twenty Ł.2s, five PWS-5s and five of R-Xs. The Rudlicki designed R-X was selected for further development, resulting in the Lublin R-XIV of which 15 were manufactured, and subsequently the Lublin R-XIII which was mass-produced for the Polish Air Force.

Lack of good fighter aircraft was the most dire problem. Flying Spads threatened rapid annihilation of the entire fighter pilot force. So in 1927 the PWS plant started work on the PWS 10 aircraft, a high wing monoplane with an in-line engine. The company failed to obtain a contract for the aircraft, though, as great expectations were placed in the recently designed PZL P.1, Puławski's revolutionary fighter. Due to planned production of this aircraft no order was placed for the PWS 10. The PWS company received a contract for licence production of Avia BH-33s, though, to be manufactured as the PWS A, while PZL undertook production of Wilbault 7 aircraft. This was planned as

Organisation of Polish Air Force, 1930

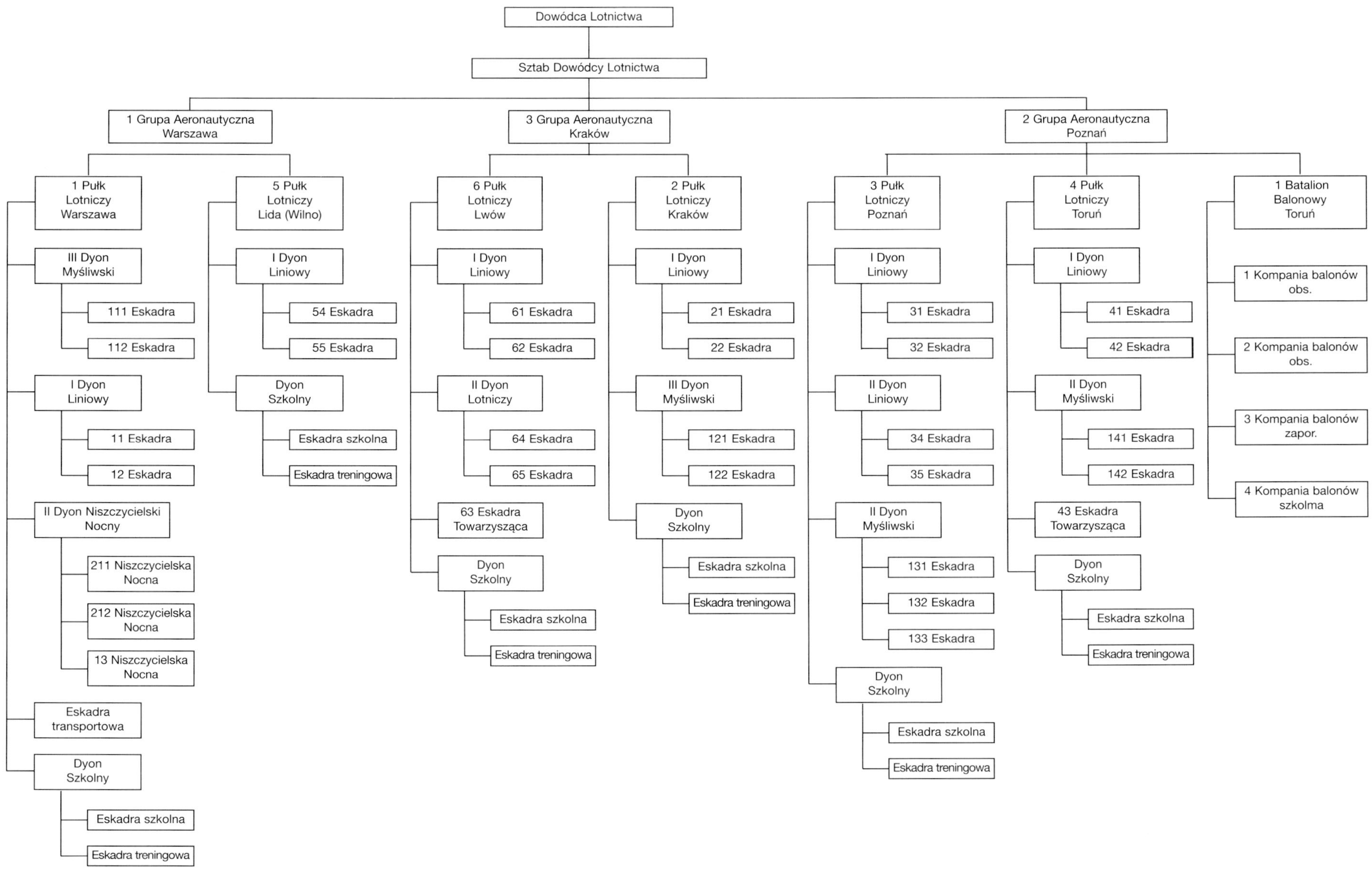

163: *A very clean Morane-Saulnier MS 35 which appears to have had an argument with the unit ambulance. Unfortunately the aircraft serial number cannot be seen*

164: Lt. Col. *Merian C. Cooper and* mjr *Ludomił Rayski. Lwów, May 1921 (Kopański)*

165: *Morane Saulnier training aircraft no. MOR. 50.32 (Kopa)*

preparation and gathering of experience for production of the aircraft designed by Puławski. However, since the aircraft's entry into production was delayed, as Puławski was developing the design into the PZL P.6, and subsequently the P.7, the PWS company received a contract for production of 80 PWS-10 aircraft, in order to replace the Spads which were unsuitable not only as combat aircraft, but also for training.

It was not until 1931 that the PZL P.7 aircraft was selected as the primary fighter for the Polish Air Force and 120 aircraft were ordered, the number later increased to 150. Eskadras would convert to these aircraft in 1933 thus making the Polish fighter force the first in the world to be equipped entirely with all-metal monoplanes. PWS 10s were relegated to training duties.

It should be noted here that the Goliath aircraft already purchased never entered first line service[1] and it was not until 22 Fokker F.VIIB/3m aircraft were purchased in 1928 that bomber eskadras were formed. 1928 was also the year of marked changes in the organisation of the Polish Air Force.

The newly created accompanying aviation was equipped at the beginning of 1930s with PZL Ł. 2 and Lublin R-XIII aircraft. Bomber aviation converted to Fokker F.VII/3m aircraft built in Poland under licence. This was a commercial type, converted for combat operations at the request of the Polish government.

In the autumn 1932 Rayski presented a new, three-year aviation development plan. This plan approved development and construction of new fighter and line aircraft prototypes.

The following year brought conversion of fighter units to the successor of the PZL P.7, the PZL P.11a, and later the PZL P.11c. This aircraft was considered at that time to be one of the most advanced fighters in the world.

The early 1930s also brought a large increase in numbers of trained airmen. Production of the Bartel BM-4h training aircraft (previously manufactured at the 'Samolot' factory, liquidated in 1930) was ordered from the PWS factory to this end. Later on this aircraft was replaced by the excellent RWD-8, with the contracts for the production of 350 machines. The PWS plant also manufactured a series of excellent training aircraft, starting with the PWS-14, followed by the PWS-16, PWS-16bis, up to the PWS-26, the latter produced until the outbreak of the war. In 1935-1936 40 PWS-18 aircraft were also turned out, this being a licence-built version of the British Avro Type 621 Tutor. The main training centre was located at Dęblin: the Centrum Wyszkolenia Lotniczego, while a Szkoła Pilotażu was based at Bydgoszcz.

Nationalisation of the aircraft industry commenced in the early 1930s, and not always in decent ways. The 'Samolot' company in Poznań was the first victim. After a fire in 1929 the government refused assistance under the pretext that the company was located too close to the German border, and the plant was closed in 1930. Subsequently the PWS factory was dealt with. In 1929-1930 this received a large government loan for development. However, from 1932 on no government orders were placed there to maintain production. At the same time an order was placed for a new training aircraft, which was replaced with another after it reached an advanced stage. This increased the company debt and in 1932 90% of PWS shares were bought out by the Aviation Department for a symbolic 1 zloty. Thus PWS became a state-owned factory. Orders for primary and advanced trainer aircraft for the air force were placed at once. Similar methods brought about the bankruptcy of the Lublin E. Plage and T. Laśkiewicz factory. In 1935 an order for 25 Lublin R-XIIIF aircraft was cancelled when these were at an advanced stage of production, on the grounds that the aircraft failed to meet the army requirements. No new designs had been ordered from the company in previous years, allowing the managers to think that the R-XIII was the aircraft that the Polish Air Force wanted. Such action by the Aviation Department led to the bankruptcy of the company and it was taken over by the treasury. From that moment the plant, now known as the Lubelska Wytwórnia Samolotów (LWS; Lublin Aircraft Factory) resumed production of Lublin R-XIIIF aircraft. Thus the RWD – DWL factory remained the only private aircraft manufacturer, turning out excellent touring RWD aircraft. The Skoda-Poland plant was also bought out by the Polish treasury and merged into the PZL company as the Wytwórnia Silników Nr 1 (WS-1; Aircraft Factory No 1). At that time also PZL erected a new plant at Okęcie. This factory was going to produce aircraft as the PZL Wytwórnia Platowców Nr 1 (PZL WP-1).

In June 1936 the Air Force had 17 line eskadras (a total of 170 Potez XXV, XXVII and Breguet XIX aircraft), 13 fighter eskadras (130 P.7 and P.11 aircraft) and 3 bomber eskadras (18 Fokker F. VII/3m aircraft), and 33 accompanying plutons in 8 eskadras (99 Lublin R-XIII aircraft). This amounted to a total of 417 aircraft in the front line.

From mid-1936 new PZL P.23A *Karaś* aircraft commenced introduction to service in first-line units, followed subsequently by its improved form, the P.23B, designed by Stanisław Prauss. The aircraft significantly improved the combat capability of line eskadras.

In June 1936 *gen.* Rayski presented a new long-term aviation development plan up until April 1942. The plan called for a total of 106 mobilisation eskadras, including 30 bomber eskadras (180 aircraft), 32 line eskadras (320 aircraft), 18 fighter eskadras (180 aircraft), 8 reconnaissance eskadras (80 aircraft), and 18 co-operation/accompanying eskadras (126 aircraft). This

166: *The MS 35 was the principal elementary flying training aircraft during the early thirties (MLP – Kraków)*

167: *A very interesting photo of a row of Morane 35 trainers which documents the considerable freedom in application of the national markings. This applied to both the arrangement of fields of the chequerboard (MS no. 32 and 12) and its position (MS 32 and 12) or absence (MS 09) (Kopański)*

168: *The Wibault 70 C1 fighter aircraft was licence-built in Poland: Państwowe Zakłady Lotnicze in Warsaw produced a total of 25 aircraft of the type (Glass)*

169: *But the Wibault 70 C1 was not a successful design and it only remained in the first line during 1930-31 (MLP – Kraków)*

170: *Wibault 70 C1 no. 3.7 from Eskadra Treningowa of 2 Pułk Lotniczy in Kraków. (Glass)*

171: *Potez XV of the Polish Air Force (MLP – Kraków)*

Organisation of Polish Air Force, 1935

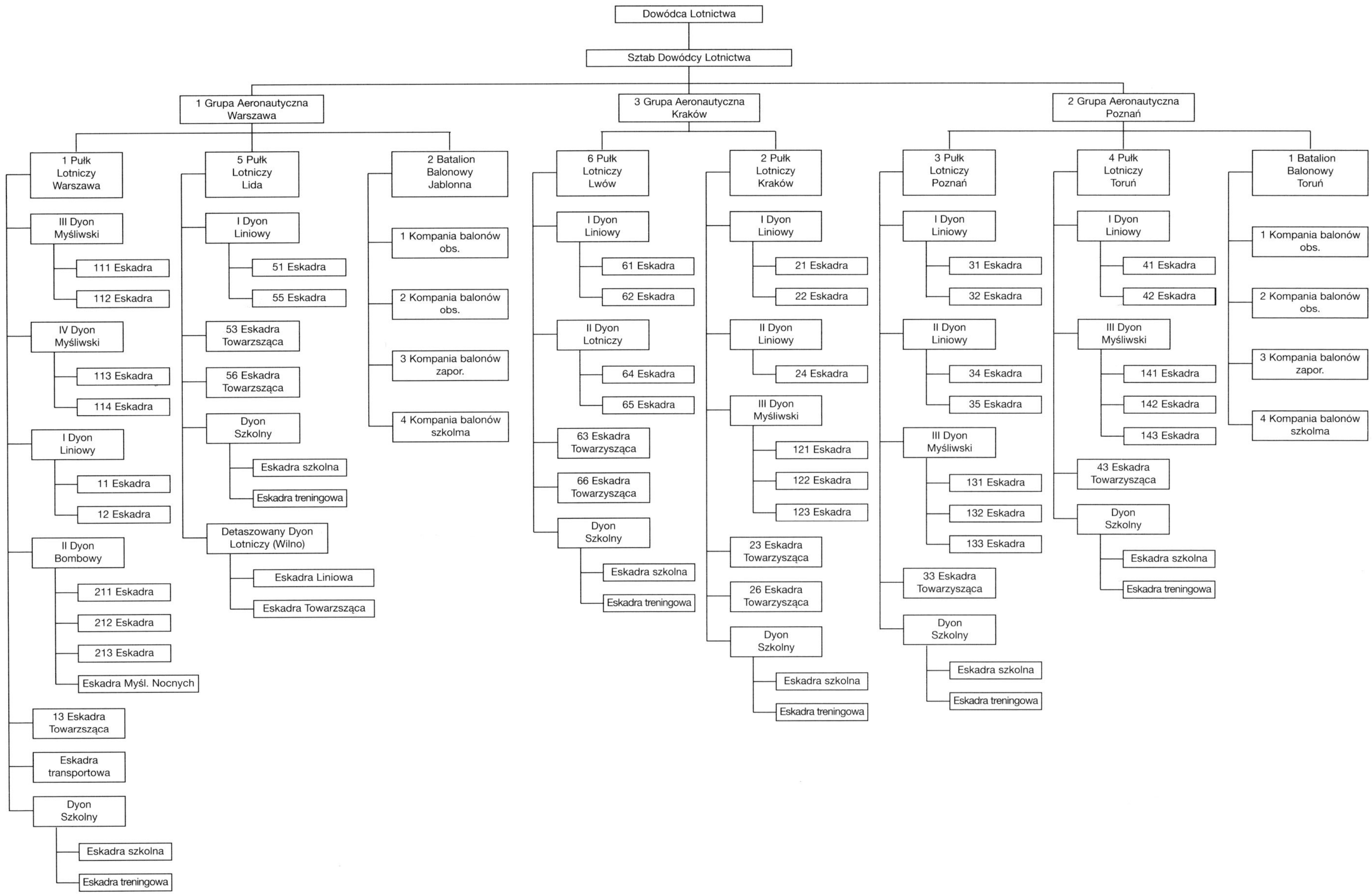

totalled 886 first line aircraft. Unfortunately, the Sztab Generalny considered this plan too costly, and ordered it to be revised. Eventually the plan was reduced by 16 line and 3 fighter eskadras. The plan stipulated that the new units would be equipped with aircraft then at the prototype stage. This applied to 6 aircraft: two each for line, bomber, and accompanying aviation. At that stage of planning no successor was to be expected for the ageing P.11 aircraft. The twin-engined P.38 *Wilk* was going to be the primary aircraft for the line aviation as well as for the planned night fighter force, and even for the pursuit aviation, a new branch of fighter aviation. According to plans this aircraft would provide 45% of the entire inventory of aircraft in the air force. This was a considerable risk as work on the *Wilk* was delayed due to problems with its engines. Lack of a suitable engine delayed introduction of the *Wilk* into service by several years, which indirectly affected the entire Polish Air Force combat value.

The final aviation development plan was approved at the 17th meeting of the Komitet do Spraw Uzbrojenia i Sprzętu (KSUS; Armament and Equipment Committee) on 13 October 1936. This was based on the Rayski plan, and was prepared, significantly, by *płk* Jan Jagmin-Sadowski, an infantry officer. This plan also included very general tactical and technical guidelines for the new aircraft in 5 branches of the air force, organisational directives for air units, and numbers and constitution of the air force in April 1941. It also listed predicted personnel losses, ammunition, bomb, and fuel consumption in wartime. The plan led to the abandoning of work on a light fighter aircraft and disbandment of the design team at PZL that studied this project. According to the KSUS plan of October 1936 the Polish Air Force order of battle in 1942 would be as follows: 78 eskadras with 642 aircraft, including: line aviation – 14 eskadras 10 aircraft each, single-seat fighter aviation – 15 eskadras 10 aircraft each, pursuit fighter aviation – 10 eskadras 10 aircraft each, bomber aviation – 221 eskadras 6 aircraft each and accompanying aviation – 18 eskadras 7 aircraft each.

The following types would be used as the aircraft in specific roles according to the stipulations and amendments of the 1936 plan (as planned for 1942):

- fighter aviation – PZL P.50 *Jastrząb*,
- pursuit aviation – unspecified type (this was connected with the P.38 *Wilk* problems),
- bomber aviation – either PZL P.37 *Łoś* or its successor,
- accompanying aviation – either LWS 3 *Mewa* or its successor,
- line aviation – PZL P.46 *Sum*.

According to the plan, conversion of the fighter aviation to the new fighter type would not start until 1940.

Reorganisation of the Air Force command structure took place during 1936. Increased authority of the Generalny Inspektor Sił Zbrojnych (GISZ) led to establishment of a new section, the Inspektorat Obrony Powietrznej Państwa (IOPP). The Inspektorat included within its competence also the inspection of air units which significantly increased the commitment of the GISZ in aircraft matters.

Also the Departament Aeronautyki was reshaped. In August 1936 it was renamed Dowództwo Lotnictwa Ministerstwa Spraw Wojskowych. The post of Dowódca Lotnictwa was established, and given to *gen.* Ludomił Rayski, the previous head of the Departament Aeronautyki. *Gen.* Gustaw Orlicz-Dreszer was appointed the first Inspektor Obrony Powietrznej Panstwa. Unfortunately, he was killed in an air crash in July 1936, and his place was taken by *gen.* Józef Zając, who was hardly an expert in aviation matters. His opinions with respect to aviation development differed significantly from those of the Dowódca Lotnictwa, *gen.* Rayski. The former believed that Poland could not afford bomber aviation, and therefore only the fighter and pursuit aviation should be developed.

Another reorganisation of air and training units took place in 1937. Zgrupowanie Myśliwskie was established in July which included both dywizjon myśliwski units of 1 Pułk Lotniczy. By orders of 19 July 1937 three-eskadra accompanying dywizjons were formed in each pułk lotniczy. A second bomber dywizjon started to be formed in 1 Pułk, and fighter dywizjons were organised in 5 and 6 Pułk. A group of air schools was established. All these changes followed from the KSUS plan, and expansion of the accompanying aviation was considered the primary task at that time.

In order to ensure continuous supplies of equipment according to the KSUS project foundations from the previous year, construction of Wytwórnia Platowców Nr 2 (PZL WP Nr 2) was started at Mielec and of Wytwórnia Silników Nr 2 (PZL WS Nr 2) at Rzeszów.

In accordance with the KSUS plan, Wsiewołod Jakimiuk (designer of the P.11c) was given the task of developing a new single-seat fighter aircraft project, designated P.50 and later named *Jastrząb*. For a year the same designer had been employed working on the PZL P.44 Wicher passenger aircraft, he was ordered to finish that project quickly and start work on the P.50. The Aviation HQ imposed relevant specifications, not in accordance with the KSUS plan guidelines, but more compatible with the concept of the ill-fated *Wilk*. Also the engine, the Bristol Mercury VIII, was imposed on the designer, and this powerplant eventually proved to be underpowered for this aircraft. The need to develop a suitable retractable undercarriage was another obstacle in the development of the P.50. Due to a lack of experience in the Polish aero industry it was decided to purchase the gear from the Dowty company of Great Britain. This was expected to significantly accelerate construction of the

172: *Potez XXVII A2 no. 41.160 belonging to the Oficerska Szkoła Lotnictwa (Kopański)*

173: *Crash of a Potez XXVII A2 no. 41.130 manufactured by PWS plant (MLP – Kraków)*

174: *Potez XXVIIs of 65 Eskadra Lotnicza during the 1929 summer exercises (Sikorski via Belcarz)*

Organisation of Polish Air Force, 1937

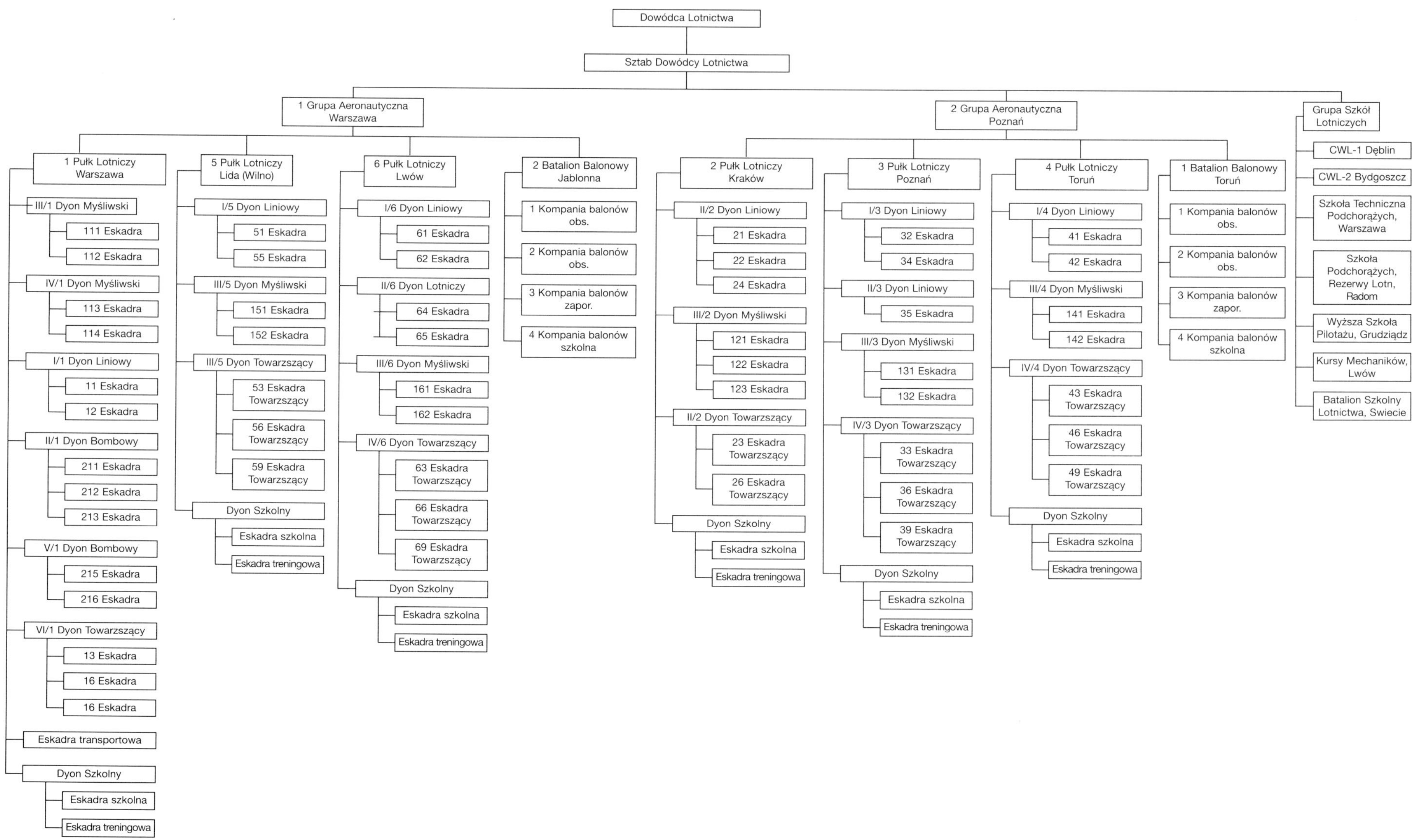

Note: III/1 Dyon Myśliwski and IV/1 Dyon Myśliwski of 1 Pułk Lotniczyt formed Zgrupowanie Myśliwskie

175: *Jupiter-powered Potez XXV of Szkoła Lotnicza at Dęblin. The airman in front of the aircraft is cadet officer Pawłowski. The aircraft's call-sign was 181 D, painted in white on the underside of wing (Glass)*

176: *Rough landing of a Potez XV no. 40.34. The half-tracked tractor visible nearby was used for aircraft movements on the airfield (MLP – Kraków)*

177: *The all-metal structure of the Wibault 70 C1 was a proving ground for Polish designers, helping them to master the new technology. But the pilots' view was unfavourable: they considered the Wibault a good training aircraft, but not a fighter (Koniarek)*

prototype. The first prototype P.50/I was to be completed by September 1938, and the second, in which a more powerful engine was to be installed, would be ready at the beginning of 1939. Although the first prototype was built in time, the Dowty undercarriage arrived only after long delay, and the prototype was not flown until the beginning of 1939. At the same time the Aviation HQ, having no option, decided to order 150 aircraft from the drawing board. Subsequently the order was increased to 500.

In the spring of 1938 the Polish Air Force reached the highest number of aircraft in its entire history so far. The total number of eskadras rose to 53, and combat aircraft to 464. This increase was achieved by depriving the air force of all its reserves, and by using mostly obsolete types of aircraft in the eskadras.

Later that same year it was found that many eskadras had virtually no combat capability. Lublin R-XIII aircraft were almost useless during the 'Zaolzie' operation, and temporarily all accompanying eskadras were withdrawn to the second line in anticipation of the forthcoming RWD-14 *Czapla* and LWS-3 *Mewa* aircraft. Due to *Karaś* overhauls and lack of spare aircraft, first line eskadras had an average of 5-6 serviceable aircraft. Also the Fokker F.VII-equipped bomber eskadras became second-line units awaiting their new *Łoś* equipment. At the turn of 1938 a total of 26 eskadras were disbanded or withdrawn from the first line due to a lack of suitable equipment, which amounted to virtually half of the air force. Only 27 eskadras retained their combat capability.

Anxious about the air force supply situation, *gen.* Zając, the Inspektor OPP, issued in November 1938 a secret report for the highest military authorities, assessing the combat capability of the air force. His report showed a substantial lack of aircraft equipment and estimated that in 1939, that with the exception of bomber aircraft (the anticipated *Łoś*), the situation in other branches of the air force would deteriorate. He stated that 1940 would be the transition year, and improvement could not be expected before 1941. According to his evaluation, should war break out in 1939 or 1940, the available equipment would be destroyed or expended within 2 to 4 weeks.

Probably it was this negative report that led to the resignation of *gen.* Rayski in January 1939. The resignation was accepted in March 1939. *Marsz.* Rydz-Śmigły , the Wódz Naczelny, appointed *gen.* J. Zając to the post of the Supreme Commander of the Aviation and Air Defence in event of a war, and *gen.* Władysław Kalkus to the post of the Dowódca Lotnictwa. At the same time an order was issued which stated that the Dowódca Lotnictwa was reporting personally to *gen.* J. Zając.

Gen. W. Kalkus was informed that the following orders for aircraft had been placed in Polish factories:

- 124 PZL 37 *Łoś* (planned end of production in April 1939);
- 160 PZL 46 *Sum* light bombers (first prototype undergoing trials, preparations for production start-up in July 1939);
- 500 P.50 *Jastrząb* (Hawk) fighters (the first prototype ready, awaiting the undercarriage, the second prototype awaiting the engine. Production of the first 50 aircraft already under way.);
- 200 LWS 3 *Mewa* reconnaissance aircraft (aircraft in production, first deliveries from August 1939);
- 130 PWS 33 *Wyżeł* (Pointer) twin-engined trainers (preparations for production to be started)
- 150 PWS 35 *Ogar* (Hound) trainers (preparations for production to be started).

Gen. Zając had a conference with the Dowódca Lotnictwa, *gen.* Kalkus, in his first day in the office, in order to accelerate deliveries of fighter aircraft, either from Polish production or from foreign purchases. This would be at the expense of stopping *Łoś* production and transferring production of training aircraft from PWS to DWL In the spring the 1937 the KSUS plan was changed, and adapted to the new air force development concept of *gen.* Zając. Pułk Lotniczy HQs, previously independent, would now form tactical formations of co-operation (army) aviation including reconnaissance units extracted from the line aviation, spotting (previously accompanying), and fighter units. The 1 Pułk Lotniczy would undergo reorganisation into an independent aviation formation. The independent aviation would consist of a bomber brigade, two line brigades and three pursuit brigades. In place of the disbanded Warsaw pułk a new, 7 Pułk Lotniczy would be formed in the autumn 1939 in Wilno.

Not until 1939 were mobilisation plans for possible war with Germany begun. Until that time all plans were based on the assumption that Russia would be the enemy. A new mobilisation plan was prepared at the end of March 1939. Each of the pułk units would during wartime reform into a baza lotnicza, providing a supply facility for units based in the vicinity of the operational base.

The increasingly tense international situation forced the Polish HQ to undertake dramatic action in order to increase the combat power of the air force. Combat capability of liaison eskadras equipped with R-XIII aircraft was restored, and some of these started to re-equip with RWD-14 *Czapla* aircraft. It was also decided to retain a batch of PZL 43A aircraft (improved version of the *Karaś*) of which 42 had been produced for Bulgaria. Eventually the latter instruction was cancelled, when the international situation improved, and the aircraft were despatched to Bulgaria. The Inspektor OPP changed his order for PZL 46 *Sum* aircraft to 300, and placed an order for 100 Fairey Battles. Production of PZL 37 *Łoś* bombers was halted by special order, to free the manufacturing capability for production of the P.50 *Jastrząb* or an improved P.24. It was also decided to purchase fighter aircraft abroad. When flight testing of the P.50 *Jastrząb* commenced it showed that the aircraft did not meet requirements and needed substantial improvement. Given the situation *gen.* Zając issued orders to halt *Jastrząb* production and introduce substantial changes to the design. Eventually however approval was granted to manufacture fifty P.50A aircraft in its original form, with the later model entering production after changes were introduced in the airframe and a new, more powerful engine acquired. Poland was negotiating purchase of the Taurus engine from the Bristol company, the engine being banned from exports at that time, and eventually never entering production anyway.

After the problems with the P.50, projects for an 'improved P.24' started to be considered. It transpired, however, that adapting the P.11c to a more powerful engine and installing an enclosed cockpit would prove a better solution. Work on this project commenced, the aircraft developing rapidly and by mid-August 1939 the prototype commenced flight trials. A decision was taken simultaneously to start production of the P.11g *Kobuz* (Hobby), as the aircraft was named, at the PWS plant.

Negotiations for the purchase of foreign fighter aircraft started in the spring. This was not a simple task, as the international situation was so perilous that most countries were preparing for war. First offers were received in June 1939. In order to evaluate the aircraft on offer, Polish test pilots went abroad. Trials included the following aircraft: Supermarine Spitfire, Hawker Hurricane, Morane MS.406, Dewoitine D.520, Bloch MB.151, Breguet 690, Potez 63, and Koolhoven FK.58. Britain agreed to sell 14 Hawker Hurricanes and 1 Spitfire. These aircraft were despatched from Britain to Poland by sea at the end of August, together with some 30 Fairey Battles. Unfortunately, these aircraft failed to reach Poland. Another offer was placed in June by the Americans who proposed various aircraft and favourable credit conditions for the purchase. The American offer was rejected due to high price and the fact that American aircraft required 100 octane fuel, not available in Poland at that time. At the end of June France also opened a credit that allowed the purchase of some 150 Morane MS 406s in express way, plus a licence for their production in Poland. The order for 130 MS 406s was signed on 8 August 1939. The first batch of Moranes was despatched from France by sea on 29-30 August.

At the same time the Aviation HQ attempted to prepare new production programmes for Polish aircraft factories. Frequent changes of directives led to chaos in production facilities and delays in work, resulting in a serious reduction of aircraft production. Equipment deliveries in 1939 were the lowest for 5 years.

Eventually by August 1939 Polish aircraft plants had reached the following positions:

PZL WP 1, Okęcie:
- five P.50A *Jastrząb* aircraft nearing completion and 25 more in various stages of construction;
- preparations for production of the P.50B with a more powerful engine, planned delivery of 200 aircraft in the autumn of 1940;
- preparations for production of 300 PZL 46 *Sum* aircraft, first deliveries in 1940.

PZL WP 2 Mielec:
- final assembly of 20 *Łoś* bombers;
- preparations for transfer of PZL 46 *Sum* production.

LWS:
- production of LWS 3 *Mewa*, 200 aircraft of which approx. 30 nearing completion, first deliveries in September 1939;
- preparations for production of the PZL P.11g *Kobuz*.

PWS
- production of the P.11g *Kobuz*, 90 aircraft, deliveries starting early 1940;
- production of a batch of 25 PWS 33 *Wyżeł* trainers;
- production of a batch of 50 PWS 35 *Ogar* trainers.

DWL[2]
- preparations for production of approx. 120 RWD 17 aircraft, first deliveries in early 1940.

Mobilisation of the air force was carried out on 23 August 1939, according to a new plan prepared by *gen.* Zając. At that time the air force had: 1,181 trained pilots, 497 observers, 219 air gunners and some 5,200 ground personnel. The equipment in mobilised units included 392 serviceable aircraft, of which 158 were fighters, 114 reconnaissance and light bombers (*gen.* Zając deciding in spring 1939 that the line aviation be divided into reconnaissance and light bomber units), 36 bombers and 84 spotting aircraft. Additionally, naval aviation had 12 warplanes with any true combat potential.

Numbers of auxiliary aircraft at the disposal of the Polish Air Force at the time of the mobilisation were: 12 transport and 94 liaison aircraft. The total number of aircraft in mobilised units was 510.

Reserves amounted to: 47 PZL 37 *Łoś* bombers in the latest stages of production, of which very few were armed, 30 RWD 14 *Czapla*, 50 PZL P.11c, 60 PZL 23 *Karaś* aircraft. Most reserve P.11c and *Karaś* aircraft were undergoing repairs. 30 PZL P.7a and some 100 Lublin R-XIII aircraft could also be regarded as a reserve, but these aircraft were hardly useful in combat operations.

1 These aircraft remained with units, but were never considered true combat machines.
2 DWL – Doświadczalne Zakłady Lotnicze.

Organisation of Polish Air Force, June 1939

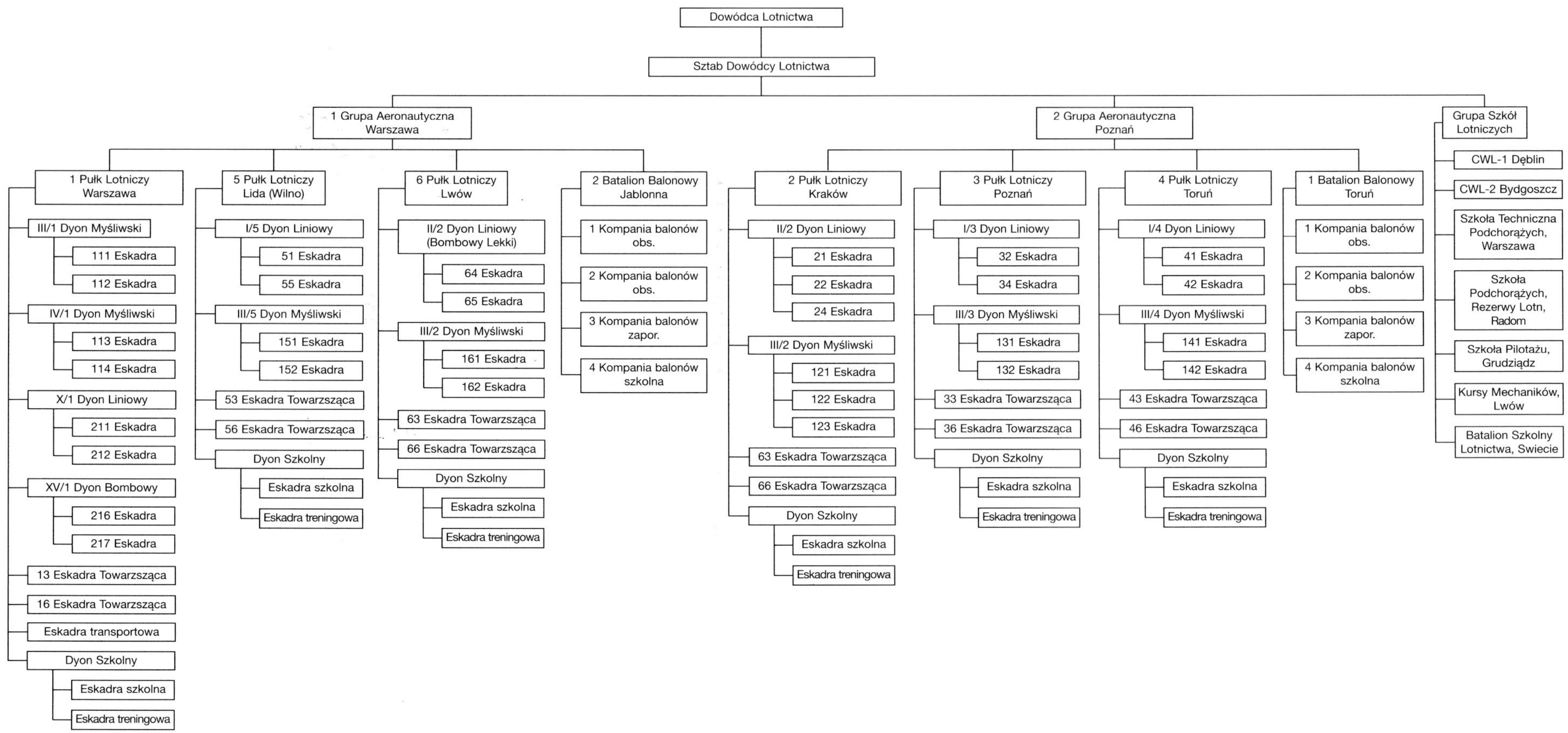

Note: III/1 Dyon Myśliwski and IV/1 Dyon Myśliwski of 1 Pułk Lotniczyt formed Zgrupowanie Myśliwskie
Note: X/1 Dyon Bombowy and XV/1 Dyon Bombowy of 1 Pułk Lotniczyt formed Zgrupowanie Bombowe

Organisation of Polish Air Force, August 1939

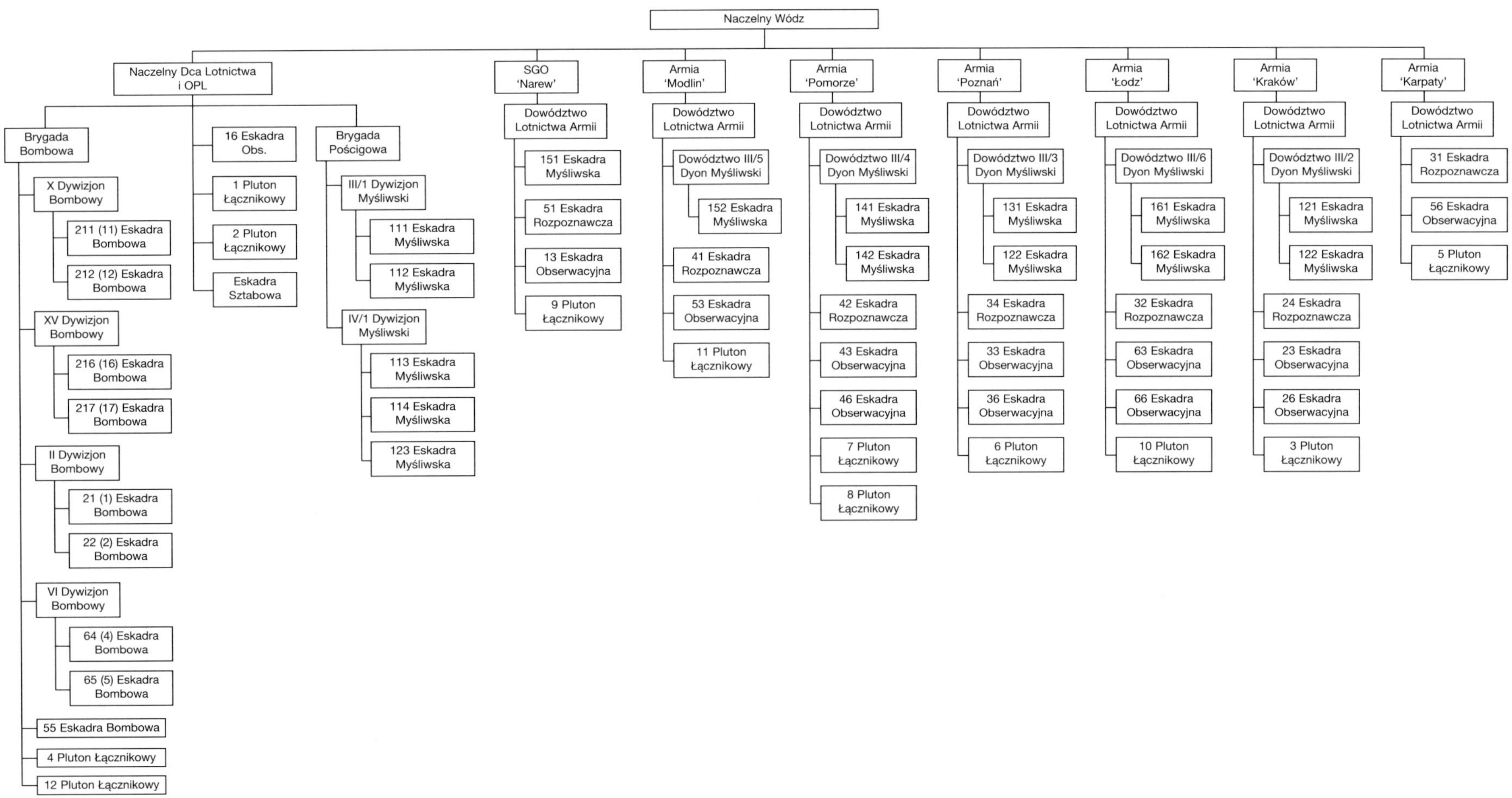

178: *The Potez XV appeared in large numbers in mid-1925, replacing the Bristol Fighters, SVA 10s, and Breguet XIVs. The photo shows the example no. 40.34 (MLP – Kraków)*

179: *The Potez XV was also licence-manufactured in Poland. A total of 135 aircraft were produced (MLP – Kraków)*

180: *Potez XXVs of Szkoła Lotnicza at Dęblin (Pawlak)*

COMBAT OPERATIONS OF THE POLISH AIR FORCE

1921 to September 1939

Aircraft of the Polish Air Force were used in combat again in May 1926 during the coup d'etat organised by *marsz.* Józef Piłsudski. Air units were used on the government side. On 12 May 1926 ground units loyal to *marsz.* Piłsudski entered the left bank of the Vistula in Warsaw and commenced attacks against the Belweder building, where the government was located at that time. The crew of the Mokotów airfield, the seat of 1 Pułk Lotniczy, organised defence of the airfield, thus defending the nearby Belweder building. Commander of the troops loyal to the government, *gen.* Rozwadowski, ordered Dowódca Lotnictwa, *gen.* Zagórski to organise air support for the government troops. The new commander of 1 Pułk, *płk pil.* Jerzy Borejsza gave orders to arm Potez XV aircraft with bombs and assemble crews. Most airmen were cut off by the attack of Piłsudski's troops, and were not able to reach the airfield, some of them probably supported the rebels and did not want to fight against Piłsudski anyway! An order was sent by the Polish Government to the pulks in Krakow, Poznań and Toruń, requesting each of them to despatch one line eskadra to Warsaw. Commercial aircraft of the 'Aerolot' airlines were also impressed. On the evening of 12 May five crews of 1 Pułk flew reconnaissance sorties in order to establish positions of troops and the area of fighting. At the same time the radio communications of the Pułk were put at the government's disposal, allowing it to control the operations of government troops. Without such aid it is probable that the troops would be defeated in a few hours. At midday on 13 May aircraft from Poznań, Krakow and Toruń arrived in Warsaw. Crews from these pulks did not enter combat that day. Aircrews from the units that remained at their respective airfields were ordered to fly reconnaissance missions for government troops advancing towards Warsaw.

181: *Potez XXVs of 34 Eskadra Liniowa in formation flight (Kopański)*

1 Pułk crews commenced operations on the morning on 13 May. The first missions were designed as a demonstration and as a deterrent, bombs being dropped on Piłsudski's troops, albeit not fused. Subsequent sorties were true combat missions with fused bombs. Attacks were launched, among others, against railway station where Piłsudski's troops were unloading. Reconnaissance and liaison missions were also flown. On 14 May aircraft from 2, 3 and 4 Pułk also entered action. Like the previous day, bombing and ground attack missions were flown, but above all reconnaissance and liaison sorties were performed. One crew from 2 Pułk was shot down when attacking artillery posts of the rebels, and was killed.

In the afternoon, due to the great success of Piłsudski's troops, air operations were halted, and on 14 May Mokotów airfield was captured by the rebels.

A total of 130 airmen participated in combat operations. 17 assault and bombing missions were flown, as well as many reconnaissance and liaison ones. Twenty-three 12.5 kg bombs were dropped. Later reports, that accused *gen.* Zagórski who ordered the air force to enter combat in defence of the government, said that air operations caused the death of 12 civilians, while 30 civilians and 8 soldiers from Piłsudski's troops were injured. After the government resigned and hostilities in Warsaw ceased, airmen from various pulks continued for several days to fly liaison missions with orders to stop troops loyal to either the government or Piłsudski in their march towards Warsaw.

Demonstration of power towards Lithuania

At the beginning of March 1938, after many border incidents, Polish-Lithuanian relations became tense. On 17 March Poland announced an ultimatum for the Lithuanian government, which called for normal diplomatic relations. Until that time the Lithuanian government refused to maintain such relations due to the unlawful, in their opinion, capture of Wilno and the surrounding area (the so-called Central Lithuania) in 1920 and subsequent incorporation of Central Lithuania into Poland.

The demand to start diplomatic relations was supported by a demonstration of Poland's military power. This included, among others, the air force, with large aviation forces grouped in Wilno, and subsequently flying formation flypasts along the Lithuanian border. Unfortunately, the action was not planned carefully. Aircraft were sent to Wilno airfield too late in the afternoon, landing there after dark. Drainage work was being carried out on the airfield at that time; the night landing (at a relatively unknown airfield) resulted in 11 aircraft crashing. The demonstration of power also involved aircraft moved to Hutniki airfield near Brody. The largest formation flypast took place on 20 March, performed by 108 *Karaś* light bombers. The emergency continued until 21 March, when the Lithuanian government signed the agreement of normal diplomatic relations with Poland, and the aircraft returned to their bases.

The 'Zaolzie' Operation

At the end of September 1938 the possibility of a Polish-Czech conflict appeared in connection with Poland's demands regarding the Zaolzie region. This area was lost by Poland in a plebiscite in 1919. With the possibility of hostilities looming, fighter aircraft from 1 Pułk Lotniczy (III/1 Dyon), 2 Pułk Lotniczy (III/2 Dyon), 3 Pułk Lotniczy (III/3) and two eskadras (161 and 162) of 6 Pułk Lotniczy were moved to an airfield at Pszczyna and to Monasterzysko airfield near Buczacz, entering the Samodzielna Grupa Operacyjna 'śląsk' ('Silesia') under *gen.* Władysław Bortnowski. Also line units of 2 Pułk Lotniczy (21, 22 and 24 Eskadra Liniowa) were sent to this area. These units would provide air cover for the operations of Polish troops if required, and engage the enemy air force. After the Czechoslovak government agreed on 2 October 1938 for Poland to take over these disputed territories (Czechoslovakia having been substantially weakened by the occupation of Sudetenland by Germany), air units did not participate in fighting, but only in a flypast organised after Polish troops entered Zaolzie. The parade was organised at Cieszyn at the beginning of October. In the second half of that month air units returned to their permanent airfields.

One should also mention the attempts to intercept German Dornier Do 17 reconnaissance aircraft which violated Polish airspace from the spring of 1939. Fighter units were ordered in July 1939 to establish fighter posts ('ambushes') along the routes of the reconnaissance aircraft flights. 1 Pułk Lotniczy organised posts along the border with East Prussia, a total of 2 sections. Dywizjon III/1 used airfields near Białystok and Grodno, and Dywizjon IV/1 near Suwałki. Aircraft of 2 Pułk organised posts at Wieluń, Częstochowa and Zawiercie along the Western border. Aircraft of 4 Pułk provided posts near Bydgoszcz, while 3 and 5 Pułk maintained aircraft at readiness at their permanent airfields. During July the aircraft were scrambled many times to intercept and visual contact was sometimes established with German aircraft, but due to the high altitude at which the Dorniers operated, and their superior speed with respect to the P.11c fighters, none was ever shot down, and at the end of July these posts were abandoned.

Also at the same time Soviet reconnaissance aircraft violated Polish airspace, but there is no written record of any contact with Polish interceptors.

182: *Breguet XIX (Kopański)*

183: *Potez XXV from 51 Eskadra Liniowa of 5 Pułk Lotniczy at Lida (Kopański)*

184: *Potez XXVs of 4 Pułk Lotniczy at Toruń. The photo was taken at Dęblin (Kopański)*

185: *A Potez XXV from the Centralna Eskadra Treningowa based at Warsaw (Kraków)*

186: *Potez XXVs from various units at the turn of the 1920s. Note that the Potez in the foreground has the new type of unit emblem, as opposed to the others (MLP – Kraków)*

187: *34 Eskadra Liniowa used Potez XXVs from 1930 until late 1936 when they were replaced by PZL P-23B* Karaś *aircraft (Kopański)*

188: *A blurred picture of a Spad 51 C1 from 111 Eskadra Myśliwska taking off from a typical Polish grass airfield. The famous 'Kosciuzsko' emblem can be clearly seen*

189: *Spad 51 C1 from 121 or 111 Eskadra Myśliwska (at the beginning of 1927 the unit number was changed) of 1 Pułk Lotniczy in Warsaw (Kopański)*

190: *50 Spad 51 C1s were used in the Polish Air Force but they failed to leave favourable impressions in the memory of Polish pilots (Kopański)*

191: *The Spad 51 C1s were replaced, together with the PWS-As (Avia BH-33s licence-built in Poland) by the ill-fated Spad 61 C1s which suffered many crashes (Kopański)*

192: *Spad 61 C1s from 131 and 132 Eskadra Myśliwska of 3 Pułk Lotniczy based at Poznań (MLP – Kraków)*

193: *This Spad 61 C1 from 131 Eskadra Myśliwska was one of the 280 Spads used by the Polish Air Force ((MLP – Kraków)*

194: *Ground-crew help to position a Spad 61 C1 for take-off (MLP – Kraków)*

PUŁK LOTNICZY HISTORIES

Peacetime, 1921-1939

1 Pułk Lotniczy in Warsaw

Formation of the Pułk commenced at Mokotów airfield in Warsaw on 29 May 1921 by the orders of the Minister Spraw Wojskowych.

Initially the Pułk included the following units:

- I Dywizjon Rozpoznawczy – 12 Eskadra Wywiadowcza, 16 Eskadra Wywiadowcza
- IV Dywizjon Rozpoznawczy – 3 Eskadra Wywiadowcza, 8 Eskadra Wywiadowcza
- III Dywizjon Myśliwski – 7 Eskadra Myśliwska, 18 Eskadra Myśliwska
- Lotniczy Dywizjon Zapasowy

These units had modest numbers of aircraft and equipment. The number of trained personnel was also small. Lack of space at Mokotów forced the unit HQ to disband IV Dywizjon, impress 3 Eskadra into I Dywizjon, and to move 8 Eskadra to 2 Pułk in Krakow. In spite of these changes some eskadras were based at other airfields: 3 and 12 Eskadra at Wilanów, 18 Eskadra at Dęblin. Eskadras returned to Mokotów airfield in 1922-1924. In 1925 deliveries of aircraft from France allowed organisation of II Dywizjon Lotniczy (13 and 14 Eskadra). Simultaneously eskadras of 6 and 11 Pułks were formed. A part of 1 Pułk personnel reinforced those units. The same year Eskadra Wywiadowcza units were renamed to Eskadra Lotnicza, and Eskadra numbering was also changed. In 1926 it was decided to build an airport and a modern aerodrome at Okęcie near Warsaw. That year II Dywizjon Lotniczy was renamed II Dywizjon Niszczycielski, with 14 Eskadra renamed 211 Eskadra Niszczycielska Nocna. Subsequent reorganisation in 1928 led to creation in the following years of a Dywizjon Szkolny consisting of Eskadra Treningowa and Eskadra Szkolna. Subsequently 212 Eskadra Niszczycielska, 213 Eskadra Niszczycielska and 113 Eskadra Myśliwska Nocna were formed. They formed part of II Dywizjon. In 1933 IV/1 Dywizjon Myśliwski with 113 and 114 Eskadra was established. The Dywizjon Niszczycielski was renamed II/1 Dywizjon Bombowy. 1934 brought disbandment of 13 Eskadra Liniowa, reformed as 13 Eskadra Towarzysząca consisting of 5 plutons. Completion of the airfield at Okęcie allowed the Pułk to move there. The airfield became the showcase of the Polish Air Force, visited by most foreign military delegations arriving in Poland. In 1936 Żwiczebna Eskadra Pilotażu was established for training of NCOs from other services. On 1 August Zgrupowanie Myśliwskie was established, which included III/1 and IV/1 Dywizjon Myśliwski. In 1937 two Eskadra Towarzysząca units and a new Dywizjon Bombowy (with two eskadras) were formed. The HQ of

195: *Inspection of a Spad 61 C1 from 122 Eskadra Myśliwska (2 Pułk Lotniczy) (Koniarek)*

the new VI Dywizjon Towarzyszący was also established. In 1938 Zgrupowanie Bombowe of II and V Dywizjon Bombowy was formed. At the same time II Dywizjon lost its 213 Eskadra, renamed Eskadra Szkolno-Treningowa.

March 1939 brought about another reorganisation. 215 and 210 Dywizjon Bombowy were formed, with the number of aircraft increased from 6 to 9, at the same time II and V Dywizjon Bombowy were disbanded.

The Pułk was disbanded when mobilisation was ordered on 23/24 August 1939, replaced by Baza Lotnicza Nr 1.

The organisational changes of the Eskadras and the aircraft used are tabulated on page 134.

Pułk commanders

May 1921–March 1922	*ppłk pil.* Camillo Perini
March 1922–May 1926	*ppłk. pil.* Antoni Buckiewicz
May 1926–April 1929	*płk pil.* Jan Sendorek
May 1929–February 1933	*ppłk. pil. inż.* Franciszek Wiedeń
March 1933–November 1935	*ppłk pil.* Władysław Kalkus
November 1935–July 1938	*ppłk obs.* Władysław Heller
August 1938–August 1939	*płk pil.* Stefan Pawlikowski

2 Pułk Lotniczy in Krakow

The formation of 2 Pułk Lotniczy in Krakow was commenced by order of the Minister Spraw Wojskowych on 20 July 1921. Organisation started at Rakowice airfield near Krakow. The Pułk originally included II Dywizjon Wywiadowczy (6 and 14 Eskadra), II Batalion Uzupełnień and II Ruchomy Park Lotniczy. In August 1922 the unit was increased by adding 8 Eskadra coming from 1 Pułk. By the orders of 29 July 1922 the Minister Spraw Wojskowych, *gen.* dyw. Kazimierz Sosnkowski, included the naval air unit into 2 Pułk Lotniczy. Thus a new unit of the Pułk was established: Detaszowany Dywizjon Lotniczo-Zwiadowczy based at Puck. *Mjr obs.* Jan Bielawski was appointed the commander of that unit. The unit was part of 2 Pułk until 1923.

The same year work commenced on expanding the airfield and constructing new hangars.

1925 brought reorganisation of the air force. Eskadra names were changed to Eskadra Lotnicza. The new 24 Eskadra Lotnicza was formed as the nucleus of II Dywizjon Lotniczy. Subsequent reorganisation of the air force in 1928 resulted in a transfer of II Dywizjon (23 and 24 Eskadra Lotnicza) to 5 Pułk Lotniczy. In exchange 2 Pułk received an Eskadra Myśliwska from the disbanded 11 Pułk. At the end of 1929 organisation of Dywizjon Szkolny started. The airfield was modernised in 1932, and received lighting for night flying. Among the interesting events during the following year was a visit by Prince Michael, the Rumanian heir to the throne. 1933 also saw the formation of the third fighter Eskadra. In 1934 24 Eskadra Liniowa was formed, and formation of Eskadra Towarzysząca also started, this unit together with 24 Eskadra constituting II Dywizjon Liniowy. Pułkowa Szkoła Pilotażu was organised in 1936, and two more Eskadra Towarzysząca units were formed in 1937. II Dywizjon Liniowy disbanded, thus establishing II Dywizjon Towarzyszący. In 1938 Pułk units participated in the 'Zaolzie' Operation.

Mobilisation in August 1939 resulted in disbandment of the Pułk, replaced by Baza Lotnicza Nr 2.

The organisational changes of the Eskadras and the aircraft used are tabulated on page 135.

Pułk commanders:

July 1921 –May 1923	*ppłk pil.* Ernest Cieślewski
May 1923–March 1924	*ppłk pil.* Jerzy Borejsza
April 1924–May 1926	*płk pil.* Jan Sendorek
May 1926–May 1929	*płk pil.* Jan Tarnawa-Malczewski
July 1929–February 1931	*mjr pil. inż.* Tadeusz Wereszczyński
February 1931–March 1939	*ppłk pil.* Edward Lewandowski
March 1939–August 1939	*płk pil.* Stanisław Nazarkiewicz

3 Pułk Lotniczy in Poznań

The Pułk was brought into existence by the orders of the Minister Spraw Wojskowych on 20 July 1921. Organisation of the Pułk commenced at Ławica airfield near Poznań. At first the Pułk included the following units:

- VII Dywizjon Wywiadowczy (1, 5 and 10 Eskadra Wywiadowcza)
- V Dywizjon Myśliwski (13 and 15 Eskadra Myśliwska)
- II Lotniczy Batalion Uzupełnień

Ławica airfield was the least damaged Pułk airfield, however its facilities required urgent repair. In 1922 a building repair and airfield expansion plan was prepared. Work commenced two years later. 1925 brought many changes, as with the other pulks. Eskadra numbering was changed and the Eskadra Wywiadowcza category was replaced with the Eskadra Lotnicza. Forming of a fourth eskadra allowed establishment of II Dywizjon Lotniczy. In the next year two more Eskadras and III Dywizjon Lotniczy were formed. This was thanks to the deliveries of aircraft purchased in France. The large number of aircraft purchased allowed formation of two fighter eskadras (IV Dywizjon Myśliwski), but a few months later it became evident that there was not a sufficient number of flying personnel and both new dywizjons were disbanded. Another reorganisation of the air force commenced in 1928, leading to the formation of Dywizjon Szkolny. In turn the Dywizjon Lotniczy category of units was renamed Dywizjon Lotniczy, and standard numbers of aircraft in eskadras were increased. In 1931 upgrade work at Ławica airfield was completed. The Pułk received new barracks and hangars, as well as many auxiliary buildings. In 1933 a

196: *A project for a Polish reconnaissance aircraft was developed by Władysław Zalewski in 1923. It was designated WZ-X. First flown in 1926, the aircraft was an equivalent of the Breguet XIX. Four were built (the prototype and three pre-production aircraft), but the type never entered series production, as the Potez XXV licence-production was preferred (Glass)*

197: *In 1928 two WZ-X aircraft participated without success in Lot Małej Ententy i Polski (Air Rally of the Small Entente and Poland). Eventually three WZ-Xs went to Polish Air Force training establishments, where one of them survived until 1939 (MLP – Kraków)*

198: *Used for training, the Bartel BM-5d had a poor reputation as an aircraft both prone to malfunctions and difficult to fly (Belcarz)*

199: *The D-1* Cykacz *(Ticker), first flown on 25 February 1925, was the first Polish sports aircraft after World War I. Its designer, Jerzy Dąbrowski, gained fame 10 years later, when he developed the excellent PZL-37* Łoś *bomber (MLP – Kraków)*

200: *PWS-A fighters were built under a Czech licence in 1928. The photograph shows aircraft of 2 Pułk Lotniczy based at Kraków (121 and 122 Eskadra Myśliwska) (Morgała)*

201: *A licence-built PWS-A at the factory airfield in Biała Podlaska (NTM Praha)*

202: *The Czech prototype of the Avia BH-33 with Walter Jupiter VI engine at Praha-Kbely factory airfield (NTM – Praha)*

203: *PWS-A 'white 4' of an unidentified unit. This interesting photo was probably taken in the second half of the thirties, as indicated by the small asymmetrically positioned national markings on top of the upper wing. In the background is a PWS-10 fighter (Glass)*

204: *The famous aerobatic trio of* kpt. *Jerzy Bajan was established in 122 Eskadra Myśliwska at the beginning of the thirties. In the foreground is 'white 1', radio call-sign 51-K, at Warsaw-Mokotów airfield in June 1932 (Glass)*

205: *The PWS-10 fighter was a competitor of the PZL P-1. Even though it proved less good, a batch of 80 machines was ordered, production starting in 1931. The photo shows aircraft of 3 Pułk Lotniczy in Poznań (MLP – Kraków)*

206: *A section of PWS-10s from 4 Pułk Lotniczy in Toruń (MLP – Kraków)*

207: *The first prototype PWS-10 was developed by Aleksander Grzędzielski and Augustyn Bobek-Zdaniewski. It was first flown in March 1930 by the factory test pilot Franciszek Rutkowski (Zdaniewski via Glass)*

third fighter eskadra in the Pułk (133 Eskadra) began to be formed. At the end of 1934 the new Eskadra Towarzysząca was established, part of II Dywizjon. 133 Eskadra Myśliwska was disbanded in 1936, its personnel moving to 6 Pułk. Pułkowa Szkoła Pilotażu was organised in the summer of 1938 at Snieciska airfield. In April 1939 35 Eskadra, one of the Pułk's oldest eskadras, was disbanded. II Dywizjon Liniowy was disbanded at the same time, 34 Eskadra moving to I Dywizjon. After mobilisation was declared 3 Pułk Lotniczy was disbanded, and Baza Lotnicza Nr 3 was established at Ławica airfield.

The organisational changes of the Eskadras and the aircraft used are tabulated on page 136.

Pułk commanders:

July 1921–March 1922	*płk pil.* Aleksander Śerednicki
April 1922–April 1925	*ppłk pil.* Camillo Perini
May 1925–June 1929	*płk pil.* Sergiusz Abżółtowski
July 1929–August 1933	*ppłk pil.* Władysław Kalkus
September 1933–October 1937	*ppłk obs.* Edward Karaś
October 1937–August 1939	*ppłk pil.* Tadeusz Jarina

4 Pułk Lotniczy in Toruń

Formation of the Pułk at Toruń airfield was started by the orders of 23 May 1924. The unit was established during a very difficult time for the Polish Air Force, lack of equipment and personnel did not assist in attaining combat capability quickly. The unit was founded on the personnel of the former Szkoła Obserwatorów and Strzelców Lotniczych at Toruń, and with volunteers from 1, 2 and 3 Pułk. Initially the Pułk included two Dywizjon Rozpoznawczy units: I Dywizjon with 41 and 42 Eskadra Lotnicza and II Dywizjon with 43 and 44 Eskadra. Buildings at the home airfield were a major problem. After receiving aircraft from France in 1925 I Dywizjon Lotniczy (change of designations took place in 1925) achieved a training capability which allowed it to participate in exercises. In March 1926 formation of a two-eskadra Dywizjon Myśliwski (123 and 124 Eskadra Myśliwska) started. This was not completed until the establishment of II Dywizjon Liniowy and conversion training of its personnel to fighter pilots. In 1928 each Eskadra Lotnicza was renamed Eskadra Liniowa. The same year formation of a Dywizjon Szkolny commenced, followed in subsequent years by that of 43 Eskadra Towarzysząca. 1931 brought completion of the airfield and unit building modernisation work. In the autumn of 1933 a third fighter eskadra was formed: 143 Eskadra Myśliwska. An experimental Eskadra equipped with British Avro (Cierva) C-30 autogiros was established in the Pułk in 1936. The Eskadra would train pilots and develop operational techniques for use of rotary wing aircraft in first line units in order to replace spotting balloons. Trials revealed, however, that due to the lack of radio communication and to the primitive construction of the autogiro, this aircraft was of little use, and in 1938 the Eskadra was disbanded.

143 Eskadra Myśliwska had been disbanded in 1937 (personnel having been moved to Wilno) while formation of another Eskadra Towarzysząca and II Dywizjon Towarzyszący commenced. Formation of Wydzielony Dywizjon Towarzyszący started in spring 1939 at Bydgoszcz airfield, including 46 and 49 Eskadra Towarzysząca. This unit would support possible operations of the Polski Korpus Interwencyjny, the corps having been formed to act against any German attempt to capture the Free City of Danzig (Gdańsk). After mobilisation 4 Pułk Lotniczy was disbanded, and Baza Lotnicza nr 4 was formed at Toruń airfield. The Wydzielony Dywizjon Towarzyszący was also disbanded.

The organisational changes of the Eskadras and the aircraft used are tabulated on page 137.

Pułk commanders:

May 1924–October 1925	*płk pil.* Roman Florer
October 1925–January 1927	*ppłk pil.* Jan Kiezuń
February 1927–January 1931	*ppłk pil.* August Menczak
January 1931–April 1934	*ppłk obs.* Władysław Heller
April 1934–May 1936	*płk pil. inż.* Stanisław Kuźminńki
May 1936–August 1939	*płk pil.* Bolesław Stachoń

5 Pułk Lotniczy in Lida

The Pułk was formed by the orders of 14 August 1928. The orders disbanded 11 Pułk Myśliwski and formed 5 Pułk Lotniczy at Lida in its place. At first the Pułk included two Eskadra Lotnicza units, soon renamed Eskadra Liniowa, from II Dywizjon of 2 Pułk Lotniczy in Krakow. In exchange two fighter eskadras of 11 Pułk were moved to Krakow. A Dywizjon Szkolny was established in the winter of 1930. At the end of 1932 part of 5 Pułk personnel were transferred to Porubanek airfield near Wilno in order to form a Wydzielony Oddział Lotniczy. The unit would consist of two eskadras: a line and an accompanying one, plus the necessary facilities. Eskadra Towarzysząca would be formed in Wilno, while the Eskadra Liniowa moved from Lida. Orders of 7 July 1933 changed the name of the unit to Detaszowany Dywizjon Lotniczy. The same orders required formation of an Eskadra Towarzysząca at Lida. A major reorganisation of the unit was completed according to the orders of 19 July 1937. The Detaszowany Dywizjon Lotniczy in Wilno was disbanded, and a two-eskadra Dywizjon Myśliwski was formed there.

The Eskadra Liniowa was moved from Wilno to Lida, while the Eskadra Towarzysząca was left there.

Formation of another Eskadra Towarzysząca started and IV Dywizjon Towarzyszący was established. In the spring of 1938 line dywizjons of 1 Pułk were assembled at Lida airfield, while fighter Dywizjons gathered at Porubanek airfield near Wilno. This was connected with the border issue with Lithuania. The Declaration of mobilisation in August 1939 led to disbandment of the Pułk, with Baza Lotnicza Nr 5 replacing it.

The organisational changes of the Eskadras and the aircraft used are tabulated on page 138.

Pułk commanders:

July 1928–January 1930	płk pil. Piotr Abakanowicz
January 1930–October 1936	płk pil. Wacław Iwaszkiewicz
October 1936–August 1939	płk pil. Jerzy Grabiński

6 Pułk Lotniczy in Lwów

The Pułk was established by the orders of 28 February 1925. Due to logistical reasons (lack of space at Lewandówka airfield as well as lack of equipment and personnel) the first units of the Pułk were formed at Mokotów airfield in Warsaw, based on equipment and personnel of 1 Pułk. II Dywizjon was formed with aircraft and personnel from 2 and 3 Pułk. The Pułk HQ moved to Lewandówka airfield at the end of May, and Pułk units reached Lwów during August. The total equipment of the Pułk consisted at that time of just 5 aircraft. As Lewandówka airfield was located among buildings, making any expansion impossible, construction of a new airfield was undertaken in 1923 at Skniłów village near Lwów. A modest budget for this investment delayed construction which finally began in 1925, after 6 Pułk had been formed. In 1928 Dywizjon Szkolny was formed, and in 1929 the Pułk moved to the unfinished Skniłów airfield. The same year formation of Eskadra Towarzysząca started. The unit received number 63, while the already existing 63 Eskadra Liniowa was renamed 65. Construction of Skniłów airfield was completed in 1933. 1934 brought further expansion of the unit. Another Eskadra Towarzysząca was formed, joining II Dywizjon.

Formation of a two-eskadras Dywizjon Myśliwski and another Eskadra Towarzysząca started at the end of 1937. At the same time IV Dywizjon Towarzyszący was established, including all three accompanying eskadras. At the end of 1938 III Dywizjon Myśliwski sent some of its aircraft as the Eskadra Korpusu Obrony Pogranicza to Sarny airfield for air protection of the fortification work there. I Dywizjon Liniowy and its Eskadras was disbanded in March 1939. Mobilisation led to disbanding of 6 Pułk, replaced by Baza Lotnicza nr 6.

The organisational changes of the Eskadras and the aircraft used are tabulated on page 138.

Pułk commanders:

March 1925–February 1929	*ppłk pil.* Camillo Perini
May 1929–April 1934	*ppłk pil.* Augustyn Domes
May 1934–August 1939	*płk pil.* Tadeusz Prauss

11 Pułk Myśliwski in Lida

Following the new concept of single-role pulks, formation of 11 Pułk Myśliwski commenced as a result of orders issued on 28 February 1925. It was assumed that the Pułk would eventually have three fighter dywizjons, each with two 10 aircraft eskadras and three aircraft in reserve. The Pułk would be based at Lida airfield. Lack of equipment and of skilled personnel, as well as the unprepared airfield at Lida, resulted in the Pułk being formed at Mokotów airfield in Warsaw, and with just one dywizjon. The Pułk did not move to Lida airfield until October 1925, but most of the personnel arrived there even later, in January 1926. Lida airfield was not properly prepared for such a large unit and the Pułk personnel spent the winter in harsh conditions. In the spring repair work was undertaken at the airfield and in the barracks, and flying training commenced. The personnel consisted mostly of young men, single status of a pilot was a pre-condition of joining the unit, so they were eager in their training to become fighter pilots, members of the elite. In a short while the unit achieved a high level of pilot training which allowed them to participate in numerous air competitions and meetings. Due to their highly proficient flying skills pilots of the unit often appeared in press articles representing the Polish Air Force. The Pułk staff equipped with Spad 61C1 aircraft took second place at a competition in Zurich in August 1927. Unfortunately, the change of organisation of pulks in 1928 led to the disbandment of the Pułk. It was dissolved by the orders of 14 July 1928.

The organisational changes of the Eskadras and the aircraft used are tabulated on page 138.

Pułk commanders:

May 1925–October 1927	*płk pil.* Jerzy Kossowski
October 1927–July 1928	*ppłk pil.* Piotr Abakanowicz

Special Eskadras (not part of regiments)

Eskadra Korpusu Ochrony Pogranicza (KOP)

When fortifications commenced construction along the Eastern border of Poland in 1936, there arose the need to provide air defence for these works. In particular there was the question of preventing aerial reconnaissance by enemy forces. To this end the commander of 1 Pułk Lotniczy, by the orders of November 1936, detached a mixed group from 12 Eskadra Liniowa and 113 Eskadra Myśliwska with a Potez XXV aircraft and a servicing unit to Sarny airfield. Since using just one aircraft could only provide limited psychological support, in the spring 1937 PZL P.7a fighters were despatched to that area also. As numerous violations of Polish airspace occurred in this region, the commander of 1 Pułk Lotniczy decided that pilots and aircraft from fighter dywizjons of 1 Pułk would operate there, changing every 3 months. The aircraft operating in that area received additional markings in form of white letters 'K.O.P.'.

From 1939 the readiness at Sarny airfield was maintained by aircraft of II/6 Dywizjon from 6 Pułk Lotniczy.

208: *The pilot's view from the cockpit of a PWS 10 peering between the engine cylinder covers. Note the ring-and-bead gunsight*

209: *Instrument panel of the PWS 10. The riffled finish to the aluminium panel is typical of the 1930s. The main instruments are the air-speed indicator, an engine RPM counter and a fuel gauge*

210: *A PWS-10 without spinner from the Szkoła Lotnicza based at Dęblin (Kopański)*

211: *Production PWS-10 no. 5.50 at factory airfield in Biała Podlaska (Kopański)*

212: *A section of PWS-10s from 4 Pułk Lotniczy in Toruń (Kopański)*

213: *Less than two years after introduction into first-line service, the PWS-10 started to be withdrawn in favour of the PZL P-7a (Kopański)*

214: *After a short period of first-line use the PWS-10 was allocated for training, where it was used until the outbreak of war (Kopański)*

215: *In 1936 fifteen PWS-10 aircraft were sold to Spain, where they were used by the nationalists in the Flying School at Léon, under the name Chiquita (MLP – Kraków)*

216: *The predecessor of the Bartel BM-5c was the the Bartel BM-4a, which served from 1927 (Glass)*

217: *The world's first aircraft with the V-tail invented by Jerzy Rudlicki – Hanriot HD-28 no. 30.83, Lublin 1931 (Archiwum Dokumentacji Mechanicznej Warsaw via Glass)*

218: *A PWS-18, or Avro 621 Tutor licence-built in Poland (Glass)*

219: *A Bartel BM-5d of the Szkoła Lotnicza at Dęblin. (Belcarz)*

220: *The Bartel BM-5d's main distinguishing feature was its Wright Whirlwind J-5 radial engine (Glass)*

221: *The Bartel BM-6a, the last design from the Samolot company. Its production was terminated when the plant closed down (Glass)*

222: *Bartel BM-5c training aircraft, first flown on 30 August 1929 (Glass)*

223: *Spad 61 C1 of 3 Pułk Lotniczy in Poznań (Kopa)*

224 Below: *Potez XXV picking-up a report from the ground (Kopański)*

225: *The successor to the PWS-12 was the PWS-14, built in a small batch of 20. It was succeeded by the PWS-16, built in the same numbers. The only external difference from the PWS-14 was the undercarriage. The photo shows aircraft of one of the flying schools (Archiwum Dokumentacji Mechanicznej – Warsaw)*

226: *PWS-16 with the early type undercarriage (Cynk via Glass)*

227: *An Eskadra of PWS-16bis trainers from the Dęblin school (Glass)*

228: *PWS-16bis no. '8 M' at Mokotów airfield in Warsaw. The photo was taken in November 1936 during the I Kurs Akrobacji Lotniczej in the Warsaw Flying Club. The aircraft was borrowed from the armed forces (Glass)*

229: *The designer and his work. Augustyn Bobek-Zdaniewski in front of a PWS-16bis. (Zdaniewski)*

230: *The PWS-26 trainer was one of the best Polish training aircraft. This machine belonged to Eskadra Treningowa of 1 Pułk Lotniczy in Warsaw (Kopański)*

231: *The PWS-26 was intended for training in aerial shooting and bombardment. It was also suited to inverted flight. Here aircraft belonging to 4 PL are shown (Kopański)*

232: *A PWS-26 of Eskadra Treningowa of 1 Pułk Lotniczy based at Warsaw (Kopański)*

233: *A PWS-26 aircraft of the Szkoła Lotnicza based at Dęblin (Kopański)*

234: *A group of unidentified officers pose for photos in front of a PWS-26. Note that only one wears the distinctive Polish 'Czapka' hat (Kopański)*

235: *Blind-flying training PWS-26 seen on the ground at Dęblin (MLP-Kraków)*

236: *PWS-26 no. 81.7. The aircraft is being piloted by the instructor. The door of the front cockpit is open (MLP–Kraków)*

Units of 1st Pułk Lotniczy 1921–1939

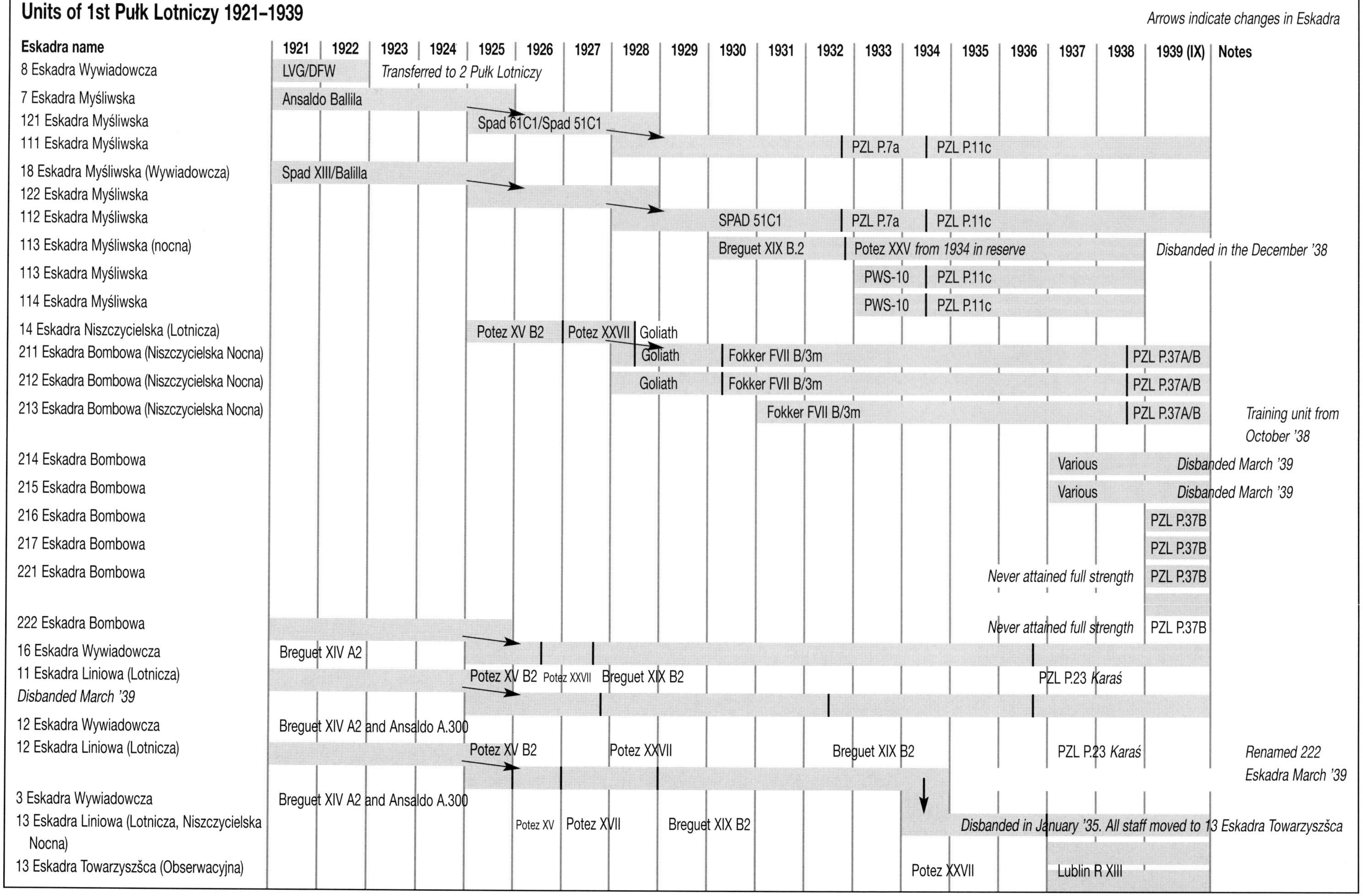

Units of 2nd Pułk Lotniczy 1921–1939

Arrows indicate changes in Eskadra

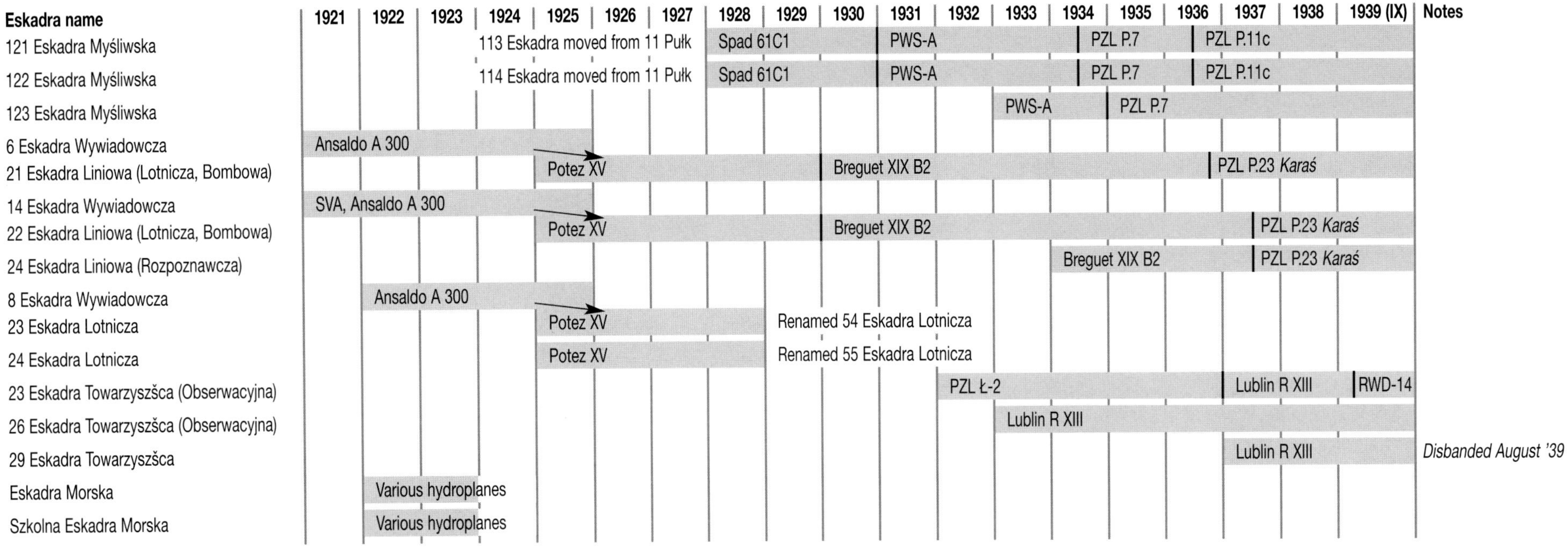

Units of 3rd Pułk Lotniczy 1921–1939

Arrows indicate changes in Eskadra

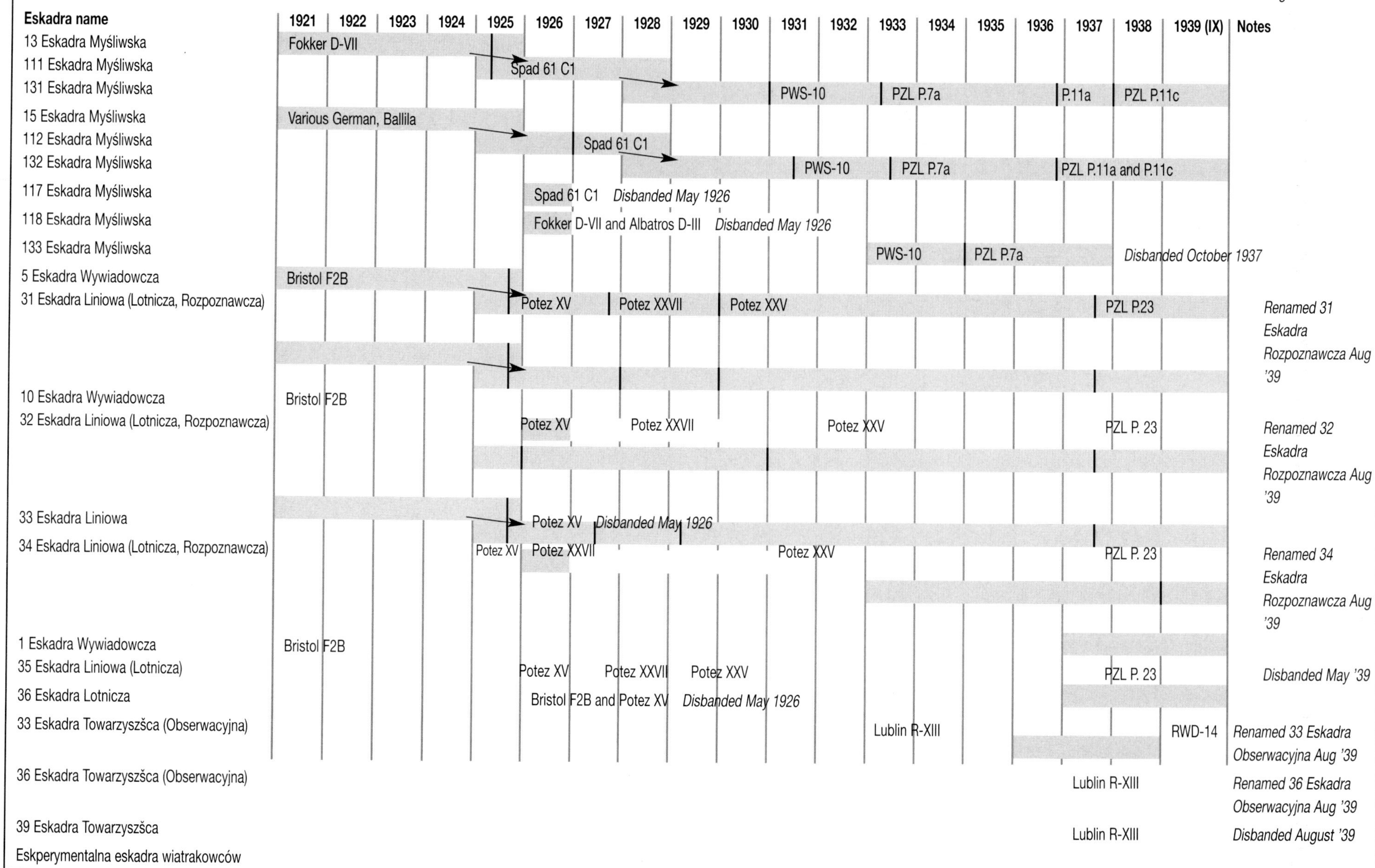

Units of 4th Pułk Lotniczy 1921–1939

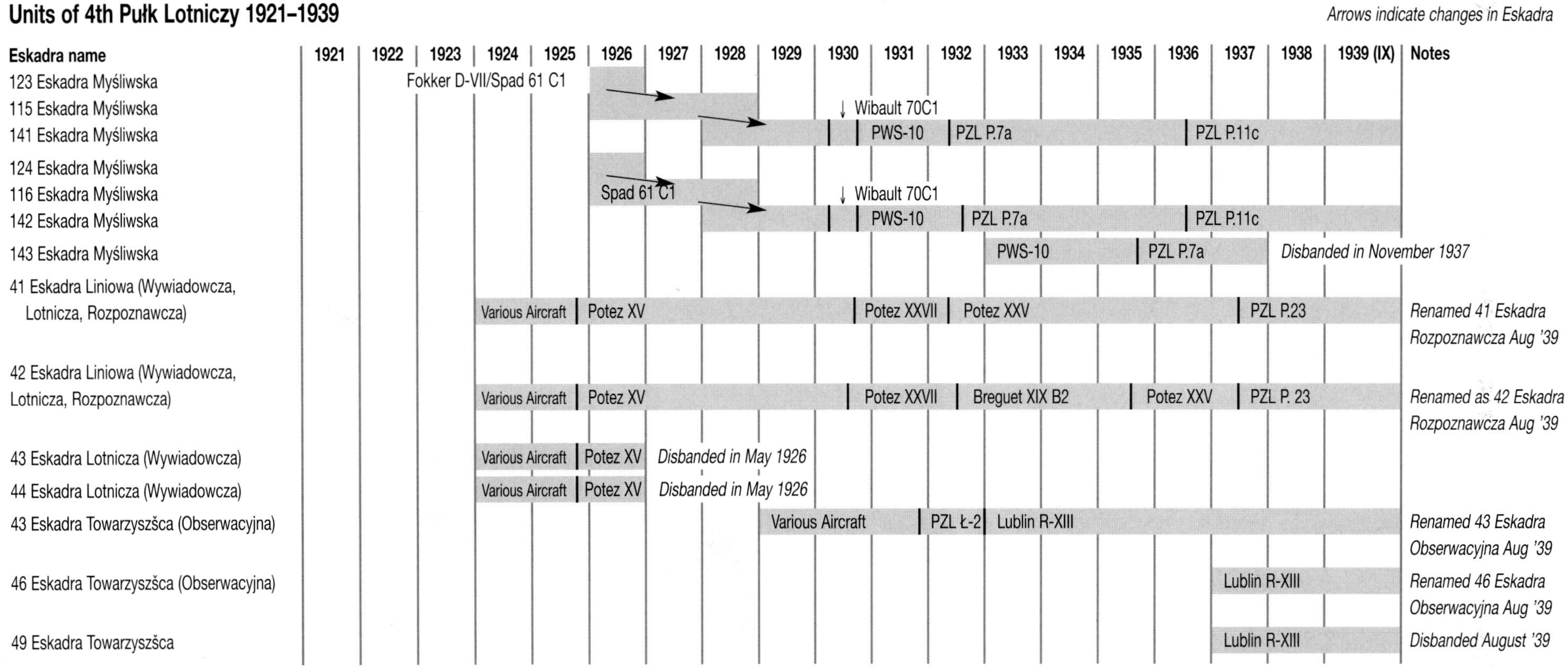

Units of 5th Pułk Lotniczy 1921–1939

Eskadra name	1921	1922	1923	1924	1925	1926	1927	1928	1929	1930	1931	1932	1933	1934	1935	1936	1937	1938	1939 (IX)	Notes
151 Eskadra Myśliwska																	PZL P.7a			
152 Eskadra Myśliwska																	PZL P.11c			
51 Eskadra Liniowa (Rozpoznawcza)													Potez XXV			Potez XV (Jupiter)		PZL P.23		*Renamed 51 Eskadra Rozpoznawcza*
54 Eskadra Liniowa					*Moved 23 Eskadra*			Potez XV			Potez XXV			*Disbanded in June 1933*						
55 Eskadra Liniowa (Samodzielna Eskadra Bombowa)					*Moved 24 Eskadra*			Potez XV		Potez XXV						Potez XV (Jupiter)		PZL P. 23		*Renamed Samodzielna Eskadra Bombowa*
53 Eskadra Towarzyszšca (Obserwacyjna)												Potez XXVII	Lublin R XIII						RWD-14	*Renamed 53 Eskadra Obserwacyjna*
56 Eskadra Towarzyszšca (Obserwacyjna)														Lublin R-XIII						*Renamed 56 Eskadra Obserwacyjna*
59 Eskadra Towarzyszšca (Obserwacyjna)																	Lublin R-XIII			*Disbanded August '39*

Units of 6th Pułk Lotniczy 1921–1939

Arrows indicate changes in Eskadra

Eskadra name	1921	1922	1923	1924	1925	1926	1927	1928	1929	1930	1931	1932	1933	1934	1935	1936	1937	1938	1939 (IX)	Notes
161 Eskadra Myśliwska																	PZL P.11c			
162 Eskadra Myśliwska																	PZL P.7a			
61 Eskadra Liniowa (Lotnicza)		initially as 63 Eskadra			Potez XV					Potez XXV								PZL P.23		*Disbanded August '39*
62 Eskadra Liniowa (Lotnicza)		initially as 64 Eskadra			Potez XV		Potez XXVII		Potez XXV									PZL P.23		*Disbanded August '39*
64 Eskadra Bombowa (Lotnicza, Liniowa)		initially as 62 Eskadra			Potez XV		Potez XXVII			Breguet XIX							PZL P.23			
63 Eskadra Lotnicza					Potez XV		Potez XXVII													
65 Eskadra Bombowa (Lotnicza, Liniowa)												Breguet XIX						PZL P.23		
63 Eskadra Towarzyszšca (Obserwacyjna)									PWS-5 & Lublin R-X		PZL Ł-2	Lublin R-XIII								
66 Eskadra Towarzyszšca (Obserwacyjna)														Lublin R-XIII						

Units of 11th Pułk Lotniczy 1925–1928

Eskadra name	1925	1926	1927	1928	Notes
113 Eskadra Myśliwska	Fokker D VII		Spad 61 C1		*Renamed 121 Eskadra Myśliwska in 2nd Pułk*
114 Eskadra Myśliwska	Fokker D VII		Spad 61 C1		*Renamed 122 Eskadra Myśliwska in 2nd Pułk*

237: *The Bartel BM-4a was the first Polish aircraft of the inter-war period to be put into series production (Kopański)*

238: *Bartel BM-5b of a training unit at Dęblin (Kopański)*

239: *From the end of 1920 the Podlaska Wytwórnia Samolotów (PWS) factory began to specialise in the production of training aircraft. The whole family stemmed from the PWS-12 of 1929 vintage. This photo shows the first prototype after initial changes (reshaped engine cowling and rounded wing tips) (Zdaniewski)*

240: *The PWS-18 received the military type number (serial prefix) 80 and individual serials ranging from 1 to 80. This is 80-14 (Kopański)*

241: *Experience gained with the PWS-18 was used when designing the indigenous PWS-16 bis (Kopański)*

242: *Between 1935 and 1936 forty PWS-18 aircraft were manufactured (Kopański)*

243: *A section of PWS-18s in flight (MLP – Kraków)*

244: *PWS-26 'blind-flyer' with a special removable cover over the rear cockpit (Kopański)*

245: *The RWD-8 was used for initial flying training. The photograph shows an aircraft of the L.O.P.P. para-military organisation, with a civil registration, SP-BJH (MLP – Kraków)*

246: *Aircraft of the Warsaw Flying Club, including RWD-8s (SP-ANR, SP-AMW, SP-ANY). Most aircraft of flying clubs were impressed immediately before the outbreak of war. They were used in liaison platoons (MLP – Kraków)*

247: *The Pre-war Polish Air Force used some 350 RWD-8 aircraft. This photograph shows RWD-8 no. 34.137 of the Szkoła Lotnicza in Bydgoszcz (Kopański)*

248: *The PWS-19 was supposed to become the successor to the Potez XXV and Breguet XIX aircraft. However, during testing in 1933 the aircraft crashed and the imminent construction of the prototype PZL-23* Karaś *resulted in abandonment of this interesting design (Glass)*

249: *The PWS-5t2 was a competitor of the PZL Ł-2 and the Lublin R-X. Poor performance resulted in only a batch of 5 aircraft being delivered for military use (compare the chapter devoted to naval aviation) (MLP – Kraków)*

250: *A group of cadet officers by a Bartel BM-4 at Radom-Sadków airfield. Seated in the middle is an instructor,* chor. *Ludwik Homa (Belcarz)*

251 Below: *Licence-built PWS-18s were used in flying schools at Krosno, Bydgoszcz, Dęblin and in small number in 4 Pułk Lotniczy (Kopański)*

252-254: *A series of three photos showing the first flight (with skis and wheels) of the prototype Lublin R-X aircraft. This took place on 1 February 1929 at the factory airfield in Lublin (NTM Praha)*

255: *The Lublin R-VIIIa bomber-reconnaissance aircraft was powered by a Lorraine-Dietrich engine and first flew in July 1928 (MLP – Kraków)*

256: *The LWS-4a* Żubr *(Bison) bomber showed much resemblance to French bombers of the thirties. It was not a success (Glass)*

257: *Lublin R-XIIID aircraft at the factory airfield in Lublin (Glass)*

258: *The PZL P-1 was the progenitor of the family of Polish fighter aircraft developed by Puławski (Glass)*

259: *The prototype of the PZL Ł-2 liaison aircraft (Ł – łącznikowy = liaison) was first flown in 1929. It was manufactured in a batch of 25. The photo shows an example known generally as 'the African' as it was used for a flight around Africa. It was piloted by kpt. Stanisław SkarŔyński, who would later cross the Southern Atlantic. The African tour took place between 1 February and 5 May 1931 (MLP – Kraków)*

260: *Even though the RWD-13 was a touring aircraft, it also found use as liaison aircraft. A dozen or so were impressed during the 1939 campaign (NTM Praha)*

WARTIME OPERATIONS

World War 2 broke out on 1 September 1939. This was a total war, in which the aim was not only to destroy enemy troops, but also to destroy his economy. Each method of achieving this aim was ruthlessly used by the aggressor. Poland became the first victim of this. The speech of Adolf Hitler to his commanders delivered at the briefing in Obersalzberg on 22 August 1939 left no doubt as to the objectives and methods of fighting against Poland. Initially Fall Weiss[1] was to begin on 26 August 1939, but due to the alliance between Poland and Britain signed on 25 August the date was postponed to 1 September. In the above mentioned speech Hitler said: *"Destruction of Poland is our first aim. Our target is not to achieve some defined line, but to destroy the human force (. . .) Have no mercy. Be brutal. Eighty million people must receive what they deserve, they deserve their existence secured. (. . .) Our first goal is to reach the Vistula and Narew rivers. Our technological superiority will break the Poles' nerves. Every new Polish army that appears should be crushed immediately, the war has to be a war of attrition".*

Indeed, the German superiority, both in quantity and quality was overwhelming. The Germans had an army of over 1.8 million soldiers, equipped with 11,000 pieces of artillery, 2,800 tanks, and some 2,600 aircraft. Poland could only resist with 1.2 million soldiers armed with 3,000 pieces of artillery, 600 tanks, and 494 aircraft of which 392 were warplanes. Any comparison (in 1939) of these two armies lacks meaning. The German war machine that had been prepared over several years was faced by a poorly equipped Polish army, which had commenced preparations to face the Third Reich a mere few months before. The pre-war Polish war doctrine assumed that the greatest danger for the state was posed by the Eastern neighbour, the USSR. Polish defence plan 'Zachód' ('West') assumed that operations would continue until an Allied counter-offensive was launched i.e. for some two weeks. History proved how naive were these assumptions. The best comment on this situation is provided by the French phrase that "nobody was going to die for Polish Danzig." The tragic situation was completed by the Ribbentrop-Molotov pact of 24 August 1939 in which the Germans and the Russians defined the new partition of Poland.

261: *Impressive shot taken during ground engine run on a PZL P-11a from 161 Eskadra Myśliwska of 6 Pułk Lotniczy in Lwów.* Ppor. *W. Gandor, the unit engineering officer is standing next to the aircraft (Kopański)*

The September 1939 campaign can be divided into several stages. The first, from 1 until 6 September is called the 'border battle' during which the Poles tried to maintain their positions at the state border. The principal German attack was directed from Silesia, Pomerania and East Prussia towards the capital city – Warsaw. Only minor containment operations were carried out at the Wielkopolska sector defended by Armia 'Poznań' under *gen.* Kutrzeba, with the intention of encircling this force. In effect Armia 'Poznań' remained the only Polish ground formation which escaped serious losses in the first days of the war and retained its operational capability. On 7 September the HQ decided to form a new front line along the Vistula and San rivers. By that time most Polish army formations were disintegrating, further affected by the chaos behind the lines. This was caused by the operations of the German air force which attacked both the retreating troops, and the evacuating civil population. Polish troops were also attacked by night, by German saboteurs of the Fifth Column. These were usually German nationals living in Poland.

On the night of 5 September government and diplomatic institutions were evacuated from Warsaw. At the same time fierce fighting continued in the coastal region, cut off from the rest of the country. On 7 September Westerplatte surrendered, the Polish military depot in Danzig, where the first shots of the Second World War had been fired. Resistance by Polish troops on the coast continued until the end of the campaign, when Hel surrendered on 2 October.

Establishing the new defence line would be difficult to achieve, although for a moment it seemed realistic. No doubt one positive factor was provided by the Polish counter-offensive on the Bzura river. On the night of 9 September joint forces of *gen.* Kutrzeba's Armia 'Poznań' and parts of *gen.* Bortnowski's Armia 'Pomorze' struck at the left flank of the German 8 Army attacking Warsaw. Initially the Polish side achieved an advantage, no doubt due to surprise. However, after 14 September, when the Germans moved additional forces from the front, the Poles started to lose the upper hand. Eventually the greatest battle of the 1939 campaign ended in a Polish defeat. During the battle, which lasted until 18 September, Polish losses amounted to over 150,000 soldiers. In spite of the increasing German superiority Polish troops continued to fight, despite fighting in difficult conditions, often without communication with other units.

17 September 1939 proved the crucial moment of the campaign, as on that day Red Army troops entered the territory of Poland to fulfil their obligations towards Germany. The Polish government, located at that time in Kołomyja on the Polish-Rumanian border, came under direct threat. When Russian troops were reported some 30 km away from Kuty where the government moved, it was decided to cross the border into exile. President Ignacy Mościcki and the Wódz Naczelny *gen.* Edward Rydz-Śmigły evacuated with the government. Even though Wojsko Polskie still had some 25 divisions, the lack of communications led to disorder. Individual formations conducted independent operations, which marked the third stage of the 1939 campaign. During this stage most troops attempted to achieve realistic goals. Most usually these consisted in trying to reach Warsaw (Armia 'Poznań', 'Pomorze', 'Łódź', 'Prusy' troops) or the so-called Rumanian bridgehead, as it was hoped Allied assistance would arrive through that country (Rumania was the only neighbour to traditionally maintain excellent relations with Poland). Quite different was the situation of those troops that found themselves encircled in the middle of the country. Usually they continued the uneven struggle against the Germans, in the end their only goal being to preserve the honour of the Polish soldier. Relatively well organised defence operations were carried out in the second half of September in the Eastern part of Poland. This followed from the fact that Korpus Ochrony Pogranicza (KOP) units that defended the Russian border did not participate in the first stages of fighting. The largest KOP formation was led by *gen.* Orlik-Rückemann who fought several skirmishes and two major battles with the Russians (at Szack on 28-29 September and at Wytyczne on 1 October). After parting with the enemy he disbanded his troops. The capital city continued to defend itself bravely until 28 September. Two days later the fortress of Modlin, some 30 km north of Warsaw surrendered. The last major formation to fight in regular combat operations was Samodzielna Grupa Operacyjna 'Polesie' under *gen.* Kleeberg. In an attempt to break through to besieged Warsaw they fought the last battle of the campaign on 2-5 October, at Kock. A separate chapter of SGO 'Polesie' operations was written by 13 Eskadra Szkolna also known as the Pluton Rozpoznawczy Lotniczy. The unit was formed by *por. pil.* Edmund Piorunkiewicz. On 18 September he assumed command of a part of the ground party of 13 Eskadra Obserwacyjna, subordinating it to SGO 'Polesie'. The unit was formed around a PWS 26 trainer aircraft found at Adampol near Włodawa. 13 Eskadra Szkolna was joined by cadet officers Bandor, Matz and Wieczorek, who brought with them two RWD 8 aircraft. On 25 September the name of '13 Eskadra Szkolna' was officially accepted, and the unit reported directly to *gen.* Kleeberg. During their short period of combat (25 September-5 October) pilots flew many reconnaissance missions over enemy troops in their unarmed aircraft. Since the aircraft had no bomb racks, the crews attacked the Germans with hand grenades. These were the last aircraft with Polish markings in the sky over Poland in 1939.

In order to properly evaluate the Polish Air Force participation in the 1939 defence war, one should go back in time and analyse the organisational structure of the Wojsko Polskie. At the time of the outbreak of war, according to the so-called wartime structure, Wojsko Polskie was commanded by the Naczelne Dowództwo, formed by reorganisation of the Główny Inspektorat Sił Zbrojnych and the Sztab Główny. This was headed by the Wódz Naczelny, *marsz.* Edward Rydz-Śmigły, with *płk dypl.* T. Munnich as his ADC. Naczelne Dowództwo included commanders of the services and branches of the army. *Gen. bryg.* S. Miller was the artillery commander, *gen. bryg.* J. Zając was the commander of the aviation and air defence, *gen. bryg.* M. Dąbkowski was the commander of the engineering forces, and *płk.* J. Kapciuk was the commander of armoured weapons. Other members of the Naczelne Dowództwo included:

262: *The Polish Air Force used six Lublin R-XVIb medical evacuation aircraft (the prototype and five production aircraft). During 1933 the Lublin R-XVIb won the Medical Aviation Competition at the VII International Air Medicine Congress in Madrid, for which it was awarded the M. Raphael trophy (Glass)*

263: *Lublin R-XIIIt, the so-called 'blind-flyer' from the Eskadra Treningowa of 4 Pułk Lotniczy in Toruń (Glass)*

264: *The Lublin R-XIV was the predecessor of the popular Lublin R-XIII. The photo shows a production R-XIV with lower fin (Glass)*

265: *Lublin R-XIIID no. 56.116 of 13 Eskadra Obserwacyjna with the crew: pilot Chęckiewicz, observer Grzeszczak (Kopański)*

266: *Lublin R-XIIID no. 56.127 with civil registration SP-AMG. This was the personal aircraft of the PAF commander* gen. *Ludomił Rayski. The aircraft was silver with red trim (MLP – Kraków)*

267: *Lublin R-XIIID no. 56.179 (underwing no. N 27) belonging to 13 Eskadra Obserwacyjna, picks up a report from the ground (Glass)*

268: *Lublin R-XIIIF no. 58.8 of the Szkoła Podchorążych Lotnictwa at Dęblin. Some 58 examples of the R-XIIIF version were produced, including the prototypes (Kopański)*

269: *A Lublin R-XIIIC from 63 Eskadra Obserwacyjna of 6 Pułk Lotniczy in Lwów. A batch of 48 aircraft of this version was manufactured (Glass)*

270: *From 1936 Fokkers were used for parachute training. The photograph shows an aircraft from 212 Eskadra Bombowa of 1 Pułk Lotniczy in Warsaw (Kopański)*

271: *Lublin R-XIIID no. 56.159 from 36 Eskadra Obserwacyjna of 3 Pułk Lotniczy in Poznań. The photo was taken during summer 1938 at Warsaw-Okęcie airfield (Glass)*

272: *Lublin R-XIIID from 53 Eskadra Obserwacyjna (Glass)*

273: *Aerobatic training Lublin R-XIV, factory no. 54-1, first flown during summer 1930 (Glass)*

(*naczelny komisarz cywilny*) (*płk*. W. Kostek-Biernacki), representative of the Wojsko Polskie Chaplain Bishop (*rev.* S. Sinkowski). *Gen.* W. Stachiewicz was the Chief of Staff, with *gen.* bryg. T. Malinowski, *płk*. dypl. I. Jaklicz and *płk*. dypl. J. Wiatr as his deputies.

Wojsko Polskie was organised in armies and operational groups.[2] This structure had a significant effect on the role played by the air force in the 1939 campaign. The pre-war concept regarding the role of the air force assumed that it would not operate as an independent service, but would be part of ground forces. Extracting some units from the army aviation to form separate tactical formations was an exception from that rule. The formations in question, Brygada Bombowa and Brygada Pościgowa, were at the disposal of the Wódz Naczelny. Brygada Pościgowa duties included air defence of Warsaw, while Brygada Bombowa would serve as the reserve of the Wódz Naczelny, to perform special duties. The remaining portion of the air force would be used within individual armies.

Furthest to the north was the Armia 'Pomorze' under *gen. dyw.* W. Bortnowski. This included: 63 infantry battalions, 25 cavalry squadrons, 312 field guns, 24 anti-aircraft guns, 26 tanks and 58 aircraft of various types, including 46 warplanes. This army's main task consisted in defence of the so-called 'Corridor', the Polish territory on the Baltic coast between Germany and the East Prussia. Plk. Bolesław Stachoń was the commander of the Lotnictwo Armii 'Pomorze'. He had the following units under his command:

- 42 Eskadra Rozpoznawcza (commander *kpt.* Wacław Waltera – 10 PZL 23B *Karaś* aircraft + 1 RWD 8)
- 46 Eskadra Obserwacyjna (commander *kpt.* Roman Rypień – 7 Lublin R-XIIID and R-XIIIC aircraft + 2 RWD 8)
- 43 Eskadra Obserwacyjna (commander *kpt.* Władysław Dawidek – 7 Lublin R-XIIID aircraft + 2 RWD 8)
- III/4 Dywizjon Myśliwski HQ (commander *kpt.* Florian Laskowski – 2 PZL P.11c + 1 RWD 8)
- 141 Eskadra Myśliwska (commander *kpt.* Tadeusz Rolski – 10 PZL P.11c)
- 142 Eskadra Myśliwska (commander *kpt.* Mirosław Leśniewski – 10 PZL P.11c)
- Pluton Łącznikowy Nr 7 (commander *ppor.* Henryk Lewandowski – 3 RWD 8)
- Pluton Łącznikowy Nr 8 (commander *ppor.* Włodzimierz Krzyżanowski – 3 RWD 8)

To the South of Armia 'Pomorze' was Armia 'Poznań' under *gen. dyw.* Tadeusz Kutrzeba. This consisted of the following units: 55 infantry battalions, 19 cavalry squadrons, 240 field guns, 18 anti-aircraft guns, 65 tanks, 2 armoured trains, 56 aircraft including 46 warplanes. Armia 'Poznań' was located in Wielkopolska region. This army's aviation was commanded by *płk*. Stanisław Kuźminski, who controlled the following units:

- 34 Eskadra Rozpoznawcza (commander *kpt.* Janusz Badowski – 10 PZL P.23B *Karaś* + 1 RWD 8)
- 33 Eskadra Obserwacyjna (commander *kpt.* Stanisław Zaleski – 7 RWD 14 *Czapla* + 2 RWD 8)
- 36 Eskadra Obserwacyjna (commander *kpt.* Bolesław Dorembiewicz – 7 Lublin R-XIIID + 2 RWD)
- III/3 Dywizjon Myśliwski HQ (commander *mjr* Mieczysław Mümler – 2 PZL P.11c + 2 RWD 8)
- 131 Eskadra Myśliwska (commander *kpt.* Jerzy Zaremba – 10 PZL P.11c)
- 132 Eskadra Myśliwska (commander *kpt.* Franciszek Jastrzębski – 10 PZL P.11c)
- Pluton Łącznikowy Nr 6 (commander *por.* Janusz Mościcki – 3 RWD 8)

Armia 'Lodz' was the next, situated to the south of Armia 'Poznań'. It was commanded by *gen.* dyw. Juliusz Rómmel. The Army was smaller than the two mentioned above. It included a total of 34 infantry battalions, 29 cavalry squadrons, 168 field guns, 10 anti-aircraft guns, 50 tanks, 2 armoured trains, 51 aircraft including 45 warplanes. *Płk*. Wacław Iwaszkiewicz was the commander of Armia 'Łódź' aviation. He had the following air units under his command:

- 32 Eskadra Rozpoznawcza (commander *kpt.* Mieczysław Ryszkiewicz – 10 PZL P.23B *Karaś* + 1 RWD 8)
- 63 Eskadra Obserwacyjna (commander *kpt.* Jan Harezlak – 7 RWD 14 *Czapla* + 2 RWD 8)
- 66 Eskadra Obserwacyjna (commander *kpt.* Albert Kubieniec – 7 Lublin R-XIIIC + 2 RWD 8)
- III/6 Dywizjon Myśliwski HQ (commander *kpt.* Stanisław Morawski – 2 PZL P.11c + 1 RWD 8)
- 161 Eskadra Myśliwska (commander *kpt.* Władysław Szcześniewski – 7 PZL P.11c, 2 PZL P.11a)
- 162 Eskadra Myśliwska (commander *kpt.* Bernard Groszewski – 10 PZL P.7a)
- Pluton Łącznikowy Nr 10 (commander *ppor.* Bohdan Arct – 3 RWD 8) – the unit failed to arrive at its operational area, the aircraft were not included in the Armia 'Łódź' aviation.

South-western Poland was defended by Armia 'Kraków' under *gen. bryg.* Antoni Szylling. It included 59 infantry battalions, 29 cavalry squadrons, 312 field guns, 40 anti-aircraft guns, 90 tanks, 2 armoured trains, 54 aircraft including 44 warplanes. *Płk*. Stefan Sznuk was the commander of Lotnictwo Armii 'Kraków'. He had the following units at his disposal:

- 24 Eskadra Rozpoznawcza (commander *kpt.* Julian Wojda – 10 PZL P.23B *Karaś*+ 1 RWD 8)
- 23 Eskadra Obserwacyjna (commander *por.* Władysław Rewakowicz – 7 RWD 14 *Czapla* + 2 RWD 8)
- 26 Eskadra Obserwacyjna (commander *kpt.* Stanisław Rzepa – 7 Lublin R-XIIID + 2 RWD 8)
- III/2 Dywizjon Myśliwski HQ (commander *kpt.* Mieczysław Medwecki – 1 RWD 8)

- 121 Eskadra Myśliwska (commander *kpt.* Tadeusz Sedzielowski – 10 PZL P.11c)
- 122 Eskadra Myśliwska (commander *kpt.* Mieczysław Wiórkiewicz – 10 PZL P.11c)
- Pluton Łącznikowy Nr 3 (commander *por.* Piotr Dunin – 3 RWD 8 + 1 Lublin R-XIII)

Armia 'Karpaty' was located South of Armia 'Kraków'. It was established on 11 July 1939. Its commander, *gen. dyw.* Kazimierz Fabrycy, had relatively modest forces at his orders. These included: 26 infantry battalions, 8 field guns and 20 aircraft. This army's aviation was commanded by *ppłk.* Olgierd Tuśkiewicz, who controlled the following units:

- 31 Eskadra Rozpoznawcza (commander *kpt.* Witalis Nikonow – 9 PZL P 23B + 1 RWD 8)
- 56 Eskadra Obserwacyjna (commander *kpt.* Marian Sukniewicz – 7 Lublin R-XIIID + 2 RWD 8)
- Pluton Łącznikowy Nr 5 (failed to arrive at its operational area)

The northern border of Poland was defended by Armia 'Modlin'. Its troops were deployed north of Warsaw and would protect Polish territory from an attack originating in East Prussia. Armia 'Modlin' was commanded by *gen. bryg.* Emil Krukowicz-Przedrzymirski, and he had at his disposal 28 infantry battalions, 37 cavalry squadrons, 180 field guns, 12 anti-aircraft guns, 26 tanks, 1 armoured train and 28 aircraft including 25 warplanes. Lotnictwo Armii 'Modlin' was commanded by *płk.* Tadeusz Prauss. The following air units were under his control:

- 41 Eskadra Rozpoznawcza (commander *kpt.* Władysław Chrzanowski – 8 PZL P.23B *Karaś*)
- 53 Eskadra Obserwacyjna (commander *kpt.* Józef Kierzkowski – 7 RWD 14 *Czapla* + 2 RWD 8)
- III/5 Dywizjon Myśliwski HQ (commander *mjr* Edward Więckowski – 1 RWD 8)
- 152 Eskadra Myśliwska (commander *kpt.* Włodzimierz Lazoryk – 9 PZL P.11c + 1 PZL P.11a)
- Pluton Łącznikowy Nr 11 (commander *ppor.* Zygmunt Cesarczyk – 5 RWD 8 + 1 Lublin R-XIII) – the unit failed to arrive at its operational area, the aircraft were not included in the Armia 'Modlin' aviation.

Apart from the above mentioned armies there was also Armia 'Lublin' (*gen. bryg.* Tadeusz Piskor), Armia 'Prusy' (*gen. dyw.* Stefan Dąb-Biernacki), Armia 'Warszawa' (established on 10 September 1939, under *gen. dyw.* Juliusz Rómmel). These formations did not have air units, apart from some ad hoc outfits. There were also smaller formations, called Samodzielna Grupa Operacyjna (SGO: Independent Operational Group)

274 Below: Marshal *Józef Piłsudski surrounded by pilots. To his left is Bajan, to his right Pokrzywka – participants of the Challenge International competition. The photo was taken at Moszcznica near Żywiec in 1934 (MLP – Kraków)*

275 Below: Płk. *Wacław Iwaszkiewicz – commander of 5 Pułk Lotniczy at Lida in 1930-1936 (Belcarz, Pęczkowski collection)*

276: *Lublin R-XIIIB (Glass)*

277: *A Lublin R-XIIID, no. 56.27, of 66 Eskadra Obserwacyjna of 6 Pułk Lotniczy and admirers. Note the dark green chameleon unit emblem*

278: *Between 1929 and 1939 the Polish Air Force used 37 Fokker F-VIIB/3m aircraft (Kopański)*

279: *The Fokkers were still used in the 1939 campaign as transport aircraft within the Brygada Bombowa (Kopański)*

280: *Fokker F-VIIB/3m aircraft of an unknown Eskadra (MLP – Kraków)*

281: *The Fokker F-VIIB/3m was also used as a night-bomber. The photograph shows aircraft from 213 Eskadra Bombowa of 1 Pułk Lotniczy in Warsaw (MLP – Kraków)*

282: *Lublin R-XIIID with Polish national markings positioned asymmetrically on top surfaces. This scheme dates from the second half of the 1930s (Kopański)*

283: *A section of Lublin XIIIDs from 43 Eskadra Towarzysz1ca of 4 Pułk Lotniczy in Toruń. The aircraft in the foreground has only the white background applied, with the unit emblem yet to be painted on (Kopański)*

284: *Lublin R-XIIID of an unknown unit from 3 PL (Kopański)*

285: *The PZL P-6, the successor to the PZL P-1, was first flown in July 1930. The main difference between these two types lay in the Jupiter VI unsupercharged radial engine (Glass)*

286: *An R-XIIID belonging to 13 Eskadra Towarzysz1ca of 1 Pułk Lotniczy in Warsaw, damaged during landing (Kopański)*

287: *The PZL P-6 was displayed at the Paris Air Show, where it attracted a great deal of interest. The original wing layout became known as the 'Polish wing'. Estonia, Greece, Portugal, Rumania, Switzerland and Yugoslavia all expressed an interest in the aircraft (NTM Praha)*

288: *The RWD-14 during trials at the Instytut Techniczny Lotnictwa. Aircraft undergoing trials had their rudders painted white (Glass)*

and Grupa Operacyjna (GO). Only one of those, SGO 'Narew', under *gen. bryg.* Czesław Mlot-Fijalkowski included air units. SGO 'Narew' was deployed in the triangle formed by the borders of Poland with Lithuania and Third Reich (East Prussia). SGO 'Narew' aviation was commanded by *ppłk.* Stanisław Nazarkiewicz. He had the following units under his control:

- 51 Eskadra Rozpoznawcza (commander *kpt.* Leopold Hrabkiewicz – 7 PZL P.23B *Karaś*)
- 13 Eskadra Obserwacyjna (commander *kpt.* Lucjan Fijuth – 7 RWD 14 *Czapla* + 2 RWD 8)
- 151 Eskadra Myśliwska (commander *por.* Józef Brzeziński – 10 PZL P.7a)
- Pluton Łącznikowy Nr 9 (commander *ppor.* Stanisław Krakowski – 3 RWD 8) – the unit failed to arrive at its operational area. Its aircraft were not included in the SGO 'Narew' aviation.

All the above mentioned air units fought as part of the so-called army aviation. Apart from them, the aircraft of the Discretionary Aviation of the Supreme Aviation HQ participated in fighting. These were reporting directly to the Dowódca Lotnictwa, *gen.* bryg. Józef Zając. These units formed Brygada Pościgowa, Brygada Bombowa and some independent units 'served' the HQ. Of these:

- 16 Eskadra Obserwacyjna was assigned between 1 and 5 September to Dowództwo Okręgu Korpusu Nr 1, and subsequently was at the disposal of the Naczelny Dowódca Lotnictwa. The Eskadra, led by *kpt.* Eugeniusz Lech, had 7 Lublin R-XIII and 2 RWD 8 aircraft.
- Pluton Łącznikowy Nr 1 was at the disposal of the Wódz Naczelny, and subsequently impressed as an auxiliary unit to Brygada Pościgowa HQ. *Por.* Henryk śliwiński was the commander of the pluton, and the unit was equipped with 3 RWD 8.
- Pluton Łącznikowy Nr 2 at the disposal of the Szef Sztabu Generalnego of the Wojsko Polskie. The pluton was commanded by *ppor.* Stanisław Filipowicz, and had 3 RWD 8 aircraft.

Eskadra Sztabowa was at the disposal of the Naczelny Dowódca Lotnictwa, *gen.* bryg. Józef Zając. The history of Eskadra Sztabowa goes back to 1929, when it was formed as Sztabowa Eskadra Treningowa (Staff Advanced Training Squadron), part of Dywizjon Szkolny in 1 Pułk Lotniczy in Warsaw. Since 1931 the Eskadra was known under the name used during the 1939 campaign. Officers working in the central institutions in Warsaw flew their training flights in the Eskadra. During the war the Eskadra was commanded by *kpt.* Henryk Wirszyłło. Equipment of Eskadra Sztabowa was formed from a motley collection of types, with two RWD 14 *Czaplas* undoubtedly the most modern among them. The Eskadra had a total of 28 aircraft which included, apart from the RWD 14: RWD 8, RWD 13, PWS 26, Lublin R-XIII, and Potez XXV.

Five fighter eskadras were extracted from the army aviation. These formed Brygada Pościgowa with *płk.* Stefan Pawlikowski in command. The Brigade included the following units:

- III Dywizjon Myśliwski HQ (commander *kpt.* Zdzisław Krasnodębski – 2 PZL P.11c) including:
- 111 Eskadra Myśliwska (commander *kpt.* Gustaw Sidorowicz – 9 PZL P.11c)
- 112 Eskadra Myśliwska (commander *kpt.* Tadeusz Opulski – 6 PZL P.11c + 4 PZL P.11a)
- IV Dywizjon Myśliwski HQ (commander *kpt.* Adam Kowalczyk – 2 PZL P.11c), including:
- 113 Eskadra Myśliwska (commander *por.* Wieńczysław Barański – 5 PZL P.11c + 5 PZL P.11a)
- 114 Eskadra Myśliwska (commander *kpt.* Juliusz Frey – 6 PZL P.11c + 4 PZL P.11a)
- 123 Eskadra Myśliwska (commander *kpt.* Mieczysław Olszewski – 10 PZL P.7a)
- Brygada Pościgowa HQ also had three RWD 8 aircraft.

Similar principles applied to formation of Brygada Bombowa. It included four eskadras of *Łoś* and five eskadras of *Karaś* bombers. For auxiliary duties these eskadras also had three RWD 8 aircraft as well as 6 more RWD 8 machines of Pluton Łącznikowy Nr 4 and Nr 12. Pluton Łącznikowy crews were dispersed among individual eskadras of the Brigade. Plk. Władysław Heller was appointed the commander of Brygada Bombowa. The Brygada was formed at the end of August 1939 from:

- Zgrupowanie Bombowe (211, 212, 216, and 217 Eskadras)

289 Below: *A pilot takes his place in the cockpit of a* Łoś *(Glass)*

- I/2 Dywizjon Bombowy Lekki (21, 22 Eskadras)
- II/6 Dywizjon Bombowy Lekki (64, 65 Eskadras) 55 Samodzielna Eskadra Bombowa

On 1 September 1939 personnel of the eskadras were informed that the war had broken out, and told of the orders of the Brygada Bombowa commander which, among others, stipulated renumbering of the eskadras previously belonging to Zgrupowanie Bombowe. According to the orders of 1 September 1939 the following number changes were introduced: 211 Eskadra to 11, 212 to 12, 216 to 16 and 217 to 17, 21 to 1, 22 to 2, 64 to 4, 65 to 5. As a result of this the organisation of Brygada Bombowa was as follows:

- X Dywizjon Bombowy (commander *ppłk.* Józef Werakso), including:
  - 11 Eskadra Bombowa (commander *kpt.* Franciszek Omylak – 9 PZL 37B and A bis + 2 Fokker F.VII)
  - 12 Eskadra Bombowa (commander *kpt.* Stanisław Wołkowinski – 9 PZL 37B and A bis + 1 Fokker F.VII)
- XV Dywizjon Bombowy (commander Stanisław Cwynar), including:
  - 16 Eskadra Bombowa (commander *kpt.* Władysław Dukszto – 9 PZL 37B *Łoś* + 2 Fokker F.VII)
  - 17 Eskadra Bombowa (commander *kpt.* Eugeniusz Prusiecki – 9 PZL 37B *Łoś* + 2 Fokker F.VII)
- II Dywizjon Bombowy Lekki (commander *mjr* Jan Biały), including:
  - 1 Eskadra Bombowa Lekka (commander *kpt.* Jan Buczma – 10 PZL P.23B *Karaś* +1 RWD 8 + 1 Fokker F.VII)
  - 2 Eskadra Bombowa Lekka (commander *kpt.* Kazimierz Słowinski – 10 PZL P.23B *Karaś* + 1 RWD 8 + 1 Fokker F.VII)
- VI Dywizjon Bombowy Lekki (commander *mjr* Alfred Peszke), including:
  - 4 Eskadra Bombowa Lekka (commander *kpt.* Mieczysław Pronaszko – 10 PZL P.23B *Karaś* + 2 RWD 8 + 1 Fokker F.VII)
  - 5 Eskadra Bombowa Lekka (commander *kpt.* Maciej Piotrowski – 10 PZL P.23B *Karaś* + 2 RWD 8 + 1 Fokker F.VII)
  - 55 Samodzielna Eskadra Bombowa (commander *kpt.* Józef Skibiński - 10 PZL 23B *Karaś* + 1 RWD 8 + 1 Fokker F.VII).

This was the inventory of the Polish Air Force at the outbreak of war. Of course some reinforcements arrived during the 1939 campaign, although these unfortunately were negligible. The course of operations will be presented further below. This listing does not include naval aviation which is discussed in a separate chapter.

The Polish Air Force was going to be used according to the guidelines prepared by the Sztab Lotniczy przy Sztabie Głównym, issued on 28 July 1939. These defined the principles of use of both army and discretionary aviation. Right at the beginning, this study remarks that *"Poor equipment of the army aeronautical forces and very limited capabilities for loss replenishment charge all the commanders in control of the aviation with the duty of the greatest possible limit in its use, and the commanders of the army aviation, air units – of scrupulous analysis of the way their duties can be performed . . . Use of the aeronautical forces should be restricted as far as possible during quiet times at the front line, to spare it for the period of fighting".* The guidelines mentioned above defined precisely the ways of using individual types of aviation. So, the line aviation would fulfil the following tasks: *"Reconnaissance is the main task of the army-assigned line aviation units. However, when the situation requires all available assets to be thrown into battle, there should be no hesitation to use also these in the capacity of bombers against the human forces of the enemy. . . They should therefore be limited to close reconnaissance, reaching no further than the areas of unloading stations and the distance of practical day advance of an armoured unit, thus more of tactical than operational nature. It is all the more necessary that the 'accompanying' aviation units, with their obsolete equipment, cannot be used for these duties".* Tasks for the army fighter aviation units were defined as precisely: *"The task of the fighters is to combat enemy aircraft operating over the army area, most of all in the combat zone, protect their own aviation operations in the combat zone, in moments critical for the ground combat, direct participation in this combat by fighting the human forces of the enemy.*

Due to lack of a well organised early warning network, fighting against enemy aviation assets heading behind the lines will only be possible by ambushes. To this end every fighter dywizjon will organise in the army territory several ambushes at the most probable directions of the enemy reconnaissance aviation. To combat enemy aircraft operating in this combat zone, as well as to protect their own forces operating in this zone, use of fighter forces should be avoided in weak but frequent operations; on the contrary – they should operate seldom, but in force, co-ordinating fighter aviation actions with the co-operation aviation operations". The accompanying aviation units would operate in particularly difficult conditions, with largely obsolete equipment. According to the guidelines: *"Accompanying aviation (with its current equipment) can only perform combat reconnaissance above its own lines, or by flying short excursions to the immediate rear of the enemy, and only during the periods of day when fighter aviation operations are the least. Points of active anti-aircraft defence should be established behind their own lines. . . These points should be known to the crews of aircraft performing combat reconnaissance; they will protect themselves under their cover during enemy fighter attacks. The accompanying aviation, with its low speed, will be vulnerable to operations of active anti-aircraft means. To reduce the effects of operations, reconnaissance of objects located behind the lines should be carried out by*

290: *The PZL P-8, a development of in-line engine powered Puławski fighters, was first flown in August 1931. The aircraft was going to be evaluated against the PZL P-7. The photo shows the second prototype, PZL P-8/II, powered by Lorraine Petrel engine, first flown at the beginning of 1932 (Glass)*

291: *PZL P-7a of 2 Pułk Lotniczy in Kraków. In the foreground is P-7a no. 6.17 of 121 Eskadra Myśliwska; behind it is a P-7a no. 6.110 of 123 Eskadra Myśliwska (Glass)*

292: *PZL P-7a fighter of the commander of a fighter Dyon in 4 Pułk Lotniczy at Toruń (Glass)*

293: *PZL P-23B* Karaś *– a PZL publicity photograph (Belcarz & Pęczkowski)*

294: *PZL P-7a from Dęblin. The pilot who stands in front of the aircraft is wearing a flying suit with NCO insignia (MLP – Kraków)*

295: *PZL P-11c fighters of various units. In the foreground are aircraft of 4 Pułk Lotniczy at Toruń (Glass)*

296: Por. *J. Dzwonek by his P-11c from 161 Eskadra Myśliwska. The turkey, applied on starboard side of the aircraft only, was a rejected unit emblem. Photograph taken at Lwów-Skniłów airfield during summer 1939 (Kopański)*

297: *P-11c 8-76 from 113 Eskadra Myśliwska of 1 Pułk Lotniczy in Warsaw (Kopański)*

298: *P-11c 8-14 from 112 Eskadra Myśliwska (Cynk)*

299: *PZL P-11a and P-11c fighters during a parade fly-past over Warsaw (Glass)*

300: *The first production example of the PZL P-24B (Belcarz & Pęczkowski)*

301: *The prototype PZL P-24. The photo is taken from a PZL factory catalogue (Belcarz & Pęczkowski)*

302: *Production P-24s for export to Turkey (Belcarz & Pęczkowski)*

303: *A formation of PZL P.7as of 4 Pułk Lotniczy led by the garishly marked aircraft of* mjr. *Leopold Pamuły. The different esadra within the pułk all wore an emblem contained within an inverted pentagon shape*

304: *PZL P-23B cockpit interior (Belcarz & Pęczkowski)*

305: *The prototype RWD-14* Czapla *(Heron) 'observation' (spotting) aircraft (Glass)*

306: *The second prototype of the LWS-3/II* Mewa *(Gull) spotting aircraft at the factory airfield in Lublin (Glass)*

307: *The PZL P-46* Sum *(Sheatfish) was to be the successor to the* Karaś. *Bułgaria expressed interest in the type, placing an optional order for 12 aircraft (Glass)*

308: *A converted* Karaś *(Carp) prototype was first flown in April 1936, under designation of PZL P-42. The main differences comprised twin fins and rudders, plus a retractable observer's cupola. After trials which failed to produce satisfactory results, the aircraft was handed over to the military. It later served as an instructional airframe at the Szkoła Podchorążych Lotnictwa in Dęblin, and was destroyed in an air raid in 1939 (Glass)*

309: *The third prototype PZL P-23/III during trials – note the probe under the starboard wing (NTM Praha)*

310: *A group of instructors and pilots at Dęblin airfield in early thirties. Fourth from right is* sierż. *Ludwik Homa. Breguet XIX and Caudron G-III are in the background (Belcarz)*

311: *PZL P-23A* Karaś *from the Eskadra Treningowa of I Pułk Lotniczy in Warsaw (MLP – Kraków)*

312: *First version of the* Karaś, *the PZL P-23A, was manufactured in a batch of 40 aircraft (Glass)*

313: *Undercarriage and observer's cupola of the PZL P-23B (Belcarz & Pęczkowski)*

314: Karaś *at Kraków-Rakowice airfield, the location today of the Polish Aviation Museum (Cynk)*

315: *The pre-war Polish aircraft industry was forced to sell badly-needed aircraft to foreign customers in order to assist the Polish economy. This is a PZL P-43, the greatly improved version of the* Karaś *sold to Bulgaria and seen in Bulgarian service*

316: Generał brygady *Ludomił Rayski, PAF commander from May 1926 until March 1939. During WW2 he flew in Britain as a ferry pilot initially, and from 1943 he was the Polish Liaison Officer to RAF Middle East (Belcarz & Pęczkowski)*

317: *Pilot's cockpit in the PZL P-23B* Karaś *(Belcarz & Pęczkowski)*

means of short excursions, aimed at the given object of reconnaissance. This kind of operations requires very detailed definition of the tasks given to aircraft crews by unit commanders". Entirely different tasks were given to the discretionary aviation at the disposal of the Wódz Naczelny. These tasks were as follows:

"a) reconnaissance for the Wódz Naczelny, particularly at the flanks of the front,
b) bomber operations with the main aims as follows:
– intervention operations on the battlefield and close rear, against human forces of the enemy,
– fighting enemy aviation, most of all bombers and fighters, on airfields,
– fighting railway and road transports of the enemy.
c) fighter aviation at the disposal of the Wódz Naczelny will be used for anti-aircraft defence of the country".

A short analysis of the German forces allows one to compare the enemy against which Polish airmen fought in Poland's skies in September 1939. The list of German Air Force units follows:

- ObdL – HQ – *Marschall* Herman Göring (9 Do 17, 17 He 111, 12 Do 17U)

- Luftflotte 1 – commander *Gen.* Albert Kesselring
  - 1. and 3. (F)/121 – (17 Do 17P)

- 1 Fliegerkorps – commander *Gen.Lt.* Ulrich Grauert
  - 2. (F)/121 – (6 Do 17P)
  - KG 1 'Hindenburg' – commander *Oberst* Ulrich Kessler (I./KG 152 – 65 He 111)
  - KG 26 'Löwengeschwader' – commander *Oberst* Hans Siburg (1./I. and II. 38 He 111H)

- KG 27 'Boelcke' – commander *Oberst* Behrendt (Stab., I., II., and III. – 69 He 111P)
- KG 53 'Legion Condor' – commander *Oberst* Stahl (I. – 29 He 111, Stab. and I. (J)/LG 2 – 37 Bf 109E, II./ZG 1(JGr 101) – 36 Bf 109)
- St.G 2 'Immelmann' – commander *Oberst* Baier (II. and III. – 67 Ju 87B + 6 Do17M)
- IV. (St.)/LG 1 – (36 Ju 87B + 3 Do 17M)
- 4. (St.)/TrGr 186 – (12 Ju 87B, C)

- LftwKdo 'Ost Preussen' – *Gen.Lt.* Wilhelm Wimmer
  - 1. (F)/120 – (12 Do 17P)
  - KG 2 'Holzhammer' – commander *Oberst* J. Fink (Stab., II., and III. – 72 Do 17Z)
  - KG 3 'Blitz' – commander *Oberst* W. Chamier-Glisczinski (Stab., II., and III. – 70 Do 17Z)
  - St. G. 1 – commander *Hptm.* W. Hozzel (28 Ju 87B + 3 Do 17M)
  - I./JG 1 – (54 Bf 109E)
  - I./JG 21 – (28 Bf 109E, C)
  - I./ZG 1 – (24 Bf 110)

- Lehr Division – commander *Gen.Maj.* Helmuth Foerster
  - 4. (F)/121 – (10 Do 17P)
  - LG 1 – commander *Oberst* A. Bulowius (Stab., II., and III. – 73 He 111)
  - I. (Z)/LG 1 – commander *Maj.* W. Grabmann (29 Bf 110)

- Luftflotte 4 – commander *Gen.* Alexander Lohr
  - 3. (F)/123 – (12 Do 17P)

- 2 Fliegerdivision – *Gen.Maj.* Bruno Loerzer
  - 3. (F)/122 – (9 Do 17P)
  - KG 4 'General Wewer' – commander *Oberst* M. Fiebig (Stab., I., II., and III. – 81 He 111P)
  - KG 76 – commander *Oberst* S. Frölich (Stab., I., and III. – 77 Do17Z, M)
  - KG 77 – (Stab., I., II., and III. – 100 Do 17M, E)
  - I./JG 76 – (45 Bf 109E)
  - JG 77 'Herz As' – (I., and II. – 79 Bf 109E)
  - I./ZG 76 – commander *Hptm.* Reinecke (29 Bf 110)

- Fliegerführer zbV (Special duties force) – *Gen.Maj.* Wolfram von Richthofen
  - 1. (F)/124 – (9 Do 17F)
  - I./St. G 2 – commander *Maj.* O. Dinort (29 Ju 87B + 3 Do 17M)
  - I./St. G 76 – commander *Hptm.* W. Sigel (33 Ju 87B + 2 Do 17M)
  - St. G 77 – commander G. Schwarzkopf (Stab., I., and II. – 65 Ju 87B + 6 Do 17M)
  - II. (Sch.)/LG2 – commander *Maj.* W. Spielvogel (37 Hs 123)
  - I./JG 20 – (20 Bf 109E)
  - I./ZG 2 (JGr 102) – commander *Hptm.* H. Genzen (40 Bf 109D, C)

- Luftgau 3 (Reich defence fighter units)
  - JG 2 'Richthofen' – commander *Oberstlt.* von Massow (48 Bf 109E, C)
  - JG 3 – (45 Bf 109E)
  - 11. (N)/LG 2 – (9 Bf 109E)

318: *Initial form of the PWS-12. (Zdaniewski)*

319: *A* Karaś *from 24 Eskadra Rozpoznawcza captured by the Germans at Kraków (Cynk via Kopański)*

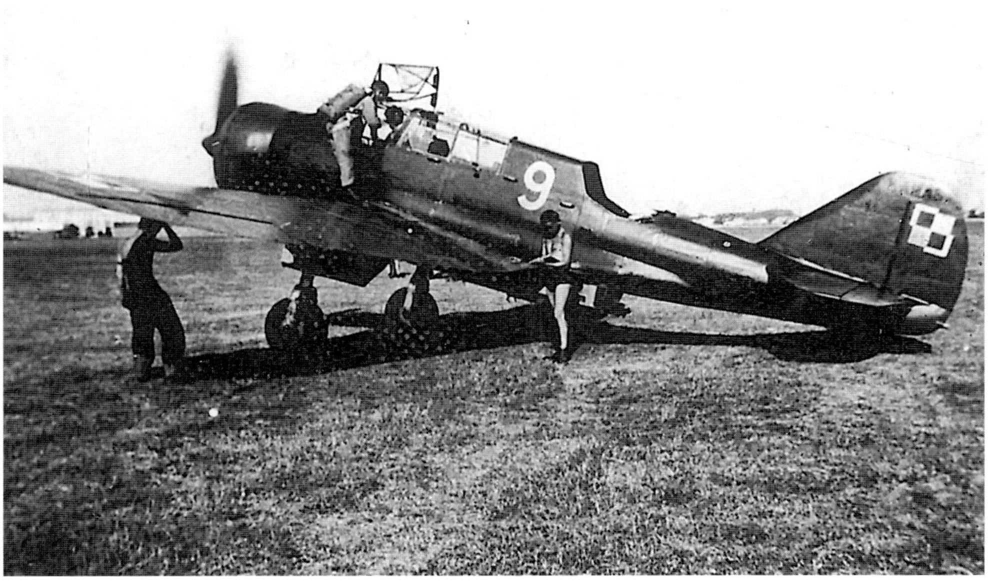

320: *A PZL P-23B* Karaś *with the undercarriage spats removed (Kopański)*

321: *The pilot of a PZL P-23B carries out engine checks*

322: *The prototype PZL P-37B during trials conducted at the Instytut Techniczny Lotnictwa*

323: *PZL P-37A* Łoś *aircraft ready to be collected by the air force, summer 1938 (Kopański)*

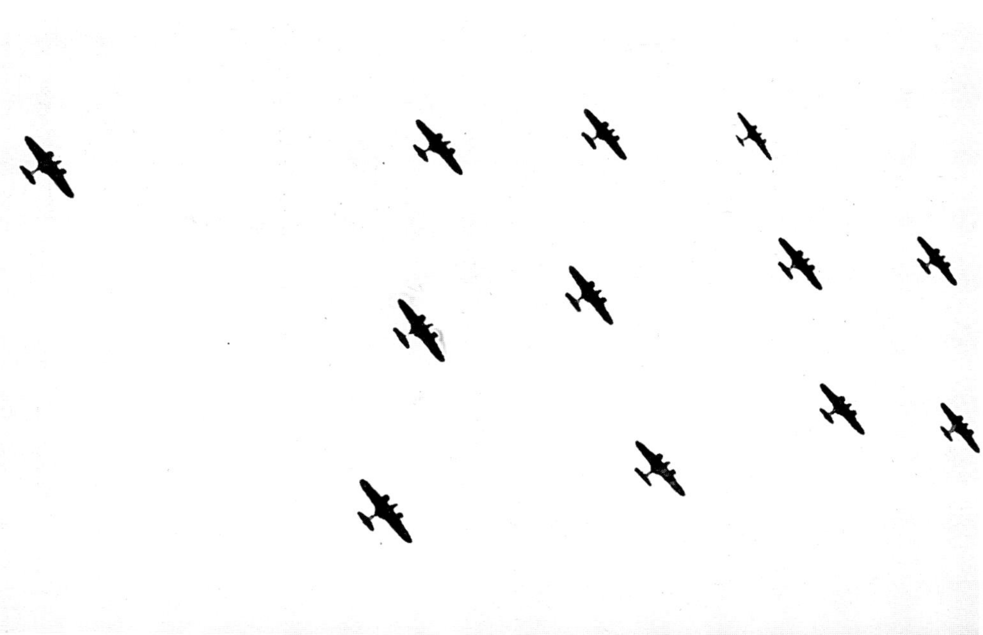

324: *A* Łoś *formation during air display over Warsaw in April 1939 (Glass)*

- Army reconnaissance units
  - Aufkl. Staffel(F)/*Gen.* d. Lw. – *Ob.* d. H. – (special unit for the 1939 campaign – 9 Do 17)
  - 3. (F)/11 – (10 Do 17P)

- Koluft AOK 3[3] – commander *Oberst* Zoch
  - 3. (F)/10 – (12 Do 17P)
  - 1. (H)/10 – (10 Hs 126)
  - 2. (H)/10 – (12 Hs 126)

- Koluft AOK 4 – commander *Oberst* Keiper
  - 4. (F)/11 – (10 Do 17P)
  - 1. (H)/21 – (10 Hs 126)
  - 2. (H)/21 – (10 Hs 126)
  - 3. (H)/21 – (11 Hs 126)
  - 9. (H)/LG 2 – (9 Hs 126 + 2 He 46)
  - 2. (F)/11 – (12 Do 17P)

- Koluft AOK 8 – commander *Oberst* von Gerlach
  - 3. (F)/31 – (12 Do 17P)
  - 1. (H)/12 – (11 Hs 126)
  - 5. (H)/13 – (9 Hs 126 + 2 He 45)

- Koluft AOK 10 – commander *Obstlt.* Lohmann
  - 7. (F)/LG 2 – (9 Do17)
  - 1. (H)/41 – (8 Hs 126)
  - 3. (H)/12 – (9 Hs 126 + 1 He 46)
  - 3. (H)/41 – (8 Hs 126)
  - 4. (H)/31 – (9 He 46 + 2 He 45)
  - 2. (H)/41 – (10 Hs 126)
  - 2. (H)/23 – (9 He 46)
  - 4. (H)/13 – (9 Hs 126 + 1 He 46)
  - 2. (H)/13 – (11 Hs 126)
  - 1. (H)/11 – (9 Hs 126 + 2 He 46)

- Koluft AOK 14 – commander *Oberst* Pistorias
  - 4. (H)/14 – (9 Do 17P)
  - 1. (H)/31 – (9 Hs 126)
  - 2. (H)/31 – (8 He 46)
  - 3. (H)/14 – (9 Hs 126)
  - 2. (H)/14 – (9 Hs 126)
  - 1. (H)/14 – (9 Hs 126 + 1 He 46)

- Naval Aviation co-operating with the 1 Fleet
  - KuFlGr 506 – (1. (M) – 12 He 60, 2. (F) – 14 Do 18 and 3. (Mz) – 7 He 59)
  - KuFlGr 706 – (Stab., 1. (M) – 11 He 60 and 3. (Mz) – 7 He 59)
  - 2. (F)/KuFlGr 606 – (10 Do 18)[4]

1 German plan of attack against Poland in 1939.
2 see map
3 Koluft AOK = Air Force HQ at the Army HQ
4 Data on numbers of aircraft in Luftwaffe units at the Polish front are based on: Jerzy B. Cynk – *Siły lotnicze Polski i Niemiec 1939* (*Air Forces of Poland and Germany 1939*), Wydawnictwa Komunikacji i Łączności – Warsaw 1989

325: *PZL P-11c aircraft from 122 Eskadra Myśliwska during air display at Warsaw-Okęcie airfield in 1938 (Kopański)*

Polish Air Force Order of Battle 1 September 1939 – serviceable aircraft

Unit	Airfield	Combat aircraft	Auxiliary aircraft
Discretionary Aviation – HQ Units			
16 Eskadra Obserwacyjna	Warsaw-Okęcie	7 R-XIII	2 RWD 8
Pluton Łącznikowy Nr 1	Warsaw-Okęcie		3 RWD 8
Pluton Łącznikowy Nr 2	Warsaw-Okęcie		3 RWD 8
Eskadra Sztabowa	Warsaw-Powsin	RWD 8, RWD 13, RWD 14, PWS 26, R-XIII, Potez XXV	a total of 28 various aircraft
Brygada Pościgowa			
Brygada HQ	Zielonka		3 RWD 8
III Dywizon Myśliwski HQ	Zielonka	2 P.11c	
111 Eskadra Myśliwska	Zielonka	9 P.11c	
112 Eskadra Myśliwska	Zielonka	6 P.11c 4 P.11a	
IV Dywizon Myśliwski HQ	Poniatów	2 P.11c	
113 Eskadra Myśliwska	Poniatów	5 P.11c 5 P.11a	
114 Eskadra Myśliwska	Poniatów	6 P.11c 4 P.11a	
123 Eskadra Myśliwska	Poniatów	10 P.7a	
Bryfada Bombowa[21]			
Brygada HQ	Dęblin		2 RWD 8
X Dywizjon Bombowy HQ	Ułęż		
11 Eskadra Bombowa	Ułęż	9 PZL 37B and PZL 37A bis	2 Fokker F.VII
12 Eskadra Bombowa	Ułęż	9 PZL 37B and PZL 37A bis	1 Fokker F.VII
XV Dywizjon Bombowy HQ	Podlodów		
16 Eskadra Bombowa	Podlodów	9 PZL P.37B	2 Fokker F.VII
17 Eskadra Bombowa	Podlodów	9 PZL P.37B	2 Fokker F.VII
II Dywizjon Bombowy HQ	Wsoła		
1 Eskadra Bombowa Lekka	Wsoła	10 PZL 23B	1 RWD 8 1 Fokker F.VII
2 Eskadra Bombowa Lekka	Wsoła	10 PZL 23B	1 RWD 8 1 Fokker F.VII
VI Dywizjon Bombowy HQ	Nosów		
4 Eskadra Bombowa Lekka	Nosów	10 PZL 23B	2 RWD 8 1 Fokker F.VII
5 Eskadra Bombowa Lekka	Nosów	10 PZL 23B	2 RWD 8 1 Fokker F.VII
55 Samodzielna Eskadra Bombowa	Marynin	10 PZL 23B	1 RWD 8 1 Fokker F.VII
ARMY AVIATION			
Samodzielna Grupa Operacyjna 'Narew' – Łomża			
Pluton Łącznikowy Nr 9	Failed to arrive in the area of operations	3 RWD 8	
51 Eskadra Rozpoznawcza	Rynek	7 PZL 23B	
151 Eskadra Myśliwska	Biel	10 P.7a	
13 Eskadra Obserwacyjna	I/13 Czerwony Bór II/13 Dobra Wola	7 RWD 14	2 RWD 8
Armia 'Modlin' – Modlin			
Pluton Łącznikowy Nr 11	Failed to arrive in the area of operations	5 RWD 8, 1 R-XIII	
41 Eskadra Rozpoznawcza	Zdunowo	8 PZL 23B	
II/5 Dywizjob Myśliwski HQ	Szpondowo		1 RWD 8
152 Eskadra Myśliwska	Szpondowo	9 P.11c 1 P.11a	
53 Eskadra Obserwacyjna	Sokolówek	7 RWD 14	2 RWD 8

Unit	Airfield	Combat aircraft	Auxiliary aircraft
		Armia 'Pomorze' - Toruń	
Pluton Łącznikowy Nr 7	Piszcz		3 RWD 8
Pluton Łącznikowy Nr 8	Toruń		3 RWD 8
42 Eskadra Rozpoznawcza	Toruń	10 PZL P23B	1 RWD 8
III/4 Dywizjon Myśliwski HQ	Markowo	2 P.11c	1 RWD 8
141 Eskadra Myśliwska	Markowo	10 P.11c	
142 Eskadra Myśliwska	Markowo	10 P.11c	
43 Eskadra Obserwacyjna	I/43 Toruń II/43 Niedzwiedż	7 Lublin R-XIII D	2 RWD 8
46 Eskadra Obserwacyjna	I/46 Czersk II/46 Biedaszkowo	7 R-XIII C and D	2 RWD 8
		Armia 'Poznań' - Poznań	
Pluton Łącznikowy Nr 6	Gniezno		3 RWD 8
34 Eskadra Rozpoznawcza	Gulczewo	10 PZL P23B	1 RWD 8
III/3 Dywizjon Myśliwski HQ	Dzierznica	2 P.11c	2 RWD 8
131 Eskadra Myśliwska	Dzierznica	10 P.11c	
132 Eskadra Myśliwska	Dzierznica	10 P.11c	
33 Eskadra Obserwacyjna	Zydowo	7 RWD 14	2 RWD 8
36 Eskadra Obserwacyjna	I/36 Gwizdowo II/36 Śnieciska	7 R-XIII C	2 RWD 8
		Armia 'Łódź' - Łódź	
Pluton Łącznikowy Nr 10	Failed to arrive in the area of operations	3 RWD 8	
32 Eskadra Rozpoznawcza	Sokolniki	10 PZL P23B	1 RWD 8
III/6 Dywizjon Myśliwski HQ	Widzew	2 P.11c	1 RWD 8
161 Eskadra Myśliwska	Widzew	7 P.11c 2 P.11a	
162 Eskadra Myśliwska	Widzew	10 P.7a	
63 Eskadra Obserwacyjna	I/63 Leknisko II/63 Bechcice	7 RWD 14	2 RWD 8
66 Eskadra Obserwacyjna	Lublinek	7 R-XIII C	2 RWD 8
		Armia 'Kraków' - Krakow	
Pluton Łącznikowy Nr 3	Rakowice		3 RWD 8, 1 R-XIII
24 Eskadra Rozpoznawcza	Klimontów	10 PZL P23B	1 RWD 8
III/2 Dywizjon Myśliwski HQ	Balice		1 RWD 8
121 Eskadra Myśliwska	Balice	10 P.11c	
122 Eskadra Myśliwska	Balice	10 P.11c	
23 Eskadra Obserwacyjna	Palczowice	7 RWD 14	2 RWD 8
26 Eskadra Obserwacyjna	I/26 Zarępice-Przyrów II/26 Sosnowiec-Klimontów	7 R-XIII D	2 RWD 8
		Armia 'Karpaty' - Rzeszów-Staromieście	
Pluton Łącznikowy Nr 5	Zaczernie		3 RWD 8, 1 R-XIII
31 Eskadra Rozpoznawcza	Werynia	9 PZL P23B	1 RWD 8
56 Eskadra Obserwacyjna	Mrowla	7 R-XIII D	2 RWD 8

326: *A section of* Karaś *aircraft from 41 Eskadra Liniowa (Rozpoznawcza) of 4 Pułk Lotniczy in Toruń (Kopański)*

327: *PZL P-37/II no. 72.2 during trials at the beginning of 1937. Note the lack of spinners. The aircraft is still unpainted (Belcarz & Pęczkowski)*

328: *PZL P-37/II no. 72.2 – side view (Belcarz & Pęczkowski)*

329: *PZL P-37B* Łoś *during trials in winter 1938/39 (Glass)*

330: *The prototype of the PZL-38/II Wilk multi-role fighter-bomber aircraft, Warsaw-Okęcie, November 1938. The photo shows the second prototype powered with Polish Foka engines (MLP – Kraków)*

331: *The PZL P-38/I with Ranger SGV-770 engines at Warsaw-Okęcie airfield, spring 1938 (MLP – Kraków)*

332: *First prototype of the PWS-33/I* Wyżeł *training aircraft at Okęcie airfield. Aircraft of the type were to be used for conversion training onto the modern twin-engine designs, such as PZL P-37* Łoś, *for example (MLP – Kraków)*

333: Łoś *bombers from 210 Dywizjon Bombowy during a staged briefing on 19 March 1939 (Kopański)*

334: *PZL P-37B* Łoś *from 210 Dywizjon Bombowy among P-11a and P-11c fighters of 1 Pułk Lotniczy in Warsaw (Cynk)*

335: *Refuelling a* Łoś *from 200 litre barrels, using a field distributor. Lack of adequate airfield support facilities, such as refuelling trucks, was a major disadvantage for the Poles. It hampered sortie rates and increased time on the ground, thereby increasing vulnerability to the Luftwaffe (Glass)*

336: Łoś *immediately after leaving the factory (MLP – Kraków)*

337: *PZL P-37B* Łoś *with white code number 10 on the fuselage (Glass)*

338: *Lublin R-XIIID from 26 Eskadra Obserwacyjna of 2 Pułk Lotniczy in Kraków. (Glass)*

339: *A PZL P-23B Karaś with the undercarriage spats removed. (Kopański)*

340: *B version* Karaś *aircraft from 11 Eskadra Liniowa of 1 Pułk Lotniczy based in Warsaw, at Lida airfield – March 1938 (Kopański)*

341 Below: *LWS-3/I at Warsaw-Okęcie airfield, March 1939 (Kopański)*

342: *The PZL P-6 was displayed at the Paris Air Show, where it raised much interest. The original wing layout became known as the 'Polish wing'. Greece, Yugoslavia, Switzerland, Estonia, Portugal and Rumania, all expressed their interest in the aircraft (NTM Praha)*

343: *The third prototype PZL P-23/III was displayed at Stockholm between 15 May and 1 June 1936. This was the first official presentation of the* Karaś *outside Poland (NTM Praha)*

UNIT HISTORIES IN THE 1939 CAMPAIGN

Lotnictwo Armii 'Pomorze'

141 Eskadra Myśliwska

The Eskadra, together with Eskadra 142, formed III/4 Dywizjon Myśliwski under *kpt. pil.* Florian Laskowski. Both Eskadras were based at Toruń, the seat of 4 Pułk Lotniczy. 141 Eskadra Myśliwska was commanded by *kpt. pil.* Tadeusz Rolski, who described the period immediately before the war in the following way: *"At the end of March we received for the first time profiles of German aircraft and their performance. They were a revelation for us, although unpleasant, but anyway presenting the real shape of things. We learned officially at that time that almost all German aircraft exceeded the relevant types of our machines in combat effectiveness. We were interested in the superiority of the German Messerschmitt 109 fighter against the Polish P.11. In level speed it was some 150 km/h better. It had also much better climbing speed and substantial fire superiority. Our P.11 was only better in manoeuvrability and ease of landing even at unprepared airfields. But that was not enough; the overall balance was in the red for Polish fighters."*[1]

Both eskadras of the Toruń Pułk were mobilised extremely early, on 18 August 1939. This was due to the fact that they were based in close proximity to the German border. From 24 August 1939 'readiness of alert' sections was introduced, with the intention of intercepting German aircraft that violated Polish airspace. These were most usually Dornier Do 17s that remained out of reach of Polish aircraft. On 30 August the Eskadra moved to a forward airfield at Markowo. The first scramble of the war took place on 1 September at approximately 11:00 a.m. The Do 17 was not intercepted, however, as the German pilot spotted the Polish aircraft and escaped from them without a problem. 141 Eskadra's first kill was achieved the same day. About 15:00 *por.* Marian Pisarek and *kpr.* Mielczyński shot down a Henschel Hs 126. *Ppor.* Skalski of 142 Eskadra also took part in the combat, and he later gave the following account of it: *"The German reconnaissance machine flew steadily on an unchanged course. The crew, obviously preoccupied with their reconnaissance, sure of themselves, do not watch the sky.*

344 Above: *Besieged Warsaw seen from the air.*

Kills attributed to 141 Eskadra Myśliwska				
1	1 September 1939	*por.* Marian Pisarek	1/2 Henschel Hs 126	10 km west of Toruń
2	1 September 1939	*kpr.* Benedykt Mielczyński	1/2 Henschel Hs 126	10 km west of Toruń
3	3 September 1939	*kpt.* Tadeusz Rolski	Junkers Ju 87	Terespol Pomorski
4	2 September 1939	*por.* Marian Pisarek	Henschel Hs 126	Kwidzyń area
5	3 September 1939	*por.* Marian Pisarek	Dornier Do 17	Kwidzyń area
6	3 September 1939	*ppor.* Lech Lachowicki-Czechowicz	Junkers Ju 87	Poczałkowo area
7	6 September 1939	*pchor.* Zygmunt Drybanski	Junkers Ju 87	Defence of bridges at Toruń
8	6 September 1939	*kpt.* Tadeusz Rolski	Henschel Hs 126	Solec Kujawski
9	6 September 1939	*por.* Jerzy Sloński	Junkers Ju 87	Narwa area

The distance between us is shrinking rapidly... Suddenly the Henschel spits at me with a chaotic observer's fire. The pilot runs for the ground. Traces of bullets enclose the entire aircraft like an octopus. I hold the stick stronger and, without losing the gunsight from view, I close on to the enemy... I push the trigger. The old Vickers guns play their perfect tune. I am exactly on the tail. No deflection needed. Long burst stops the gunner's fire, the propeller slows down its revs rapidly. A fraction of a second – and the last, short burst from direct distance, and then I recover my machine violently up, in order to avoid collision and the gunfire... of por. *Pisarek and* kpr. *Mielczyński".*[2]

In spite of this account of Skalski's the victory was credited to Pisarek and Mielczyński. A somewhat different account of the combat was given by Skalski in his 'Written report' now held in the Polish Institute and Sikorski Museum in London.[3] He wrote there: *"Upon coming out of the clouds... I saw 500 m below a Henschel Hs 126. . . At the same time* por. *Pisarek and kpr. Mielczyński were the first ones to get onto his back, shooting in passing – subsequently me and* pchor. *Pniak have kept after it until it crashed on the ground".* It is worth noting that this event has an aftermath. After the Henschel was shot down, Skalski landed beside it, dressed the wounds of the crew and took them prisoner. Many years after the war, thanks to the help of Renate Marsch, a German journalist who worked in Poland, Skalski met one of the members of that crew, Leutnant Wimmer. Both airmen became celebrities on a T.V. programme.

The next day proved tragic for 141 Eskadra Myśliwska. Armia 'Pomorze' aviation HQ ordered a low level attack in force of the full Dywizjon (Eskadra 141 and 142) against an unarmoured-motorised group moving along the Brodnica-Grudziądz road. The Dywizjon commander, *kpt.* Laskowski, who passed this order on to Eskadra commanders realised that the HQ decision was senseless, and he decided he would lead 141 Eskadra to the attack, while 142 Eskadra would provide a sweep in the same area at that time. 141 Eskadra lost 4 pilots and 4 aircraft in the attack, including the Dywizjon commander, *kpt.* Florian Laskowski. *Kpt.* Tadeusz Rolski, the commander of 141 Eskadra Myśliwska was appointed the new commander of III/4 Dywizjon Myśliwski. On 3 September the Eskadra defended the Vistula crossings at Chełmno from the air, during which *kpt.* Rolski shot down a Ju 87. That evening 141 and 142 Eskadra changed airfields, moving to Kaczkowo. The following day (4 September) they moved again, this time to Poczałkowo. That same day pilots of 141 Eskadra shot down 2 Ju 87s (*por.* Pisarek and *pchor.* Lachowicki-Czechowicz). And once again a move to a new airfield – Osięciny. 5 September was a day of rest, used for necessary repairs. During the following day the Eskadra again provided air cover for the Vistula crossings (*pchor.* Z. Drybański shot down a Ju 87) and escorted Lublin R-XIIIs of 43 Eskadra Obserwacyjna. Due to the modest force of the Eskadra it was decided that 2-3 aircraft patrols would operate in the R-XIII area of operations. During such a sortie *kpt.* Rolski shot down a Henschel Hs 126 on 6 September.

The same evening Dyon III/4 was ordered to transfer into the structure of Brygada Pościgowa and change airfields at the same time. On 7 September the surviving aircraft left, fulfilling the orders. During 8-17 September sporadic patrol missions were flown and airfields changed. The main reason for a reduced intensity of flying lay in the lack of fuel. On 17 September five surviving P.11c fighters flew to Rumania. 141 Eskadra Myśliwska pilots shot down a total of 8 German aircraft (4 Ju 87 + 3 Hs 126 + 1 Do 17) for the loss of 7 machines (including aircraft of the Dywizjon HQ).

142 Eskadra Myśliwska

The history of 142 Eskadra was closely connected with that of Eskadra 141 described above. It too was mobilised on 18 August 1939. According to the orders, its commander, *kpt.* Mirosław Leśniewski, set out an alert section to intercept German aircraft that violated Polish airspace. Eskadra aircraft took off several times at the end of August, but to no effect. On 30 August the aircraft flew to the forward airfield at Markowo, leaving only the alert section at Toruń airfield. During landing at the forward airfield the Eskadra commander 'lost' a tyre, but thanks to the alertness of the fitters who fired a flare to warn him, he landed without damage to his machine. The first scramble of the Eskadra in section force took place before midday on 1 September. The section, led by *ppor.* S. Skalski, failed to intercept a reconnaissance Dornier Do 17. The alert section left behind at Toruń was

Kills attributed to 142 Eskadra Myśliwska				
1	2 September 1939	*kpt.* Mirosław Leśniewski	Dornier Do 17	Covering 141 Eskadra which attack ground targets, sweep in Grudziądz-Brodnica area
2	2 September 1939	*ppor.* Stanisław Skalski	2 Dornier Do 17	Sweep in Grudziądz-Brodnica area
3	2 September 1939	*pchor.* Stanisław Kogut	Dornier Do 17	Sweep in Grudziądz-Brodnica area
4	2 September 1939	*pchor.* Karol Pniak	Dornier Do 17	Sweep in Grudziądz-Brodnica area
5	2 September 1939	*kpr* Stanisław Wieprzkowicz	Dornier Do 17	Sweep in Grudziądz-Brodnica area
6	3 September 1939	*ppor.* Stanisław Skalski	Henschel Hs 126	Patrol over Chelmno-Swiecie area
7	3 September 1939	*ppor.* Paweł Zenker	Henschel Hs 126	Patrol in Dubielno-Lisewo area
8	3 September 1939	*por.* Stanisław Zielinski	Henschel Hs 126	Patrol in Grudziądz area
9	4 September 1939	*kpt.* Mirosław Leśniewski	Messerschmitt Bf 110	Poczalkowo area
10	4 September 1939	*ppor.* Stanisław Skalski	Junkers Ju 87	Poczalkowo area
11	4 September 1939	*pchor.* Karol Pniak	Junkers Ju 87	Poczalkowo area

subjected to a Luftwaffe attack. After that the alert section aircraft joined the Eskadra at Markowo airfield. 2 September was the day of glory for the Eskadra. Pilots of 142 were fortunate that, unlike their colleagues of 141, they did not have to strafe the German armoured-motorised column. Their task of air protection for the attacking 141 Eskadra was fulfilled perfectly when they destroyed 6 Do 17s without loss. A double victory was achieved by *ppor.* Skalski. The latter added to his score the following day when he shot down a Henschel Hs 126. This was an imposing start of the career of a true ace.[4] The same day *ppor.* Paweł Zenker shot down another Hs 126. He reported the fact as follows: *"I closed in onto the enemy aircraft – it was a Henschel. I fired a long burst at the tail. It started making turns. For a moment I dropped off its tail – because the enemy closed the throttle down.* Pchor. *Pniak and* kpr. *Klein fired from behind. I got onto its tail again – it continued to make turns. At an altitude of some 400 m it started emitting smoke. Flying perpendicularly towards the ground – on hitting the ground it exploded and burnt. This was in Dubielno-Kornatowo-Lisewo area. . ."* More or less at the same time por S. Zieliński shot down another Henschel Hs 126 in Grudziądz area, thus increasing the Eskadra score to 9 machines.

The first days of the war revealed another problem, suffered by many Polish air units (and most other air forces). The problem consisted of extremely accurate fire from Polish anti-aircraft artillery. The Head of Armia 'Pomorze' aviation wrote in the orders of 2 September at 19:00: *"Again it was found that several of our own aircraft were shot at and destroyed by our own troops. I remind you of the order to recognise aircraft first. I order immediate promulgation of relevant orders to prevent further destruction of our own aircraft equipment".*[5] Fortunately 142 Eskadra had no such problems, unlike the eskadras that flew much slower aircraft.

4 September entered the Eskadra history, as the day that it participated in an air battle (together with two sections of 141 Eskadra Myśliwska) in the Poczałkowo area, where the new airfield of Eskadra 141 and 142 was located. The aircraft scrambled and intercepted a formation of Dornier and Junkers bombers with Bf 110 cover. The Eskadra pilots shot down 2 Ju 87s (*ppor.* Skalski and *pchor.* Pniak) and a Bf 110 (*kpt.* Leśniewski). *Kpt.* Mirosław Leśniewski, the Eskadra commander was wounded when, after shooting down a Bf 110 he fell victim to two other German fighters. The pilot managed to land his burning machine, from which he was rescued by local inhabitants. After that action on 5 September *por.* Wacław Wilczewski was appointed the new commander of 142 Eskadra. The next morning a pair of aircraft (*por.* Skalski, *kpr.* Śmigielski) attacked a German pontoon bridge across the Vistula. The same day the Eskadra provided air cover for bridges at Toruń. On 7 September Eskadra 142 together with 141 flew to Kierz airfield near Lublin. On the 9th of that month the aircraft moved to a new landing ground at Ostrozec, where two P.11c fighters were damaged when landing after dark. During 8-16 September aircraft of the Eskadra flew few missions, due to lack of fuel. On 17 September the three surviving P 11s flew across the border and were interned in Rumania. During the 1939 campaign the Eskadra scored 12 victories (6 Do 17 + 3 Hs 126 + 2 Ju 87 + 1 Bf 110) for the loss of 7 aircraft and the first commander of the Eskadra (*kpt.* Leśniewski died of wounds on 15 September 1939). The remaining three aircraft were evacuated with five P.11s of 141 Eskadra Myśliwska.

42 Eskadra Rozpoznawcza

The Eskadra was mobilised on 24 August 1939. It had 10 *Karaś* aircraft commanded by *kpt. obs.* Wacław Waltera. The aircraft were based at the Pułk airfield in Toruń until the outbreak of war, when three of them moved to a forward airfield at Zdunowo. The remaining aircraft were temporarily based at Toruń. On 1 September Eskadra aircraft flew reconnaissance sorties along the state border, also reconnoitring the area 10-15 km into the Reich. Subsequent raids against the Toruń airfield led to 5 more *Karaś* aircraft being moved to the airfield at Zdunowo, leaving 2 at the disposal of the Armia 'Pomorze' aviation commander, *płk.* B. Stachoń. On 2 September 42 Eskadra lost its first aircraft, shot down by the Polish anti-aircraft artillery. On 3 September the bad luck continued. 141 Eskadra fighters attacked and shot down in error one of 42 Eskadra's *Karaś*. The observer of the crew, *ppor.* Mazurkiewicz, died of wounds the following day. That day aircraft of the Eskadra reconnoitred the German airfield at Pila (Schneidemuhl), but this was not attacked. On 4 September the crew of *pchor. obs.* Pfelger, *kpr. pil.* Wojciechowski, and *kpr. strz.* Jasiński spotted a German armoured column 12 km west of Koronowo. A raid by 4 *Karaś* aircraft followed, these bombing the HQ of the German formation. On 5 September a change of airfield took place (Folbórz near Włocławek). The same day one *Karaś* (no. '6') left for repair at PZL in Warsaw. It did not return to the Eskadra, as it was destroyed during an air raid at Okęcie. On 6 September Eskadra crews flew two reconnaissance missions without loss. At the end of that day an order was received to ferry the aircraft to Butlerów airfield, with a simultaneous change of assignment for the Eskadra which would now report to the commander of the Wódz Naczelny's Aviation. This order was carried out on 8 September, when the Eskadra was incorporated into VI Dywizjon Bombowy Lekki. On 11 September all serviceable aircraft together with three pilots transferred to VI Dywizjon, while the remaining personnel crossed the Rumanian border on 17-18 September. During its short wartime history the Eskadra flew 23 combat missions, dropped some 3 tonnes of bombs, lost 3 aircraft and 4 airmen.

43 Eskadra Obserwacyjna

Similar to other units of the Toruń based 4 Pułk, 43 Eskadra was also put at readiness much earlier than the units further inside the country. Full readiness was achieved by the Eskadra on 26 August 1939. The commander, *kpt. obs.* Władysław Dawidek did not command the entire Eskadra, as for tactical reasons it had been divided into two plutons. Pluton I/43 under *por. obs.* E. Siedlecki (4 Lublin R-XIIID + 1 RWD 8) remained at the disposal of the Armia 'Pomorze' commander, while II/43 (commander *por. obs.* T. Jasionowski – 3 R-XIIID + 1 RWD 8) was required to co-operate with the commander of Grupa Operacyjna 'Wschód'. On the morning of 1 September the Eskadra commander together with Pluton II/43 left for Niedzwiedź landing ground, leaving Pluton I/43 at Toruń. This airfield, as with other bases of the Polish Air Force, was extensively bombed from the first moments of the war. Therefore Pluton I/43 moved to nearby Katarzynki airfield on the evening of 1 September. Simultaneously it was ordered to reconnoitre the Nakło, Brodnica, and Grudziądz areas. Both aircraft despatched were lost. One was shot down by Polish anti-aircraft defences, the other was shot down by German aircraft. The same day reconnaissance missions were flown by the aircraft of Pluton II/43. On 2 September Pluton I/43 was reinforced with three Lublin R-XIIIs (together with crews) from I/46 Pluton of 46 Eskadra Obserwacyjna. From 3 until 5 September both plutons flew extensive missions as ordered by the HQs of co-operating units, and changing their landing ground. On the evening of 5 September one of Pluton II/43's R-XIIIs crashed while landing at Poczałkowo. Subsequent days meant more missions. 10 September was the first day of rest and both plutons were reunited, again forming an Eskadra at Lubien airfield. In spite of the reinforcements mentioned earlier, the Eskadra was not in a good shape – it had just 4 R-XIII and 1 damaged RWD 8. On 11 September the Eskadra resumed reconnaissance missions. One of those – flown by *por. obs.* Pszczółkowski and *ppor. pil.* Elsner deserves particular mention: "*. . .On 13 September 1939 he performed a reconnaissance mission of the area south of M. Piątek. When crossing the front line the aircraft was shot at and one round, which perforated two steel tubes of the fuselage, hit* ppor. *Elsner, stopping near his backbone. In spite of the wound* ppor. *Elsner continued the flight. Upon completion of the mission, in spite of the observer's order*[6] *he did not land immediately behind the front line, but at the Eskadra airfield, and lost consciousness upon landing. . .* ppor. *Elsner died in hospital*".[7]

On 15 September, during a ferry flight from Luszyn to Brzezie the last R-XIII of I/43 Pluton crashed. The following day the last of the 1939 campaign's 65 combat missions was flown. Evacuation of the personnel and surviving aircraft to Lublin was scheduled for 17 September, however. only one arrived there, but the Baza nr 4, which was the destination of the evacuees, had been evacuated itself. Due to lack of fuel the crew joined the ground party of 151 Eskadra Myśliwska, with which they were evacuated to Rumania. All Eskadra aircraft, including reinforcements, were destroyed or lost.

46 Eskadra Obserwacyjna

The mobilisation process of 46 Eskadra was carried out in a similar fashion and at the same time as that of Eskadra 43. As with 43 Eskadra, no. 46 (commander *kpt. pil.* Roman Rypson) was divided into two plutons. Pluton I/46, under *por. obs.* T. Pokoniewski was put at the disposal of the commander of Pomorska Brygada Kawalerii, moving immediately to Czersk airfield. Pluton II/46, under *por. obs.* S. Osiadacz, was assigned to the commander of 15th Infantry Division, and deployed to Biedaszkowo airfield. Both plutons left Toruń for their new airfields at dawn on 30 August 1939. During the first days of the war crews flew mostly reconnaissance for the Polish ground units, mainly observing German and Polish troop movements, and delivering reports. On the evening of 2 September, due to the worsening situation at this section of the front, the commander of Pomorska Brygada Kawalerii ordered the evacuation of I/46 Pluton to Toruń, where it joined I/43 Pluton Obserwacyjny.[8] Subsequent days meant hard work with constant landing-ground changes and increasing problems with serviceability of the badly worn equipment (at the outbreak of war the Eskadra had seven Lublin R-XIIIs). At that time Eskadra 46 flew missions mainly for the 15th and 26th Infantry Divisions. On 11 September, due to the counter-attack of Polish forces (Battle on Bzura river) the Eskadra flew several reconnaissance sorties. This is how one of the observers of 46 Eskadra Obserwacyjna recalled that day: "*. . .The next day, on 11 September, the Eskadra commander,* kap. pil. *Rypsoń wakes us up at*

345: *Somewhere over Poland. He 111 crew (NTM Praha)*

346: *Shot down Do 17P*

347: *A rare radio-equipped P.11c from 1 or 3 Pułk Lotniczy, captured by the Germans (Kopański)*

348: *Vistula bridges seen from the cockpit of a German Henschel Hs 126 reconnaissance machine (NTM Praha)*

349: *PZL P.23B* Karaś *from 41 Eskadra Rozpoznawcza of 4 Pułk Lotniczy in Toruń. The aircraft is fitted with two camera guns – one is mounted above the cockpit, and the other is in the gunner's post (Kopański)*

350: *A* Karaś *of 3 Pułk Lotniczy in flight (Kopański)*

dawn and orders an immediate briefing... We are going to fly several reconnaissance sorties in all directions, both in the morning and afternoon. I am assigned a morning reconnaissance missions in the Toruń-Inowrocław-Koło area... The commander wants general information about German movements in that area. The reconnaissance has to be carried out at 2,000 m... Fitters roll out the aircraft. Fill up the fuel, fit the machine gun on the mount, put four ammunition magazines in the cockpit. I collect my observer's equipment – the map, note-book, pencils. We take off straight ahead from the barn. The aircraft jumps at the uneven ground and gets airborne... Both I and the pilot watch the air carefully... During the last days the Luftwaffe virtually disappeared from our area. We thought some units were deployed to the Western front, releasing the Eastern front. What we saw this morning, proves this is not the case... We realise our 'R'[9] *is virtually defenceless. What can a single machine gun do? One attack would be enough to send us down. No chance of escape. And that damned altitude of 2,000 m. Protects us only from the fire of our own infantry, who love to shoot at Polish aircraft.*[10] *At Kruszwica I recognise a long motorised column... My pilot, kpr. Musiał, turned his head in all directions, looking out for the enemy. I am puzzled by the silence of the Germans... Could they take the 'R' for one of their own aircraft? The pilot shows something to port. I turn around. I can see two aircraft. They fly above,on an almost parallel course. The speed leaves no doubt that they are Messerschmitts. At the moment they cannot see us, as I am against the ground and under the sun. But once they spot us, no trace of us will be left. The pilot understands the situation perfectly and quickly heads for the nearest cumulus... Ten minutes later we land at Kłóbka. 'We were lucky', says Musiał taking off his parachute. He means the Messerschmitts...''*[11]

During 12-14 September crews of 46 Eskadra flew only a few reconnaissance sorties. Those on 14 September were particularly important, as they obtained intelligence giving the Armia 'Pomorze' HQ an idea of the actual situation at the front line. On 17 September the remaining three R-XIIIs were evacuated east, but all three crews failed to reach Polish lines. Thus the Eskadra lost its last serviceable aircraft. The remaining personnel tried to break through to Warsaw together with the remains of Armia 'Poznań' and 'Pomorze'. Some were captured by the Germans. During the 1939 campaign pilots of 46 Eskadra Obserwacyjna flew a total of 53 combat missions, losing 2 killed and all aircraft destroyed.

Pluton Łącznikowy Nr 7

Liaison plutons were intended to supplement line units and were formed with reserve pilots. Their tasks included mainly liaison sorties for the unit to which they were assigned. Pluton Łącznikowy Nr 7 was mobilised at the airfield of 4 Pułk Lotniczy in Toruń. During the 1939 campaign it was commanded by *ppor. rez. pil.* H. Lewandowski, who had at his disposal 3 RWD 8 aircraft. On 31 August the Pluton left for Piszcz airfield, where it would remain at the disposal of the commander of the 9th Infantry Division. Already on the first day of the war the Pluton commander's RWD 8 was lost, shot down by Polish troops. The pilot was lucky to be saved by one of his pilots, who recognised the machine when overflying the location of the forced landing and picked up the CO. On 3 September *płk.* B. Stachoń, the commander of Armia 'Pomorze' aviation ordered Pluton Łącznikowy Nr 7 to join Pluton Łącznikowy Nr 8 to form the so called Eskadra Łącznikowa under *por. obs.* J. Eichstaedt. Thus the short combat history of this Pluton came to an end.

Pluton Łącznikowy Nr 8

The Pluton was formed in Toruń, where it was based until 2 September. Initially it had three RWD 8 aircraft, which at first remained at the disposal of Armia 'Pomorze'. Its first losses were suffered on 1 September following a German air raid at Toruń, and the day after when two RWD 8s were shot down. If it were not for reinforcements, and the decision to merge with Pluton Łącznikowy Nr 7, the unit would probably have ceased to exist. On 4 and 5 September crews of the, by then, Eskadra Łącznikowa flew several liaison missions, losing 1 aircraft. On 10 September the crew of *ppor.* Krzyżanowski and *kpr. mech.* Halas flew a liaison sortie to the Supreme HQ in Warsaw. Unable to find the Armia 'Pomorze' HQ location they could not return and they landed at Warsaw, where the crew was posted to join Pluton Łącznikowy Naczelnego Dowódcy Lotnictwa. There is no further data of the fates of Eskadra Łącznikowa (Plutons Nr 7 and 8), It is only known that after the loss of all aircraft the personnel were impressed into 43 Eskadra Obserwacyjna.

Lotnictwo Armii 'Poznań'

131 Eskadra Myśliwska

Like the Toruń eskadras, the eskadras of 3 Pułk Lotniczy in Poznań were mobilised before those in other parts of Poland. This was because of the short distance from the national border. Mobilisation of 131 Eskadra Myśliwska was carried out during 23-24 August 1939. Eskadra 131 together with 132 formed III/3 Dywizjon Myśliwski commanded by *mjr pil.* Mieczysław Mümler. He decided the tactics to be used during the first days of the war by both fighter eskadras. These operated in section strength from ambush posts located at various operational positions. The aim of this tactic was to cover a wide area of operations with relatively small forces. On the morning of 31 August 1939 the aircraft of III/3 Dywizjon Myśliwski flew to Dzierznica airfield near Nakło. Only one ambush post (from 132 Eskadra Myśliwska) was left at Poznań Ławica airfield. At the outbreak of war *kpt. pil.* Jerzy Zaremba was 131 Eskadra commander, having at his disposal 10 PZL P.11c aircraft. On 1 September the Eskadra suffered its first loss. *Pchor.* Kortus was seriously injured during take-off and was

Kills attributed to 131 Eskadra Myśliwska				
1	2 September 1939	*ppor.* Włodzimierz Gedymin	Dornier Do 17	Kórnik area
2	2 September 1939	*ppor.* Włodzimierz Gedymin	Heinkel He 111	Zlotniki village
3	3 September 1939	*kpt.* Jerzy Zaremba	Heinkel He 111	Wolsztyn area
4	3 September 1939	*ppor.* Lech Grzybowski	Heinkel He 111	Kobylepole ambush post
5	4 September 1939	por. Zbigniew Moszynski	1/2 Heinkel He 111	Znin ambush post
6	4 September 1939	pcho. Mirosław Nowak	1/2 Heinkel He 111	Znin ambush post
7	6 September 1939	*ppor.* Włodzimierz Gedymin	Heinkel He 111	Patrol on Słupea-Klodawa line
8	11 September 1939	*ppor.* Lech Grzybowski	Messerschmitt Bf 110	Osiek Maly ambush post, within 132 Eskadra Myśliwska

taken to a hospital. The same day pilots of 131 Eskadra formed two ambush posts: at Gułtowy (3 P.11c) and at Kobylepole (2 P.11c). Taking off from the latter *ppor. pil.* Włodzimierz Gedymin shot down a Do 17 on 2 September, its crew bailing out. That was a great day for Gedymin as less then hour later an He 111 was added to his score. Unfortunately, the P.11c of *ppor.* Wróblewski was lost, when in his pursuit of German aircraft he reached as far as Lodz, where he had to land due to lack of fuel. *Ppor.* Gedymin, whose aircraft was flown by *ppor.* Wróblewski, recalled: "*. . .During lunch I can hear the sound of an 'eleven' taking off. Upon return to the airfield I find out that Wróblewski scrambled to chase a bomber formation passing by. He scrambled in my aircraft, with my map case and my hat. I never saw the hat, nor the map case, nor the aircraft. Much later, when I was lying in a hospital in Warsaw, I was visited by Wróblewski. Naturally he was in civvies and hiding from the Germans. I learned that he chased the formation as far as Łódź, in vain. Here his fuel ended. He landed at Aleksandrowice, at VI Dywizjon Myśliwski airfield. They refuelled him and he took off to return. When circling the airfield he decided to test the guns. He fired one burst and his aircraft went on fire. Probably the fuel tank was shot through and leaking fuel resulted in the explosion. Wróblewski bailed out. . .*".[12] On 3 September a new ambush post was established at Gebarzewo, including pilots of both 131 and 132 Eskadra. Taking off from there *ppor.* Maliński of 132 shot down an He 111 on 3 September. Pilots from the Kobylepole post achieved substantial success. The commander, *kpt.* Zaremba, was credited with a Heinkel He 111, and *ppor.* Grzybowski shot down another He 111. During that combat *kpt.* Zaremba was seriously wounded and he had to give Eskadra command over to *por.* Zbigniew Moszyński (on 4 September 1939). The latter achieved his first victory the same day, when he shot down an He 111 together with *pchor.* Nowak (a new ambush post at Znin). On 4 September airfields were changed twice (Witkowo and Kleczew). The following day some posts were closed, with only the one at Gebarzewo retained. On 5 September the airfield was changed again, this time to Babiak landing ground near Kolo. Another move followed the same day, to the nearby Osiek Maly airfield. 6 September was another day of fierce fighting for the Eskadra. When patrolling the Slupca-Klodawa area an He 111 was shot down by *ppor.* Gedymin who was wounded in combat. On 7 and 8 September the Eskadra escorted *Karaś* aircraft from 34 Eskadra Rozpoznawcza. On 11 September an ambush post was set up at Osiek Maly airfield. *Por.* Grzybowski of this post shot down a Bf 110. Two days before, the orders of *mjr* Mümler had been read out. It stated that some pilots of 131 Eskadra would be impressed into Eskadra 132. The remainder would leave with the ground party or fly their machines to Baza Nr 3 at Lublin for overhaul. However, they never reached their destination and after joining the ground party of III/I Dywizjon Myśliwski they crossed the Rumanian border. The rest of the personnel were captured by the Soviets.

Total: 8 aircraft shot down. Losses: 3 pilots wounded, 2 prisoners of war, 1 missing. 3 aircraft destroyed, 6 transferred to 132 Eskadra Myśliwska + 1 to 111 Eskadra Myśliwska.

132 Eskadra Myśliwska

Eskadra 132 initially closely co-operated with Eskadra 131 as described above. Thus pilots of both eskadras participated in ambush posts organised in the Armia 'Poznań' area of operations. 132 Eskadra was based at the same airfields and at the same time as Eskadra 131. *Kpt.* Franciszek Jastrzębski was the commander of 132 Eskadra Myśliwska during the 1939 campaign. After mobilisation on 23-24 August the Eskadra awaited its orders at Ławica airfield in Poznań. Together with no. 131 it moved on the morning of 31 August to an advanced airfield, leaving only an airfield defence section at Poznań with three P.11c aircraft. A pilot of this section, scrambled during a German raid, achieved the first victory for III/3 Dywizjon Myśliwski and for 132 Eskadra Myśliwska: *kpr.* Wawrzyniec Jasiński shot down a Bf 109, while *ppor.* Mikołaj Kostecki-Gudelis was credited with another probably destroyed. Upon landing and rearming aircraft of *ppor.* Kostecki-Gudelis' section were moved to Dzierznica airfield. The next day pilots operating from the ambush post at Kalisz shot down 2 Heinkel He 111s. On 3 September 1939 *ppor.* Paweł Łuczyński took command of the ambush post at Gębarzewo with five P.11c (including two from 131 Eskadra) at his disposal. Pilots of this post managed to shoot down an He 111. On 4 September *ppor.* Łuczyński shot down a reconnaissance Do 17. The following day *pchor.* Jan Pudlewicz shot down an He 111. He scrambled at the sight of the incoming German aircraft, and one of those fell as his victim. The next day (6 September) brought further victory. On 7 September a section of P.11c's led by *por.* Kazimierz Wisniewski (III/3

Kills attributed to 132 Eskadra Myśliwska				
1	1 September 1939	kpr. Wawrzyniec Jasiński	Messerschmitt Bf 109	Poznań-Ławica
2	2 September 1939	*kpt.* Franciszek Jastrzebski	Heinkel He 111	Kalisz ambush post
3	2 September 1939	*pchor.* Jan Pudelewicz	Heinkel He 111	Kalisz ambush post
4	3 September 1939	*pchor.* Jan Maliński	Heinkel He 111	Gebarzewo ambush post
5	4 September 1939	ppor. Paweł Łuczyński	Dornier Do 17	Gebarzewo ambush post
6	5 September 1939	*pchor.* Jan Pudelewicz	Dornier Do 17	Near Ślesin
7	7 September 1939	*pchor.* Jan Maliński	Messerschmitt Bf 109	Combat with the escort of He 111s in Kalisz-Kolo area
8	9 September 1939	*pchor.* Alfons Kabat	Messerschmitt Bf 109	Krośniewice area, a Bf 109 of I.(J)LG2 shot down
9	11 September 1939	*kpt.* Franciszek Jastrzębski	Messerschmitt Bf 109	Combat over Lubań airfield
10	11 September 1939	*pchor.* Stefan Wapniarek	Messerschmitt Bf 109	Combat over Lubańn airfield
11	13 September 1939	kpr. Kazimierz Mazur	Heinkel He 111	Szadki area
12	14 September 1939	kpr. Kazimierz Mazur	Henschel Hs 126	Patrol in Żychliny area
13	15 September 1939	*pchor.* Stefan Wapniarek	Henschel Hs 126	Piatek area
14	16 September 1939	shared (Jastrzębski, Oiewiński, Nowak)	Henschel Hs 126	Patrol Łęczyca-Sochaczew

Dywizjon Myśliwski tactical officer) attacked a formation of Heinkel He 111s without noticing the Messerschmitt escort. An air combat ensued, during which *pchor.* Jan Malinski shot down one aircraft, being himself wounded and losing his P.11c (from which he bailed out). The same day *ppor.* Paweł Łuczyński was captured by the Germans when his aircraft crashed in territory controlled by the Germans. Combat missions alternated with airfield changes (compare with the 131 Eskadra Myśliwska history). On 9 September *pchor.* Witold Jaroszka was killed during his first combat sortie of the war, shot down by a Bf 109. That evening Eskadra 131 was formally disbanded, part of its personnel and aircraft reinforcing 132 Eskadra. On 11 September pilots of the Eskadra fought a dramatic combat: "*...About 17: 00 a patrol Bf of 109s overflew the airfield north of Kamienna farm, performing a regular 'merry-go-round'. The readiness section of the Dywizjon removed the masking branches and scrambled immediately. Other pilots jumped into their machines and after a couple of minutes 7 fighters were airborne... the Germans engaged... Eventually a trail of smoke appeared behind one of the Bf 109s. The aircraft fell to the ground. A moment later another Bf 109 emitting heavy smoke dropped towards the front line, where it crashed near the only artillery battery at the line of combat. Ammunition of the Poles was running short. They started to land... A moment later all was clear – two P.11s failed to return...*".[13]

Kpt. Franciszek Jastrzębski and *pchor.* Stefan Wapniarek obtained kills in that combat. Two P.11c's were lost, their pilots escaping without harm. The number of Eskadra aircraft available was increased by repairing a machine of Brygada Pościgowa, whose pilot was forced to land near Lubien on 6 September. Mümler shot down another He 111. On 13 September 132 Eskadra aircraft flew reconnaissance missions during which a Henschel Hs 126 (*mjr* Mümler) and a Do 17 was shot down (*pchor.* Nowak – victory credited to the disbanded 131 Eskadra, as Nowak used to be its pilot). Another Hs 126 was shot down on 14 September by *kpr.* Kazimierz Mazur. Last victories of the Eskadra fell to *pchor.* Stefan Wapniarek, who shot down an Hs 126 (15 September 1939) and the section of *kpt.* Jastrzębski. On 16 September the commander of III/3 Dywizjon, *mjr* Mümler, passed the orders of Armia 'Poznań' HQ to evacuate the following day surviving aircraft and personnel to Baza Nr 3 in Lublin. Only one P.11 reached the Polish-Rumanian border (*mjr* Mümler). The remaining aircraft were lost during evacuation (3 P.11c).

Losses: 2 killed, 2 wounded, 1 missing, 2 in custody. 17 aircraft destroyed (10 original + 7 from reinforcements)

Mjr Mieczysław Mümler (commander of III/3 Dywizjon Myśliwski) and *por.* Kazimierz Wiśniewski (Dywizjon tactical officer) also flew combat missions with Eskadra 131 and 132. They had at their disposal two P.11c aircraft. Mümler brought down two aircraft: a Heinkel He 111 on 12 September while patrolling the Słupca-Klodawa line and a Henschel Hs 126 the following day, while on a general patrol.

Losses: 1 pilot in custody, 1 P.11c destroyed. 1 evacuated.

34 Eskadra Rozpoznawcza

The unit was mobilised on 23-24 August 1939. *Kpt. obs.* Janusz Badowski commanded the Eskadra, which included 10 *Karaś* aircraft and 1 RWD 8. On the morning of 31 August the Eskadra moved to Gulczewo airfield. On the first day of the war crews flew reconnaissance missions, for among others, the 26 Infantry Division. These continued the following day, with several aircraft being shot at by the Germans, as well as by their own troops (aircrew known to participate included *por.* Noetzel, *por.* Michałak, *por.* Górecki and *pchor.* Żmichowski). On 3 September the Eskadra moved to Kazimierz Biskupi airfield.[14] Some aircraft moved directly, several others took off for reconnaissance sorties from the old airfield, subsequently landing at the new one after completing their missions. That day the first *Karaś* was lost, the observer, *por.* Grekowicz-Grochowski being killed. The badly damaged *Karaś* hit a building at Cielcza near Jarocin during a forced landing. Unfortunately, another crew assigned the same task was similarly unlucky, their *Karaś* was seriously damaged by ground fire and it too crashed following a forced landing. The wounded crew were captured by the enemy. A third crew managed to accomplish the mission, albeit not without problems. The *Karaś* was attacked by a Polish P.11, its pilot then fortunately realising his mistake. *Karaś* aircraft were often mistaken for Stukas (especially by the ground defences) because of the undercarriage, so similar at first sight to that of the Ju 87. Considering the overwhelming superiority of the Germans in the air there is nothing strange in the behaviour of Polish soldiers who preferred to shoot at the apparent enemy rather than wait for positive identification. On 4 September Eskadra crews flew 4 reconnaissance missions without loss. In the evening the unit changed airfields, moving to Ozorzyn near Babiak. On 5 September the Eskadra accomplished three sorties without loss, although another P.11 attacked the crew of *por. obs.* Zdzisław Gliszczyński. The following day 34 Eskadra lost two *Karaś* aircraft. One crashed during an evening ferry flight to a new airfield, killing two crew members. The other aircraft was shot down by Messerschmitt Bf 109s. Eskadra tactical officer, *por. obs.* Stanisław Martyni described the incident as follows: "... *During the return flight, over Borecznia village near Kolo, at an altitude of over 1,500 m the crew was attacked by 4 Bf 109 aircraft. As a result of the attack by Messerschmitts the Polish aircraft caught fire.* Por. *Górecki bailed out at an altitude of approx. 1,000 m, but German pilots open fire on the airman and shot him in the air. Dead* por. *Górecki had numerous traces of bullets. The pilot* – kpr. *Pingot – was probably heavily wounded or killed, as he did not even try to bail out and burnt with his aircraft. The tail gunner* – kpr. *Wilkowski – bails[ed] out at an altitude of only 300 m, suffering leg injuries. Being an eyewitness of the German barbarism he returned to the Eskadra...*"[15]

On 7 September only a few reconnaissance missions were flown, before moving again, this time to Lubień. The following day the Eskadra lost another aircraft, which was badly shot-up by a Bf 109, returning to the airfield with difficulty, so it was sent back for repair. On 9 September 34 Eskadra aircraft reconnoitred German forces in the Skierniewice-Sochaczew and Głowno-Lódź-Ozorków-Łęczyca areas for Grupa Operacyjna of *gen.* Knoll-Kownacki, who was preparing to counter-attack (at the Bzura river). The following day crews of the Eskadra flew reconnaissance in the battle area and again on 11 September. On the latter day the *Karaś* of *por. obs.* Franciszek Michałak was lost, when due to appalling weather it encountered problems returning to the airfield. On 12 and 13 September only three reconnaissance missions were flown before changing airfields again (Wola Raciborska near Kutno). On 13 September Polish troops shot down in error a *Karaś* of 34 Eskadra Rozpoznawcza which was sent for repair. On 14 September 34 Eskadra Rozpoznawcza and 33 Eskadra Obserwacyjna with *Czapla* aircraft were combined. That day these merged units changed their base twice (Brzozów, Luszyn). 34 Eskadra had only 3 *Karaś* aircraft and an RWD 8 left. One *Karaś* was destroyed on the ground on 15 September at Luszyn airfield. The following day the Eskadra's RWD 8 was transferred to Pluton Łącznikowy Nr 6, and the remaining two *Karaś* aircraft returned to Brzozów, where one was destroyed, and the other damaged in a bombing raid. On 17 September repair of the damaged *Karaś* was commenced, but another artillery inflicted further damage and the idea was abandoned. Grounded personnel of the Eskadra were ordered to get through to Warsaw. During the 1939 campaign 34 Eskadra crews flew a total of 48 combat missions. Losses – 4 killed, 2 wounded, 4 missing. All aircraft (10) destroyed.

33 Eskadra Obserwacyjna

Mobilisation of this Eskadra was carried out on 24-26 August 1939. This Eskadra was one of the few equipped with RWD 14 *Czapla* aircraft. The Eskadra consisted of two plutons, each assigned to a different infantry unit at the outbreak of war. Pluton I/33 (I Pluton of 33 Eskadra) was put at the disposal of 26 Infantry Division, and Pluton II/33 was assigned to 25 Infantry Division. The first forward airfield for 35 Eskadra aircraft was at Zydowo. At that airfield the plutons were separated: no. I/33 left for Sielec landing ground, and no. II/33 to Dębe airfield. On 3 September Polish AA defence shot down a *Czapla* of Pluton I/33. The crew survived. The same day both plutons changed airfields, I/33 moving to Szczepanowo-Lesniczówka landing ground, and II/33 to an airfield at Turek. On 4 September I Pluton lost two more *Czaplas*, destroyed in a collision whilst landing at a new airfield near Inowroclaw. The following day Pluton II/33 lost an aircraft, most probably shot down by German AA defences north of Turek. On 9 September both plutons were merged, but by that time aircraft numbers had been reduced to 3 *Czaplas* and 1 RWD 8. During all this time the Eskadra flew for Armia 'Poznań'. On 10 September another change of airfield took place (Krośniewice), and two days later yet another (Wola Raciborska). Shrinking territory and extensive activity by the German air force led to yet further changes of airfields (14 September – Brzozów Stary, 15 September – Luszyn, 16 September – Brzozów Stary). On 16 September a badly damaged *Czapla* crashed during landing after a combat sortie. On 17 September evacuation commenced. During the 1939 campaign the Eskadra flew 44 combat missions, losing all its aircraft. Throughout operations 4 airmen were killed, 8 others went missing or were captured by the Germans.

36 Eskadra Obserwacyjna

During the 1939 campaign this Eskadra was divided into plutons which operated respectively for the Army HQ (Pluton I/36) and for Wielkopolska Brygada Kawalerii (Pluton II/36). Both plutons flew Lublin R-XIII aircraft. During the first two days of the war crews of both plutons flew missions for their units without loss.

351: *The Warsaw area photographed by German airmen from a Henschel Hs 126 (NTM Praha)*

352: *P.7a of 4 Pułk Lotniczy at Toruń (MLP – Kraków)*

353: *P.7a from 141 or 142 Eskadra Myśliwska (MLP – Kraków)*

354: *Wing of a, probably, Ju 87 shot down over Warsaw (Kopański)*

355: *PZL P.37 Łoś of X Dywizjon Bombowy photographed on 31 August 1939 at Ułęż airfield (Kopański)*

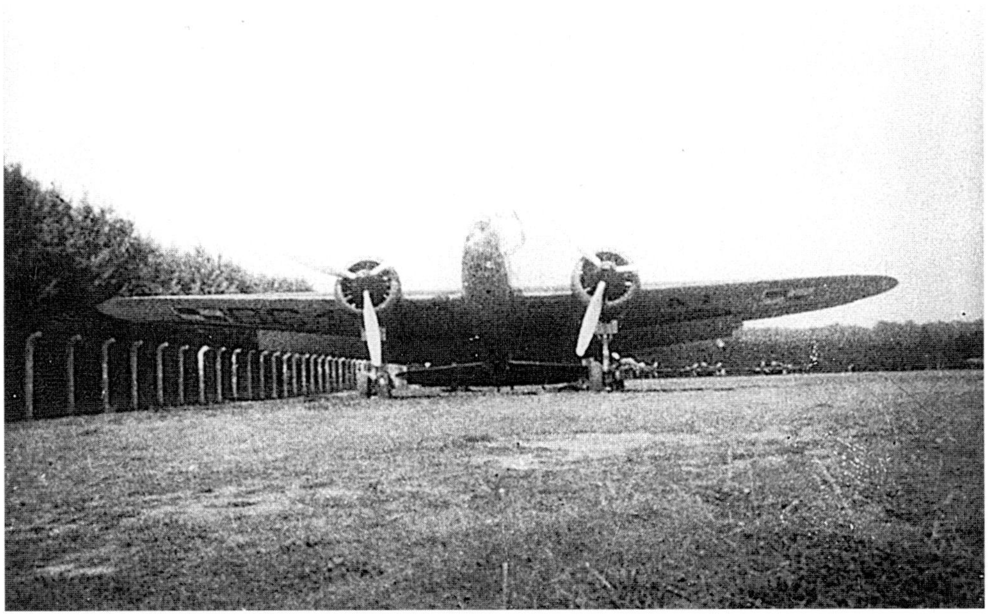

356: *Damaged P.11c fighters from 113 and 114 Eskadra Myśliwska in front of the hangar of 1 Pułk Lotniczy in Warsaw (Koniarek via Kopański)*

On 3 September Pluton II/36 suffered its first loss caused by Polish artillery which shot down the crew of *ppor. obs.* Cezary Kowal, *plut. pchor.* Roman Białasik in the Kłodawa area. On the evening of 5 September both plutons were merged. By 8 September crews had flown several spotting missions. From that day on the Eskadra was assigned to Grupa Operacyjna of *gen.* Knoll-Kownacki. At that time 1 Lublin was lost (11 September). During 12-14 September the Eskadra again flew missions for the Army commander, changing airfields several times. During the 1939 campaign these were, in sequence: Poznań-Ławica, Gwiazdowo (I/36), Śnieciska (II/36), Kleczew, Cienin, Niwka, Strzelce, Luszyn, Brzozów Stary. Eskadra losses amounted to 7 Lublin R-XIIIDs, including 2 lost during evacuation. Personnel losses included 1 killed, 3 wounded, 2 in custody, 5 missing. The combat effort amounted to 40 combat missions.

Pluton Łącznikowy Nr 6.

Commanded by *por. rez.* Janusz Mościcki it flew missions for the commander of Armia 'Poznań'. On 7 September an RWD 8 was lost. Two remaining machines were evacuated after 17 September. One of these was shot down on 20 September at Terespol.

Lotnictwo Armia 'Łódź'

161 Eskadra Myśliwska

Eskadra 161 was part of III/6 Dywizjon Myśliwski, based at Lwów. When mobilised, it attained combat readiness on 25 August 1939, the ground crews subsequently leaving for the new airfield at Widzew (today a part of Lódź). 161 Eskadra aircraft arrived there on 31 August, one of which crashed during landing. The Eskadra had 10 PZL P.11c + 2 P.11a fighters of the Dywizjon HQ. The first day of the war brought no success to Eskadra pilots, even though they engaged German aircraft. On 2 September pilots scrambling from ambush posts shot down 2 German aircraft: a Hs 126 (*ppor.* Dzwonek) and a Bf 110 (1/2 for *ppor.* Koc). Moreover *ppor.* Koc shared a Bf 110 shot down with a 162 Eskadra pilot. Losses were heavy though, – 3 aircraft, 2 pilots killed and 1 wounded. On 3 September the Eskadra lost its RWD 8 liaison aircraft, which was shot down during a liaison sortie. On 4 September the Dywizjon suffered severe losses in combat with German Bf 109s – 5 aircraft were lost (including 1 of 161 Eskadra) and 3 damaged. To make up for this the Eskadra received a P.11c which returned from repair in Warsaw. On 6 September 161 Eskadra's location was changed to Drwalewo airfield. The same day a probable victory was credited to *plut.* Franciszek Pretkiewicz, who attacked an He 111 near Grójec. Due to the difficult situation at this sector of the front the commander of Armia 'Lódź' aviation asked the Naczelny Dowódca Lotnictwa, *gen.* Zając for further guidelines. In response *gen.* Zając sent the following cable to the Army HQ: *"The Supreme Commander ordered the air party of III/6 Fighter Dyon to move today to Matczyn airfield (17 km S-W of Lublin)."*

Evacuation was carried out according to the orders of 7 September. In addition, the aircraft that had been abandoned at Drwalewo airfield (R-XIII and RWD 8) flew off together with the P.11s. On 8 September the remaining aircraft of III/6 Dywizjon Myśliwski were assigned to Dywizjon IV/1 of Brygada Pościgowa. On 9-15 September the Eskadra activities were virtually limited to further moves, mainly due to lack of fuel, a common problem in mid-September 1939. This was slightly improved on 16 September, when the ground party reached the Dywizjon at Litiatyn airfield. The same day *ppor.* Tadeusz Koc shot down a Soviet R-5 reconnaissance aircraft at Delatyń village. This was the last victory of the Eskadra in the 1939 campaign. On 17 September the Eskadra left Polish territory.

Losses: 3 killed, 2 wounded. 8 aircraft destroyed.

162 Eskadra Myśliwska

The other fighter eskadra of 6 Pułk Lotniczy fought in Armia 'Łódź' as well. Movements by this unit mirrored Eskadra 161. The main difference lay in the fact that 162 Eskadra used the much older PZL P.7a aircraft. Their combat value was negligible. Strange as it way seem, though, it was 162 Eskadra that gained credit for more kills than the P.11-equipped no. 161. On 1 September Eskadra pilots didn't achieve any victories, although they participated in air combat. The following day the Eskadra took part in an air battle against Bf 110s in the Pabianice area. Victories were obtained by *kpr.* Jan Malinowski and *ppor.* Czesław Główczyński (shared with *ppor.* Koc of 161 EM). It is worth noting that *ppor.* Główczyński flew the P.11c of the Dywizjon III/6 commander. Three aircraft were lost that day (2 from Polish AA fire and 1 crashed during landing). On 3 September Główczyński added another aircraft to his score, and there is a certain degree of doubt about the actual type involved. The pilot reported shooting down a Junkers Ju 86, but it seems unlikely that he actually encountered this type of aircraft in 1939 over Poland. It could probably have been a Do 17. Another victory for the Eskadra was achieved that day by *kpr.* Zdzisław Urbańczyk, who shot down a Henschel Hs 123 of II.(Schl.)/LG 2. On 4 September the Eskadra lost no less than four 4 P.7a's including 3 on the ground. Before this

Kills attributed to 161 Eskadra Myśliwska

1	2 September 1939	*ppor.* Tadeusz Koc	1/2 Messerschmitt Bf 110	shared with *ppor.* Główczyński of 162 Eskadra in Pabianice area
2	2 September 1939	*ppor.* Jan Dzwonek	Henschel Hs 126	shot down in Wieluń area
3	6 September 1939	*plut.* Franciszek Predkiewicz	1/2 Heinkel He 111	shared with kpr. Urbańczyk of 162 EM in Grójec area. KG4 aircraft
4	17 September 1939	*ppor.* Tadeusz Koc	Polikarpov R 5 (Soviet)	shot down in Delatyń area

Kills attributed to 162 Eskadra Myśliwska

1	2 September 1939	kpr. Jan Malinowski	Messerschmitt Bf 110	shot down in Łódż area
2	2 September 1939	*ppor.* Czesław Główczyński	1/2 Messerschmitt Bf 110	shot down in Łódż area, shared with *ppor.* Koc of 161 EM
3	3 September 1939	*ppor.* Czesław Główczyński	Junkers Ju 86(?)	Cjhojny area
4	3 September 1939	kpr. Zdzisław Urbańczyk	Henschel Hs 123	
5	4 September 1939	*ppor.* Zdzisław Zadrozinski	Dornier Do 17	Łódż area
6	6 September 1939	*ppor.* Czesław Główczyński	Heinkel He 111	Grójec area
7	6 September 1939	kpr. Zbigniew Urbańczyk	1/2 Heinkel He 111	Grójec area, shared with *plut.* Prędkiewicz of 161 EM

happened though *ppor.* Zdzisław Zadrozinski shot down a Do 17 near Łódź. Moments later the Polish pilot was shot at and hit by Bf 109s of I./ZG2(JGr102), suffering wounds. Subsequently the Bf 109s attacked and destroyed 3 P.7a's on the airfield (these aircraft had returned from the ambush post and could not be refuelled before the attack). On 5 September Dywizjon III/6 received orders to move to Drwalewo airfield, which was carried out the following day. Even though the intensity of flying on 6 September was low, the Eskadra suffered its heaviest losses. Due to a German air raid on the Eskadra ground party two pilots were killed (*st. szer.* Z. Brzeźniak, *st. szer.* Michał Krzyszowski) and another two (i.e. *ppor.* Szubert) were seriously wounded, a car driver was also killed. A section led by *ppor.* Główczyński scrambled against this raid from Drwalewo. Pilots of the section shot down 2 He 111s of KG4 (one by Główczyński, the other shared by *plut.* Franciszek Prędkiewicz of 161 EM and *kpr.* Zbigniew Urbańczyk). On 7 September aircraft of III/6 moved to Matczyn airfield near Lublin and were assigned to IV/1 Dywizjon Myśliwski of Brygada Pościgowa. At that time 162 Eskadra had only one serviceable P.7a. The Eskadra's eventual fate was the same as that of 161 Eskadra described above. The last P.7a of 162 Eskadra was impressed into the Eskadra Rozpoznawcza formed on 16 September (from P.7a aircraft of the former Brygada Pościgowa). Together with the Eskadra it was evacuated to Rumania.

Losses: 3 killed, 1 wounded. 9 PZL P.7a destroyed.

32 Eskadra Rozpoznawcza

The Eskadra was based at Poznań Ławica airfield before the war, as part of 3 Pułk Lotniczy. It received a mobilisation assignment to Armia 'Łódź'. The Eskadra ground party left Poznań on the night of 26 August 1939. The air party flew on 31 August to the distribution airfield at Lublinek near Łódż, and then to Sokolniki near Ozorków. The first combat mission took place on 1 September about 8.30 a. m., when the crew of *por. obs.* Alfons Nowak reconnoitred the southern part of the Army area of operations. During the mission the *Karaś* was attacked by the fighter cover of a German armoured-motorised formation. The pilot escaped into the clouds, the gunner suffering slight leg wounds. The next *Karaś* also encountered German fighters and had to escape. The same day two more combat missions were flown, keeping watch over the extensive movement of German formations (the Armia 'Łódź' area of operations was one of the principal areas of the German attack). On 2 September an unusual event took place. When returning from the morning sortie, the reconnaissance *Karaś* of *pchor. obs.* Adam Kandzior encountered a German Henschel Hs 126, which was shot down by *kpr. pchor. rez.* Czesław Maślankiewicz. This happened at Kaczanowice. The same day 32 Eskadra crews flew two more reconnaissance sorties. On 3 September the Eskadra suffered its first losses. The crew of *ppor. obs.* Ludwik Dembek was shot down during an attack against a German motorised column at Wielun. All on board were killed. The remaining tasks (including leaflet dropping at Wroclaw by the crew of *por. obs.* Karol Gębik) were carried out that day without loss. On 4 September the Eskadra lost two more *Karaś* aircraft, the crew of *pchor. obs.* Adam Kandzior being shot down by a Bf 110 (no survivors). The other *Karaś* force-landed at Ozorków due to engine seizure, the crew returning to the Eskadra.

The next day, 5 September, proved the most tragic of the 1939 campaign. A section of *Karaś* aircraft that took off from Skotniki airfield was attacked and shot down by Messerschmitt Bf 110s of 2./ZG 76. Victories over Polish *Karaś* aircraft were credited to Oblt. Falcke, Lt. Fahlousen and Lt. Uellenbeck.[16] The downed aircraft had serials 44.109, 44.122, and 44.132. Five Polish airmen were killed in this brief encounter. The same day another *Karaś* crashed at the airfield, when returning from a reconnaissance mission. On 6 September two crews flew reconnaissance missions for the Army HQ. In the afternoon four surviving *Karaś* aircraft and one RWD 8 flew to a new airfield at Piastów near Radom, followed on 7 September by yet another move of the Eskadra, this time to Karczmiska airfield near Kazimierz on Vistula where another *Karaś* crashed during landing, fortunately the crew was unhurt. 8 September was a day of rest for the Eskadra, as no orders were received. The following day the *Karaś* of *por. obs.* Bronisław Wojciechowicz was shot down by Messerschmitts. The remaining two aircraft flew to Marianów airfield that day. On 11 September the Eskadra moved to another landing ground (Borki near Radzyń Podlaski), where the commander received orders to disband the unit. The remaining 2 *Karaś* aircraft were to be transferred to VI Dywizjon Bombowy. After 14 September the Eskadra personnel were evacuated. During the 1939 campaign 32 Eskadra Rozpoznawcza crews flew 28 combat mission losing 14 killed, 2 wounded and 8 PZL P.23B *Karaś* aircraft.

63 Eskadra Obserwacyjna

Similar to the fighter eskadras of 6 Pułk Lotniczy, 63 Eskadra Obserwacyjna received its mobilisation assignment to Armia 'Łódź'. The eskadra was divided into two plutons to act independently. Pluton I/63 was placed at the disposal of the commander of Grupa Operacyjna 'Piotrków', while Pluton II/63 would become the reserve of the commander of Armia 'Łódź' aviation, *płk. pil.* Wacław Iwaszkiewicz. The Eskadra arrived in the area of operations on 31 August 1939. Pluton I/63 operated from Leknisko airfield, and no. II/63 from Bechcice airfield. The first combat mission took place on 2 September, but due to poor weather the task was not accomplished. The same aircraft took off in the afternoon. The *Czapla* encountered a German fighter, which however had trouble aiming at the much slower Polish aircraft. Ironically, at that very moment Polish AA artillery opened fire and shot down their own aircraft. The crew was killed. On 3 September a move was made to the airfield at Dłutów. That day the Eskadra flew typical spotting missions, without loss. On 4 September II Pluton flew several liaison sorties. On 5 September a *Czapla* returning from a combat mission was forced to land in Łódź when its fuel tank was shot through; the civilian population, suffering constantly from German air raids, mistook the Polish aircraft for an enemy and lynched one of the crew members. The damaged aircraft, with no possibility of repair, was burnt by the pilot (the badly beaten observer was in hospital). After a few further rapid airfield changes both plutons met at Kamień near Białobrzegi. Pluton I/63 was reinforced by a Lublin R-XIIIC taken from Lublinek airfield where the Eskadra had one of its stopovers. At the same time one of Pluton II/63's *Czaplas* was shot down by its own troops. This was hastily repaired and rejoined the Eskadra on 8 September. On 9-13 September only a few missions were flown, changing airfield only once (Górka Polonka near Łuck). On 14 September the Eskadra commander received orders to prepare the personnel for conversion to new equipment, the change taking place at the Polish-Rumanian border. Surviving aircraft would equip the planned Dywizjon Rozpoznawczy, to be formed from surviving remnants of Eskadra Obserwacyjna 63, 66, 13, and 53. On 17 September a *Czapla* crashed at Złoczów, after it had been shot at by German aircraft, while later that day German AA defences shot down the *Czapla* of *por.* Barański. On 18 September the crew of *por.* Kazimierz Zerębecki was ordered to deliver documents from the Wódz Naczelny for *gen.* Sosnkowski. Upon completion of the task the aircraft force-landed at Stanisławów due to lack of fuel. The crew burnt the aircraft, before making for Rumania.

During wartime operations the crews flew 36 combat missions, losing 2 airmen killed, 1 wounded, 1 missing, and 5 aircraft.

66 Eskadra Obserwacyjna

The Eskadra was mobilised on 25 August 1939. Together with Eskadra 63 it found itself on 31 August at Lublinek distribution airfield near Łódź. As opposed to no. 63 which flew *Czaplas*, 66 Eskadra was equipped with Lublin R-XIIIDs. The Eskadra was divided into two plutons, each operating with a different ground unit. Pluton I/66 was assigned to the commander of the 10th Infantry Division, and no. II/66 to the commander of Wołyńska Brygada Kawalerii. On 1 September both plutons reconnoitred new landing grounds and attempted to contact the units to which they were assigned. On 2 September Pluton I/66 lost its first aircraft, it having been struck by both German and Polish AA fire. The aircraft crashed, and the crew was taken to hospital. The following day the pluton lost another machine which, after being hit, landed in no-man's-land between the front lines. The aircraft was burnt by its crew. Another Lublin was lost on 3 September, when an aircraft of Pluton II/66 was attacked by Messerschmitts. The wounded pilot lost consciousness, but the aircraft was successfully landed by the observer: "*...The seriously wounded pilot fainted and fell onto his controls. I did not bail out, but landed, flying the aircraft from the rear cockpit...*"[17]

During this short period Eskadra aircraft changed locations several times. On 5 September the commander of 66 Eskadra Obserwacyjna, *kpt. obs.* Albert Kubieniec received orders to move the Eskadra to the Wódz Naczelny's reserve. On 6 September the Eskadra moved to Polkowszczyzna airfield near Nałęczów. On 11-14 September aircraft flew missions on the orders of *płk.* Iwaszkiewicz, commander of Armia 'Łódź' aviation. On 15 September the Eskadra was transferred near to the Rumanian-Polish border (to Stasin), where its remnants would join the Dywizjon Obserwacyjny then being formed. During 15-18 September 66 Eskadra Obserwacyjna crews flew several missions. The last 2 Lublins flew to Rumania on the evening of 18 September 1939.

The Eskadra lost 3 airmen wounded with 2 moremissing, and 5 aircraft destroyed.

Pluton Łącznikowy Nr 10

This Pluton failed to arrive at its operational area. This was mainly due to the fact that it was mobilised at the airfield of 5 Pułk Lotniczy in Lida, located a long way from the Armia 'Łódź' operational area. On 3 September the Pluton lost its first aircraft. Between 6 and 9 September the commander of the Pluton, *ppor. rez.* Bohdan Arct flew courier missions for the Chief HQ. In effect the Pluton ceased to exist on 10 September when its last aircraft was lost.

Lotnictwo Armii 'Karpaty'

31 Eskadra Rozpoznawcza

The Eskadra was mobilised on 23 August 1939 at Poznań-Ławica airfield of 3 Pułk Lotniczy. Four days later it moved to Skniłów airfield at Lwów. During the move the *Karaś* of *ppor. obs.* Olgierd Łuczkowski was damaged during a forced landing at Zamość, to such extent that it required factory repair. The War assignment for the Eskadra was to the southern part of the front line, where Armia 'Karpaty' operated. Armia 'Karpaty' was one of the few not to have its own fighter units, and the aviation forces allocated were unimpressive. This was due to the fact that the Army was not positioned on the expected direction of the main German attack. At Lwów the commander of 31 Eskadra Rozpoznawcza, *kpt. pil.* Witalis Nikonow, received orders to move his unit to Werynia airfield near Mielec. As the airfield was not technically prepared for Eskadra aircraft, they did not arrive there until 31 August, when the shortcomings were taken care of. On 1 September two crews of the Eskadra flew a reconnaissance over German forces in Slovakian territory, bringing back useful intelligence. However a planned bombing raid was not made, as HQ did not want to attack the territory of a foreign country. On 2 September 3 *Karaś* aircraft again flew over Slovakia, this time failing to observe any major German activity. On 3 September the southern direction was still the priority for the HQ. The first crew despatched to that area was shot down shortly after take off by Polish defences at Tarnów. A similar fate befell the next *Karaś*, but this one managed to get back to the airfield. A third *Karaś* was more fortunate, its crew spotting a German armoured column on the road from Chabówka-Nowy Targ. A bombing raid was as a consequence ordered which surprised the Germans who suffered major losses. One*Karaś* failed to return from the sortie (its crew was captured), and another was damaged on landing. On 4 September Eskadra aircrew flew two reconnaissance sorties to the south, a day during which the unit moved to a new airfield at Rękawek near Rzeszów. 5 September was a day in which a machine returning from a reconnaissance sortie suffered an engine failure and the crew had to bail out, but also saw the delivery to 31 Eskadra of two RWD 8 and one med-evac RWD 13 aircraft. On 6 September Eskadra aircraft flew two attacks against German troops that had been located the day before. The first was carried out from high level but with no positive result, other than one *Karaś* lost, when it landed due to a malfunction and was burnt by its crew. A low level attack was however a success. In the evening the remaining aircraft returned to Werynia airfield. On 6 September the Eskadra received reinforcements from Skniłów airfield (the base of 6 Pułk Lotniczy) in the form of two RWD 14 *Czaplas*. On 7 September several reconnaissance missions were flown, while the liaison RWD 8s searched for new landing grounds. Eventually Cieszanów village near Rawa Ruska was selected, and Eskadra aircraft flew there in the evening; during its landing one of the *Czaplas* suffered undercarriage failure. Problems with communications at the new airfield resulted in no flying on 8 September but on subsequent days Eskadra *Karaś* aircraft flew reconnaissance over the Vistula crossings. On 11 September the Eskadra received reinforcements in the form of 4 *Karaś* aircraft, taken from the disbanded 55 Samodzielna Eskadra Bombowa, however, these aircraft failed to arrive at the Eskadra, as they were unable to locate the new airfield (because the Eskadra had had to move from Cieszanów to Batiatycze). In this situation the pilots decided to fly to Skniłów airfield at Lwów, where the aircraft were lost during German raids. On 12 September the Eskadra lost another *Karaś*, shot down by Messerschmitts. During 13-15 September no flights were made, other than those required in order to move location again (Kozłówka near Brzezany). On 16 September two reconnaissance missions were flown and two unarmed *Karaś* aircraft were collected at Stanislawów airfield. On 17 and 18 September the remaining aircraft were evacuated to Rumania (4 *Karaś* + 1 *Czapla* aircraft). During the 1939 campaign 31 Eskadra Rozpoznawcza crews flew 48 combat missions dropping 8 tonnes of bomb. Losses: 6 killed, 4 missing. 8 aircraft were lost (not counting the four 55 Eskadra *Karaś* aircraft which failed to reach 31 Eskadra Rozpoznawcza).

56 Eskadra Obserwacyjna

The Eskadra was mobilised at its home airfield of 5 Pułk Lotniczy in Lida on 24 August 1939. It received an assignment to Armia 'Karpaty', even though according to previous plans it was going to join the aviation of Armia 'Modlin'. Flying Lublin R-XIIIDs, the unit landed at Mrowla airfield near Rzeszów on 1 September. In the first days of the war the Eskadra flew various missions (liaison, reconnaissance, mail, strafing missions, as well as searching for shot down Luftwaffe aircraft crews). On 4 September an RWD 8 was lost, shot down by Polish AA fire while another RWD 8 was transferred away on 5 September to Pluton Łącznikowy Nr 5. The following day the Eskadra lost two Lublins, and another was damaged. On 7 September the Eskadra flew reconnaissance missions in Tarnów and Nowy Sącz area, and over Slovakia. In the evening the airfield was left, moving instead to Nienadowa. On 8 September the Eskadra was joined by the pilot of the Pluton Łącznikowy mentioned above. 9 September brought another move, this time to Stubno airfield near Przemyśl. In the following days the Eskadra flew reconnaissance missions, moving in concert with the front line. On 11 September the Eskadra received reinforcements in form of two R-XIIIs, a *Czapla*, an RWD 8 and an RWD 17. The following day the RWD 17 crashed, while being flown to Lublin by *por. obs.* Mieczysław Gorzeński, the remaining crews flew reconnaissance missions in the Lwów area identifying German armoured columns. On 13 September another change of airfield occurred (Markowce near Stanislawów). By 17 September the Eskadra was flying fewer and fewer missions until it was ordered to evacuate, this being accomplished on 17 and 18 September. Eventually two *Czaplas* and the Lublin R-XIIIs flew to Rumania. During the 1939 campaign 56 Eskadra Obserwacyjna flew 71 combat and 15 liaison missions, losing 2 aircrew wounded, 2 missing, and 9 aircraft destroyed.

357: *A PZL P.37* Łoś *damaged in an air raid against Małaszewicze base (Kopański)*

358: Karaś *of 21 Eskadra Rozpoznawcza at Kraków airfield. The unit emblem and Polish national marking on the rudder have been cut out by German 'souvenir hunters' (Kopański)*

359: *PZL P.37B* Łoś *with traces of numerous bullet hits – guarded by a German soldier (Karl Kössler)*

360: *Fragments of the engine of a Ju 87 shot down in the first days of the war over Warsaw (Kopański)*

361: *Aircraft captured by the Germans at Dęblin airfield. Left to right: PZL P.23A* Karaś, *Potez XXV, RWD-8, PZL P.11a (with a non-standard code number '999'), Potez XXV with Jupiter engine, and an RWD-14* Czapla *fuselage standing on its nose (Kopański)*

Pluton Łącznikowy Nr 5

Was formed from reserve airmen of 3 Pułk Lotniczy at Lublinek airfield near Łódź. It had three RWD 8 aircraft. On 1 September it moved via Lwów to Zaczernie near Rzeszów, as the reserve unit of Armia 'Karpaty' HQ. The Pluton flew mainly liaison missions. On 4 September an RWD 8 was lost, shot down by Polish troops. On 5 September the Pluton received the liaison machine of 56 Eskadra Obserwacyjna as a replacement. On 6 September the commander, *ppor. rez. pil.* Jerzy Gerlicz flew to Warsaw, where he received another courier task, to fly to *gen.* Kutrzeba, the commander of Armia 'Poznań'. Upon returning to the capital (9 September 1939) he received documents for *gen.* dyw. Langer, the commander of Lwów defences. During the mission the aircraft was forced to land due to damage inflicted by Messerschmitts. As the absence of the commander was getting longer, and the remaining aircraft were lost during operations, the commander of Armia 'Karpaty' aviation ordered the remaining two pilots of the Pluton to 56 Eskadra Obserwacyjna (8 September 1939).

Lotnictwo Armia 'Kraków'

121 Eskadra Myśliwska

Eskadra 121 together with nos. 122 and 123 formed III/2 Dywizjon Myśliwski before the war. Mobilisation assignments impressed 123 Eskadra into Brygada Pościgowa. Mobilisation of the Krakow Pułk was carried out on the night of 26 August 1939. Both Eskadras (121, 122) moved on 31 August to Balice airfield near Krakow. (Aircraft allotted to the ambush post located near Bielsko-Biała did not go to Balice.) On 1 September at approximately 7:00 a.m. a section of P.11c fighters scrambled from Balice (together with a section from 122) led by the commander of III/2 Dywizjon Myśliwski, *kpt.* Mieczysław Medwecki but fell under the guns of Stukas from I./StG 2 'Immelmann' returning from Krakow, who literally shot to pieces the aircraft of the Dywizjon commander (which probably hit in its fuel tank, exploded in mid-air). Medwecki was the first Polish (and Allied) airman to be shot down in the Second World War. Shortly afterwards *ppor. pil.* Władysław Gnyś shot down two Do 17Es of KG 77, probably the first German aircraft shot down over Poland. Half an hour later III/2 Dywizjon aircraft engaged a German bomber formation. During the combat *sierż.* Leopold Flanek shot down an He 111. The pilots from the ambush post near Bielsko-Biała (Aleksandrowice) added two further aircraft to the Dywizjon scoreboard. *kpr. pil.* Jan Kremski shot down an He 111, and together with a pilot of 122 Eskadra (*plut.* Antoni Markiewicz) a Henschel Hs 126. On 2 September 3 aircraft of the Eskadra, together with machines of no. 122, attacked a formation of Stukas from StG 2 but the pilots of 121 Eskadra failed to score in this combat. The same day the Eskadra received a single replacement (a P.11c) from Baza Nr 2 in Krakow. On 3 September the Eskadra attacked a group of He 111s: a P.11c was lost (*ppor.* Wacław Król bailed out safely), but the Eskadra scoreboard was increased by an He 111 shot down by *ppor.* Tadeusz Nowak and *sierż.* Leopold Flanek. Moreover, *st. szer.* Tadeusz Arabski shot down a Do 17. On 3 September the entire III/2 Dywizjon Myśliwski moved by the orders of the Naczelny Dowódca Lotnictwa to Podlodów airfield near Dęblin. The following day only a few patrols were flown, without contact with the enemy. On 5 September *ppor.* Wacław Król, together with *kpr.* Piotr Zaniewski shot down a Dornier Do 17 over Borowina airfield near Dęblin. In the evening the Eskadra moved to Kraczewice airfield near Opole Lubelskie. On 6 September the Eskadra flew no missions. On 7 September Eskadra aircraft flew patrol missions. During one of those the Eskadra commander, *kpt.* Tadeusz Sędzielewski was shot down and killed in an uneven combat with three Bf 109s of JGr. 102. Two more aircraft of 121 Eskadra landed in fields, the aircraft of *st. szer.* Marian Futro was forced to land due to lack of fuel. The following day the pilot, still in search of fuel, met a German patrol and was shot dead (the aircraft was captured by the Germans). On the morning of 9 September the Eskadra flew 5 patrol missions, and in the afternoon moved to Strzelce airfield near Hrubieszów. On 10-11 September III/2 Dywizjon Myśliwski aircraft flew a total of 6 reconnaissance missions without encountering the enemy. On 12 September the Dywizjon was assigned to Brygada Pościgowa. On 14 September III/2 Dywizjon flew to Werby airfield, and thence to Petlikowice near Buczacz. The further fate of the Eskadra was connected with those of Brygada Pościgowa, with which it was evacuated to Rumania.

Losses: 3 pilots killed, 6 P.11c's destroyed.

Kills attributed to 121 Eskadra Myśliwska

1	1 September 1939	*ppor.* Władysław Gnyś	2 x Dornier Do 17	Olkusz area
2	1 September 1939	*sierż.* Leopold Flanel	Heinkel He 111	Kety area
3	1 September 1939	*kpr.* Jan Kremski	Heinkel He 111	Trzyniec area
4	1 September 1939	*kpr.* Jan Kremski	1/2 Henschel Hs 126	Shared with plut A. Markiewicz of 122 EM
5	3 September 1939	*ppor.* Tadeusz Nowak *sierż.* Leopold Flanek	Heinkel He 111	KG4 aircraft shot down over Puszcza Niepolomicka
6	3 September 1939	*st. szer.* Tadeusz Arabski	Dornier Do 17	Olkusz area
7	5 September 1939	*ppor.* Wacław Król *kpr.* Piotr Zaniewski	Dornier Do 17	Dęblin area

Kills attributed to 122 Eskadra Myśliwska				
1	1 September 1939	*plut.* Antoni Markiewicz	1/2 Henschel Hs 126	ambush post at Aleksandrowice, shared with kpr. Jan Kremski of 121 EM
2	2 September 1939	*kpt.* Mieczsław Wiórkiewicz	Junkers Ju 87	some sources credit this victory to plut Markiewicz Antoni
3	2 September 1939	*ppor.* Blesław Własnowolski *plut.* Władysław Majchrzyk	Junkers Ju 87	Chrzanów area

122 Eskadra Myśliwska

Activities of 122 Eskadra Myśliwska in September 1939 were closely connected with those of III/2 Dywizjon Myśliwski, and thus also with Eskadra 121, described above. This unit, assigned to Armia 'Kraków', was commanded by *kpt. pil.* Mieczysław Wiórkiewicz. During first days the Eskadra operated within this Army. After 4 September 122 Eskadra moved to the Dęblin group of airfields as the reserve of the Naczelny Dowódca Lotnictwa. This decision resulted in the fact that, unlike the remaining fighter units, the Eskadra failed to take an active part in combat. Also, it was probably the only one that suffered no losses. From 12 September the Eskadra was part of Brygada Pościgowa, with which it was evacuated to Rumania. Victories are listed in the table above.

24 Eskadra Rozpoznawcza

Mobilisation of the Eskadra was carried out on 24-25 August 1939. The unit was assigned to Armia 'Kraków'. On 31 August Eskadra *Karaś* aircraft moved to Klimontów airfield near Krakow. On 1 September Eskadra aircraft reconnoitred the enemy on the Army's flanks, and the following day movements of the unit already located were watched. The Army HQ decided to carry out a bomber attack against the German columns, six aircraft of 24 Eskadra receiving an escort of P.11c fighters from 122 Eskadra Myśliwska. The task was accomplished by 5 *Karaś* aircraft as one had force-landed due to engine failure. The next day *Karaś* aircraft attacked an armoured column near Rabka, during the raid the aircraft of *ppor. obs.* Tadeusz Prędecki was shot down, only the pilot surviving. After dropping their bomb load the *Karaś* bombers strafed the column. On 3 September the commander received orders to move to Ułęż airfield. Thus after flying 23 combat missions for Armia 'Kraków' the Eskadra was moved to the reserve of the Naczelny Dowódca Lotnictwa. On 4 September the Eskadra did not fly, while the following day it only flew two short reconnaissance missions. 6 September was another day of rest, and on the 7th only three reconnaissance missions were flown. On 8 September the Eskadra received assignment to Armia 'Lublin', then being formed and also took delivery of two *Karaś* aircraft brought to the Eskadra from Krzywda airfield near Luków, where they had been stored without crews. On 9 September the Eskadra flew 1 reconnaissance mission, and in the afternoon it moved to the new airfield at Luszczów near Lublin. On the evening of 10 September the Eskadra was ordered to reconnoitre German troops on the right bank of Vistula between Sandomierz and Puławy, plus other units regrouping on the southern flank of operations of Armia 'Poznań' (on 9 September this Army commenced the greatest battle of the campaign). Since these orders were delivered late in the evening, they were carried out the following day, on 11 September. The next day crews flew reconnaissance missions for the Naczelny Dowódca Lotnictwa and for the Commander of Armia 'Lublin'. The targets included fords across the Vistula and Bug, as well as Warsaw suburbs. On 13 September these missions continued, during the course of the two days 2 *Karaś* aircraft crashed (those flown by the crews of *ppor.* Jeżewski and *ppor.* Bidziński). From 13 September the Eskadra was assigned to the disposal of the Commander of Armia 'Lublin', this being of rather theoretical significance (the following day the Eskadra changed its deployment, being virtually unable to co-operate with this army). When landing at Kniahinin airfield near Młynów another *Karaś* crashed. On 15 September the crew of *por. obs.* Roman Miarczyński, *por. pil.* Tadeusz Nowierski, *ppor. obs.* Władysław Zborowski flew the Eskadra's most spectacular mission during the 1939 campaign. The crew delivered mail from the Wódz Naczelny, *marsz.* Rydz-Śmigły to the Commander of Armia 'Warszawa', *gen.* Rómmel. The aircraft landed under German fire and after refuelling took off for the flight back which was uneventful, but for the shelling at take off. The same day an LWS 3 *Mewa* was flown from Pińsk (the type was going to be the successor of the RWD 14 *Czapla*, but failed to enter service in substantial numbers). On 16 September the Eskadra moved to Uzyniec airfield some 25 km east of Kniahinin, flying reconnaissance missions in the Chełm-Zamość area. The *Mewa* was shot down on 17 September near Horodenka by Soviet troops (that was the first day of the Russian intervention to fulfil the Ribbentrop-Molotov pact). Three evacuated *Łoś* bombers were also stored at Uzyniec airfield with 24 Eskadra aircraft. When evacuation was ordered, the Eskadra tactical officer, *por. obs.* Aleksander Bujalski ordered the *Łoś* aircraft burnt, to prevent these from falling into enemy hands (Eskadra personnel had not been trained on the type which differed considerably from the obsolete *Karaś*). However *kpr. pil.* Stanisław Mierniczek asked *por.* Bujalski permission to ferry a *Łoś* to the new airfield at Gwoździec Stary near Horodenka. In spite of the obvious problems, the flight ended successfully. The aircraft had spent only a few hours at the new airfield when the Eskadra was ordered to evacuate to the Cernautsi area in Rumania. After dark Eskadra aircraft left Polish territory.

During the campaign the Eskadra flew 57 combat missions dropping 8 tonnes of bombs. Losses: 2 killed, 1 wounded, 1 missing. 9 *Karaś*, 1 *Łoś*, and 1 RWD 8 aircraft flew to Rumania.

23 Eskadra Obserwacyjna

Before the outbreak of war the Eskadra was based at 2 Pułk Lotniczy airfield in Krakow, armed with 2-seater RWD 14 *Czapla* reconnaissance aircraft. The unit was assigned to Armia 'Kraków' (1-8 September 1939), then to Armia 'Karpaty' (9-11 September 1939), and eventually to Grupa Armii 'Małopolska' (after 12 September 1939). During the first days of the war, while still flying for Armia 'Kraków', the Eskadra operated with Grupa Operacyjna 'Bielsko' and 'Boruta'. Between the 1st and 3rd of the month crews flew over the southern part of the front, in the Zakopane, Cieszyn, and Nowy Targ areas, losing 1 machine which crashed during landing after it had been hit by anti-aircraft fire (both German and Polish). Other airfields used by the Eskadra at that time included: Palczowice near Zatora (31 August), Balice (3 September), Pobiednik (3 September). On 4 September fighter and reconnaissance eskadras of Armia 'Kraków' moved together with the HQ, which appointed the commander of 23 Eskadra, *por. obs.* Władysław Rewakowicz, to the post of the co-ordinator of 23 and 26 Eskadra Obserwacyjna combat operations. The same evening the airfield was changed to Kszczonów near Nowy Korczyn. Damaged aircraft that could not be evacuated were burnt at the old airfield. From Kszczonów the Eskadra flew reconnaissance over the Busko and Sandomierz areas, spotting numerous enemy formations. The situation threatened the northern flank of the army, and also the airfield of the Eskadra. This led to the decision to change airfields again, moving on 7 September 1939 to Werynia near Kolbuszowa. 2 crews stayed at the old airfield to work for the army commander. After two days both crews rejoined the Eskadra, which was then based at Szczucin airfield. From 9 September the Eskadra reconnoitred the situation at the front line for Armia 'Karpaty'. At that time the Eskadra was reinforced by a *Czapla* ferried in from Dęblin by *ppor.* Tadeusz Kaszycki. From 12 September Armia 'Karpaty', merged with Armia 'Kraków' and Armia 'Lublin', formed Grupa Armii 'Małopolska' for which the Eskadra would now operate. During that period the intensity of flying diminished significantly due to lack of fuel. On 17 September the commander of the Eskadra received orders to evacuate to Rumania (5 *Czapla* aircraft were left).

During the campaign the Eskadra flew 92 combat missions without losses in personnel (only two slightly wounded, who stayed with the unit). 6 aircraft were lost (4 *Czaplas* and 2 *Mewas*).

26 Eskadra Obserwacyjna

The Eskadra operated within Armia 'Kraków'. At the moment of the mobilisation it was divided into two plutons, no. I/26 operating for the Commander of the 7 Infantry Division, and no. II/26 for the commander of the Grupa Operacyjna 'Slask'. On 1 September the commander of Pluton I/26, *por. obs.* Leon Wrzeszcz was killed (together with his pilot, *st. sierż.* Adam Baran). His post was taken over by *por. obs.* Władysław Szymik. Also Pluton II/26 lost one Lublin R-XIIID, which was sent back for repair to Baza Lotnicza Nr 2 in Krakow. Bad luck dogged the commanders of Pluton I/26. *Por.* Szymik, appointed on 1 September, was killed the following day during a combat mission in the Częstochowa area. The pilot bailed out safely and rejoined the unit after a few days. Pluton II/26 aircraft suffered considerable damage from ground fire, leading the Pluton commander, *por. obs.* Stanisław Król to send pilots to Krakow to bring new aircraft (eventually one Lublin R-XIII was obtained from Baza Nr 6 at Lwów). Pluton I/26 was in a difficult situation, miraculously avoiding being encircled and captured by the enemy. The only serviceable Lublin of I/26 Pluton flew to Mielec. Two more Lublins from Baza Nr 6 at Lwów helped to make up the losses of Pluton II/26. High losses by both plutons resulted in much reduced combat activity on their part. When transferred to Armia 'Karpaty' on 9 September the Eskadra had only 3 Lublin R-XIIIs and an RWD 8 left. On 12 September the Eskadra received reinforcements in the form of two LWS 3A *Mewas*. These would not stay for long with the unit, as one crashed the same day at Medyka airfield near Przemyśl, (the other was burnt on 17 September at Zagwóźdź airfield near pod Stanisławów, unable to be evacuated due to lack of fuel). The aircraft of *ppor.* Mieczysław Łapa (*pil. kpr.* Andrzej Duda) crashed on 12 September during a forced landing. That evening the unit made an emergence departure from the airfield at Lwów, due to the threat of an attack by German armoured troops. By 18 September the Eskadra flew few missions, losing its last RWD 8 (17 September 1939). Evacuation to Rumania was ordered for the next day. However, due to dense fog and threat from the enemy, all aircraft were burnt (1 RWD 14 *Czapla*, 3 Lublin R-XIII and 1 LWS 3 *Mewa*). Eskadra personnel left Poland on the ground. Losses: 4 killed, 1 wounded, 1 missing, all aircraft destroyed.

Pluton Łącznikowy Nr 3

The Pluton was formed during the last week of August at Rakowice airfield in Krakow. It was placed at the disposal of Armia 'Kraków' HQ. Apart from the standard equipment of liaison plutons, i.e. RWD 8s, Pluton Nr 3 also had a Lublin R-XIII. It was transferred to 26 Eskadra Obserwacyjna on 3 September. That day Pluton aircraft were directed to find two P.11c fighters that had force-landed due to lack of fuel. One of these, that of *st. szer.* Tadeusz Arabski, was located and refuelled. The attempt to find the other one was unsuccessful. During the return flight the search aircraft was fired at by German troops and had to make a forced landing (the aircraft crashed and was burnt by its crew). On 7 September the commander of the Eskadra, *por. rez. pil.* Piotr Dunin was shot down during a courier flight to Warsaw (he would return to the Pluton on 12 September

1939) whilst *plut. pchor. rez.* Roman Stadtmuller, flying in the opposite direction, was shot down over Zawichost by German AA defences. Equipment losses were made up on an *ad hoc* basis by impressing aircraft found on airfields in the army's area of operations. On 14 September *kpr.* Wacław Korwel was killed whilst landing. The last tasks were accomplished by the pluton between 15 and 18 September, subsequently evacuating to Rumania.

Lotnictwo Armii 'Modlin'

152 Eskadra Myśliwska

Prior to the outbreak of war the Eskadra was part of 5 Pułk Lotniczy at Lida. War mobilisation of the Eskadra took place at Porubanek airfield near Wilno, from which the aircraft flew to Jaszuny airfield on 24 August. Thence on 31 August the Eskadra moved via Warsaw to Szpondowo airfield, becoming part of Armia 'Modlin' aviation. Eskadra 152, together with 151, was used to form III/5 Dywizjon Myśliwski under *mjr* Edward Więckowski. Immediately prior to the outbreak of war the Eskadras were assigned to different formations. *Mjr* Więckowski, the commander of III/5 Dywizjon, stayed with 152 Eskadra. For the unit's pilots the war commenced on the afternoon of 1 September. Their first task was to provide air cover for the Modlin fortress. During a German raid pilots of two sections lost their nerve and started a pursuit of enemy aircraft heading for Warsaw. The pursuit caught up with the Germans close to the city, simultaneously with the aircraft of Brygada Pościgowa. Eskadra pilots shot down a Heinkel He111, and shared two more with Brygada Pościgowa pilots. Losses:1 P.11c shot down, 4 badly shot up. There was no flying on 2 September. On 3 September *kpr.* Marian Belc shot down a Bf 109, and *kpr.* Stanisław Brzeski a German spotting balloon. The following day 152 EM aircraft escorted 41 Eskadra Rozpoznawcza bombers during the return flight of which another balloon was shot down (*ppor.* Jan Bury-Burzymski). AA fire punctured *kpr.* Brzeski's fuel tank, forcing him to land. From midday on 4 September until 6 September the Eskadra changed airfields every day (Kroczewo, Poniatów, Wieruchów). 7 September was the last day of Eskadra operations for Armia 'Modlin'. That day a section of P.11s flew a reconnaissance mission over Bugo-Narew river area. From 8 September the Eskadra was re-assigned to report to the commander of Brygada Pościgowa, moving to Kierz airfield. The same day the Eskadra flew 6 patrol sorties in the Lublin-Dęblin-Góra Kalwaria area. On 9 September patrol sorties continued, with a Heinkel 111 shot down (the section of *ppor.* Bury-Burzymski) losing the P.11 of *kpr.* Antoni Joda. In the evening the Eskadra received orders to move to Zielonka airfield in order to reinforce the air defence of Warsaw. Since the remaining units of Brygada Pościgowa failed to received the orders in time, they moved south-east, to the Wołyń region. Thus on 10 September 152 Eskadra was the only air defence of Warsaw, on which day a reconnaissance and cover mission was flown for the HQ column of Armia 'Modlin', losing one aircraft shot down by He 111 gunners. On 11 September the Eskadra flew to Brześć, and on 12 September to Ostrozec airfield near Łuck. The remaining period of the 1939 campaign was spent by the Eskadra moving together with Brygada Pościgowa. On 17 September 1939 the last two Eskadra aircraft crossed the border of Poland.

41 Eskadra Rozpoznawcza

Before the war the Eskadra was part of 4 Pułk Lotniczy in Toruń. After the mobilisation, carried out on 26 August, its crews remained at readiness. The move planned for 31 August was cancelled owing to bad weather, but commenced the following day although it had to leave two aircraft behind as they were undergoing repair. After landing at Mokotów airfield the aircraft arrived at their eventual destination at Zdunów near Zakroczym, becoming part of Armia 'Modlin' aviation. No combat missions were flown on 1 September. On 2 and 3 September the Eskadra flew reconnaissance missions in the border area and the railway station at Niedenburg (Nidzica) was bombed. The 4 September saw 6 aircraft of the Eskadra ordered to bomb enemy troops. A waterlogged airfield prevented the aircraft from carrying full bomb loads, even so one *Karaś* failed to lift off, and another crashed. Returning crews were faced with the same problem. Two more crews crashed their aircraft. In the evening the unit moved to Warsaw Mokotów airfield. 3 damaged *Karaś* aircraft were burnt. On 5 September the Eskadra was due to receive reinforcements from the PZL Okęcie works. At least 6 PZL P-43A aircraft of the batch of 42 ordered in 1938 by Bulgaria were still at Okęcie. At the outbreak of war it was decided to erect the aircraft, already crated for shipment. The last one was undergoing assembly on 5 September. The P-43A was an export version of the *Karaś* with a more powerful Gnome Rhone GR 14N-01 engine. Eskadra pilots who went to Okęcie airfield found 3 PZL P-43As there. At the same time a German air-raid started,

Kills attributed to 152 Eskadra Myśliwska

1	1 September 1939	*ppor.* Jan Bury-Burzymski	Heinkel He 111	shot down in Warsaw suburb
2	1 September 1939	Shared	2 x 1/2 Heinkel He 111	shared with Brygada Pościgowa pilots
3	3 September 1939	kpr. Marian Belc	Messerschmitt Bf 109	Zenbok area
4	3 September 1939	kpr. Stanisław Brzeski	Spotting balloon	
5	4 September 1939	*ppor.* Jan Bury-Burzymski	Spotting balloon	
6	9 September 1939	Shared	Heinkel He 111	*ppor.* Bury-Burzymski section

361: *A burnt-out* Łoś *engine photographed at Małaszewicze (Kopański)*

362: *P.11c captured by the Germans. The aircraft has an interesting and mysterious camouflage scheme. The aircraft's tail was damaged and probably that is why the Germans retouched a new tail, never seen on a P.11c, prior to publication of the photos*

363: Karaś *no. 44.126 captured by the Germans, photographed at Okęcie airfield (Cynk)*

364: *Damaged* Karaś *after capture by the Germans (MLP – Kraków)*

365: *LWS-4 Żubr destroyed at Dęblin in a German air raid (Kopański)*

during which the aircraft were damaged. *Por. obs.* Czesław Malinowski of 41 Eskadra learned from one of the factory technicians that a batch of five[18] P-43As assembled previously were located at another (forward) airfield in Warsaw, at Bielany. The information proved correct and the Eskadra was reinforced by 5 new aircraft. The aircraft went together with the Eskadra to Zielonka airfield near Warsaw. From the morning of 6 September Eskadra aircraft flew reconnaissance missions, shooting down a German spotting balloon. Unfortunately two aircraft were lost due to damage. On 7 September the Eskadra lost two more aircraft (including one with its crew) although the crew of *pchor. obs.* Fabian Pokorniewski was credited with probably shooting down an attacking Messerschmitt Bf 109. On 8 September a German armoured column was located, and the following day it was bombed by the crew of *por.* Malinowski. On 9 September, while changing airfields (Krzesk) another *Karaś* crashed and the following day a *Karaś* lost its propeller during take-off and the aircraft crashed. Moreover, during a ferry flight to a new airfield at Siennica, Messerschmitts shot down a PZL P-43A. On 11 September the Eskadra did not fly due to lack of fuel. Thus on the morning of 12 September the Eskadra had only one serviceable aircraft, a PZL P-43A. It took off for Brześć, but during the flight it was attacked by two Bf 109s, and managed to escape, unfortunately, during landing the aircraft turned over in a bomb crater. The unit, deprived of all its equipment had now lost its combat value. Most personnel entered Rumania on 18 September. During the campaign 32 combat missions were flown, dropping 2 tons of bombs. Losses: 6 killed, 13 aircraft destroyed.

53 Eskadra Obserwacyjna

Mobilisation of the Eskadra was carried out on 24 August 1939 at Porubanek airfield near Wilno, the unit then moved the aircraft to Biała Waka near Wilno. After a week the Eskadra moved, via Warsaw, to Sokołówek airfield near Ciechanów and thus became part of Armia 'Modlin'. The Eskadra was divided, Pluton I/53 being placed at the disposal of Nowogródzka Brygada Kawalerii. On the first day of the war a *Czapla* of Pluton II/53 was lost when it crashed on landing. On 2 September Pluton II/53 flew missions for the 20th Infantry Division and Mazowiecka Brygada Kawalerii. On 3 September three of four Pluton I/53 crews returned to Sokołówek airfield (one crew continued to operate with Nowogródzka Brygada Kawalerii). The same day missions were flown for the 8th Infantry Division, losing one *Czapla* of Pluton I/53 to Polish AA fire. On 4 September the Eskadra moved to Zawady airfield near Modlin, landing at Szpondowo on the way. On 5 September it moved to Poniatówek airfield near Jablonna. On 4 and 5 September two damaged *Czaplas* and an RWD 8 were burnt before leaving various airfields. During the days that followed the Eskadra flew missions for various units of Armia 'Modlin'. On 8 September the *Czapla* of *por. obs.* Kazimierz Nowak was shot down by gunners of three Do17s (the pilot was killed, the observer severely wounded). On 11 September the remaining equipment was evacuated to Brześć on the Bug river. During the flight two *Czaplas* and an RWD 8 were attacked by German aircraft (reported as Ju 86s, but that seems improbable) and the RWD 8 was shot down, its crew missing. On 13 September, in view of the high losses the Eskadra was reorganised by transferring 5 officers, 12 NCOs, and 28 men together with the last 2 *Czaplas*. However, the worsening situation at the front line resulted in the crews not being used in full. Eventually both aircraft were lost. The first was abandoned in mid-air by the crew on 17 September 1939 (they could not find a suitable landing place, and the fuel was almost used up), while the other was burnt by its crew, when on 20 September 1939 they could not take off due to adverse weather, and whilst threatened by Ukrainian guerrillas. During the 1939 campaign Eskadra crew flew 42 combat missions losing 4 airmen killed and all aircraft.

Pluton Łącznikowy Nr 11

The Pluton was formed at 6 Pułk Lotniczy airfield at Skniłów near Lwów. On 1 September 2 RWD 8 and 1 Lublin R-XIII aircraft were lost in a German raid. The Pluton remained at Skniłów until 5 September, when the ground party went to Modlin. By the orders of the Commandant of Baza Nr 6 the air party was reporting to Dowództwo Obrony Lwowa and stayed there. There is no further data on the fate of that unit, but it is known that it never operated for Armia 'Modlin' to which it had been assigned at the outbreak of war.

Lotnictwo Samodzielnej Grupy Operacyjnej 'Narew'

151 Eskadra Myśliwska

Mobilisation of the Eskadra was carried out on 24 August 1939. Mobilisation orders assigned the Eskadra to Samodzielna Grupa Operacyjna 'Narew' that operated at the northern flank of the Polish forces. It was one of the few fighter eskadras equipped with the obsolete PZL P.7a aircraft, most often described in the following manner: "*. . . Everybody has known for a long time that the P.7s were no good for war at all. It is not even worth mentioning how slow they were. What was worse, their machine guns usually jammed after a few shots were fired. Poor Brzeziński*[19] *tried to operate this junk like a real fighter unit. He at once lost one of his pilots in a totally fruitless attack against bombers. . . As a result the HQ ordered 151 Eskadra to fly only reconnaissance missions. These proved their sense. . .*"[20]

Combat missions were initially flown from Biel landing ground near Ostrów. 1 September did not abound with flights. During one of the few the section of *por.* Marian Wesolowski escorted a reconnaissance aircraft (*Karaś* of 51 Eskadra Rozpoznawcza) which located a German airfield at Szczytno. On 2 and 3 September a few scrambles were made to intercept enemy aircraft, but no contact was made. On 4 September *kpr.* Tadeusz Kwalkowski was shot down over enemy territory, bailing out and listed as missing. On 5 September *pchor.* Marian Łukaszewicz damaged a Dornier Do 17, which would prove to be the only damage caused to Luftwaffe aircraft by the Eskadra. On 7 September the Eskadra changed airfields, moving to Ceranów near Wegrów, at the same time changing its role to one of purely reconnaissance. The following day it moved to another airfield, this time Adamków near Brześć on the Bug. From 9 September the Eskadra flew reconnaissance missions for the Supreme Aviation HQ and on 11 and 12 September a total of 4 P.7a aircraft was lost. On 12 September another change of airfields took place with 5 aircraft reaching Litiatyn, but flying then ceased for the next three days. On 16 September, following a reorganisation of the avarious units, pilots and aircraft of (among others) 151 Eskadra formed the Eskadra Rozpoznawcza. The following day the last 4 P.7a's (the aircraft of *ppor.* Wiktor Szulc having been written off) of the Eskadra were evacuated, together with the aircraft of Brygada Pościgowa, to Rumania.

51 Eskadra Rozpoznawcza

This *Karaś* Eskadra was arguably the most unfortunate of all eskadras flying this type of aircraft. Even before the outbreak of war 3 aircraft were lost when they crashed whilst changing airfields. The Eskadra was mobilised at the airfield of 5 Pułk Lotniczy in Lida on 25 August 1939, with assignment to SGO 'Narew'. Bad luck remained with the unit when on 1 September it lost two *Karaś* aircraft (1 crashed when taking off for a combat mission, the other during a change of airfield). Thus after the first day of the war Eskadra 51 had only 5 serviceable *Karaś* aircraft left (50% of the original number). On 2 September only 2 reconnaissance missions were flown, though without loss. The following day a bombing raid was flown, with an enemy armoured group as the target, since this was not located, bombs were dropped on a secondary target. In the evening two *Karaś* aircraft flew photo reconnaissance over enemy territory. On 4 September reconnaissance missions continued, and additionally one of the aircraft successfully bombed a rail echelon at Biała Piska railway station. On 5 September, following a reconnaissance, 3 *Karaś* aircraft bombed a motorised column on the Chorzele-Przasnysz route. On 6 September the Eskadra moved to Ceramowo airfield and also bombed a large German column on the route Janowo-Krzynowloga. During the raid one *Karaś* was attacked by German fighters (the raid was flown by single aircraft), the crew of which lost their bearings and landed near Skierniewice when during landing the aircraft was spotted by a formation of Ju 87s that strafed and destroyed it. The following day there was no flying, while equipment and armament was moved from the previous airfield. On 8 September only two reconnaissance missions were flown for SGO 'Narew' HQ. Then on the 9th the Eskadra changed airfields twice more (Rogów, Małaszewicze), and on 11 September it moved again to an airfield near Pruzany (no flying occurred on 10 September). From 12 until 16 September no combat missions took place, but in spite of that another *Karaś* crashed near Łuck while changing airfields (13 September 1939). Throughout the campaign one *Karaś* of 51 Eskadra flew sorties for the Commander of Obóz Warowny and Commandant of Baza Lotnicza nr 5 in Lida. This was an aircraft sent back from the Eskadra for repair to Lida just before the outbreak of war. After repair the aircraft was left at Lida and operated from there. The aircraft continued to fly until 17 September when it exploded in mid-air en route to bomb a motorised column (the bombs exploded due to aircraft vibrations). Of the entire Eskadra only one *Karaś* (that of *por. obs.* Bolesław Jarkowski) survived, it having operated since 15 September from Lawrów airfield. During the campaign the Eskadra flew some 22 combat mission and 4 liaison sorties, dropping 4 tonnes of bombs, losing 4 airmen killed and 9 missing.

13 Eskadra Obserwacyjna

The Eskadra was part of 1 Pułk Lotniczy and was mobilised at Okęcie airfield on 23-24 August 1939. The unit, equipped with 7 RWD 14 *Czapla* and 2 RWD 8 aircraft, moved to Czerwony Bór airfield on 28 August 1939. The following day Pluton II/13 was placed at the disposal of the commander of Oddział Wydzielony 'Suwałki' and moved to Dobra Wola airfield near Suwałki. On 1 September Pluton I/13 flew reconnaissance over the border area, while the airfield of Pluton II/13 was bombed by the Germans, forcing the HQ to change airfields. On 2 September both plutons continued reconnaissance missions. A *Czapla* of II/13 Pluton broke its undercarriage during landing while returning from a mission and was burnt the following day during evacuation of the airfield. On 3 September another *Czapla* of Pluton II/13 was shot down, and both airmen were killed. On 5 September an aircraft of Pluton I/13 force-landed due to lack of fuel (the crew rejoined the Eskadra on 7 September 1939). On 9 September the Eskadra flew a few reconnaissance missions, locating enemy armoured troops on virtually each of these sorties. On 10-11 September the Eskadra lost communications with the HQ of SGO 'Narew' and attempted to re-establish it. On 12 September the Eskadra received orders to transfer to the disposal of the commander of the newly formed Front Północny, *gen.* Dąb-Biernacki. On 13 September the *Czapla* of *kpt. obs.* Feliks Misiewicz (commander of Pluton I/13) was lost during a ferry flight to a new airfield at Jeleniec near Łuków. The new landing ground proved to be under threat from German troops, which led yet again to evacuation. 2 *Czaplas* were lost, both shot down by Bf 109s (one of these rejoined the Eskadra after a forced landing and provisional repair). The following days were chaos for the Polish forces, communications with HQ were interrupted repeatedly, yet despite this situation 13 Eskadra managed to fly on 15 and 16 September a few missions for the commander of the Łuck defences. On 18 September the last two crews

366: *PZL P.11c no. 8.70 of* por. *Hieronim Dudwał (3 kills in September 1939) captured by the Germans (Glass)*

367: *The same P.11c with national markings on top of the wing overpainted – a non-standard feature on Polish aircraft. The damaged fairing behind the cockpit was repaired with unpainted sheet duralumin (Kopański)*

368: *One of 28 PWS-26 aircraft sold in 1940 by the Germans to Rumania (Bernard)*

369: *A crash-landed PZL P-37 Łos surrounded by German sightseers. This is the same aircraft as seen in photo 359. Most operational Polish aircraft were identified by numbers but some, it seems, carried letters*

370: *PZL P.7a in German markings (MLP – Kraków)*

371: *An RWD-13 captured by the Luftwaffe was used during the war as a hack at the Fieseler factory (Karl Kössler)*

372: *Abandoned civilian-registered Bartel BM-4h trainers in a damaged Polish hangar. One is registered SP-APR*

373: *A captured PZL P-37 in German markings surrounded by various artillery pieces on display in Germany*

374: *Luftwaffe troops inspecting the remains of various abandoned Polish aircraft. Nearest is a PWS 16 or 26, while an RWD 8 in civilian markings and a PZL 23 numbered '13' can be seen in the background. The location may be Dęblin*

evacuated to Rumania. The ground party of the Eskadra, on their way south, came under command of *por. pil.* Edmund Piorunkiewicz, who organised it into the so-called '13 Eskadra Szkolna'.[21] During the 1939 campaign Eskadra crew flew a total of 45 combat missions, losing 3 killed, 3 wounded and 5 missing.

Pluton Łącznikowy Nr 9

Was formed at 5 Pułk Lotniczy airfield in Lida with assignment to SGO 'Narew'. The first week of the war was spent by the Pluton waiting for orders. These failed to materialise until the end of the campaign. During that time airfields were changed several times, performing a small number of courier missions meanwhile. On 18 September the Pluton evacuated to Latvia.

'Discretionary Aviation' of the Supreme Commander

Brygada Pościgowa

The Brygada was the only large formation of fighter aviation during the 1939 campaign. It was formed for the air defence of Warsaw. It included the following fighter eskadras: 111, 112 (both of III/1 Dywizjon Myśliwski), 113, 114 (IV/1 Dywizjon Myśliwski), 123 (from III/2 Dywizjon Myśliwski). All, except no. 123 were equipped with PZL P.11c and P.11a aircraft. Eskadra 123 used the obsolete PZL P.7a's. *Płk. pil.* Stefan Pawlikowski, the last pre-war commander of 1 Pułk Lotniczy in Warsaw, was appointed the commander of Brygada Pościgowa. *Ppłk. pil.* Leopold Pamuła was his deputy. Between 1 and 6 September the brigade defended the skies over Warsaw. From 7 September it was withdrawn to the so-called Lublin group of airfields, where during following days it underwent a reorganisation, by incorporating into the brigade some Army eskadras. These included: 152 Eskadra Myśliwska from 8 September 1939, 141, 142, 161 and 162 Eskadra Myśliwska from 9 September 1939, 121 and 122 Eskadra Myśliwska from 12 September 1939. 151 Eskadra Myśliwska was the last incorporated into the brigade (on 16 September 1939). That day Brygada Pościgowa was reorganised by reforming its eskadras into two Dywizjons: Warszawski (22 P.11s) and Krakowski (24 P.11s) plus the Eskadra Rozpoznawcza with eight PZL P.7a aircraft. The following day, 17 September, brought evacuation to Rumania. Probably 52 aircraft, including 10 PZL P.7a were evacuated with the brigade.[22]

Brygada Bombowa

In the spring of 1939 a new concept for the application of aviation into a conflict was established. Within this plan it was determined that a large force of bomber aircraft should be formed. Specific guidelines, which modified this plan, were not published until July 1939. The bomber group (later named Brygada Bombowa) was given the following tasks, in accordance with the guidelines as they then stood.

- *intervening operations at the battlefield and close rear, against human forces of the enemy*
- *attacking enemy aviation, most of all bombers and fighters, at airfields*
- *attacking railway and road transport of the enemy*
- *reconnaissance of the targets of bomber aviation operations will be generally carried out by the discretionary aviation of the Wódz Naczelny, using mostly army reconnaissance aviation.*[27]

375: *Shot-down* Karaś *44.217 of 41 Eskadra Rozpoznawcza of 4 Pułk Lotniczy, visited by a* Storch *crew.*

Date	Deployment	Victories	Losses
1 September	111, 112 - Zielonka 113, 114, 123 - Poniatów	*por.* Gabszewicz A. (IV/1 HQ) - He 111 *por.* Palusiński J. (111) - He 111 *kpt.* Kowalczyk A. (IV/1HQ) - He 111, Do 17 *ppor.* Dudwał H. (113) - He 111 *por.* Okrzeja S. (112) - He 111, Do 17 *kpt.* Frey J. (114) - 1/2 He 111 *ppor.* Czerniak J. (123) - 1/2 He 111 *por.* Borowski J. (113) - Bf 109 *ppor.* Radomski J. (113) - Bf 109 *ppor.* Sawicz T. (114) - Bf 109 *ppor.* Daszewski J. (112) - Ju 87 *ppłk.* Pamuła L. (BP HQ) - Bf 109 *plut.* Kiedrzyński W. (114) - 1/2 Bf 109 *ppor.* Miksa W. (114) - 1/2 Bf 109 shared - He 111	*st. szer.* Olewiński B. (114) *# *ppor.* Palusiński J. (111) *# *ppor.* Szmejl S. (114)# *st. szer.* Horn Z. (113)* *kpt.* Olszewski (123)+# *ppor.* Szszka F. (123)*# *ppor.* Danek A. (123)*#[23] *ppor.* Czternastek S. (123)# *ppor.* Kawnik E. (123)< *kpr.* Flamme H. (123)< *kpt.* Sidorowicz G. (111)*< *por.* Gabszewicz A. (IV/1 HQ)*# *ppor.* Radomski J. *113)*< *ppłk.* Pamuła L. (BP HQ)*# *ppor.* Dudwał H. (113)<
3 September	ditto	*por.* Januszewicz W. (111) - Bf 110 *por.* Cebrzyński A. (111) - Bf 110	*kpt.* Krasnodębski Z. (III/1 HQ)*# *ppor.* Feric M. (111)*# *ppor.* Maciński J. (111)< *st. szer.* Szope H. (111)< *ppor.* Stoga R. (114)#
4 September	111, 112 - Zaborów near Leszno Warszawskie 113, 114, 123 - Radzików near Błonie	*por.* Januszewicz W. (111) - Ju 87 *ppor.* Kalpas R. (113) - Do 17 *ppor.* Dudwał H. (113) - Do 17 *ppor.* Sawicz T. (114) - Do 17	*ppor.* Drecki W. (111)-*# *por.* Szalowski J. (114)*# *st. szer.* Nowakiewicz E. (123)<[24]
5 September	ditto	*por.* Januszewicz W. (111) - Ju 87 *ppor.* Strzembosz W. (111) - Bf 110 *por.* Barański W., *ppor.* Dudwał H., *plut* Kazmierczak M. (113) - Ju 87 *por.* Borowski J., *ppor.* Kalpas R., *ppor.* Radomski E., *ppor.* Chalupa S., *pchor.* Kratke T. (123) - He 111[25]	*por.* Okrzeja S. (112)+# *ppor.* Nowakowski W. (112)*# *st. szer.* Gallus P. (112)< *kpr.* Górecki B. (112)< *por.* Januszewicz W. (111)< *ppor.* Maxiński J. (111)< *st. sierż.* Kolcon J. (111)<
6 September	ditto	*por.* Januszewicz W. (111) - Ju 87 *ppor.* Czerniak J. (123) - He 111 *ppor.* Szmejl S. (114) - He 111 *kpt.* Kowalczyk A. (IV/1 HQ) - He 111 *por.* Lapkowski W., *ppor.* Marciniak J., *szer.* Wieraszkia W. (112) - He 111 *por.* Barański W., *por.* Borowski J., *st. szer.* Lipinski W. (113) - He 111 *ppor.* Klawe W., *st. szer.* Adamek M. (113), *plut.* Kiedrzyński W. (114) - Ju 87 *ppor.* Sawicz T., *st. szer.* Zieliński J., *kpr.* Niewiara A. (114) - Do 17Z	*st. szer.* Nowak L. (112)# *kpt.* Opulski T. (112)< *ppor.* Stoga R. (114)+# *plut.* Kazmierczak M. (113)+# *por.* Barański W. (113)< *st. szer.* Lipinski W. (113)< *st. szer.* Adamek M. (113)< *kpr.* Niewiara A. (114)< *ppor.* Bozek W. (123)<[26]
7 September	111, 112 Kierz near Lublin 113, 114, 123, Bełżyce, subsequently Radawiec Duży near Lublin		
8 September	152 Kierz 161, 162 Radawiec Duży		
9 September	111, 112, 141, 142 Ostrożec 113, 114, 123, 161, 162 - Mlynów near Dubno 152 - to Zielonka near Warsaw (evening)	*ppor.* Lapkowski W. (112) - He 111 *ppor.* Feric M. (111) - Hs 126 *ppor.* Bury-Burzymski J. (152) - He 111	*ppor.* Lapkowski W. (112)< *kpr.* Joda A. (152)< *ppor.* Stefankiewicz H. (113)< *ppor.* Pniak K. (142)< *ppor.* Czapiewski J. (142)<

Date	Deployment	Victories	Losses
10 September			*st. szer.* Popek M. (152)<
11 September	111, 112, 161, 162 - Łuszczów near Lublin 141, 142 - Brześć	*ppor.* Wróblewski A. (111) - He 111	
12 September	113, 114, 123 - Luszczów, Młynów 121, 122 - Strzelce 111, 112 - Strzelce 141, 142, 152 - Ostrożec		
13 September	161, 162 - Jabłonna near Lublin		
14 September	111, 112 - Werby, Denysów 121, 122, 123 Werby, Petlikowice 161, 162 - Liliatyn		*st. szer.* Dąbrowski B. (114)*#
15 September	141, 142, 152 - Liliatyn		
16 September	151 - Liliatyn 141, 142 - Petlikowice	*ppor.* Dudwał H. (113) - Hs 126	
17 September	111, 112, 113, 114, 121, 122, 123, 141, 142, 151, 152, 161, 162 - evacuation to Rumania	*ppor.* Koc T. (161) - R-5 unidentified pilot - 2 x SB	*ppor.* Zatorski S. (113)+#

* = wounded; + = killed; ^ = missing; # = aircraft destroyed; < aircraft damaged

Brygada Bombowa was formed virtually at the outbreak of war and included the following air units:

- X (210) Dywizjon Bombowy with:
- 11 (previously 211) Eskadra Bombowa - 9 PZL P.37B *Łoś*
- 12 (previously 212) Eskadra Bombowa - 9 PZL P.37B *Łoś*
- XV (215) Dywizjon Bombowy with:
- 16 (previously 216) Eskadra Bombowa - 9 PZL P.37B *Łoś*
- 17 (previously 217) Eskadra Bombowa - 9 PZL P.37 *Łoś*
- II (1/2) Dywizjon Bombowy Lekki with:
- 1 (previously 21) Eskadra Bombowa - 10 PZL P.23B *Karaś*
- 2 (previously 22) Eskadra Bombowa - 10 PZL P.23B *Karaś*
- VI (II/6) Dywizjon Bombowy Lekki with:
- 4 (previously 64) Eskadra Bombowa - 10 PZL P.23B *Karaś*
- 5 (previously 65) Eskadra Bombowa - 10 PZL P.23B *Karaś*
- 55 Samodzielna Eskadra Bombowa - 10 PZL P.23B *Karaś*

Final evacuation of the Brygada Bombowa to Rumania took place on 17-18 September 1939. During the operations *Karaś* crews dropped some 61 tonnes of bombs, and shot down at least 7 Bf 109s, while *Łoś* crews dropped 119 tonnes of bombs, and shot down three Bf 109s and an He 111.[31]

Eskadra Sztabowa

The Eskadra Sztabowa was established in 1929 as the Sztabowa Eskadra Treningowa. Logistically it reported to 1 Pułk Lotniczy. The change of name to Eskadra Sztabowa took place in 1931, and the unit's main task was to fly training sorties with officers working in the central institutions in Warsaw. After mobilisation it reported to the Naczelny Dowódca Lotnictwa, *gen.* J. Zając. On 1 September the Eskadra under *kpt.* Henryk Wirszyłło moved to Powsin airfield 12 km south of Warsaw, although three aircrews stayed with ground-crews at Mokotów airfield. At the outbreak of war the Eskadra had 28 aircraft of various types (including RWD-8, RWD-13, PWS-26, RWD-14 *Czapla*). On 3 September two RWD-8s were lost. On 5 September *kpt.* Wirszyłło received orders to form an eskadra with 7 aircraft and put it at the disposal of *gen.* J Głuchjowski – First Bice-Misiter Spraw Wojskowych, moving it to Świdnik airfield near Lublin. Due to very poor concealment and the large number of aircraft at this location he decided to find a new airfield (Krupe near Krasnystaw). The remaining personnel, led by *kpt.* Roman Czerniawski, together with 19 aircraft, moved via Świdnik to Gurków airfield. Since the section of Eskadra detached for *gen.* Głuchowski failed to contact him, *kpr.* Wirzyłło decided on 9 September to fly to Ławrów airfield near Łuck, where contact was made with the HQ. At that time the Eskadra had 25 aircraft, 25 pilots, 7 observers, 10 technicians, and 14 soldiers.[32] On 14 September it was decided to evacuate 5 aircraft to Jarosławicze airfield, and the remaining 20 to the Buczacz area. On 15 September aircraft flew to Dworzyszcze, and on 16 September to Jagielnica near Czortków. The

376: *Loading bombs into an early He 111 – note the extended ventral turret*

377: *Shot down* Karaś *no. 44.217 from 41 Eskadra Rozpoznawcza of 4 Pułk Lotniczy in Toruń*

378: *An unidentified German airfield in use by a Gruppe of Junkers Ju 87B* Stukas

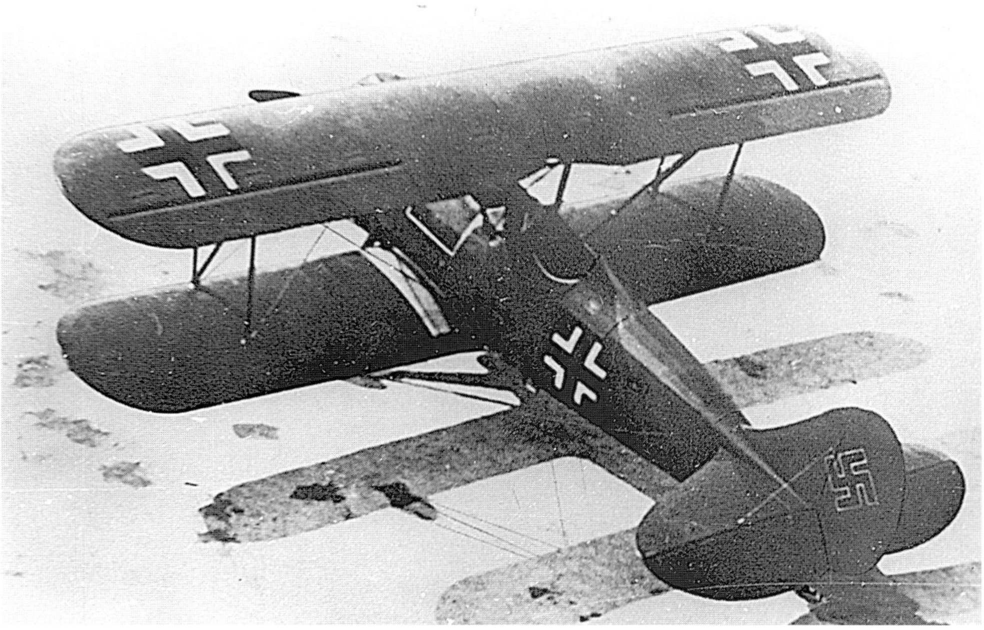

379: *A PWS-26 repaired and flown by the Germans in Mielec aircraft factory. Some of the captured PWS-26s were sold to Rumania (Konarski)*

380: *In 1940 the Germans made a propaganda film about the 1939 campaign, entitled 'Kampfgeschwader Lützow'. The PZL P.11 role was played by Czech Avia B-534 biplanes, which received fancy emblems for the occasion (Nowarra via Petr Buchar)*

381: *A Do-17P damaged by Polish AA fire*

The combat record and losses of Brygada Bombowa

Date	Deployment	Number of sorties	Losses – shot down + damaged	No. of aircraft on given day: morning + reinforcements
2 September	X – Ułęż	4	1 (12 EB)	18
	XV – Podlodów	0	-	18
	II – Wsoła, Kamień	2	1 (1 EB)	20
	VI – Nosów, Franopol	19	2 (4 EB), 4 (5 EB) + 4 dam. (4 EB)	20
	55 – Marynin	0	-	10
3 September	X – Ułęż, Kuciny-Dzierzanowo	1	-	17
	XV – Podlodów, Stara Wieś	0	-	18
	II – Wsoła, Kamień	33	2 (1 EB), 4 (2 EB)	19
	VI – Ząbków	1	-	14
	55 – Marynin	9	2	10
4 September	X – Kuciny	26	1 (11 EB), 6 (12 EB)	17
	XV – Stara Wieś	29	2 (17 EB)	18
	II – Wsoła, Kamień	4	0	13
	VI – Ząbków	0	0	14
	55 – Marynin	0	0	8
5 September	X – Kuciny, Grójec	0	1 (11 EB) on the ground	10
	XV – Stara Wieś	9	1 (? EB) on the ground	16
	II – Podlodów, Ułęż	4	-	13
	VI – Ząbków	8	1 (5 EB)	14
	55 – Marynin	4	-	8
6 September	X – Ułęż	0	-	9
	XV – Popielowo	1	-	15 + 1
	II – Podlodów, Marianów	1	-	13
	VI – Ząbków	0	-	13
	55 – Marynin	2	-	8
7 September	X – Gnojno	0	-	9
	XV – Popielowo	10	3 (16 EB), 2 (17 EB)	16 + 1
	II – Marianów	10	2 (1 EB)	13
	VI – Ząbków	22	1 (5 EB)	13
	55 – Marynin	2	1	8
8 September	X – Gnojno	0	-	9
	XV – Popielowo	6	-	12
	II – Marianów	5 1 (1 EB)	11	
	VI – Ząbków	5	1 (4 EB)	12
	55 – Marynin	8	-, 1 damaged	7
9 September	X – Gnojno	0	-	9 + 3
	XV – Podlodów	0	1 (17 EB)	12
	II – Marianów	4	-	10
	VI – Franopol	2	-	11
	55 – Matynin	9	-	6
10 September	X – Gnojno	4	1 (12 EB)	12
	XV – Wielick	0	-	11
	II – Marianów[28]	3	1 (1 EB0	10 (9 to VI DB)
	VI – Franopol	0	-	11 + 9 (from II DB)
	55 – Marianów[29]	1	2	6 (4 to 31EB)
11 September	X – Grojno	4	1 (11 EB)	11
	XV – Wielick	0	-	11
	VI – Falenicze, Wielick, Falenicze	0	-	20

Date	Deployment	Number of sorties	Losses - shot down + damaged	No. of aircraft on given day: morning + reinforcements
12 September	X - Gnojno	14	1 (11 EB)	10
	XV - Wielick	4	1 (17 EB)	11 + 3
	VI - Chołopecze	8	1 (5 EB)	20 + 3 (from 42 ER)
13 September	X - Gnojno	1	-	9
	XV - Wielick	4	1 (17 EB)	11 + 3
	VI - Chołopecze	8	1 (5 EB)	20 + 3 (from 42 ER)
14 September	X - Gnojno	0	-	9
	XV - Wielick	4	1 (16 EB)	13
	VI - Hutniki	8	3 (4 EB)[30]	21
15 September	X - Wielick	0	-	9 + 1
	XV - Wielick	1	1 (17 EB)	12
16 September	X - Wielick	0	-	10
	XV - Wielick	8	1 (17 EB)	11
17 September	X - Gwoździec Stary	0	1 - burnt by its crew	10, 9 left
	XV - Buczacz	0	1 - burnt by its crew	10, 9 left

following day the evacuation to Rumania was accomplished, via Podgajce landing ground. During the war, in spite of disorder due to a lack of precise assignments for the Eskadra, its crews flew 5 combat (reconnaissance) missions and over 50 liaison sorties, losing 7 aircraft and 4 airmen wounded.

16 Eskadra Obserwacyjna

The Eskadra was mobilised on 25 August 1939 at Okęcie airfield. During the campaign the Eskadra reported to the commander of Okreg Korpus Nr 1 (1-5 September 1939), and subsequently to the Naczelny Dowódca Lotnictwa. For the first five days of the war the Eskadra didn't fly operationally, but changed location several times. One Lublin R-XIIID was lost, when it crashed during landing and subsequently had to be burnt due to lack of repair facilities. The following days offered little in the way of flying activity for the Eskadra. During the campaign the Eskadra flew only about a dozen missions. All the equipment was lost, mainly due to damage caused when landing and other failures with the aircraft.

382: *PZL P.11a from 112 Eskadra Myśliwska, which in September 1939 was part of Brygada Pościgowa in defence of Warsaw (Kopański)*

Wartime air units

During the war operational air units were formed spontaneously, usually to support the operations of ground units. The kind of operations they performed were many and various. Brief details are listed in the table:

Unit name	Period of activity	Commander and number of personnel	Number and type of aircraft	Notes
Pluton Lotniczy Warszawskiej-Brygady Pancerno-Motorwej	3/9/39-18/9/39	*kpt. obs.* Julian Łagowski Pilots: 6; Observers: 5; Gunners: 1	5-6 September - 2 Potez XXVB2[33] 6-15 September - 2 PZL P.23A *Karaś*[34] 15-18 September - 2 RWD-8	1 RWD-8 crashed on take-off on 16/9 at Lwów
Eskadra Ćwiczebna Obserwatorów SPL Dęblin	21/8/39-19/9/39 Approximately 50?	*kpr. pil.* Jan Kryniewicz	I Pluton - 15 various types II Pluton - 15 RWD-8 III Pluton - 7 Lublin R-XIII IV Pluton - Potex XXV B2	All aircraft were captured by the Red Army at Potoczyska airfield[35]
Eskadra Ćwiczebna Pilotażu Nr 3 SPL Dęblin	1/9/39-16/9/39	*kpt. pil.* Jan Czerny Pilots: 12 SPL instructors + ? cadet officers	17 PZL P.23A *Karaś*[36] 6 PZL P.7a	Evacuation of the equipment and personnel to Rumania
Rezerwowa Eskadra Rozpoznawcza SPL Dęblin	6/9/39-17/9/39	*kpt. obs.* Maksymilian Brzozowski Pilots: 12; Observers: 10	7 PZL P.23A *Karaś*	Losses: 3 PZL P.23A Kills: 1 Bf 109
Wyższa Szkoła Pilotażu Grudziądz-Ułęż	1/9/39-18/9/39	*kpt. pil.* Stanisław Brzezina (acting) Pilots: 30 instructors + ? cadet officers	8 PZL P.7a 10 PWS-10 15 PWS-26 8 Lublin R-XIIIC 1 PZL P.11g *Kobuz*[37]	Kills: 2 He 111
Oddział Lotnictwa Mysliwskiego Bazy Nr 3	3/9/39-17/9/39	*kpt. pil.* Jerzy Orzechowski Pilots: at least 8	PZL P.11c? RWD-8	Losses: 1 RWD-8
Eskadra Łącznikowa Dowództwa Obront Lwowa	7/9/39-17/9/39	*kpt. pil.* Roman Czerniawski Pilots: 6 Observers: 2 + ?	RWD-13	
1 Plutron Łącznikowy Naczelnego Dowódcy Lotnictwa	2/9/39-18/9/39	*por. pil.* Jan Michalowski Pilots: 3 + ?	3 RWD-8	Losses: 1 RWD-8
II Pluton Łącznikowy Naczelnego Dowódcy Lotnictwa	5/9/39-11/9/39	*kpt pil.* Janusz Araszkiewicz Pilots: 4	2 RWD-8 1 Lublin R-XIII	After the loss of aircraft the personnel were impressed into I Pluton Łącznikowy Naczelnego Dowódcy Notnictwa
Pluton Łącznikowy Prezydium Rady Ministrów	31/8/39-?	*chor. pil.* Antoni Wolniczek Pilots: ?	3 Lublin R-XIIIC	Lack of information about the Pluton operations
Zespół Lotniczy Dowództwa Obrony Warszawy	16/9/39-27/9/39	*ppłk.* Mateusz Iżycki Pilots: 4 + ?	1 PZL P.11a 1 PZL P.7a 2 Lublin R-XIIID 9 RWD-8 2 Bak powered gliders 1 DH Moth 1 PZL-5	Losses: 1 Lublin R-XIII Evacuation: - PZL P.11a (23/9)[38] - DH Moth (23/9 - PZL P.7a (24/9)[39] - PZL-5 (25/9)[40] - PZL-46 *Sum*[41]
13 Eskadra Szkolna	25/9/39-6/10/39	*por. pil.* Edmund Piorunkiewicz Pilots: 3; Observers: 2	1 PWS-26 2 RWD-8	The last air unit of the 1939 campaign

Czech airmen also participated in the fighting of 1939. After the fall of Czechoslovakia some 1,000 airmen arrived in Poland. 190 of them stayed there, while the rest left for France in 6 transports. 93 of those who stayed joined the Wojsko Polskie on 31 August 1939. Some found their way to the Czechoslowaxka Eskadra Rozpoznawcza which commenced its formation on 4 September 1939 at Góra Puławska airfield near Puławy, with 60 airmen and 11 aircraft (Potex XXV and RWD-8). During the 1939 campaign the crews flew about a dozen reconnaissance sorties. The unit was captured by the Red Army on 17 September 1939. Five airmen volunteered to join I Pluton of Eskadra Cwiczebna Obserwatorów under *por. obs.* Zbigniew Osuchowski.[42] According to Czech sources personnel losses amounted to 4 killed and 6 wounded.

Fighter units on 1 September 1939

Dywizjon	Eskadra	PZL P.11c	PZL P.11a	PZL P.7a
III/1 (Brygada Pościgowa)	HQ	2	-	-
III/1 (BP)	111	7	2	-
III/1 (BP)	112	6	4	-
III/2 ('Armia Kraków')	121	10	-	-
III/2 ('Armia Kraków')	122	10	-	-
III/3 ('Armia Poznań')	HQ	2	-	-
III/3 ('Armia Poznań')	131	10	-	-
III/3 ('Armia Poznań')	132	10	-	-
III/4 ('Armia Pomorze')	HQ	2	-	-
III/4 ('Armia Pomorze')	141	6	4	-
III/4 ('Armia Pomorze')	142	10	-	-
III/5 (SGO 'Narew')	151	-	-	10
III/5 ('Armia Modlin')	HQ	-	-	-
III/5 ('Armia Modlin')	152	10	-	-
III/6 ('Armia Łódź')	HQ	2	-	-
III/6 ('Armia Łódź')	161	7	2	-
III/6 ('Armia Łódź')	162	-	-	10
IV/1 (Brygada Pościgowa)	HQ	2	0	0
IV/1 (BP)	113	5	5	-
IV/1 (BP)	114	6	4	-
IV/1 (BP)	123	-	-	10
TOTAL		**107**	**21**	**30**

Reconnaissance (ER) and Spotting (EO) Eskadras on 1 September 1939

Eskadra	Assignment	P.23B *Karaś*	Lublin R-XIIID	RWD-14 *Czapla*
13 EO	SGO 'Narew'	-	-	7
16 EO	Discretionary Aviation	-	7	-
23 EO	Armia 'Kraków'	-	-	7
24 ER	Armia 'Kraków'	10	-	-
26 EO	Armia 'Kraków'	-	7	-
31 ER	Armia 'Karpaty'	9	-	-
32 ER	Armia 'Łódź'	10	-	-
33 EO	Armia 'Poznań'	-	-	7
34 ER	Armia 'Poznań'	10	-	-
36 EO	Armia 'Poznań'	-	7	-
41 ER	Armia 'Modlin'	8	-	-
42 ER	Armia 'Pomorze'	10	-	-
43 OR	Armia 'Pomorze'	-	7	-
46 OR	Armia 'Pomorze'	-	7	-
51 ER	SGO 'Narew'	7	-	-
53 EO	Armia 'Modlin'	-	-	7
56 EO	Armia 'Karpaty'	-	7	-
63 EO	Armia 'Łódź'	-	-	7
66 EO	Armia 'Łódź'	-	7	-
TOTAL		**64**	**49**	**35**

383: *Two of at least ten RWD 14* Czaplas *which reached Rumania at the end of September 1939, seen here in Rumanian air force markings*

Bomber aviation on 1 September 1939			
Eskadra	**Assignment**	**P.37B *Łoś***	**P.23B *Karaś***
1 (21) EB	II Dywizjon/Brygada Bombowa	–	10
2 (22) EB	II Dywizjon/Brygada Bombowa	–	10
4 (64) EB	VI Dywizjon/Brygada Bombowa	–	10
5 (65) EB	VI Dywizjon/Brygada Bombowa	–	10
11 (211) EB	X Dywizjon/Brygada Bombowa	9	-
12 (212) EB	X Dywizjon/Brygada Bombowa	9	-
16 (216) EB	XV Dywizjon/Brygada Bombowa	9	-
17 (217) EB	XV Dywizjon/Brygada Bombowa	9	-
55 Samodzielna EB	Brygada Bombowa	–	10
TOTAL		**36**	**50**

Air Victories of Polish Pilots			
no.	**Name**	**Unit**	**Number of kills**
1.	*ppor.* Stanisław Skalski	142 EM[43] / III/4 DM[44]	4
2.	*por.* Wojciech Januszewicz	111 EM / BP[45]	4
3.	*ppor.* Hieronim Dudwał	113 EM / BP	3
4.	*ppor.* Włodzimierz Gedymin	131 EM / III/6 DM	3
5.	*kpt.* Adam Kowalczyk	IV/1 DM (HQ)/BP	3
6.	*por.* Marian Pisarek	141 EM / III/4 DM	3
7.	*ppor.* Czesław Główczyński	162 EM / III/6 DM	$2\frac{1}{2}$
8.	*ppor.* Tadeusz Sawicz	114 EM / BP	$2\frac{1}{3}$
9.	*ppor.* Władysław Gnyś	121 EM / III/2 DM	2
10.	*kpt.* Franciszek Jastrzębski	132 EM / III/3 DM	$2\frac{1}{3}$
11.	*kpt.* Mirosław Leśniewski	142 EM / III/4 DM	2
12.	*ppor.* Jan Malinski	132 EM / III/3 DM	2
13.	*kpr.* Kazimierz Mazur	132 EM / III/3 DM	2
14.	*mjr.* Mieczysław Mümler	III/3 HQ	2
15.	*por.* Stefan Okrzeja	112 EM / BP	2
16.	*ppor.* Karol Pniak	142 EM / III/4 DM	2
17.	*ppor.* Jan Pudlewicz	132 EM / III/3 DM	2
18.	*kpt.* Tadeusz Rolski	141 EM / III/4 DM	2
19.	*ppor.* Henryk Szczęsny	Wyższa Szkoła Pilotażu	2
20.	*ppor.* Stefan Wapniarek	132 EM / III/3 DM	2

The table includes only pilots with at least 2 confirmed kills. Fractions under $\frac{1}{3}$ were not counted.

Number of Polish Air Force front-line aircraft on 1 September 1939	
Fighter aircraft	158
Reconnaissance and spotting aircraft	148
Bomber aircraft	86
TOTAL:	392

1 Tadeusz H. Rolski – *Uwaga, wszystkie samoloty!* (*Attention, All Aircraft!*). Instytut Wydawniczy PAX. Warsaw 1974.
2 Stanisław Skalski – *Czarne krzyże nad Polską* (*Black Crosses over Poland*). Wydawnictwo MON. Warsaw 1975 (7th ed.)
3 LOT A II 15/1a. 16 Polish Institute and Sikorski Museum, London.
4 Stanisław Skalski ended the war at the rank of a Wing Commander with 22 enemy aircraft to his credit.
5 Adam Kirowski – *Lotnictwo polskie w 1939 roku* (*Polish Air Force in 1939*). Wydawnictwo MON. Warsaw 1962.
6 In the pre-war Polish Air Force it was the observer who commanded the aircraft.
7 From the decoration application filed by the Eskadra commander, W. Dawidek on 12 February 1947 in London. Via J. Pawlak – *Polskie eskadry w wojnie obronnej 1939* (*Polish Eskadras in the Defensive War of 1939*).
8 This move was somewhat affected by the fact that the Pluton's ground party had been captured by the Germans at Chelmno.
9 Popular informal name of Lublin R XIII.
10 The overwhelming superiority of the Luftwaffe from the very beginning of the war led to the notion among Polish ground troops that everything in the sky had to wear black crosses. Compare also footnote no.18.
11 Collective. *Lotnicy września* (*September Airmen*). Chapter "Maszerujemy do decydującej bitwy" ("We March for the Decisive Battle") – Kazimierz Sławinski. Instytut Wydawniczy "Nasza Ksiegarnia". Warsaw 1972.
12 Włodzimierz Gedymin – "Pod wielkopolskim niebem" ("Under the Sky of Wielkopolska"). From the book *Lotnicy września*.
13 A letter from *mjr* Mümler, commander of III/3 Dywizjon to J. Pawlak – *Polskie eskadry w wojnie obronnej 1939*.
14 Some sources claim the airfield was at Kleczew. The authors tend to accept the version documented by J. Pawlak.
15 Written account of Stanisław Martyni via J. Pawlak – *Polskie eskadry w wojnie obronnej 1939*.
16 Tomasz Kopański, Krzystof Sikora – *P.23 Karaś*, AJ Press, Danzig, 1996.
17 J. Pawlak – *Polskie eskadry w wojnie obronnej 1939*, based on a written account of Tadeusz Sokoliński (observer who was forced to land), PI&SM London.
18 According to the account of *por.* Czesław Malinowski, there were at least 8 P-43As at Okęcie and Bielany airfields. However, according to the exports analysis by A. Glass and W. Mazur (*Militaria* 1/99) 36 out of the 42 aircraft ordered had been despatched to Bulgaria, which throws doubt on the account of Malinowski as regards the number of P-43As still in Poland in 1939.
19 *Por pil.* Józef Brzezinski was the commander of 151 Eskadra Myśliwska.
20 Janusz Kędzierski – *Z kabiny obserwatora* (*From the Observer's Cockpit*). Wydawnictwo MON, Warsaw 1975.
21 As mentioned in the introduction of this chapter.
22 The exact number is difficult to establish, as aircraft of III/3 Dywizjon Myśliwski and those of training units were being evacuated at the same time.
23 He died of wounds on 18 March 1940.
24 Upon repair it returned to the unit.
25 In their report the Polish pilots erroneously claimed the aircraft as an Bf 110. In fact it was an He 111 of I./KG 152.
26 Undercarriage damaged during ferry flight to another airfield.
27 Quote from the 'general guidelines of air force use" developed by the Air Staff at the General Staff. Issued on 28 July 1939.
28 On 10 September it was decided to transfer four PZL P.23s of 1 Eskadra Bombowa and five of 2 Eskadra Bombowa to VI Dywizjon Bombowy. The personnel of II Dywizjon Bombowy would go to Rumania in order to collect Allied aircraft there.
29 Four *Karaś* aircraft would be transferred to 31 Eskadra. However, upon arrival at Cieszanów airfield it was found that 31 Eskadra had in fact left. Therefore *por. obs.* Jerzy Sukiennik, who led the unit, decided to continue to Lwów, where all aircraft were destroyed in an air raid.
30 The remaining aircraft of VI Dywizjon Bombowy were twice bombed at Hutniki airfield, on 14 and 15 September. As a result the unit lost all aircraft, and its personnel were orderd to proceed towards the Rumanian border.
31 On 7 September 1939 the crew of *kpt.* Dukszto from 16 Eskadra Bombowa attacked a Heinkel He 111 flying below and shot it down thanks to the element of surprise.
32 *Krótki zarys wojennej pracy eskadry sztabowej w czasie od 1/9–17/9 1939* (*Short Outline of the War Operations of the Eskadra Sztabowa between 1/9–17/9 1939*) by *kpt. pil.* Henryk Wirszyłło on 30 November 1939 in Paris.
33 The Potez aircraft were sent back to the Eskadra Ćwiczebna Pilotów of Szkoła Podchorążych Lotnictwa at Dęblin.
34 Grounded due to lack of fuel at Radziechowo airfield at Lwów (15 September 1939)
35 With exception of the aircraft of I Pluton (RWD-8, PWS-26) led by por obs Zbigniew Osuchowski.
36 On 6 September 1939 two *Karaś* aircraft with crews were transferred to Pluton Lotniczy of Warszawska Brygada Pancerno-Motorowa (Armoured-Motorised Brigade *Warsaw*).
37 This was a prototype, i.e. PZL P.11c with a 625 kW (850 hp) PZL-Bristol Mercury VIII engine. A decision was made to produce this version because 150 engines of the above type were in military storage. Initially they were intended to be used in the new PZL P-50 *Jastrząb* Polish fighter. However, in view of the unsatisfactory performance of that latter type, and the German threat, it was decided to build a batch of 90 P.11g aircraft. Externally the P.11g *Kobuz* differed from the P.11c with a reshaped engine cowling and a fully enclosed cockpit. The prototype was evacuated when the factory was requisitioned and armed by the air force. On 14 and 15 September *por.* Henryk Szczęsny scored two victories in it.
38 Two pilots: *ppłk.* M. Iżycki and *mjr* E. Wyrwicki, flew to Hungary in this aircraft.
39 The aircraft with two airmen on board (*kpr. pil.* Stanisław Rochmanski and *kpt. obs.* Franciszek Rybicki) was shot down by Red Army troops before reaching the Rumanian border. Both airmen were captured by the Soviets.
40 The aircraft flew to Hungary with two gliders on tow.
41 The PZL P-46 *Sum* was a development of the ubiquitous *Paraś*. 300 *Sums* had been ordered on 28 March 1939. The second *Sum* prototype was evacuated on 17 September to Rumania. On 26 September, under the pretext of ferrying the aircraft from Bucharest to the IAR factory at w Brasov the aircraft was 'hi-jacked' to besieged Warsaw with the orders for the commander of the defence of the city, *gen* Rómmel. The following day the *Sum* flew from Warsaw to Kowno (Kaunas) in Lithuania.
42 They included *plut. pil.* Josef Frantisek who later became an ace with the RAF. He was killed in the Battle of Britain with 17 victories to his credit, having flown with 303 (Polish) Squadron.
43 EM - Eskadra Myśliwska
44 DM - Dywizjon Myśliwski
45 BP - Brygada Pościgowa

384: *Destroyed railway line seen from the cockpit of an Dornier Do 17*

POLISH NAVAL AVIATION

After the First World War Poland initially had no access to the sea. This was only acquired in 1920, when in line with the Versailles Treaty the country received lands north-west of Danzig (Gdańsk). This was a narrow strip of coast along the Hel Peninsula, some 30 km long. The foundations of Polish naval aviation, however, had been laid over a year earlier. In May 1919 a staff section was established at the Departament Spraw Morskich Ministerstwa Spraw Wojskowych, which in 1921 became the Referat Lotnictwa Morskiego. It was headed by *por. mar.*[1] *pil. obs.* Karol Trzaska-Durski. Two questions were regarded as priorities: finding properly trained military staff, and providing suitable equipment for the future naval aviation. Naval aviation personnel came mainly via the ex-Russian imperial naval air service, and Austro-Hungarian air forces. Since at the time the future Referat Lotnictwa Morskiego was established (1919) Poland did not yet have access to the sea, it was decided to focus on aircraft equipment for the river monitor flotilla based at Pińsk in Polesie region. Purchase of 6 Oeffag hydroplanes from the Wiener Neustadt factory was considered. This idea never came to fruition, however.

The Versailles Treaty regulations gave the legal opportunity to take over the territory of Pomorze Gdańskie (Gdańsk Pomerania) from the Germans. On 10 February 1920 Polish troops reached Puck, where the Germans had left a naval aviation base. The same day a symbolic act of marriage to the sea was performed. *Gen.* broni Józef Haller, standing by the hydroplane slipway in the Puck base, threw a golden ring into the waves of the Baltic Sea. I Batalion Morski under *kpt. mar.* Konstanty Jacynicz was the first military unit to be stationed at the base. The base included 4 hangars, a grass airfield of 700 × 350 m, and the sole concrete way for handling of wheeled hydroplanes in Poland, size 800 × 10 m. The location was very convenient for a hydroplane base. Puck is located on the bay coast, with calm waters, thus enabling relatively easy take-offs and landings. Apart from the above mentioned facilities, the base had no air equipment, apart from some scrapped aircraft, which the Germans failed to remove to bases at Pilau (Pilawa), Danzig (Gdańsk) or (Mrzeżyno). They had the right to do this according to the Versailles Treaty. The commander of the I Batalion Morski, *kpt. mar.* K. Jacynicz ordered the formation of a Pluton Lotniczy within the unit, with *kpt. pil.* Wiktoryn Kaczyński as the commander. The Pluton would bring the airfield to usable condition. On 27 May 1920 Kaczyński was appointed commandant of the naval aviation unit at Puck, and on 1 July 1920 it was renamed Baza Lotnictwa Morskiego, reporting to Dowództwo Wybrzeża Morskiego. Lack of aircraft resulted in closer inspection of the wrecks left behind by the Germans. Thanks to the efforts of Polish technicians, two of these were made serviceable. Thus a Friedrichshafen FF 33H floatplane and a Fokker D VII fighter became the first aircraft of the Polish naval aviation. The Friedrichshafen, flown by *chor. pil.* Andrzej Zubrzycki, took off for the navy's inaugural flight over the Bay of Puck on 15 July 1920. This date became the unit day.

385: *LeO H135B3 from Eskadra 'Rugia' in 1930. Note the unit emblem – known as światowid.* Por. pil. *K. Szalewicz (in naval uniform) is standing next to the emblem (Konarski)*

386: *View of aircraft workshops, with hangars in the background. Puck, early twenties (MLP – Kraków)*

387: *Review of the Baza Lotnictwa Morskiego by the Dowódca Wybrzeża Morskiego* płk. mar. *J. Świrskiego – 20 August 1920 (Konarski)*

388: *Friedrichshafen FF 33 E no. 8 on Puck port canal (MLP – Kraków)*

389: *Friedrichshafen FF 33E takes off from Zatoka Pucka waters (Olejko)*

390: *The same aircraft in the Puck base, on a trolley (Olejko)*

391: *Cadets of the Morska Szkoła Pilotów in front of a Hansa Brandenburg NW no. 6. Puck 20 October 1921 (Konarski)*

392: *Hansa Brandenburg NW no. 6 leaving Puck base, 1920 (Olejko)*

393: *Another Albatros B IIa, this time no. 3, in the Puck hangar (Konarski)*

394: *Nieuport Macchi M 9 no. 2-3 at the airfield in Puck (Olejko)*

395: *A group of sailors at Puck by the first Macchi M 9 to be assembled, no. 23931. The aircraft is in a pre-1923 colour scheme. Until that time the Macchis continued to wear Italian roundels on wing and fuselage (MLP – Kraków)*

The Fokker was less fortunate, as it was burnt by unidentified persons (probably members of a German nationalist organisation) at the airfield in Danzig (Gdańsk) Wrzeszcz (Danzig-Langfuhr).

First purchases for the naval aviation were made in Danzig (Gdańsk), which had the status of a free city. With help from the company of Ing. Utgoff, four floatplanes (three Friedrichshafens in FF 33E, FF 33L, and FF 49b versions, and a Lübeck Travemünde F 4) were bought. At the same time a training Albatros B II was transferred to Puck from Szkoła Obserwatorów at Toruń. During the inspection of the base by the Dowódca Wybrzeża Morskiego *kmdr* Jerzy Świrski on 20 August 1920 the unit boasted 6 aircraft of various types.

July 1920 also brought the decision to establish an Eskadra Szkolna with the task of conversion training for land aviation pilots, and subsequently of training for officers and men from other services. Subsequently the unit received more aircraft: Sablatnig F 5, Hansa Brandenburg NW hydroplanes and DFW C IV (two), Albatros D V, Albatros B II (two) landplanes. These aircraft formed the nucleus of the Morska Eskadra Obserwacyjna, under *kpt. pil.* Władysław Misinski. The main task of the Eskadra was to patrol the Polish border, both at sea and on land.

A naval aviation development plan was prepared at the end of 1920, with the intention of a dynamic development. However, the realities were such that the plan would never be fulfilled. Air accidents during 1921 resulted in the loss of the Friedrichshafen FF 33L, FF 49b and one Albatros B II. This reduced the inventory to 8 aircraft, and these were far from new (for example the Friedrichshafen FF 33H was earmarked for scrapping in 1920). It may be noticed that the first purchases for the Polish naval aviation were an attempt to bring it to combat readiness as quickly as possible, but it is hard to define a concept of its shape. The first attempt to unify the equipment of the naval aviation followed in 1921, as in 1920 the Italian Military Mission in Poland had offered to sell Italian Nieuport Macchi M 7 and M 9 hydroplanes. The Italian offer was accepted at the end of 1920, when orders started to be placed for aircraft equipment via the Rodolfo Prokopowski company of Rome. On 3 December that year order no. 351/20 for 5 new Nieuport Macchi M 9 aircraft plus spares was placed. A subsequent order (no. 93/21) from early February 1921 called for two more Macchi M 9 and 9 of the new FBA S 4 hydroplanes plus spares. The spares were planned to be used to assemble three more Macchi M 9 and 4 FBA S4 hydroplanes. The total purchase was brought to Poland at the end of July 1921 on the Italian ship *Rosaalba*. According to the contract the aircraft would be erected by the Italians (this did not apply to the aircraft to be assembled from spares), but they delayed conclusion of the contract. In spite of numerous letters, arrival of the experienced Italian fitters was postponed. As a result, at the beginning of 1922 the Polish started assembly of seven Macchi M 9s themselves! Official reception of the first aircraft took place on 10 April 1922. However, the condition of the aircraft raised some questions. At the end of June that year the Italian team finally arrived, but included only one pilot, Adolfo Frigeiro, and one fitter, Vittorio Pradolini. They decided to dismantle the assembled aircraft and re-assemble these again. The first one was complete on 14 July and an unofficial first flight was made. However, the verdict was poor, as the condition of the aircraft, stored for almost a year in unheated hangars, left much to be desired. The situation with the FBA S4 was even worse. After the first one was erected (14 July 1922) it was found that these too required a major inspection. In the case of the FBA this was never done, and eventually at the beginning of 1923, due to excessive cost this idea was dropped. The Macchis were more fortunate, as they would be overhauled. Work on the first five M 9s was completed at the beginning of second half of 1923. Stress testing was carried out, and the M 9s were certificated for use. In October 1923 one of the machines crashed, killing the crew of two. After that accident the remaining aircraft were sent back to the Centralne Zaklady Lotnicze in order to be strengthened. The Macchis remained in first line use until the end of 1926, without gaining the enthusiasm of their pilots.

Meanwhile changes in the organisation of the Polish naval aviation took place. In November 1921 the Lotnictwo Morskie was established. This was achieved by merging the Baza Lotnictwa Morskiego with Morska Szkoła Pilotów (both located in Puck). In 1922 the unit was situated in a difficult organisational position. Due to subsequent reorganisations it had double reporting lines: to the Navy and to the Departament IV Żeglugi Powietrznej of the Ministerstwo Spraw Wojskowych. This problem was solved personally by the Minister Spraw Wojskowych, *gen. dyw.* Kazimierz Sosnkowski who, by the orders of 29 July 1922, incorporated the unit into 2 Pułk Lotniczy based in Krakow, in southern Poland. The name of the unit was changed to: Detaszowany Dyon Lotniczo-Zwiadowczy based at Puck. *Mjr obs.* Jan Bielawski was appointed the commander of the new unit. A tragic accident occurred on 15 August 1922 during the Soldier's Day ceremonies which included an air show. Bombing with live munitions from a Lübeck-Travemünde F4 floatplane was one of the display features. A manually dropped 12.5 kg bomb exploded among the public, killing 5 and injuring 13 people. The crew was expelled from the service.

1923 brought another change of the unit's name. By the orders of the Ministerstwo Spraw Wojskowych of 16 March the Morski Dywizjon Lotniczy was formed. Logistically it reported to Departament IV Żeglugi Powietrznej of the Ministerstwo Spraw Wojskowych, and for training and operational purposes it reported to Dowództwo Floty i Służb Nabrzeżnych. *Plk. obs.* Antoni Leonkow was appointed the new commander. The same year the Head of Departament Żeglugi Powietrznej of the Ministerstwo

396: *Albatros B II no. 12 at Puck airfield – 1921 (Konarski)*

397: Por. pil. *A. Stempkowski in the cockpit of Albatros D V 'white 5'. The photo was taken at Puck (Konarski)*

398: *Friedrichshafen FF 33E no. 8 in a hangar of Baza Lotnictwa Morskiego in Puck (Konarski)*

399: *Left to right:* plut. pil. *S. Stankiewicz and Italian airmen in front of the same Macchi M 9 (no. 2-3), 14 November 1924 (Konarski)*

400: *Aerial view of the base at Puck. The photo was taken at the turn of 1925. A Swedish Junkers can be seen at the bottom (MLP – Kraków)*

401: *A group of officers from Morski Dywizjon Lotniczy by a Lioré et Olivier LeO H 13B. The photo was taken in late 1920s (Konarski)*

Spraw Wojskowych *Gen.* Francois-Leon Leveque included new hydroplanes in a major order for air equipment from France. In 1924 he was replaced by *gen. bryg.* Włodzimierz Ostoja-Zagórski. This change did not affect realisation of the French contract. After the unfortunate purchase of Italian aircraft Polish naval aviation was in a very difficult situation in terms of equipment. Four Lioré et Olivier LeO H-13B short range reconnaissance flying boats were the first to arrive in Poland. They were brought in November 1924 by ORP 'Warta' military transport vessel. They were erected in March 1925 and received numbers in the range 1-1 to 1-4. At the same time numbers were issued for the overhauled Macchi M 9s (2-1 to 2-8). LeO H 13Bs were first flown by a factory pilot, Lucien Bourdin, who had supervised their assembly. *Ppor. pil.* A. Stempkowski was the Polish test pilot.

Before the LeO H 13Bs were introduced into service in August 1924, Morski Dywizjon Lotniczy suffered another loss. The Lübeck Travemünde F 4, flown by *chor. pil.* A. Zubrzycki caught fire in flight. The aircraft was destroyed, and its pilot drowned.

Largest deliveries of equipment from France took place in 1926-27. Deliveries to Puck during that time included 6 Schreck FBA-17HE2 flying boats, 12 Schreck FBA-17HMT2 (including two which received civil registrations, and the names LOPP and Lubliniak), 8 Latham 43 HB3 patrol-bomber and 4 CAMS 30E training-reconnaissance flying boats. These aircraft received the following serials: FBA-17HE2 (4-1 to 4-4), FBA-17HMT2 (5-1 to 5-10), Latham (3-1 to 3-8), CAMS (2-1 to 2-4). The latter were designated with the same numbers as the Macchi M 9s as the Macchis were withdrawn from service and the CAMS's took over their serials. Lioré et Olivier LeO H-135B3s were the last type to be introduced into service in the Dywizjon, delivered in 1927, and serialled 6-1 to 6-7.

At that time primary duties of the Dywizjon included patrolling of Polish territorial waters, warship co-operation, submarine detection, and rescue missions if necessary.

A new internal structure of the unit was introduced in 1926. I and II Eskadra Morska Obserwacyjna were formed: no. I for short range reconnaissance, and no. II for long range reconnaissance. Both achieved combat capability on 1 July 1926. In February of the subsequent year another change of the unit commander took place. This post was given to the former head of the Referat Lotnictwa Morskiego Departamentu Spraw Morskich who laid foundations for the naval aviation (as early as 1919), *kmdr por. pil. obs.* Karol Trzaska-Durski. He understood the special nature of naval aviation, contributing a lot to the future of the unit. Previous commanders came mostly from the land based aviation which led to conflicts in the chain of command. Unfortunately, 1927 saw the beginning of a series of flying accidents in the Morski Dywizjon Lotniczy. *Kpt. pil. obs.* Jan Malicki was killed on 23 May 1927 during aerobatics in the Schreck FBA 17HMT2 amphibian no. 5-1. The Schreck FBA 17HE2 no. 4-1 crashed during landing on 5 December 1929 due to an error of judgement of height by the pilot, *por. pil.* Kazimierz Szalewicz. The observer, *ppor.* Zygmunt Kawecki-Dolęga was killed in the crash. On 11 April 1930 another Schreck FBA 17HE2, no. 4-3, crashed. *Ppor. pil. obs.* Zygmunt Majewski and a fitter, Bernard Łukaszyk, were killed. Accidents in 1930-31 took two more lives.

The end of the 1920s was not marked only by accidents, but also by systematic expansion of the unit, which underwent organisational changes. By 1928 the Dywizjon included Morska Eskadra Wielosilnikowa, Morska Eskadra Obserwacyjna, Sekcja Žwiczen, Park Lotniczy, Oddział Portowy, Sekcja Radiolotnicza, and Sekcja Foto. In 1930, together with another change of title, a system of emblems was introduced. I Eskadra Liniowa received the name 'Wiking' and an emblem in the form of a dragon's head as fitted on a Viking boat. The Eskadra used Latham 43HB3 flying boats. II Eskadra Liniowa 'Rugia', flying LeO H13Bs and LeO H135B3s used an emblem of Swiatowid, a pagan god. Eskadra Szkolna which used Schreck FBA 17 HE2 and FBA 17HMT2 amphibians carried an emblem in the form of a question mark.

In 1928 a small outfit was extracted from the Dywizjon and posted inland. That was the establishment of the Rzeczny Pluton Lotniczy, the history of which is described below. The second half of the 1920s was also the period when Polish naval aviation was visited by many European airmen. Poland was visited by aircraft from the following countries: Italy (Macchi M19-1925), Denmark (Brandenburg HM 1-1925 and 1926), Britain (Blackburn Iris, Saro Valkyrie, Supermarine Southampton in 1927 and 1930), Germany (Dornier Wal-1929), France (1931), Czechoslovakia (1934), Latvia (1933 and 1936), and Sweden (1934 and 1936). Polish aircraft also visited other countries.

As time went by aircraft wear increased. Extensively used equipment was becoming dangerous to operate, and it was necessary to replace it. However, the economic situation during the Great Depression did not favour the process and at the beginning of the 1930s Poland had no funds available for this. On the other hand, growing numbers of write-offs for technical reasons resulted in an embarrassing situation in Morski Dywizjon Lotniczy. The gap was to be filled in 1930 by delivery of five Bartel BM 5c trainers (used in the naval Dywizjon as Bartel BM 300), but this was hardly even an interim solution as, apart from their original role, it has to be remembered that they were landplanes and could not be fitted with floats.

Polish naval aviation found itself in a difficult situation again, as it had been at the beginning of the 1920s. Even though the HQ received various offers from aircraft factories, these rarely got beyond the project stage. The most promising proposal seemed to be the one

402: *Unofficial first flight of the aircraft no. 23931 on 14 July 1922 (MLP – Kraków)*

403: *Nieuport Macchi M 9 no. 2-5. Aircraft of the type had their serials applied without separating the type prefix. Thus the Macchi M 9 had the serial applied as '25', rather than '2-5'. The photo was taken in the Puck hangar (MLP – Kraków)*

404: *Lübeck Travemunde F 4, early 1920s (Konarski)*

405: *Transporting the LeO H 13B no. 2 (4-2) (MLP – Kraków)*

406: *Beaching of the LeO H 13B no. 4-1 (MLP – Kraków)*

407: *LeO H 13B flying boat on a slipway at Puck base, late 1920s (Konarski)*

408: *LeO H 13B no. 4 in flight over Puck (MLP – Kraków)*

409: *CAMS 30E flying boat at the beach in Gdynia. Note the different way of serial application than on the Macchi M 9 (Konarski)*

410: *Hanriot HD 28S used in the Morski Dywizjon Lotniczy. This was a medical version of the training aircraft. The aircraft used around 1928 in Puck was designated 30-14S (Konarski)*

411: *Officers from the Puck unit by a Lioré et Olivier LeO H 135B3 (Konarski)*

412: *Lioré et Olivier LeO H 135B3 from Eskadra Obserwacyjna, Puck 1929 (Konarski)*

413: *One of the British aircraft – Saro A3 N 186 Valkyrie – visiting the base at Puck on 24 August 1927 (Konarski)*

414: *Another visit of a British design in Poland. A Latvian Fairey Seal on 24 June 1934 (Konarski)*

415: *Latham 43HB3 from Eskadra 'Wiking' on the beach at Gdynia (Konarski)*

416: *Hoisting a Latham 43HB3 flying boat from the water (Konarski)*

from Lublin-based Zakłady Mechaniczne Plage i Laśkiewicz. Initially the company offered to licence-build Fokker aircraft or those from one of the French companies (CAMS, LeO, Villiers). When this idea did not meet a favourable response, the Lublin company offered in 1930 to convert their Lublin R-VIII aircraft, already used by the land based aviation, for naval use. According to the order from Kierownictwo Marynarki Wojennej from 1931 the Plage i Laśkiewicz company would convert four Lublin R-VIIIs. Conversion would include the prototype, powered by an 18-cylinder Lorriane-Dietrich18 Kd engine, and three production R-VIIIa's with Hispano-Suiza 12 Lb engines. As compared to the land-based version, the naval variant had floats and a reshaped rudder. Eventually three aircraft were converted, and the fourth was reduced to spares. The Lorriane-Dietrich-powered aircraft was designated Lublin R-VIII bis and received the code number 801. The two remaining ones were designated R-VIII ter, and coded 802 and 803. Another name sometimes applied to this version was Lublin R-VIII hydro. The aircraft entered service in 1933, and two of them survived until the 1939 campaign. At the same time the Lublin company was working on a new aircraft for the land-based aviation – the Lublin R-XIV. The company also prepared a naval variant of the aircraft, designated Lublin R-XV, but the military authorities expressed no interest. Lublin R-XIV became the forerunner of the R-XIII. The latter's prototype was converted from the last of the batch of 15 R-XIVs, which received the type number 54 and consecutive serial numbers 1 to 15. It is interesting to note that the same aircraft, no. 54-15 would be converted to a floatplane version in the autumn of 1931. Tested in Morski Dywizjon Lotniczy it earned favourable opinions, which led to the placing of the first order for a batch designated Lublin R-XIII bis/hydro. This included three aircraft, coded 701, 702, 703. The prototype R-XIII no. 54-15 (in fact a Lublin R-XIV) was later re-converted to land-based standard. During trials at Puck it was coded 700.

Interestingly, this aircraft was involved in an unlikely incident. During trials at the Instytut Badan Technicznych Lotnictwa flight testing was conducted by a well known aerobatic pilot, *płk.* Jerzy Kossowski. During an aerobatic performance the control stick locking bolt broke, leaving the stick in the hands of the pilot. *Płk* Kossowski bailed out safely, and the aircraft landed itself, coming to a halt in a ditch. This event led the designer, Jerzy Rudlicki, who previously omitted the number XIII as unlucky, to choose this designation for the converted version of the Lublin R-XIV. Thus one of the most widely used Polish pre-war aircraft was born (a total of 285 R-XIVs and R-XIIIs were built). Another order for Morski Dywizjon Lotniczy equipment was placed with the Plage i Laśkiewicz company on 5 May 1933. It called for 10 Lublin R-XIIIs in the ter/hydro version. The aircraft delivered to Puck were coded 704 to 713. As compared to the R-XIII bis/hydro version (aircraft nos. 701-703) which had wooden floats, the ter/hydro had all-metal Short's floats. Another order, for 6 R-XIII Gs, was placed a year later. Moreover, the company declared it would deliver one aircraft in the land-based version, to make up for the failure to fulfil the Lublin R-VIII bis/hydro contract. As mentioned before Morski Dywizjon Lotniczy failed to receive its fourth R-VIII hydro (no. 804) at that time.

The R-XIII G did not differ much from the R-XIII ter. The aircraft received numbers 714 to 719, and the land-based version number 720. They were delivered during 1934, and the last R-XIII G arrived at the unit on 15 April 1935. The aircraft were ferried to the Dywizjon by air, by the unit's pilots. Usually they were ferried by *por. pil.* Adolf Stempkowski, *por. pil.* Józef Rudzki, and *por. pil.* Roman Borowiec.

To complete this review of Polish naval aircraft of the early 1930s, we have to mention one more type, the Lublinie R-XX twin-engined torpedo-reconnaissance floatplane. The offer to build this aircraft was made to the Navy in mid-1931. The competition included the PZL 18, and the PWS 62. In 1932 the R-XX was selected, and the completed prototype was shipped to Puck in mid-1934. Upon assembly there it was found that the aircraft was tail-heavy and required modification. After these were introduced it was test flown in 1935, and subsequently accepted into the inventory of the Dywizjon at Puck with number 806. The same year a contract was signed for construction of 6 more. This was never fulfilled, however. At the end of November 1935, due to continuous problems with the prototype and to the bankruptcy of the Plage i Laśkiewicz company the contract was cancelled. The Lublin R-XX prototype survived until the outbreak of war. The unserviceable, hangared aircraft was comandeered by the Germans. Its fate is not known. Thus in 1930s the Polish naval aviation used mainly Polish designed aircraft. The core consisted of Lublin R-XIIIs, light aircraft with rather short range (approximately 450 km). During their operation there were several incidents where these aircraft were forced to alight at sea due to lack of fuel. On 5 March 1934 the Lublin R-VIII ter/hydro nr 803 flown by *por. pil.* Roman Borowiec had to alight near Hel. The aircraft was cruising on the Puck-Libawa-Gotland-Puck route. Upon passing Libau (Libawa) the pilot headed for Gotland, but due to worsening weather he decided to turn back. This extended journey resulted in a forced landing. The aircraft was located and subsequently towed back to Puck by the ship ORP *Mewa.* A similar event happened on 10 August of the same year. Lublin R-XIII ter/hydro from Eskadra Szkolna, flown by *por. pil.* Eligiusz Ceceniowski had to alight near Gdynia due to lack of fuel. Aircraft of the naval Dywizjon and torpedo-boat ORP *Kujawiak* were despatched to search for it. Once located the aircraft was towed to Hel, but another aircraft had to alight due to lack of fuel during the rescue operation. This was Lublin R-XIII ter/hydro nr 710 flown by *por. pil.* Kazimierz Szalewicz which alighted at (Pilawa) Pilau in East Prussia, part of the German Third Reich. The crew was arrested, and subsequently released after the personal intervention of

417: *Latham 43HB3 no. 3-1 rolled on a trolley towed behind a tracked tractor (Konarski)*

418: *The tractor with its crew photographed by the Latham no. 3-1 (Konarski)*

419: *Forward fuselage of the Latham 43HB3 with an emblem of the Eskadra Szkolna. Puck – 13 August 1930 (Konarski)*

Göring. The aircraft returned three days later with its crew to Puck. A number of airmen who participated in a large naval-air exercise during the autumn of 1936 were less fortunate, however. Three Lublin R-VIIIs and 6 Lublin R-XIIIs participated. In the exercise during which a sudden change of weather occurred, the heading and force of the wind changing. All the aircraft, with exception of the R-XIII G/hydro nr 714 flown by *bosman pil.* Edmund Piotrzkowski, were forced to alight at sea. Three R-XIIIs alighted relatively close to the coast and there was no problem saving these. The remaining two R-XIIIs alighted some 70 miles north of Hel but whilst landing on rough seas, float supports were broken, pushing the floats under the wings, which prevented sinking. The aircraft were half-filled with water. The crews were rescued by German fishing boats, which attempted to take the aircraft in tow. During these towing attempts the aircraft started to sink, and the boats' engines were not powerful enough to tow the R-XIIIs. Given the situation the crews cut off the lines and both aircraft sank. The heavier Lublin R-VIIIs and their crews were more fortunate. They avoided major damage during alighting on rough seas. Two were towed to the Bay of Puck by a Polish destroyer, and the third drifted to the German port of Pilawa (Pilau).

As already mentioned, in 1928 a small unit was extracted from the naval aviation, under *por. pil. obs.* Ludwik Baczyński. On 10 May 1928 the commander of Morski Dywizjon Lotniczy, kmdr. *ppor. pil. obs.* Karol Trzaska-Durski issued official orders to form Pluton Rzeczny Wodnopłatowców. By subsequent orders of 24 July 1928 the Pluton was reporting to Flotylla Pinska, while remaining organisationally within the structures of the naval aviation. Ferrying of equipment commenced on 4 June 1928, when two Schreck FBA-17HMT2 amphibians, serials 5-2 and 5-4 flew to Pińsk. Schreck FBA-17HMT2 nr 5-8 was the third to arrive there, on 23 June. These were not the first aircraft to alight on the Pina river. During two previous years aircraft of the naval Dywizjon participated in exercises in this area. Amphibians were the most suitable equipment, as they had a shallow draught. Rzeczny Pluton Lotniczy was based at Port Wojenny in Pińsk. The primary problem for the personnel of the unit was the lack of proper engineering facilities. There were no hangars. Tarpaulin hangars were brought to Pińsk in an attempt to solve the problem. Eventually, out of eight as planned, at least one was actually brought. A real hangar was not complete until 1932. At the turn of 1928 Schreck no. 5-4 was sent back to Puck, replaced by another machine. At the same time expansion of the unit was under consideration for the first time, from 1 to 3 plutons plus HQ aircraft (a total of 10 aircraft). This plan was not put into practice at that time, however. Primary duties of the Pluton included naval artillery spotting and co-operation with land-based units. In June 1929 the Schreck FBA 17 HMT2 nr 5-7 crashed, and was consequently written off. Initially the force of the Pluton was between 2 and 4 aircraft. On 22 March 1930 the commander was changed, with *Ppor. obs.* Karol Białowąs appointed the new commander. In the summer of that year it was decided to test the possibility of using land-based aircraft. To this end two PWS 5T2 aircraft of 43 Eskadra Towarzysząca, from 4 Pułk Lotniczy were moved to Pińsk. However, the problems caused by the marshy ground resulted in abandonment of this concept. Another change in command took place in 1931, when *por. obs.* Władysław Dawidek was appointed commander. In 1932 the unit received the Lublin R-XIII bis/hydro no. 701. The aircraft was delivered by rail. It featured flat-bottom wooden floats. In April 1933 the aircraft crashed. Struts broke during landing so the floats fell off and the aircraft started to sink. Quick action saved the aircraft which had its floats replaced with all-metal ones after the accident. Soon after that the unfortunate R-XIII no. 701 suffered further damage. During take-off its pilot hit a log floating under the surface, which punctured one of the floats. This incident led *kontradm.* Unrug to file a critical note which resulted in withdrawing this type of aircraft from the Pińsk area. 1933 saw expansion of organisational structures. The Pluton was expanded into the Rzeczna Eskadra Lotnicza, from 1 January 1934 reporting organisationally do Flotylla Pinska. In 1935 *kpt. mar. pil. obs.* Stefan Kryński was appointed the new commander, he would later be the ADC to the President of Poland. In August 1935 Schrecks nos. 5-2 and 5-6 were both damaged within a week. Together with the Schreck no. 5-11 they were struck off charge in February 1936. The equipment of the Eskadra was badly worn by that time, as most aircraft had been in use for at least 10 years, the unit having only two amphibians left (nos. 5-3 and 5-10), also under repair. At the beginning of 1936 three more Schrecks moved to Pińsk (nos. 5-4, 5-8, 5-9) and the Lublin R-XIII G/hydro no. 718 with wheel undercarriage. In the autumn of 1936 *ppor. obs.* M. Tymosławski with *st. bosman pil.* H. Wiechciński, flying the R-XIII violated Soviet airspace, which led to an official protest note to the Polish government. The situation in terms of equipment did not change by the end of 1937. No aircraft were lost, but their condition deteriorated at a steady pace. Attempts to cure this situation included probing of the American, French, and British markets. In June 1936 *kpt. pil. obs.* Stefan Kryński went to Britain. The Poles were interested in two types of aircraft: Vickers Supermarine Walrus and Saunders Roe A 17 Cutty Sark. Air Ministry assistant S/Ldr Boyle considered that in his opinion neither of the aircraft would meet the Polish requirements. In spite of that *kpt.* Kryński met representatives of both companies. He was at Southampton on 3 July 1936, and at Cowes on the Isle of Wight the following day with both companies he made initial flights, and found that the Walrus had too deep a draught, while the Cutty Sark had too long a take-off run for the Polish conditions. The explanation was simple – the British did not need river-based aircraft, only sea-based ones. Eventually it was the lack of funds, and not the lack of suitable equipment, that led to temporary disbandment of the Eskadra Rzeczna at Pińsk. Under orders from Szef Kierownictwa Marynarki Wojennej the last commander of the Eskadra, *kpt. obs.* Eustachy Szczepaniuk, disbanded the unit at the end of 1937. Disassembled aircraft were sent

420: *Latham 43HB3 no. 3-4. The personnel in front of the aircraft are probably from I Eskadra (Olejko)*

421: *Latham on a transport trolley in the Puck base. Serial of the aircraft unknown (Olejko)*

422: *Schreck FBA 17HE2 flying boat no. 4-4 (Olejko)*

423: *Schreck FBA 17HMT2 patrol flying boat no. 5-3. The photo was taken at Pińsk, the base of Rzeczna Eskadra Lotnicza (Konarski)*

424: *Schreck FBA 17 HMT2 no. 5-2 hoisted in the Pińsk port (Konarki)*

425: *Lublin R XIII bis/hydro no. 702 used for blind flying training, 1933 (Konarski)*

426: *Schreck FBA 17HMT2 no. 5-2 under a canvas tent-hangar. The photo was taken in Polesie province. Note the tank fitted to the side of the fuselage next to the cockpit. It was used to carry anti-mosquito agent (Konarski)*

427: *'A military aeroplane' always makes a nice background for a souvenir photo. In the background is the Schreck FBA 17HMT2 no. 5-5. Note the way the undercarriage is retracted (Olejko)*

428: Kpt. mar. *W. Macioch, Commandant of the Naval Port at Pińsk, by the Schreck FBA 17 HMT2 no. 5-4 (Konarski)*

429: *PWS 5T2 aircraft from 43 Eskadra Towarzysz1ca which was technically part of 4 Pułk Lotniczy in Toruń but operated in 1930 over Polesie within the Rzeczna Eskadra Lotnicza. Stachów nad Prypeci1, 21 July 1930 (Konarski)*

back to Puck by rail. Even though attempts were made to reform the unit, this was not made until the outbreak of war.

A concept to equip some vessels with on-board catapults, hoists and aircraft was put forward at the end of the 1920s. At that time two designs were developed to fulfil this demand. The first, built at the beginning of 1930 was the PZL-H amphibian (later designated PZL-12), designed by Zygmunt Puławski, the creator of the famous P-fighters. Initially the amphibian was developed as a private venture, built at the company's expense. The aircraft was first flown by its designer in February 1931 in Warsaw, but on 21 March tragedy struck. During another test flight the aircraft crashed in the centre of Warsaw, killing Puławski. The accident resulted in abandonment of further work on the design. At the same time Jerzy Nikol started project work on an amphibian designated A-2. Wind tunnel tests were completed in 1934, and construction of the prototype commenced in 1936 in Morski Dywizjon Lotniczy workshops at Puck. This was completed in the spring of 1939, and the prototype was first flown on 4 March. Further testing continued until the outbreak of war. After the 1939 campaign the amphibian, anchored at Hel, was also commandeered by the Germans. After overhaul it was used as D-GOTZ at Rostock.

1937 again painfully revealed equipment shortages. The aircraft in use were nearing the end of their useful life, and attempts to find and purchase proper equipment abroad were ineffective. In this situation the HQ of the Navy decided to adopt a temporary solution, purchasing five RWD 17W aircraft. The RWD 17 was first flown in 1937 with an in-line engine. The floatplane variant, designated by the 'W' suffix was developed a year later. Initially designated RWD 17bis it received a 160 hp Bramo Sh 14a radial engine. The prototype RWD 17W was first flown with wheeled undercarriage and registered as SP-BPB. After successful tests on floats the navy decided to purchase the aircraft. They were produced prior to the outbreak of war, but none arrive at the coast. Only the prototype was in Morski Dywizjon Lotniczy. After the outbreak of war it was evacuated to the Hel Peninsula, where it was hidden in woods on its wheeled trolley. The aircraft survived in its hiding place virtually until the end of the siege of the Peninsula. On 30 September 1939 two officers attempted to use it to escape to Sweden. Unfortunately, the aircraft, flown by *ppor. mar.* Juliusz Bilewicz, crashed a few minutes after take-off. The unfortunate airmen were rescued.

Undoubtedly the greatest emotions were raised before the war by the purchase of Cant Z 506B floatplanes in Italy. The very selection of the type of aircraft was controversial. It was argued whether or not an aircraft of this class would be useful in the Baltic Sea. If we look at the planned supplies to the naval aviation in general, then a certain concept appears. The Navy leaders assumed that apart from the Cants other new types would be introduced into service. These would include the previously mentioned RWD 17Ws, Nikol A-2 amphibians and two more types: the maritime version of the LWS 3H *Mewa* trainer-spotter and the RWD 22 reconnaissance-torpedo aircraft. Work on the latter was at the design stage, and the prototype construction would not start until the outbreak of war. The following numbers of aircraft were planned to be introduced into service at the end of the 1930s: eighteen Cant Z 506Bs, six RWD 17W, sixteen LWS 3H *Mewas*, twelve RWD 22, and several Nikol A-2 amphibians.

As regards the Cant deal, one can notice that the Italian market fell within the Navy's area of interest already in the first half of the 1930s. At that time Italian companies placed many trade offers. In 1937 the Italians presented another offer, including specifications of the following aircraft: Caproni 124, Cant Z 501, Z 506, Z 508, Fiat MF 6, MF 10, Macchi MC 72, MC 77, and Aero Macchi C 94. The offer was reinforced by the written proposal for the Cant Z 506. The Italian offer had competition from the Dutch (Fokker T IVa and T VIIIW). But the performance of the Z 506 was superior, although it was more expensive. At the end of 1937 the decision to start talks with the Italians was taken. Initially the negotiations were delayed due to differing views on the terms of payment. Eventually the contract for purchase of six Cant Z 506 floatplanes was signed on 30 July 1938. According to the contract Poland would receive the aircraft in three batches of two aircraft each. They were planned to be delivered on 26 June, 11 July, and 26 July 1939. In the spring of 1939 Szef Kierownictwa Marynarki Wojennej decided to purchase 12 more Cant Z 506. However, this plan was not fulfilled due to the outbreak of war. At the beginning of July the first group of airmen left Warsaw to collect the aircraft on order. The delay in departure was caused by the manufacturer. Unfortunately, upon arrival they found that the Italians were still not ready. It is possible that these delays were due to the fact that the Italians were allies of Hitler's Germany, which at that time was preparing for war against Poland. Eventually, after much trouble, the crew virtually hijacked their aircraft, flying it to Poland. Their decision was forced by subsequent changes of heart by the Italians. In one case an apparent engine malfunction was found which, according to the personnel of CRDA (Cantieri Riuniti Dell Adriatico) required replacement. When the repair team was joined by a Polish technician it was found (by Slovene technicians working at the repair) that the engine worked correctly and it could be accepted. Trials were scheduled for 27 August 1939. Facing the increasingly tense international situation, *kpt. pil.* Roman Borowiec, the commander of the crew of the first Cant decided (without arrangement with the Italians) to fly to Poland. The route led over Belgrade and Budapest. After a four-hour flight the Cant alighted at the Bay near Puck on 27 August 1939 at 15:30. However, the combat value of the new aircraft of the Polish Navy was small, as it had no armament (neither guns, nor torpedo-bomb racks). No other aircraft of the type arrived in Poland until the outbreak of war (or after). On 1 September the base at Puck was bombed. The Cant was lucky to avoid damage. The aircraft was then evacuated to Hel. Two armourers who delivered bomb racks of Władysław Świątecki design to Puck, and were scheduled to fit these to the Cant, were evacuated together with Dywizjon personnel. One of them, Jerzy Rakowski, was killed in an air raid at Hel the same day. During this raid two crew members were in the aircraft anchored at the Bay of Danzig (Gdańsk). Attempting to escape they jumped into the water, trying to swim away from the aircraft. The Cant was attacked by three Ju 87s which dropped their bomb loads without result. Subsequently they attacked the helpless airmen swimming in their life vests near the aircraft. One of them, *bosman radio* Władysław Wzorek, when jumping into the water caught his sidearm belt on a protruding part of the fuselage, and suffered a spine injury. This initially prevented him from feeling any pain and when the Stukas left, both crew members managed to swim back to the aircraft with great difficulty. It was then that *bosman radio* W. Wzorek lost consciousness. After being dragged to the land he was found to be dead. During his funeral another raid started. Exploding bombs 'resurrected' the dead, shocking the undertakers! That same evening it was decided to evacuate the Cant inland, in order to arm it. Anyway the large bare metal aircraft was easy prey for the enemy. The following morning the aircraft took off, taking the surviving technician from the bomb-rack fitting team. Their destination was the Siemien lake near Parczewo. The lake was selected due to its proximity to Lublin, the location of the W. Świątecki factory which manufactured the bomb racks. The Cant was still using the fuel from Monfalcone. During the flight the fuel ran out and the pilot was forced to alight on the Vistula near Dęblin. After refuelling, on 6 September the Cant eventually arrived at its destination. Even though camouflaged with tree branches, it was located by German reconnaissance aircraft on 9 September. As a result of that it was destroyed on 11 September 1939. Thus ended the short history of the most modern aircraft of the Polish Navy.

Attempts to reinforce Polish naval aviation prior to the outbreak of war failed. In effect the Order of Battle of Morski Dywizjon Lotniczy was far from that envisaged in the original plan. On 1 September 1939 the Poland Navy had the following aircraft: Lublin R-VIII ter/hydro (two), Lublin R-XIII bis/ter/G/hydro (ten), Lublin R-XIII bis/hydro (one), Lublin R-XIII G/hydro on wheels (one), Schreck FBA 17HE2 (one liaison aircraft of the commander of Morski Dywizjon Lotniczy), RWD 17W (one), Nikol A-2 (one), Cant Z 506B 'Airone' (one), RWD 13 (two impressed aircraft from flying clubs). In addition one engineless Lublin R-VIII and one RWD R-XX with unserviceable engines were still at Puck.

At the outbreak of World War Two the Polish naval aviation had 285 personnel, including 15 pilots, 10 observers, and 10 gunners.

1 Mar. – marynarki – Polish Navy.

430: *Puck base, early 1920s (Konarski)*

431: *Marshy terrain gave PWS 5T2 pilots much trouble. Stachów nad Prypecil, 22 July 1930 (Konarski)*

432: *At the beginning of the 1930s Bartel BM 5c training aircraft were introduced to the naval aviation units. The Navy used five of these under the designation of Bartel BM 300. They were difficult to fly. The photo shows one of the aircraft, damaged in an accident on 13 June 1933. In front of the aircraft is* por. mar. pil. *Adolf Stempkowski (Konarski)*

433: *One of three Lublin R VIIIs introduced into service in 1932. The photo shows aircraft no. 802 on a transport trolley (Konarski)*

434: *Another Lublin R VIII, no. 803 (Glass)*

435: *A section of Lublin R VIIIs in flight over the ORP* Generał Haller *gunship, 1937 (Konarski)*

436: *Lublin R XIII ter/hydro no. 704. The first aircraft from the largest batch ordered in 1934. The photo was taken at the Copenhagen roadstead during a visit of Polish aircraft to Denmark in July 1934 (Glass)*

437: *Lublin R XIII bis/hydro no. 701 damaged at Pińsk. 8 June 1933 (Konarski)*

438: *Lublin R XIII bis/hydro no. 703 from the first batch of the aircraft, delivered in 1932. The photo was taken in 1933 (Konarski)*

439: *Beaching Lublin R XIII ter/hydro no. 710 (Olejko)*

440: *Crashed 1934 Lublin R XIII ter/hydro no. 705 (Olejko)*

441: *The same Lublin during 'unloading' on a wharf. The accident of 24 April 1934 cost the life of* bosman pil. *W. Walkowiak, who fell out of the cockpit because he was not strapped in (Konarski)*

442: *Crewmen* por. pil. *Kołodziejek and* st. bosm. obs. *T. Benetkiewicz receive a pre-flight briefing – in the background is R XIII ter/hydro no. 706 (Konarski)*

NAVAL AVIATION IN THE 1939 CAMPAIGN

Tension between Poland and the Third Reich was already clear from the spring of 1939 and the intensity of flying at the Polish-German border rose on both sides. Poland's access to the coast was of a special nature (see the map). Its peculiar character lay in the fact that Polish territory divided Germany in effect. The Pomeranian 'corridor' that belonged to Poland was located between the bulk of Germany and the territory of East Prussia. In fact the German demand for an ex-territorial motorway through Poland, and the Polish refusal, was one of the direct causes of the war.

Morski Dywizjon Lotnicyzy maintained a continuous combat readiness. New recruits were being trained, and then sent on specialist courses. At the same time a new system of long range reconnaissance was developed. It covered the area from the so-called Ławica Slupska in the west, up to the German port of Pilau (Pilawa) in East Prussia. Usually a few flights a day were flown, providing continuous monitoring of German shipping. These missions were flown by Lublin R-XIIIs, which carried out spying missions 'by the way'. The Germans were not passive, either, frequently violating Polish airspace. In one case the Polish Lublin R-XIII G/hydro no. 714 performed the role of a fighter, successfully chasing away the German LZ-130 airship from Polish territory. In April 1939 the Dywizjon lost a Lublin R-XIII which crashed at Swarzewo. Usually at the beginning of May each year a three-aircraft Pluton Samolotów Towarzyszacych was detached from the unit at Puck, the aircraft being converted to wheeled undercarriage and subsequently moving to Rumia-Zagórze airfield. Another accident occurred during night flying on 19 May 1939 at 23:00 when a crew failed to locate the airfield and crashed into trees. The crew escaped unhurt, but the aircraft was written off. On 7 August 1939 one R-XIII patrolling its assigned sector observed a large passenger ship, identified as *Hansesstadt Danzig*. The pilot wanted to take a clear picture of the vessel, and approached it at a very low level. During a sharp turn it side-slipped and crashed into the sea. The Dywizjob thus lost the Lublin R-XIII ter/hydro no. 712. The crew was picked up by a boat from the German ship, and subsequently transferred to the police in the Free City of Danzig. Thus the modest inventory of Morski Dywizjon Lotniczy was reduced by two aircraft.

443: *Lublin R XIII G/hydro on wheels, damaged during landing on a soggy airfield at Puck (Konarski)*

Pilots of the Danzig flying club mobilised on 24 August 1939, formed on the 31st of that month the Pluton Łącznikowy Dowódcy Lądowej Obrony Wybrzeża, led by *ppor. rez. pil.* Edmund Jereczek. The Pluton took over two civil RWD 13 aircraft, registered as SP-ATB and SP-BML. The Pluton was reinforced by R-XIII G/hydro no. 718 of Morski Dywizjon Lotniczy.

The main base of the naval aviation had been thoroughly reconnoitred by the Germans, so in the event of war it was assumed that the unit would be evacuated to the Hel Peninsula. After 30 August part of the storage facilities and Oddział Obrony Lądowej moved to Hel. The aircraft stayed at Puck. On the morning of 1 September 1939, about 6:00 a.m., the first German bomber formation arrived over Puck. This consisted of some 20 Heinkel He 111s from KG 1 of Luftflotte 1. They attacked the base of the Dywizjon, the railway station, and a target ship anchored in the Bay of Puck. Four people were killed, and over a dozen wounded in the raid. The Dywizjon commander, *kmdr. por. pil.* Edward Szystkowski, was among the dead, passing command to *kmdr. ppor. pil.* Kazimierz Szalewicz before he died. Immediate evaluation of the flying equipment to Hel was ordered, as there was no anti-aircraft defence left at Puck by that time. The aircraft were anchored along the Peninsula on the Bay side. The aircraft were left in full view, providing an easy target for enemy aircraft. The RWD-17W was an exception, being on land and hidden in woods. The Nikol A-2 amphibian was anchored in the naval port at Hel. The aircraft were only protected by artillery batteries located at the Peninsula. Against total air superiority, in terms of both quantity and quality, operational capabilities of the unit were largely limited even on the first day of the war. The situation grew worse with the death of the commander and the chaos caused by the unit's evacuation. An idea to bomb the *Schleswig Holstein* battleship, anchored in Danzig, and shelling the Polish posts at Westerplatte was not put into life as most of the Lublin R-XIIIs were damaged in a raid by two Heinkel He 59s that took place on the evening of 2 September. The following day the Germans resumed raids, and as a result the strafed Lublins were sunk in the coastal shallows. Only the R-XIII G/hydro no. 714

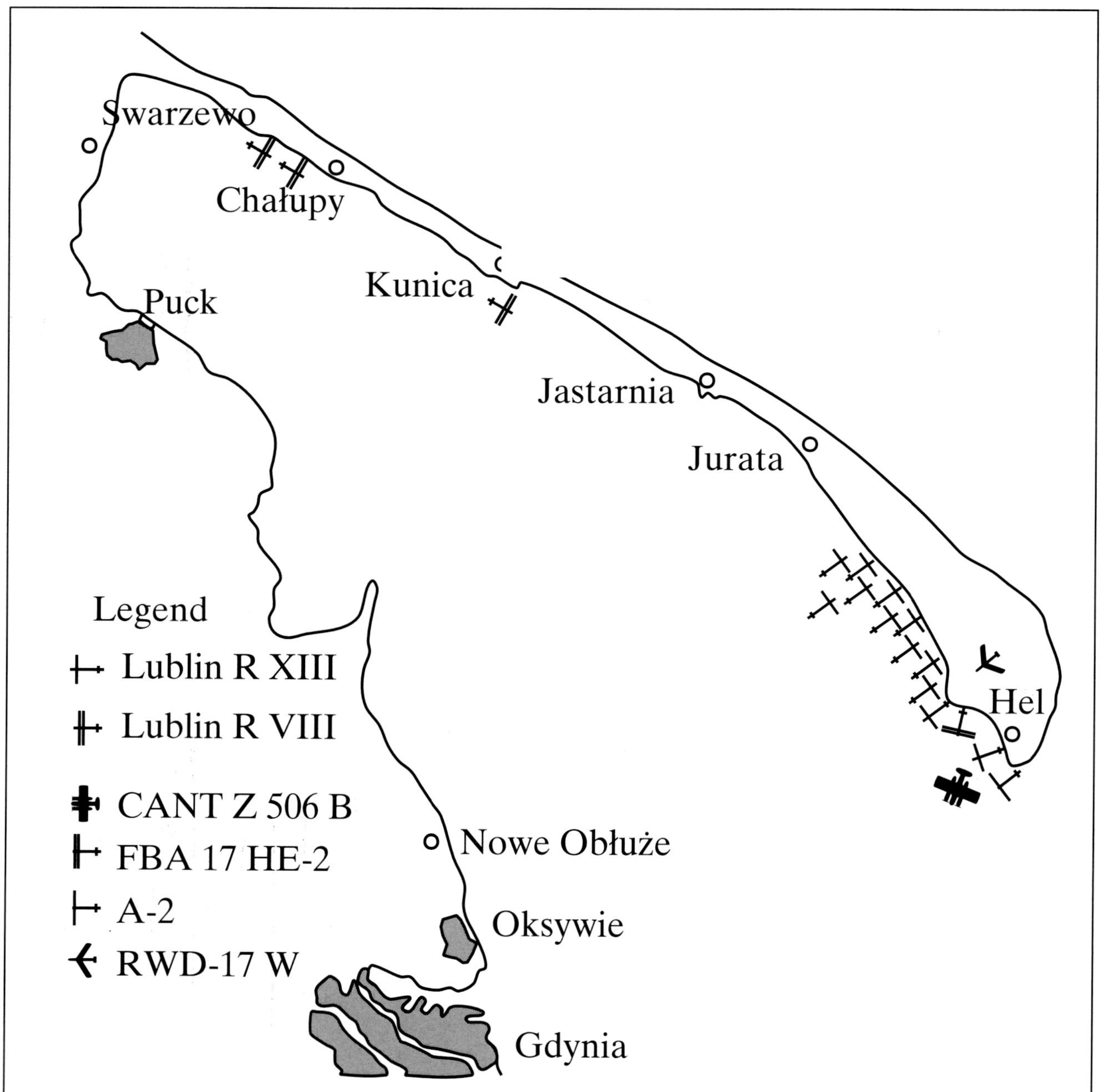

444: *Another view of the same aircraft shown on page 247 (Konarski)*

445: *Lublin R XX during flight trials (Konarski)*

446: *R XX at Puck airfield (Konarski)*

447: *Lublin R XX prototype on its transport trolley (Konarski)*

survived the ordeal. The same day the Cant Z 506B left to travel inland, most ground crews of the unit were to fight alongside ground troops that defended the Peninsula. A surviving Lublin R-XIII was used for the first time on the evening of 6 September, when it flew an hour's reconnaissance flight over the Bay of Gdańsk. The crew consisted of *por. pil.* Józef Rudzki and *por. pil. obs.* Zdzisław Juszczkiewicz. The flight was uneventful, and activity of small enemy naval craft was detected. Following this successful flight the R-XIII no. 714 took off for another the next night. This time the aircraft, flown by the same crew, was armed with six 12.5 kg bombs, with which it would attack the *Schleswig Holstein* battleship at Danzig. Upon arrival it was found that the ship had left its previous location. The R-XIII crew noticed a night parade organised in Danzig by the Germans to celebrate the victory over the Polish posts at Westerplatte, the Poles attacked, bombing and then strafing the surprised Germans. Subsequently they returned without problem to their temporary base. These were the only combat missions flown by aircraft of Morski Dywizjob Lotniczy in September 1939. The following day the Germans made a revenge attack against Hel with Ju 87s of 4./186 Trägerstaffel. During the raid the last serviceable R-XIII, no. 714, and the Schreck FBA 17HE2 were destroyed. Thus on 8 September the RWD 17W and Nikol A-2 were the only airworthy machines, with the exception of the aircraft of Pluton Łącznikowy Dowódcy Lądowej Obrony Wybrzeża. The above mentioned Pluton was merged into the Kompania Sztabowa on 1 September 1939 by the orders of Dowódca Lądowej Obrony Wybrzeąa, *płk.* Stanisław Dąbek. Initially the aircraft of the Pluton were based at the commercial airfield in Rumia. That is where they were caught (together with two 'Lot' Polish Airlines aircraft) by the German raid on the first day of the war at 6:00 a.m. After the raid a Lublin R-XIII G/hydro reinforcing the Pluton arrived at Rumia. The raid did not cause major damage, but accelerated departure of the passenger aircraft inland. Another raid carried out by the Germans the same afternoon failed to inflict damage except for bomb craters. After 4 September the anti-aircraft defences left the airfield, so the Pluton commander ordered the observer's machine gun of the Lublin R-XIII removed and mounted on a fixed base near the hangar. This provisional post shot down a Junkers Ju 87 on one of the following days, its crew becoming prisoners of war. The Pluton still remained unused. On 9 September the situation became difficult, when the airfield area came under direct enemy fire. The Pluton commander, *ppor. pil.* Edmund Jereczek, unable to contact his HQ decided to evacuate to the reserve airfield at Nowe Obłuże north of Gdynia. Using a short-lived counter-attack by the Polish infantry as cover, the pilots started the engines of their aircraft, and took off straight through the open hangar doors (since the first raid on the morning of 1 September 1939 the aircraft were hidden in old flying club hangars at one side of the airfield). On 13 September *płk.* Dąbek ordered evacuation of both RWD 13s to Sweden. The Lublin R-XIII would fly to Hel with a report. At that time the nearby base at Puck was already in use by German aircraft. Both RWD 13s took off the same day at 12:30. Immediately after take-off the aircraft started to climb through clouds. When passing through these the pilots lost contact. Given this situation each undertook individual attempts to escape. The first RWD 13, SP-BML, flown by *ppor. pil.* E. Jereczek managed after flying over 450 km landed at Visborglatt on the island of Gotland. The crew was interned, and the aircraft impressed by the Swedes, who used it until 1952. The other RWD 13, SP-ATB, flown by *szer. pil.* Wacław Zarudzki was forced to turn back due to problems with the engine. It landed back at Nowe Obłuże airfield after an hour's flight.

The last surviving aircraft. the Lublin R-XIII G/hydro no. 718, was going to fly on 17 September 1939 an evacuation flight and report to Warsaw. Flown by *mat* Stefan Czerwiński the aircraft took off that day at about 22:00. Soon after take-off the aircraft crashed into the sea for unknown reasons. The pilot was killed, while an unidentified infantry *kapitan* survived. The RWD 17, SP-BPB, surviving at the Hel Peninsula, was the last aircraft of the Polish aviation at the coast. It crashed on 30 September 1939 in the hands of *ppor. pil.* Juliusz Bilewicz during an attempt to fly to Sweden.

During the 1939 campaign the Polish naval aviation flew a total of 27 missions, including 3 combat sorties in a combined time of 13 hours 15 minutes. The activity of the naval aircraft was therefore negligible. This was due to several factors. The most important lay in the overwhelming superiority of the German air force, both in quantity and quality. The efforts of the few who continued in their resistance is all the more praiseworthy. Land fighting in defence of the Hel Peninsula involved some 300 soldiers of the Morski Dywizjon Lotniczy at Puck, led by the unit's officers.

448: *Lublin R XX floatplane (Konarski)*

449: *Crash of the R XIII ter/hydro no. 711. July 1936 (Konarski)*

450: *The crew of R XIII ter/hydro no. 713 before a reconnaissance sortie (Konarski)*

451: *The Nikol A 2 was planned to become the shipborne aircraft of Polish warships. This all-wood aircraft first flew on 4 March 1939, and proved to be very successful, but the war prevented any production, the single prototype being destroyed in September 1939 (Konarski)*

452: *Nikol A 2 amphibian built in the workshops of Morski Dywizjon Lotniczy (Konarski)*

453: *Nikol A 2 amphibian first flown on 4 March 1939 (Konarski)*

454: *PZL 12H amphibian prototype of 1931. The famous designer Zygmunt Puławski, creator of the family of excellent fighter aircraft featuring the 'seagull' wing, was killed in an accident of this prototype (Olejko)*

455: *The prototype Brahmo-powered RWD 17W training aircraft. The aircraft has civil registration SP-BPB (Glass)*

456: *Prototype RWD 17W tested in the spring of 1939 by the Morski Dywizjon Lotniczy at Puck. This was the last aircraft flying over the Polish coast. It crashed soon after take-off on 30 September 1939 (Konarski)*

457: *An Italian CANT Z 506 B floatplane. Before the war Poland purchased a single aircraft of the type. Unfortunately, no photo of the aircraft in Polish markings is known to exist (Giorgio Apostolo via A.Olejko)*

458: *A wreck of a Lublin R XIII at Hel Peninsula, October 1939 (Konarski)*

459: *Burnt out and sunk Lublin R XIII (Konarski)*

460: *Lublin R VIII ter no. 802 destroyed at Kunice in September 1939 (Konarski)*

461: *RWD 13 SP-BML, the only Polish aircraft used on the coast that was neither destroyed, nor fell into German hands. The aircraft, flown by* ppor. pil. *E. Jereczek landed at the Swedish island of Gotland after a brave flight on 13 September 1939. The photo was taken at Rumia airfield before the war(Konarski)*

462: *Lublin R VIII ter with floats damaged by German strafing in early September 1939 (Konarski)*

463: *The RWD 13 SP-ATB did not have as much luck as the other aircraft of the type. After a common take-off for Sweden on 13 September it was forced to turn back due to technical problems. Upon return the unserviceable aircraft was used as a target for the German artillery at Kępa Oksywska. 15 September 1939 (Konarski)*

BALLOON FORCES

First attempts to form balloon forces were undertaken in the I Korpus Polski in Russia, in the autumn of 1917. *Ppłk* Hipolit Łossowski formed a balloon unit. In free Poland an attempt to form an aeronautic unit was made, but a lack of equipment led the authorities to abandon the idea, until having incorporated Wielkopolska, where suitable equipment was captured (2 Parseval Drachen spotting balloons, an Alpina horse winch and several hundred cylinders of hydrogen) to change the situation. The Commander of Wojska Lotnicze, *płk pil.* Gustaw Macewicz, ordered Aleksander Wańkowicz in April 1919 to organise balloon forces in Poznań, but apart from the lack of equipment above all, skilled personnel were not available. In order to overcome these difficulties Oficerska Szkoła Aeronautyczna was established in Poznań. The Szkoła started its activities on 21 May 191. It was active until 1924, after which only special, *ad hoc* courses were organised in the balloon battalion in Torun.

In May 1919 balloon units started to be formed. The I Grupa Aeronautyczna was organised, consisting of three kompania balonowa troops. Command of the Grupa was taken by *kpt.* Jan Wolszlegier. On 23 July 1919 *płk* Aleksander Wańkowicz performed the first flight of a tethered balloon in Poland. The unit received its new equipment, purchased in France and Austria, at the end of 1919. This included balloons and Caquot Type R balloon winches, as well as field hydrogen plants. The new equipment and the first group of trained officers allowed the balloon force to expand. At the beginning of 1920 Batalion Uzupełnień was established, consisting of two kompanias and a park ruchomy. The same year aeronautical units went to the front line. I Grupa Aeronautyczna under *kpt. obs. bal.* Edmund Wolszlegier headed for the Lithuanian-Byelorussian Front, II Grupa Aeronautyczna under *por. pil.* Sławomir Bilek operated in the Polesia region, and III Grupa Aeronautyczna under *por. obs. bal.*[1] Konstanty Kamieński moved to Toruń. The Batalion Uzupełmień stayed at Poznań. The stable situation at the front line in the winter and spring of 1920 allowed for the use of balloons. Balloon units co-operated with artillery and provided monitoring of the front line. After the Red Army offensive started, rapid changes of the situation at the front line rendered spotting balloons virtually useless. In that situation *płk* Wańkowicz united all battalions (all names were changed from grupa to battalion) into one Pułk Aeronautyczny, fighting as an infantry unit. The Pułk distinguished itself at the front line in the critical period of August–September 1920.

After the armistice the Pułk was reformed into battalions, deploying these as follows:

- I Baon – Poznań, commander *płk.* pil. Aleksander Wańkowicz
- II Baon – Jablonna, commander *ppłk* Marceli Chybczyński
- III Baon – Toruń, commander *płk.* pil. Feliks Bołsunowski
- IV Baon – Krakow, commander *kpt.* Florian Rudnicki-Sipaylo
- V Baon – Brześć on Bug, commander *mjr* Roman Błażewski.

1923 brought reorganisation of balloon units. The number of units was reduced to one Battalion in Toruń. In 1923 a subsequent unit was established at Jablonna. Balloon equipment was manufactured in that town.

Balloon Battalions consisted of two Kompania Balonów Obserwacyjnych units, one Kompania Balonów Zaporowych and one Kompania Szkolna. The Battalions also included auxiliary companies. Each Kompania Obserwacyjna had one spotting tethered balloon with equipment, and 163 officers and men. Kompania Zaporowa included 2 Plutons each with 5 pairs of barrage balloons. Mobilisation plans called for 10 Kompania Balonów Obserwacyjnych units and 5 Kompania Balonów Zaporowych units.

This structure of aeronautical units remained until the mobilisation in August 1939. The mobilisation involved 7 spotting balloon companies and 5 barrage balloon companies. Only 6 spotting balloon companies were prepared for war operations, equipped with Polish WBS 'BD' balloons. These units received assignment to Armia 'Pomorze', 'Poznań', 'Łódź' one company each, Armia 'Modlin' – 2 companies, and 1 company to

464: płk *Wańkowicz was pilot of the first tethered balloon flight in Poland on 23 July 1919 and went on to command I Baon*

1: LLOYD C II. Aircraft with 'Kraków' type Polish national insignia. Probably with Austro-Daimler (160hp) engine

2: RUMPLER CI. No C.4607 with white-red badges – 'Warsaw' type early Polish national insignia. Aircraft as seen in photo taken 01/12/1918

3: RUMPLER CI. As seen on the photo taken on 21/11/1918 when ppor. pil. *Witold Zdisław Piechowski died, in a crash in this aircraft*

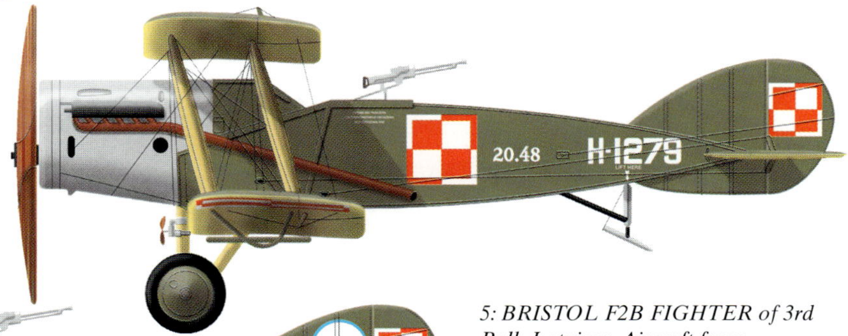

4: BRISTOL F2B FIGHTER of 1 Eskadra Wywiadowcza. Polish – Bolshevik War

5: BRISTOL F2B FIGHTER of 3rd Pułk Lotniczy. Aircraft from unknown Eskadra. Every Eskadra in 3rd Pułk had its own geometrical symbol, but which Eskadra had which symbol is not known

6: DFW CV. Aircraft after repair in Stacja Lotnicza Ławica- Poznań

7: DFX CV of 12 Eskadra Wywiadowcza. During a flight with sierż pil. *Kazimierz Burzyński, the observer was the flying commander of 15 Regiment Poznań Ułans* płk. *Władysław Anders, later the well known Polish commander of the Polish Army in Italy in 1944–1945*

SCALE: 1/72

8: ALBATROS CIII of 1 Eskadra Wywiadowcza. Personal aircraft of por. pil. *Stanisław Pawluae. During war in 1919 aircraft was shot down and crash landed but later was repaired and re-entered service*

9: DH-9 – only serial known is H4315

10: ALBATROS C XII. Number 1 from unknown unit. Note different insignias

11: ALBATROS J I. No 217/8 of 1 Wielkopolska Eskadra Polna. Note Polish insignia – late version

12: A-300-4 of 2 Pułk Lotniczy Kraków, 1924

13: HANNOVER CL II. First aircraft built in Poland. It was adopted by por. pil. Inż. *Karol Słowik. Aircraft was built in Centralne Warsztaty Lotnicze as 001/1919. Aircraft crashed in July 1919 killing Karol Słowik*

14: HANNOVER CL V no 9671/18 probably after repair by CWL. Mokotów airfield. Warsaw 1919

SCALE: 1/72

15: LVG CV no 1591/17 with name 'Stasia' of 13 Eskadra Wywiaclowcza. Ławica Airfield Poznań 1919

16: LVG CV with unknown number with name 'Halka' and 'Zosia' of 12 Eskadra Wywiadowcza (earlier 1 Wielkopolska Eskadra Polna), 1919

17: LVG CV of 5 or 6 Eskadra Wywiadowcza with original insignia on the rudder. Earlier aircraft was in Lwowska Ill Grupa Lotnicza

18: LVG C V with unknown number. Aircraft with winter engine cowling. 17 Eskadra Wywiadowcza

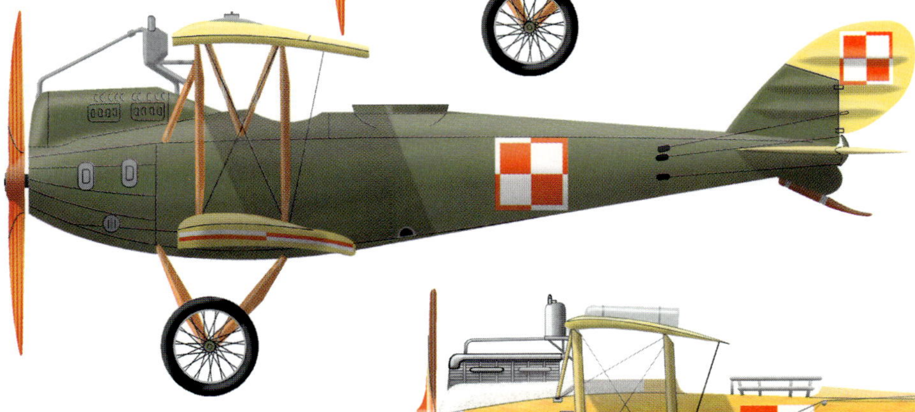

19: OEFFAG C II Probably of 2 Eskadra Wywiadowcza. As seen on the photo taken at Lwów, November 1918

20: SVA 10. Aircraft No 30 of Szkoła Pilotów in Grudziądzu

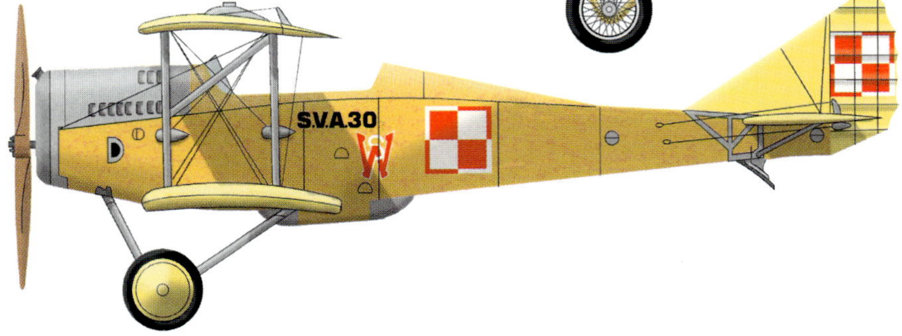

SCALE: 1/72

21: BRANDENBURG C 1 no 64.61 of Lwowska Grupa Lotnicza. Aircraft captured in 1919. Ukrainian origin

22: SALMSON 11A2 with unknown personal or Eskadra insignia

23: SALMSON 11A2 of 1 Eskadra Wywiadowcza received from 582 Eskadra Salmsonów. Used on Latvian-Bielonisian Front

24: LUBLIN R XIII D of 26 Eskadra Obserwacyjna, 2 Pułk Lotniczy w Krakowie. Wings number 15-K, black

25: LUBLIN R XIII D no 56.73 of 64 Eskadra Towarzysząca, 6 Pułk Lotniczy

26: BREGUET XIV A2 of 16 Eskadra Wywiadowcza, 1920

SCALE: 1/72

27: ALBATROS D III with red nose – Pułaski flight of 7 Eskadra Myśliwska. Pilot por. *Harmon C. Rosison, 1920*

28: ALBATROS D Ill (OEF) of Wyższa Szkoła Pilotażu, Grudziądzu

29: Above: SOPWITH CAMEL no 5234 of 7 Eskadra Myśliwska. 1920. It was the private aeroplane of por. pil. *Kenneth Murray. After war was bought by Polish Government*

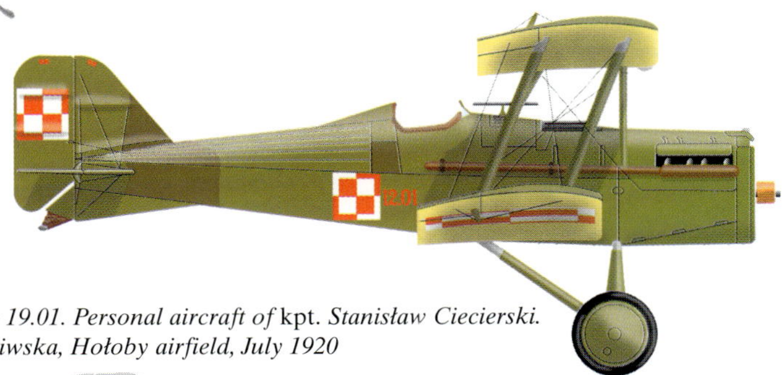

30: Right: SE-5a no 19.01. Personal aircraft of kpt. *Stanisław Ciecierski. 7 Eskadra Myśliwska, Hołoby airfield, July 1920*

31: SE-5a, G-EBIC of kpt. Pil. *(ex RAF) James G. C. Worledge. Aircraft with special smoke equipment used for skywriting. Kraków 1926*

*32: SPAD 7C1 no S.1473 of 1 Oddział Awiacyjny Bojowy (*kpt. *Grochowalski). Aircraft with Russian insignia*

33: SPAD 7C1 no 11543 of 3 Pułk Lotniczy Poznań. As seen in a photo taken on 11/05/1921

34: SPAD 13C1 of 3 Pułk Lotniczy, Poznań

SCALE: 1/72

35: SPAD 13C1 no 24.2 of 4 Pułk Lotniczy, Toruń. Aircraft in original French camouflage

36: Below: ANSALDO A-1 BALILLA. Personal aircraft of S. Pawlikowski. Aeroplane from Italian supplies, but with Polish factory Plage i Laśkiewicz badge on the fin

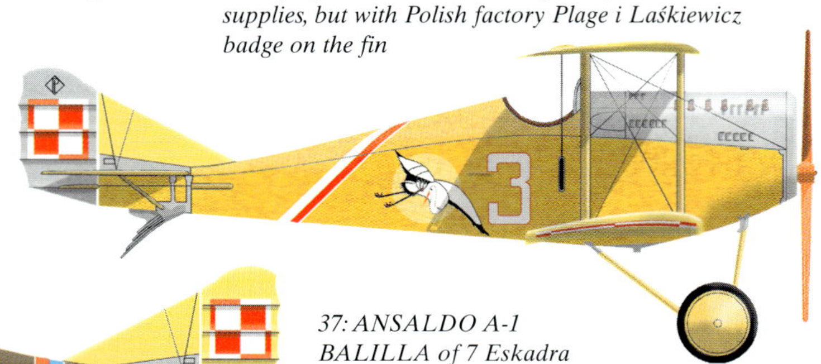

37: ANSALDO A-1 BALILLA of 7 Eskadra Myśliwska. Aircraft built in Plage i Laśkiewicz factory in Lublin

38: ANSALDO A-1 BALILLA of 7 Eskadra Myśliwska. Aircraft built in Italy

39: ANSALDO A-1 BALILLA of 7 Eskadra Myśliwska. Original Italian aircraft with factory code BA 26

40: FOKKER D VII of 13 Eskadra Myśliwska. Polish checkers on lower wings rotated

41: FOKKER D VII of 15 Eskadra Myśliwska, no unknown. Polish checkers on lower wings rotated

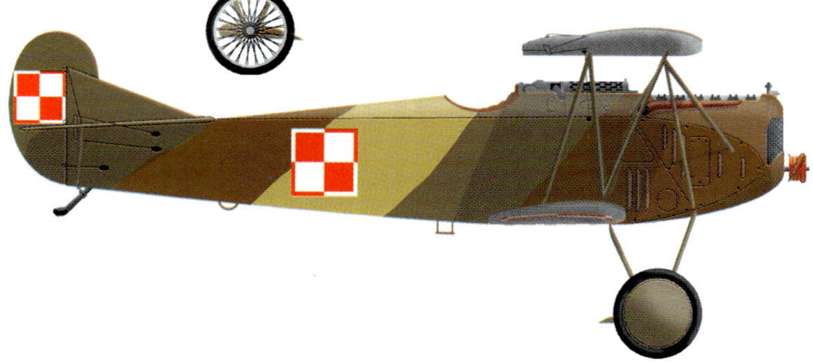

42: FOKKER D VII in postwar three- colour camouflage, 1924

SCALE: 1/72

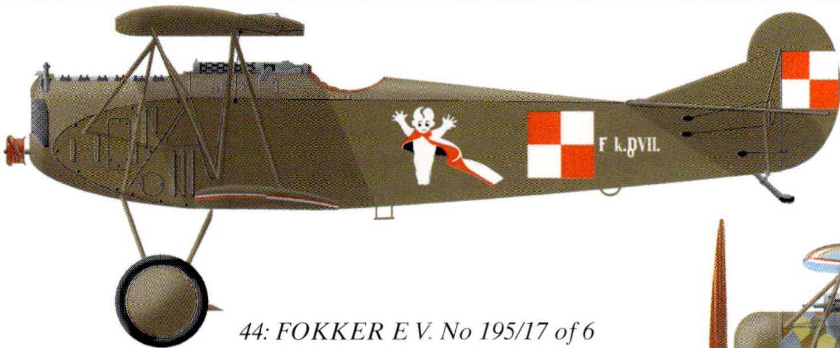

43: FOKKER D VII of 15 Eskadra Myśliwska. No unknown. Personal insignia BiBABo figure

44: FOKKER E V. No 195/17 of 6 Eskadra Lotnicze with personal emblem of por. *Stefan Stec. Later aircraft was repainted in one colour – dark green*

45:
Above: FOKKER E V of 15 Eskadra Myśliwska. Number unknown

46:
Below: F14 BUZZARD painted in white and red stripes. Personal aircraft of gen. bryg. pil. *Włodzimierz Zagórski*

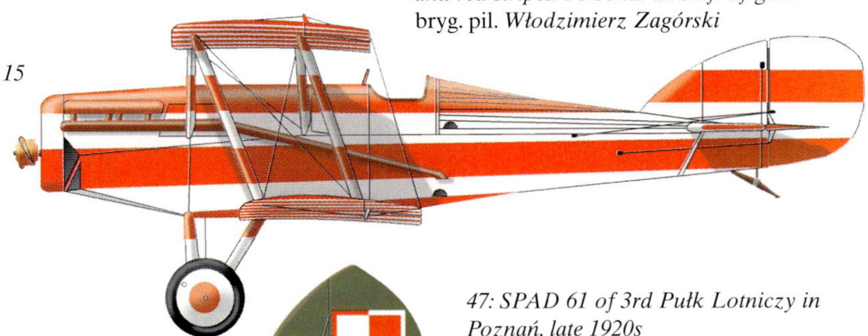

47: SPAD 61 of 3rd Pułk Lotniczy in Poznań, late 1920s

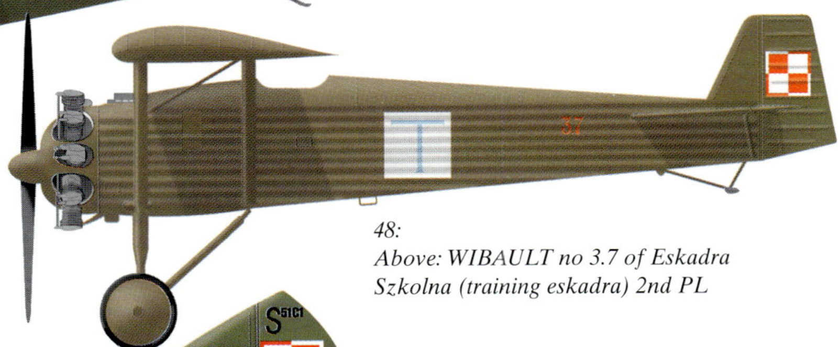

48:
Above: WIBAULT no 3.7 of Eskadra Szkolna (training eskadra) 2nd PL

49: SPAD 51 of 111 Eskadra Myśliwska, 1st Pułk Lotniczy

50: AVIA BH33 PWS-A of 122 Eskadra Myśliwska, 2nd Pułk Lotniczy

SCALE: 1/72

51: PWS-10 no 5.10, of 141 Eskadra Myśliwska 4 Pułk Lotniczy Toruń. Eskadra commander's plane. "11 T" under wing

52: PWS-10 no. 5.44 T'3' of 133 Eskadra Myśliwska, 3 Pułk Lotniczy Poznań. "62-P" under the wing

53: PWS-10 of 141 Eskadra Myśliwska, 4 Pułk Lotniczy Toruń. Eskadra commander's plane – red stripe on the fin with white trim

55: PWS-10 of 3 Pułk Lotniczy Poznań, exercises temporary camouflage 1931

55: PWS-10. '32' of Centrum Wyszkolenia Lotniczego Oficerów Lotnictwa in Dęblin. Overall aluminium dope. Red fin and wheel discs

56: PZL P.7a no 2 of 112 Eskadra Myśliwska 1st Pułk Lotniczy. White stripe on the fin. Radio number 72-N in white

SCALE: 1/72

57: PZL P.7a personal aircraft of Ludomił Rayski. White-red chevron on the fuselage

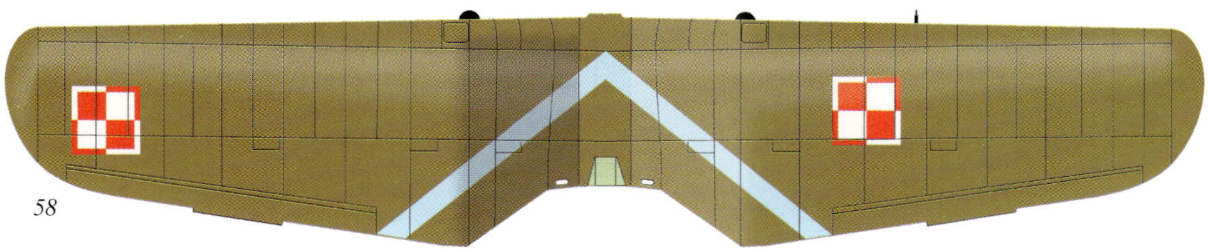

58

59: PZL, P.7a individual number 1 of 123 Eskadra Myśliwska 2nd Pułk Lotniczy. Blue stripe on the fuselage and upper surfaces of the wing (above)

60: PZL P.7a individual no 5 of 122 Eskadra 2nd Pułk Lotniczy. Blue stripe on the upper wing. Serial no 6.10 in red

61: PZL P.7a individual no 9 of 161 Eskadra Myśliwska 6th Pułk Lotniczy in Lwów

62: PZL P.11a, personal aircraft of mjr *Józef Kepiński, chief of training in the Szkoła Podchorlżych Lotnictwa in Dęblin 1938–1939. Emblem behind cockpit appears to be that of the SPL*

SCALE: 1/72

63: PZL P.11a. In this aircraft mjr *Edmund Warwick took* ppłk *Mateusz Iżycki from besieged Warsaw on 23.09.1939 to Hajduboszonney in Hungary. On the next day Polish national insignia were painted over in white*

64: PZL P.11a of 114 Eskadra Myśliwska, with white stripe on the fin

65: PZL P.11a serial no 7.22 of 111 Eskadra Myśliwska. Aircraft belonged to KOP (Korpus Obrony Pogranicza)

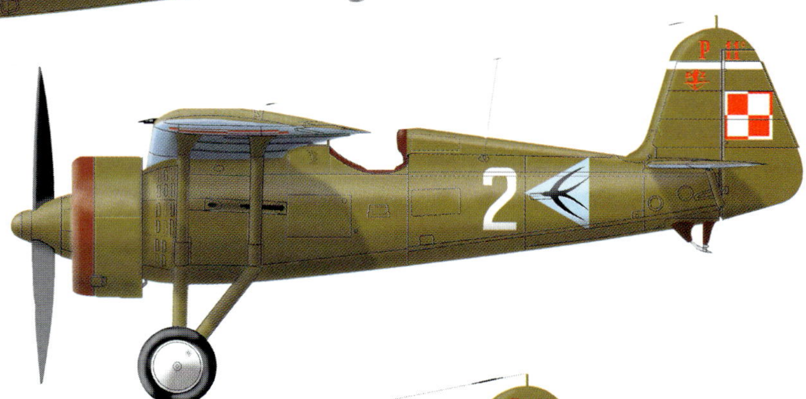

66: PZL P.11c of 114 Eskadra Myśliwska. White radio call no 72-N. White stripe on the fuselage and white wheel disks (1938–1939)

67: PZL P.11c serial no 8.115 of 121 Eskadra Myśliwska. Pilot ppor. *Wacław Król 1939*

68: PZL P.11c of 141 Eskadra Myśliwska

SCALE: 1/72

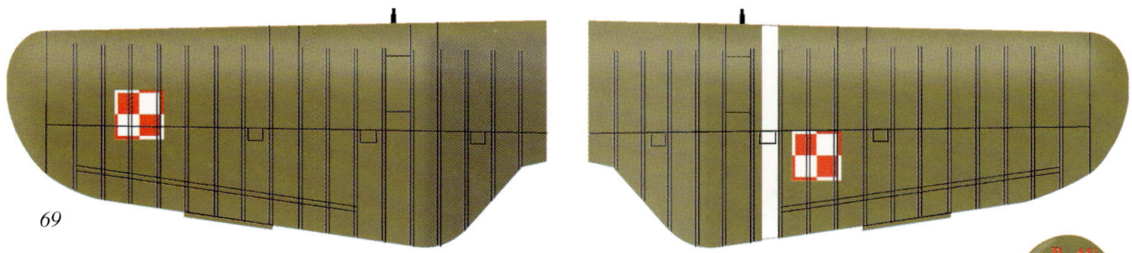

69

70: PZL, P.11c, serial no 8.70 of 113 Eskadra Myśliwska. Pilot ppor. *Hieronim Dudwał. Radio call no 170-N. White stripe on the right wing. September 1939*

71

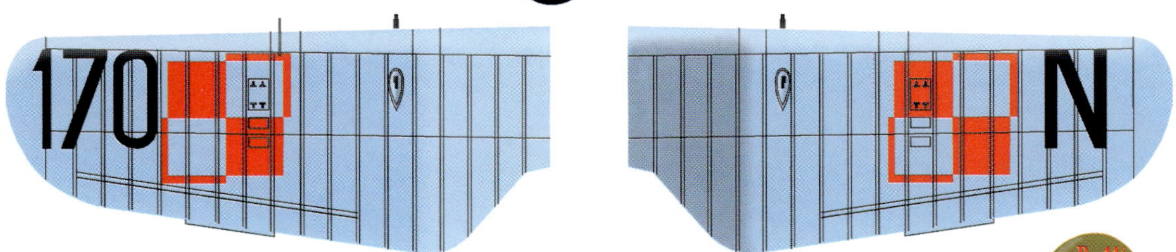

72: PZL P.11c, personal aircraft of gen. Ludomił Rayski during visit to Sweden in 1936

73: PZL, P.11c of 113 Eskadra Myśliwska. Radio call no 48-P

74: LWS 14b Czapla of 13 Eskadra Obserwacyjna

SCALE: 1/72

75: BREGUET XIV A2 serial no 10.21 of 3 Eskadra Wywiadowcza in Baranowicza. Aircraft in standard French camouflage. Rudder – grey. Painted over French national insignia

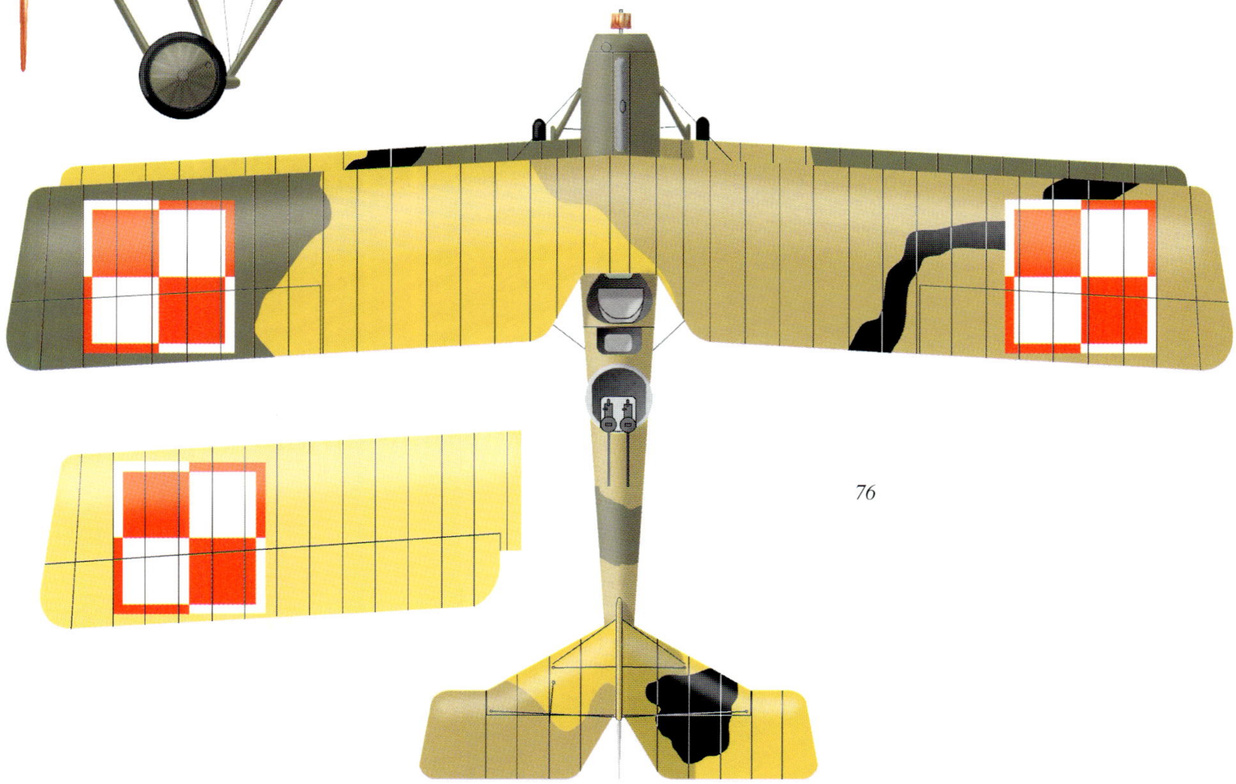

76

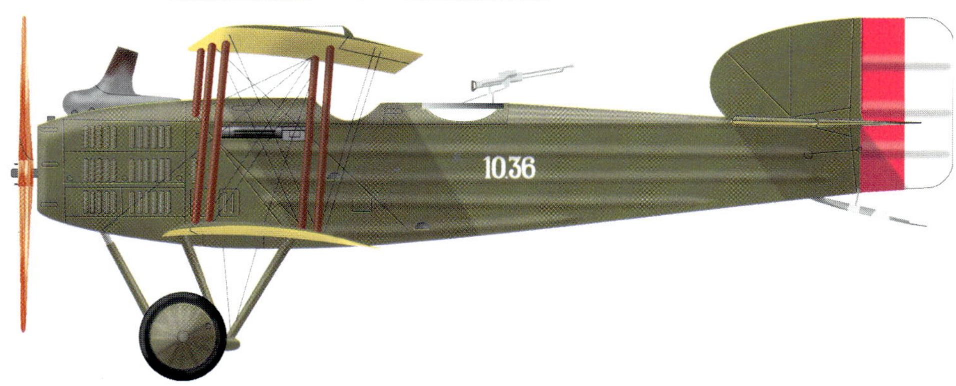

77: BREGUET XIV A2 serial 10.36 of Eskadra Wojsk Litwy Îrodkowej (Central Lithuania) in Wilno December 1920. Aircraft in dark green uppersurfaces with natural linen undersurfaces, or light blue. The national insignia is that of 'Central Lithuania' – purple and white

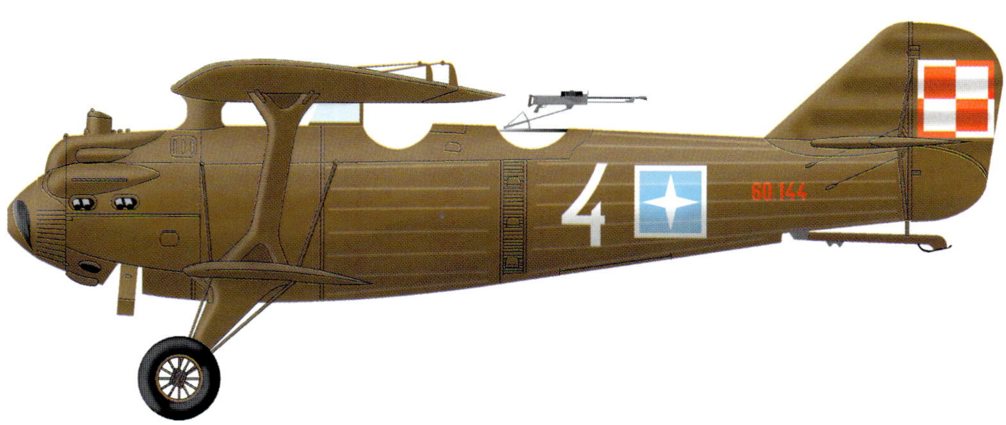

78: BREGUET XIX of 22 Eskadra Liniowa 2nd Pułk Lotniczy at Kraków, September 1933

SCALE: 1/72

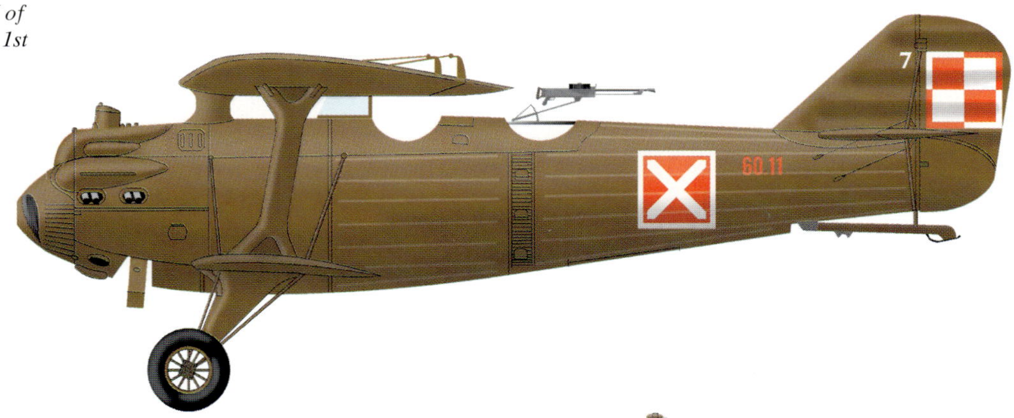

79: BREGUET XIX of 11 Eskadra Liniowa 1st Pułk Lotniczy, 1933

80: POTEZ XV A2, serial no 447. With por. pil. *Stanisław Pawluae aircraft took part in The Second Alps' Flight.*

81: POTEZ XXVII A2 serial no 41.107 of 42 Eskadra

82: POTEZ XXV of 32 Eskadra Liniowa, 3rd Pułk Lotniczy

83: FOKKER F-VII B/3m of 211 Eskadra Niszczycielska, 1st Pułk Lotniczy

SCALE: 1/72

84

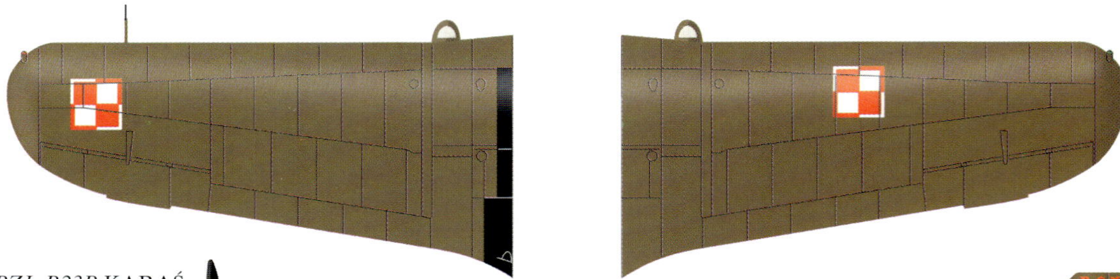

85: *PZL P.23B* KARAŚ, *of 24 Eskadra. September 1939. Radio call no 941-K in white*

86: *PZL P.23B* KARAŚ *serial no 44.214 of 41 Eskadra, Toruń, spring 1939. Radio call no 05-T in black*

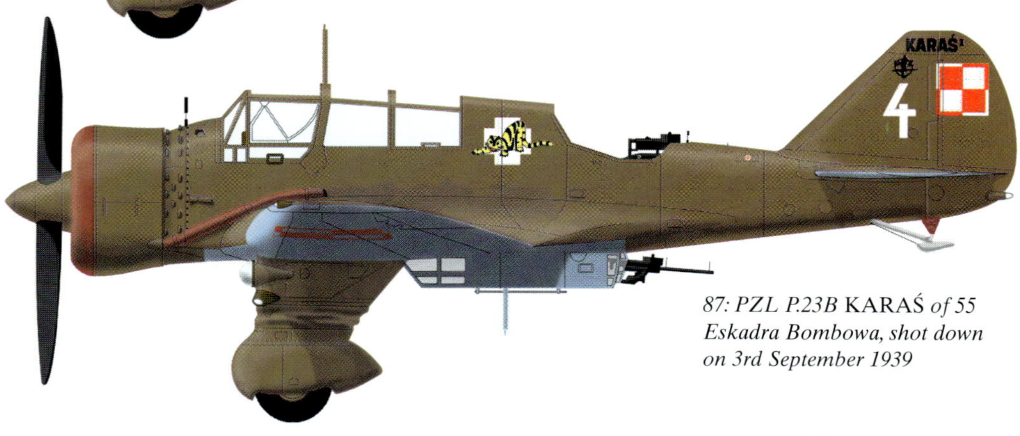

87: *PZL P.23B* KARAŚ *of 55 Eskadra Bombowa, shot down on 3rd September 1939*

88: *PZL P.23B* KARAŚ, *serial no 44.62 of 22 Eskadra during Zaolzie incorporation, autumn 1938. Radio call no 25-K*

SCALE: 1/72

89: *PZL P.23B* KARAŚ*, personal aircraft of 12 Eskadra commander. Warsaw 1938. Radio call no 08-N.*

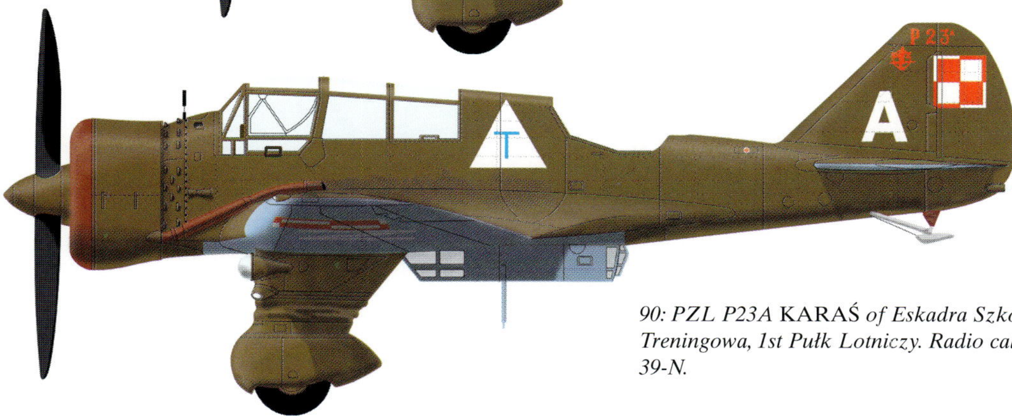

90: PZL P23A KARAŚ *of Eskadra Szkolna i Treningowa, 1st Pułk Lotniczy. Radio call underwing no 39-N.*

SCALE: 1/72

91: GOTHA GIV of 21 Eskadra Niszczycielska

92: FRIEDRISCHAFEN G.III serial 354/17 (ex 506/17) after overhaul in Ruchomy Park of 3rd Pułk Lotniczy, winter 1925–1926. Ławica airfield. Aircraft was sent to 3 PL. Was used for 3-5 years as the last Friedrischafen in the world

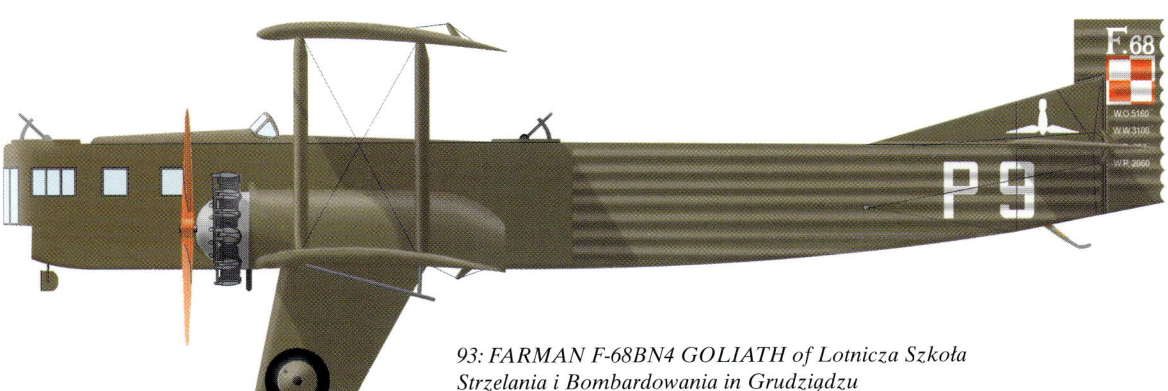

93: FARMAN F-68BN4 GOLIATH of Lotnicza Szkoła Strzelania i Bombardowania in Grudziądzu

SCALE: 1/96

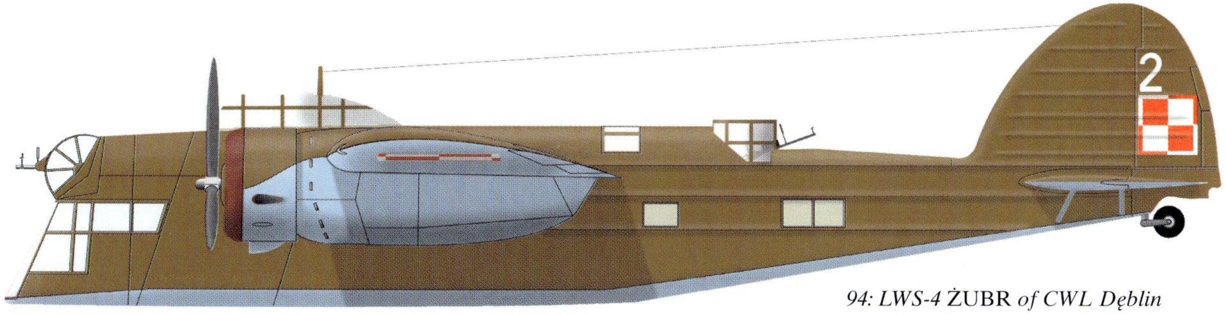

94: *LWS-4 ŻUBR of CWL Dęblin*

95: *PZL P.37A ŁOŚ. Serial no 72.11. Founded by Polish banks personnel and sent to 212 Eskadra Niszczycielska, 1st Pułk Lotniczy*

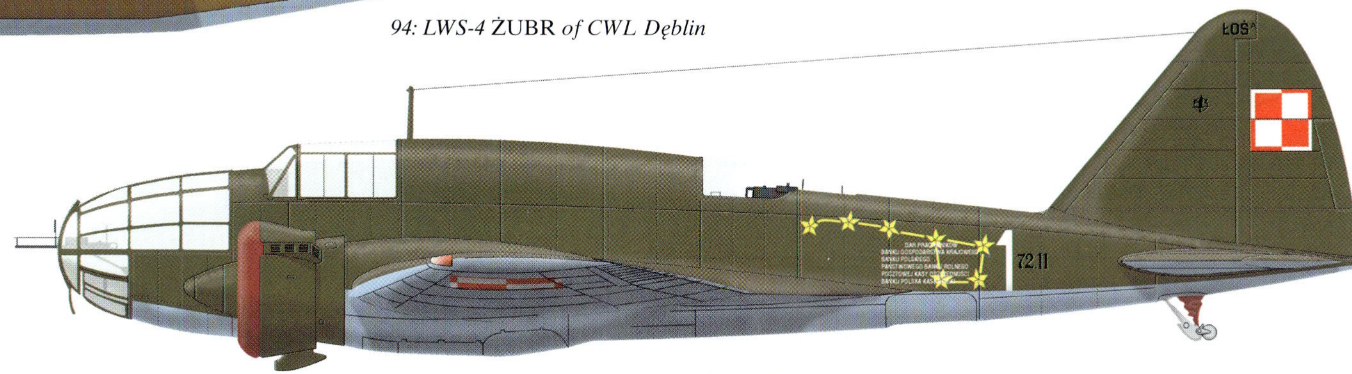

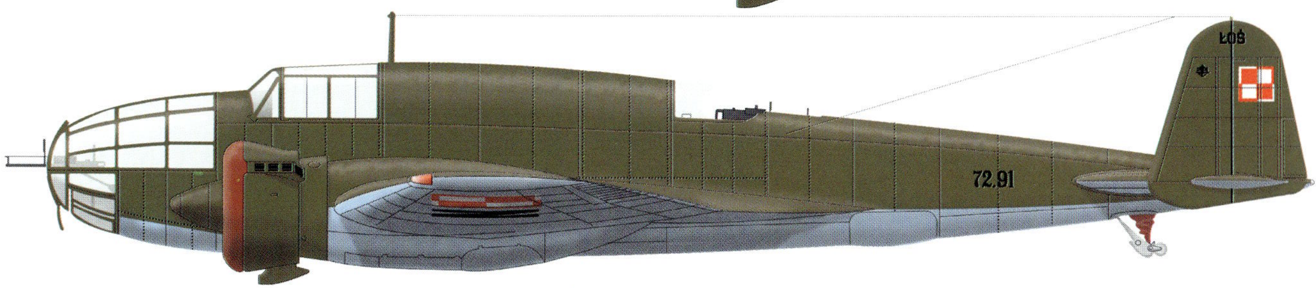

96: *Left: PZL P.37B ŁOŚ, serial no 72.91 of 1st Pułk Lotniczy. Underwing radio call no 864-N in black*

97: *Right: PZL P.37B ŁOŚ, of 12 Eskadra Bombowa. The only one known with a unit emblem*

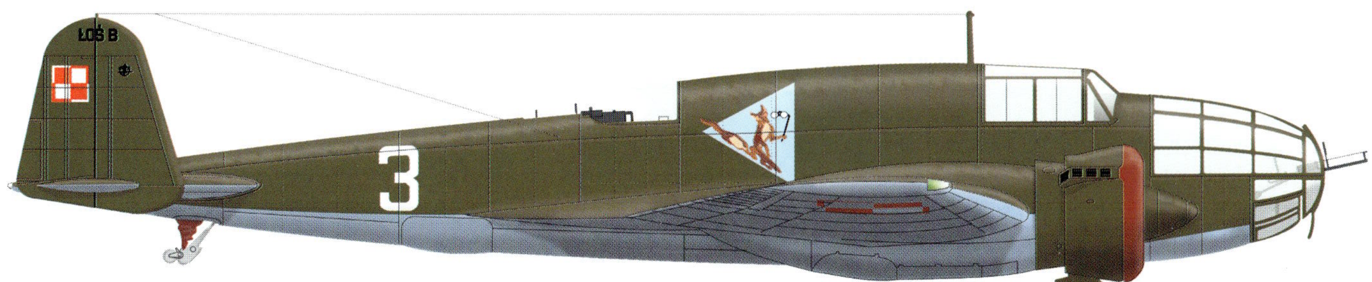

SCALE: 1/96

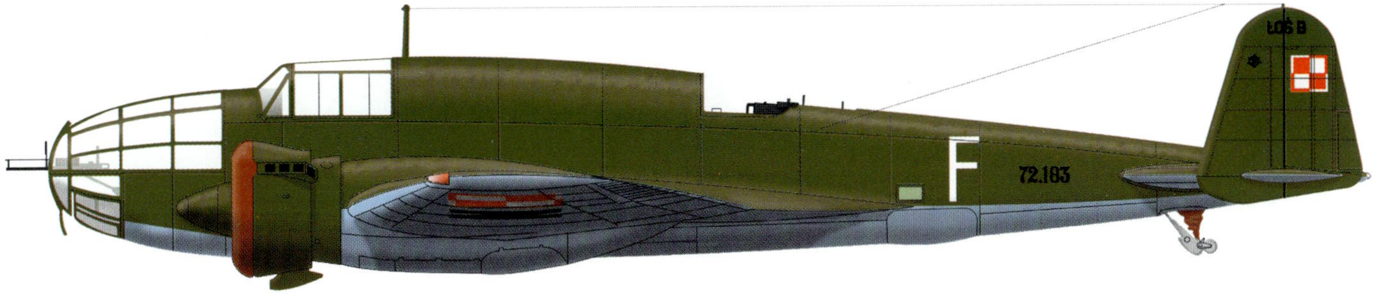

98: *PZL P.37B ŁOŚ, of 16 Eskadra Bombowa with individual letter F in white.*

99: *PZL P.37B ŁOŚ, of 17 Eskadra Bombowa with individual letter M in white, September 1939.*

100: *LeO H-135B2, probably of Morska Eskadra Obserwacyjna*

101: *LATHAM-43 HB-3 of 1 Eskadra Liniowa "Wiking".*

SCALE: 1/96

102: NIEUPORT MACCHI M-9 of MDLot at Puck, 1922

103: SCHRECK FBA-17HE2 of Eskadra Szkolna MDLot at Puck

104: LUBLIN R-XIII TER, serial no 704 of MDLot in Puck

105: LUBLIN R-MI1 TER, serial no 710 of M13Lot at Puck

106: ALBATROS B II-a of Szkoła Obserwatorów i Strzelców Lotniczych at Toruń (1920s)

SCALE: 1/72

107: LUBLIN R-VIII BIS serial no 802 of MDLot at Puck

108: ALBATROS B II-A of Wyższa Szkoła Pilotażu in Poznań

109: BRANDENBURG B 1 (HANSA), built in 1915 in Kuk Fliegerarsenal FW with red letter Z – first Polish National insignia, used in Krakow before red-white checker was approved

110: CAUDRON C III, unknown pilot's school

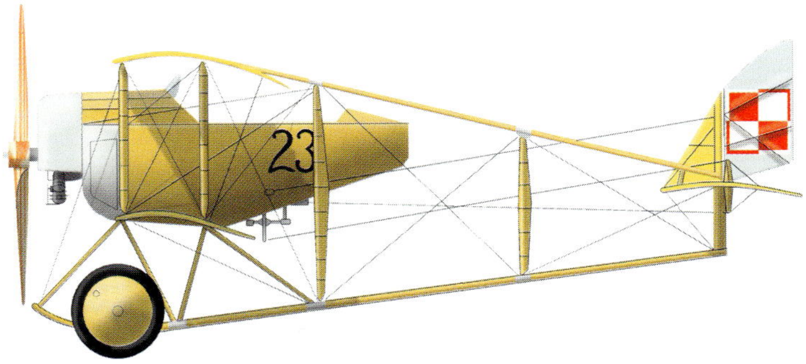

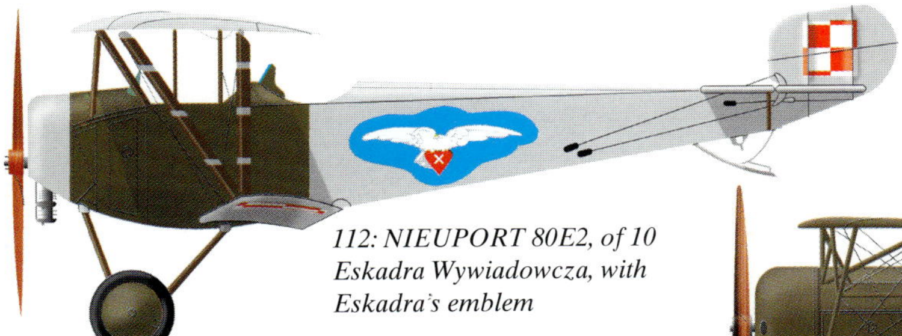

112: NIEUPORT 80E2, of 10 Eskadra Wywiadowcza, with Eskadra's emblem

113: MS-30, unknown unit

SCALE: 1/72

114: HANRIOT HD-14, serial no 30.145 of CWL at Dęblin

115: BARTEL BM-4a, individual no 3 of Szkoła Podchorlżych Lotnictwa at Dęblin

116: BARTEL BM-4h, serial no 33.40, individual no 32 of Szkoła Podchorlżych Lotnictwa at Dęblin

117: BARTEL BM-5a, serial no 53-42 of Szkoła Podchorlżych Lotnictwa at Dęblin

118: PWS-16, serial no 59-10 with radio call, under wing no 11-M of Szkoła Podoficerów Pilotów

119: PWS-18, with unknown no, of SPL at Dęblin. Underwing no 64-R

120: PWS-18, serial 80.7 of Eskadra Treningowa in 4th Pułk Lotniczy. Underwing no unknown

SCALE: 1/72

121: *PWS-26, serial 81.36 of SPL, at Dęblin*

123

122: PWS-26, serial no 81.20 of SPL at Dęblin

124: PWS-26 used for blind flying at SPL at Dęblin

125: RWD-8 PWS, serial no 34.27 of Centrum Wyszkolenia Lotniczego at Dęblin

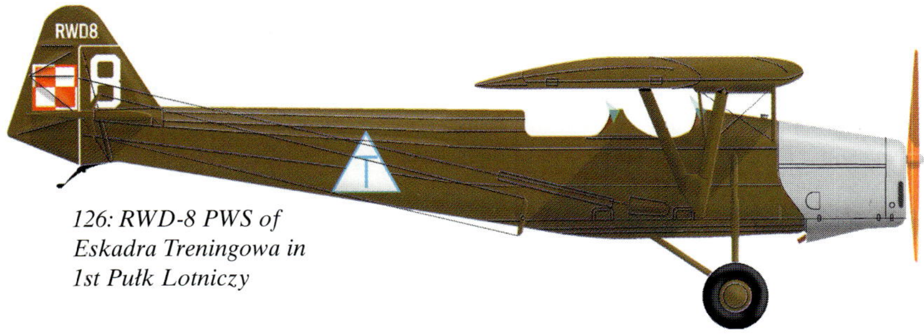

126: RWD-8 PWS of Eskadra Treningowa in 1st Pułk Lotniczy

127: RWD-8 PWS, serial no 34.147 of Centrum Wyszkolenia Lotniczego at Dęblin

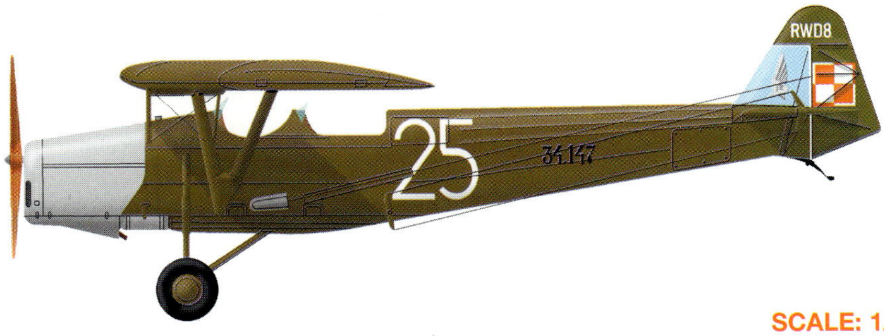

SCALE: 1/72

128: *Spitfire Mk IA L1066 was prepared for despatch to Poland in July 1939 but was never delivered, being diverted instead to Turkey. No pictures are known to exist of it at that time so it is shown here as it might have looked, finished in standard RAF fighter camouflage of the time. The Polish markings are entirely conjectural but most British exports of the period were factory-finished in the markings of their intended customer*

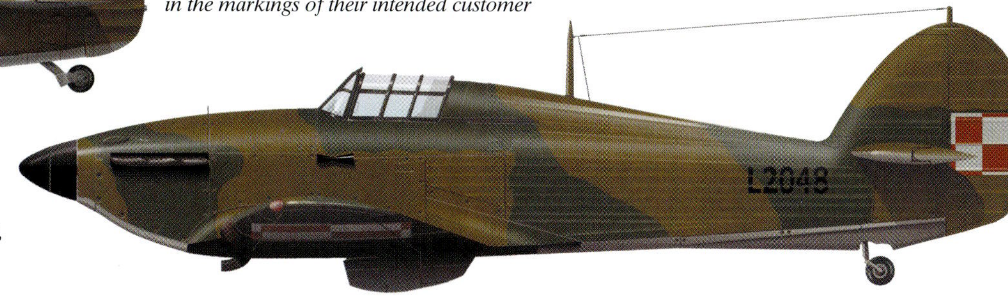

129: *Hurricane Mk I L2048 WAS sent to Poland and reached there in July 1939, so there are stronger grounds for believing that it received national markings, as did those Hurricanes delivered to Belgium and Yugoslavia. It was in fact shipped back to the UK in late August 1939, being struck off charge in January 1940*

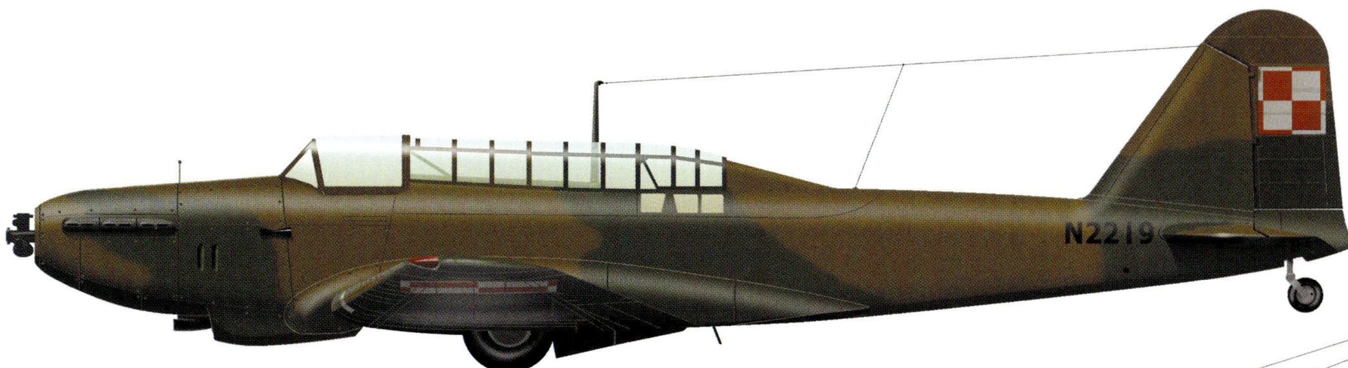

130: *Fairey Battle N2219 was one of those ordered by Poland. Shipped out of the UK on 10 August 1939 bound for Poland, nothing further is known. As Fairey were keen to sell the Battle, the balance of probability is that it too received Polish markings*

131: *There are no known photos of the sole Cant Z.506 to reach Poland, but if earlier Italian practice with export aircraft was followed it would probably have been finished in overall aluminium paint with the typical red lightning stripe on the fuselage. Whether or not it ever received the Polish chessboards is unknown, but Italian attention to detail may well have ensured that it did*

SCALE: 1/96

POLAND 1918-1920

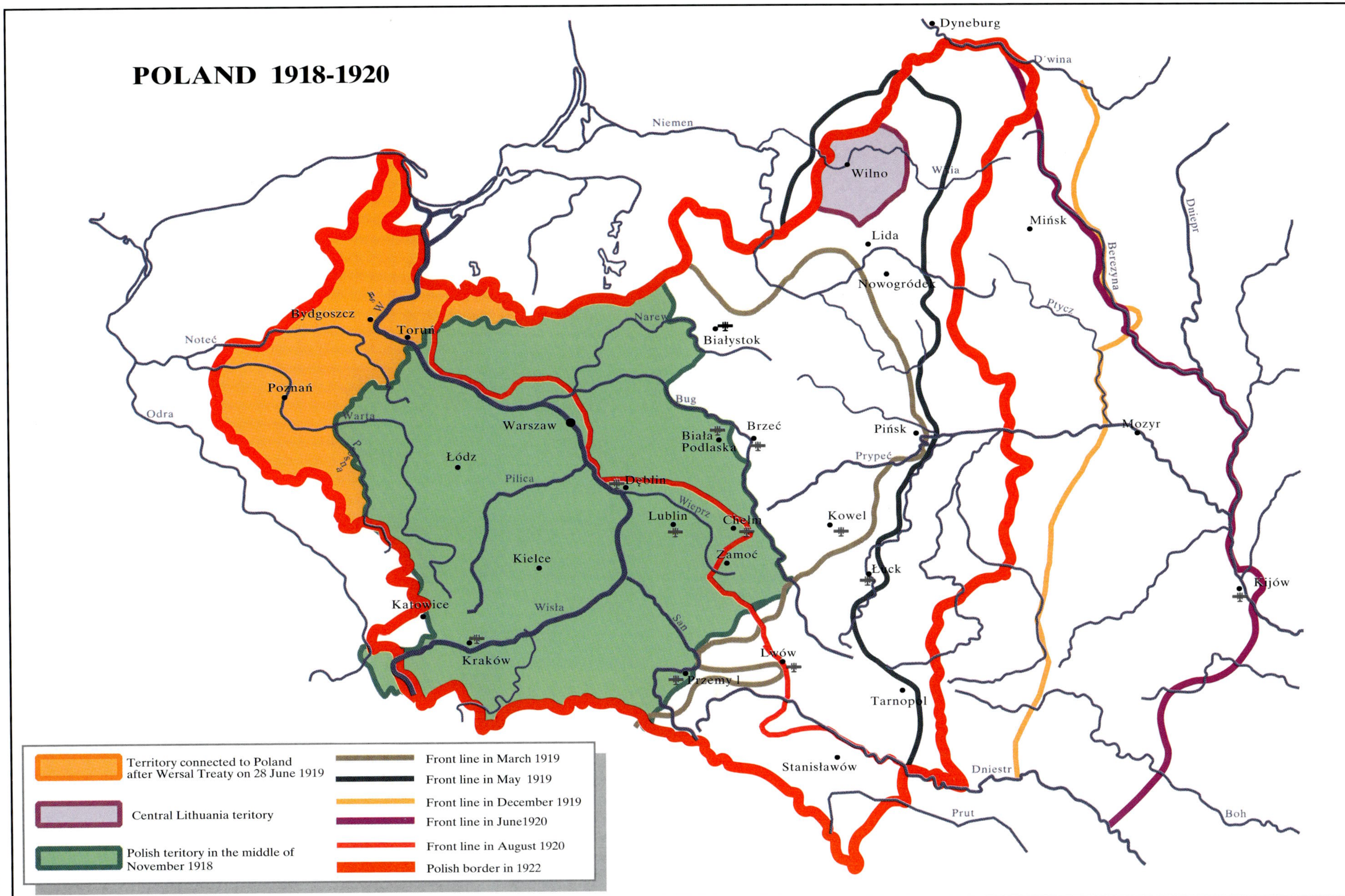

Aerial Bases August 1939

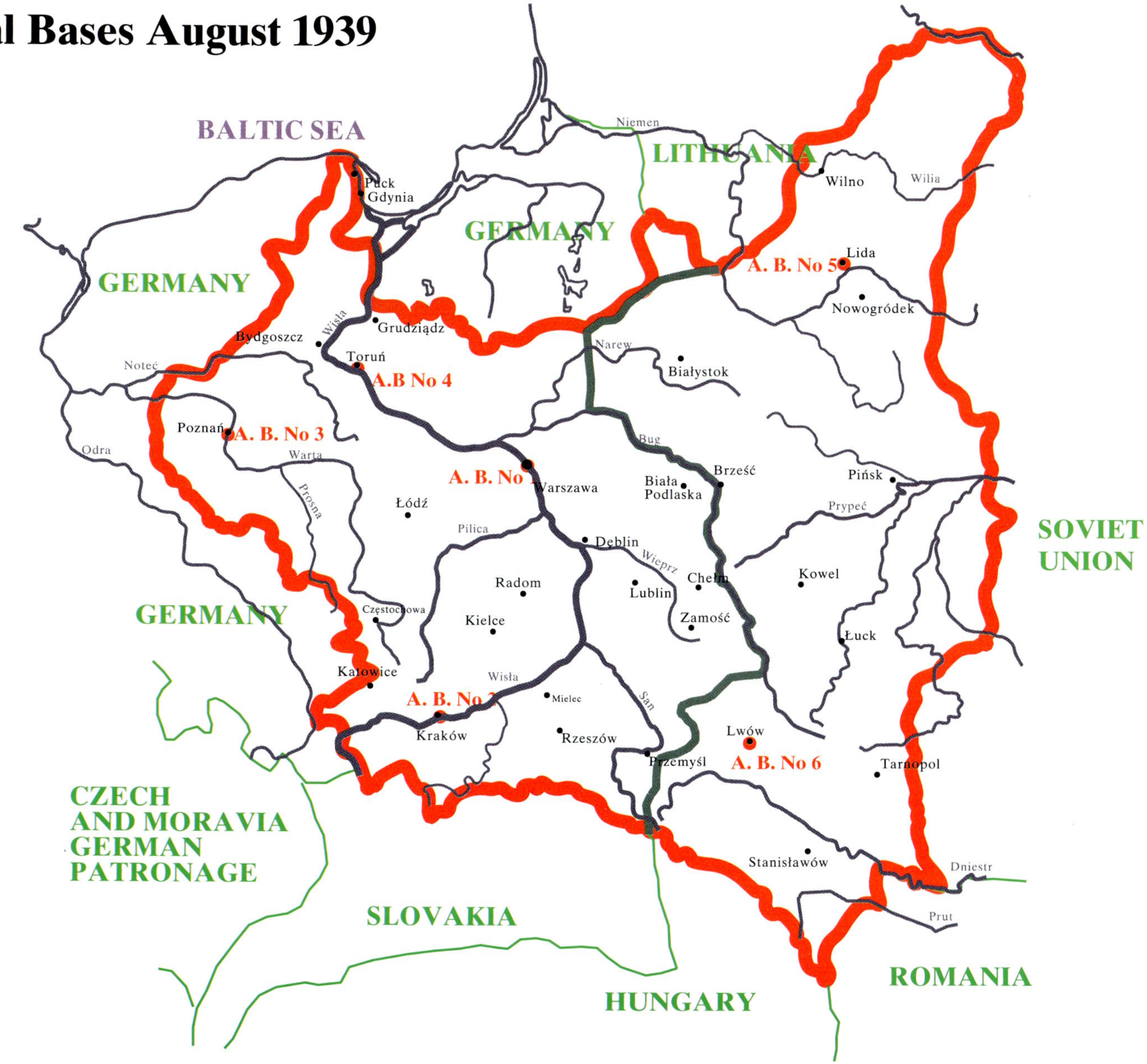

Fighter unit locations, 20 August 1939

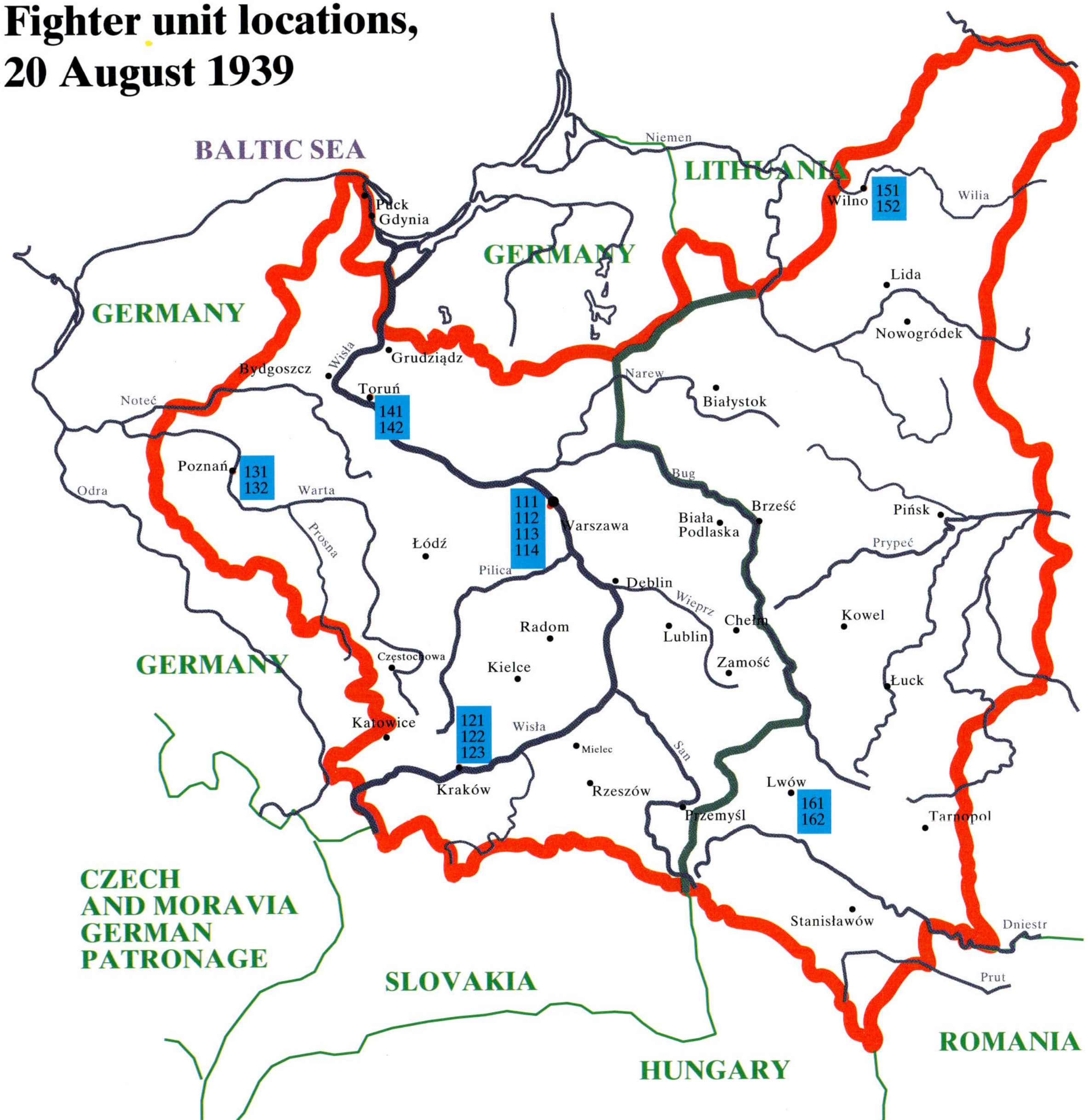

Eskadry myśliwskie (fighter units)	
111, 112, 113, 114	Warszawa-Okęcie
121, 122, 123	Kraków-Rakowice
131, 132	Poznań-Ławica
141, 142	Toruń
151, 152	Wilno-Porubanek
161, 162	Lwów-Sknilów

German Invasion routes, September 1939

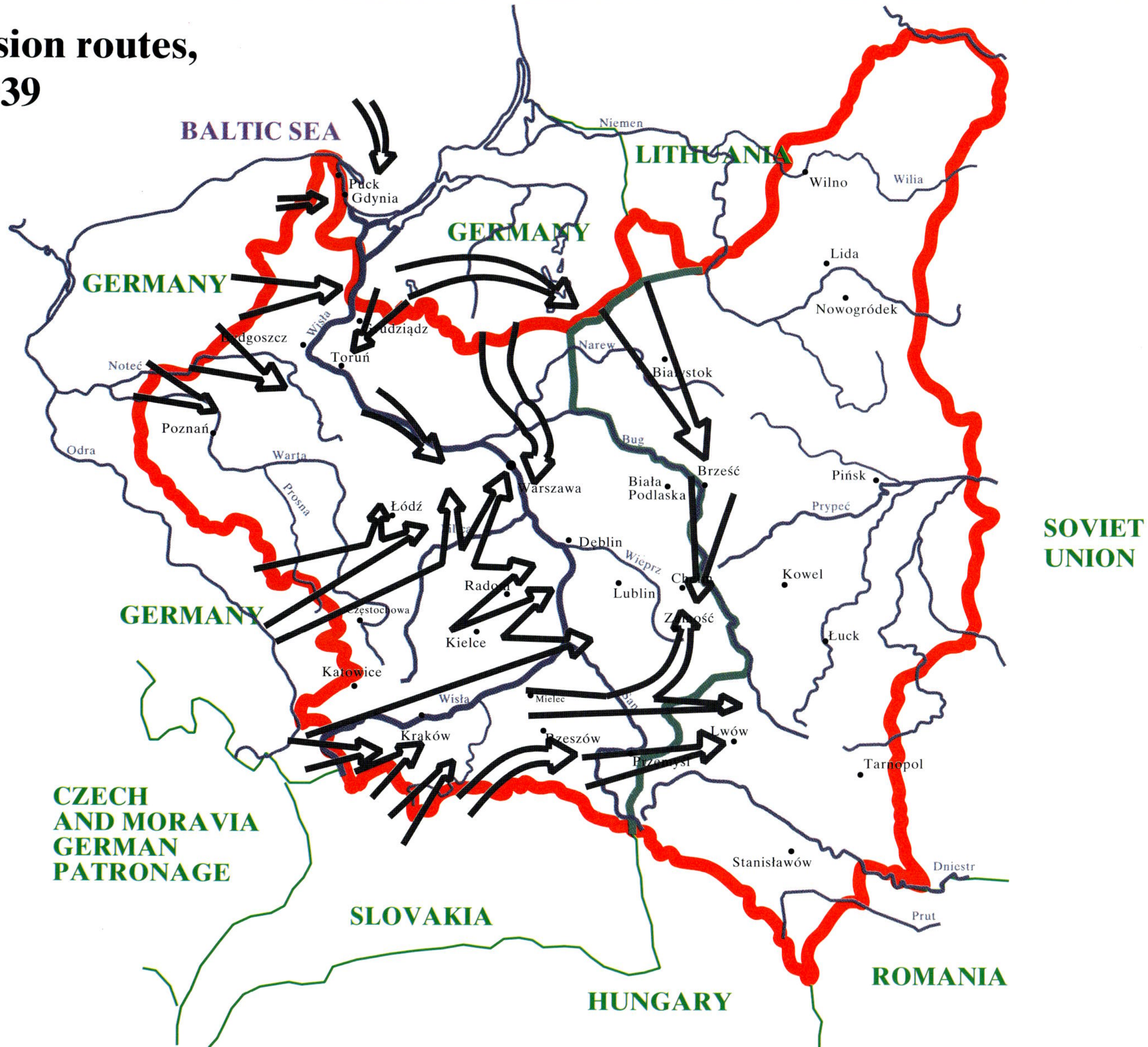

Location of Polish Air Force Units on 1 September 1939

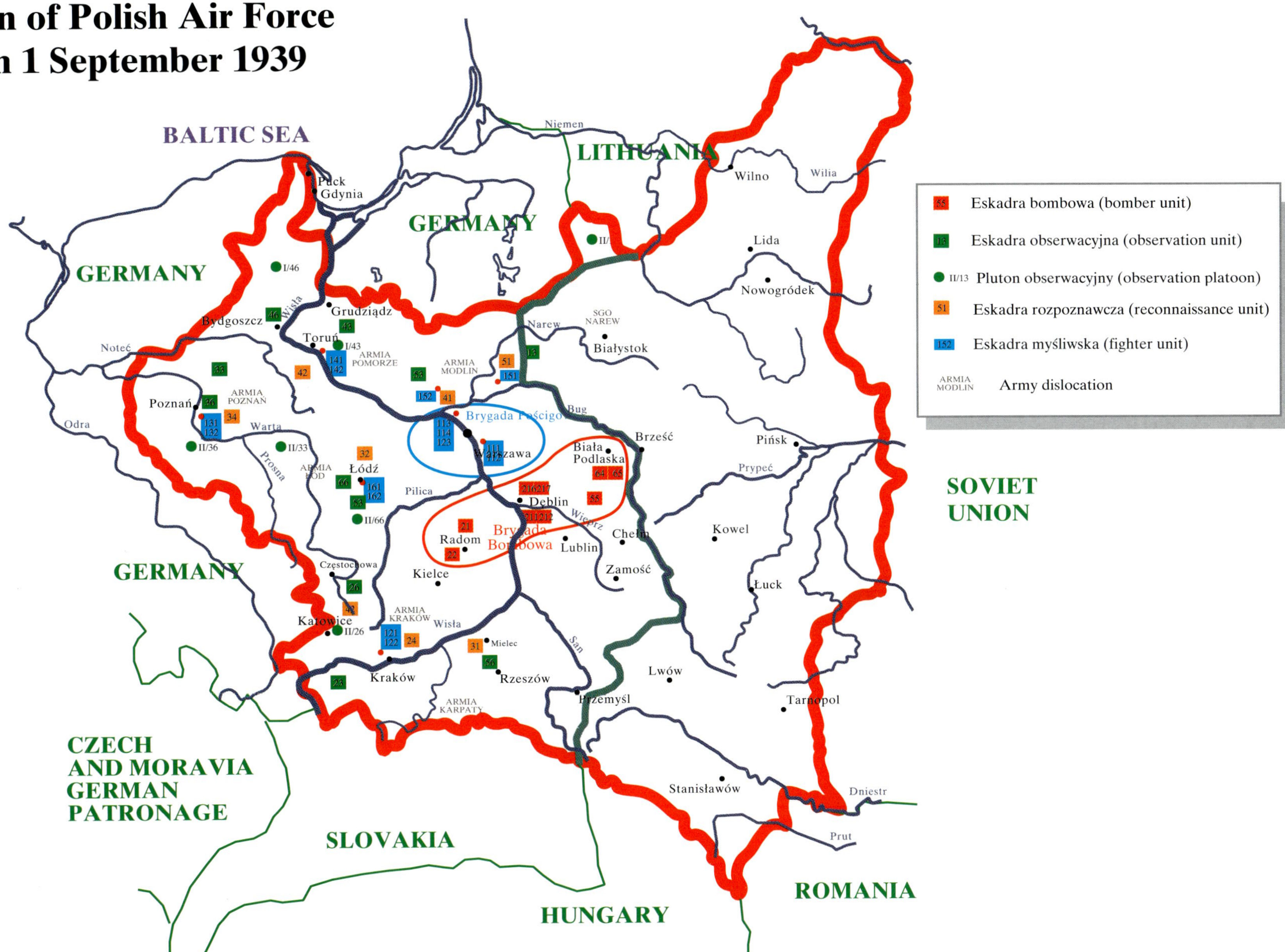

Fighter unit locations
1 September 1939

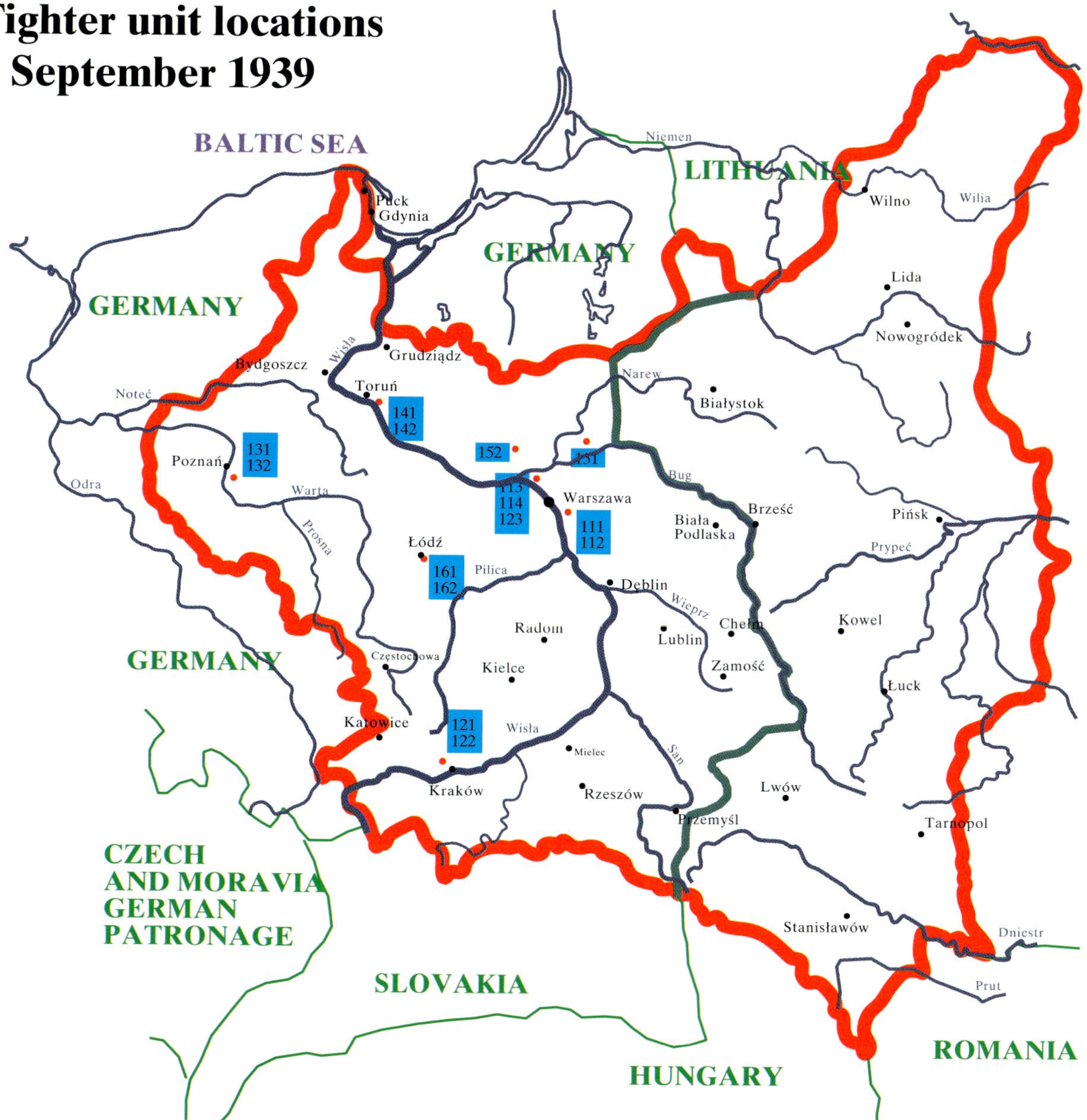

Eskadry myśliwskie (fighter units)	
111, 112	Zielonka
113, 114, 123	Poniatów
121, 122	Kraków -Balice
131, 132	Dzieżnica
141, 142	Marynów
151	Biel
152	Szpondów
161, 162	Łódź - Widzew

Fighter unit locations
4 September 1939

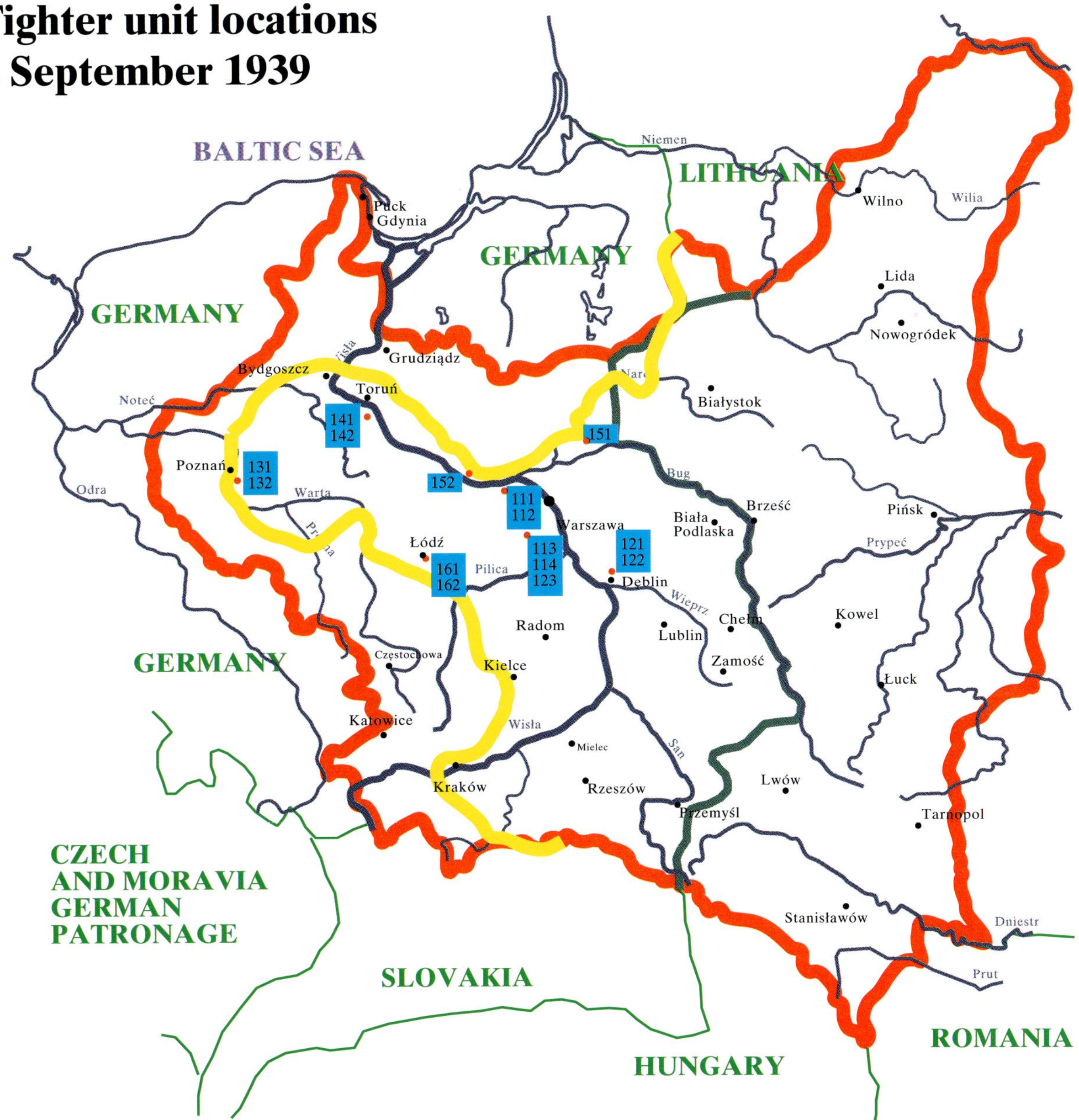

Eskadry myśliwskie (fighter units)	
111, 112	Zaborów
113, 114, 123	Radików
121, 122	Podolów
131, 132	Kleczew
141, 142	Poczołkowo
151	Biel
152	Kroczewo
161, 162	Łódź - Widzew

Fighter unit locations 6 September 1939

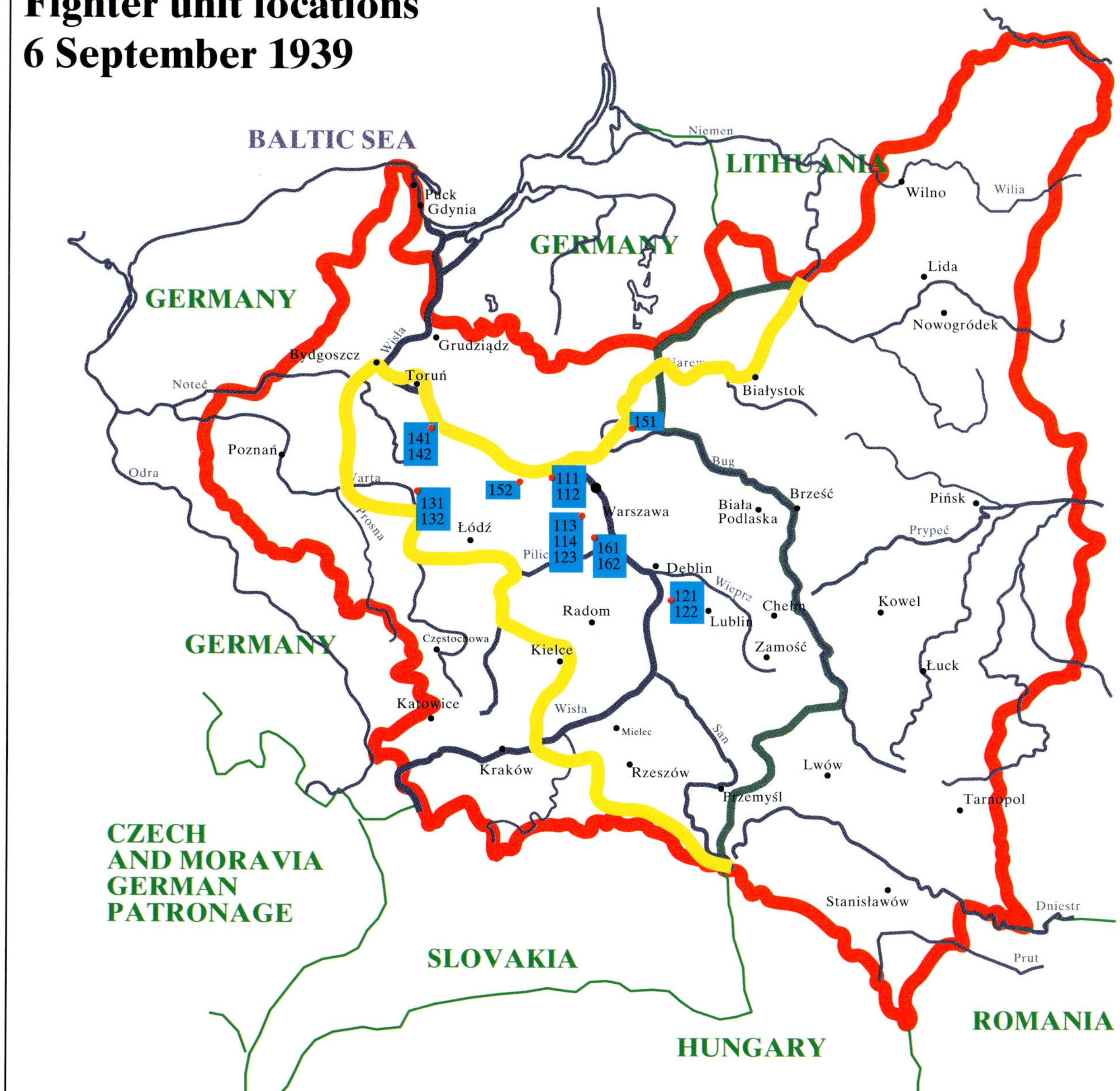

Eskadry myśliwskie (fighter units)	
111, 112	Zaborów
113, 114, 123	Radików
121, 122	Kraczewice
131, 132	Osiek Mały
141, 142	Osięciny
151	Biel
152	Wieruchów
161, 162	Drwalewo

Fighter unit locations 8 September 1939

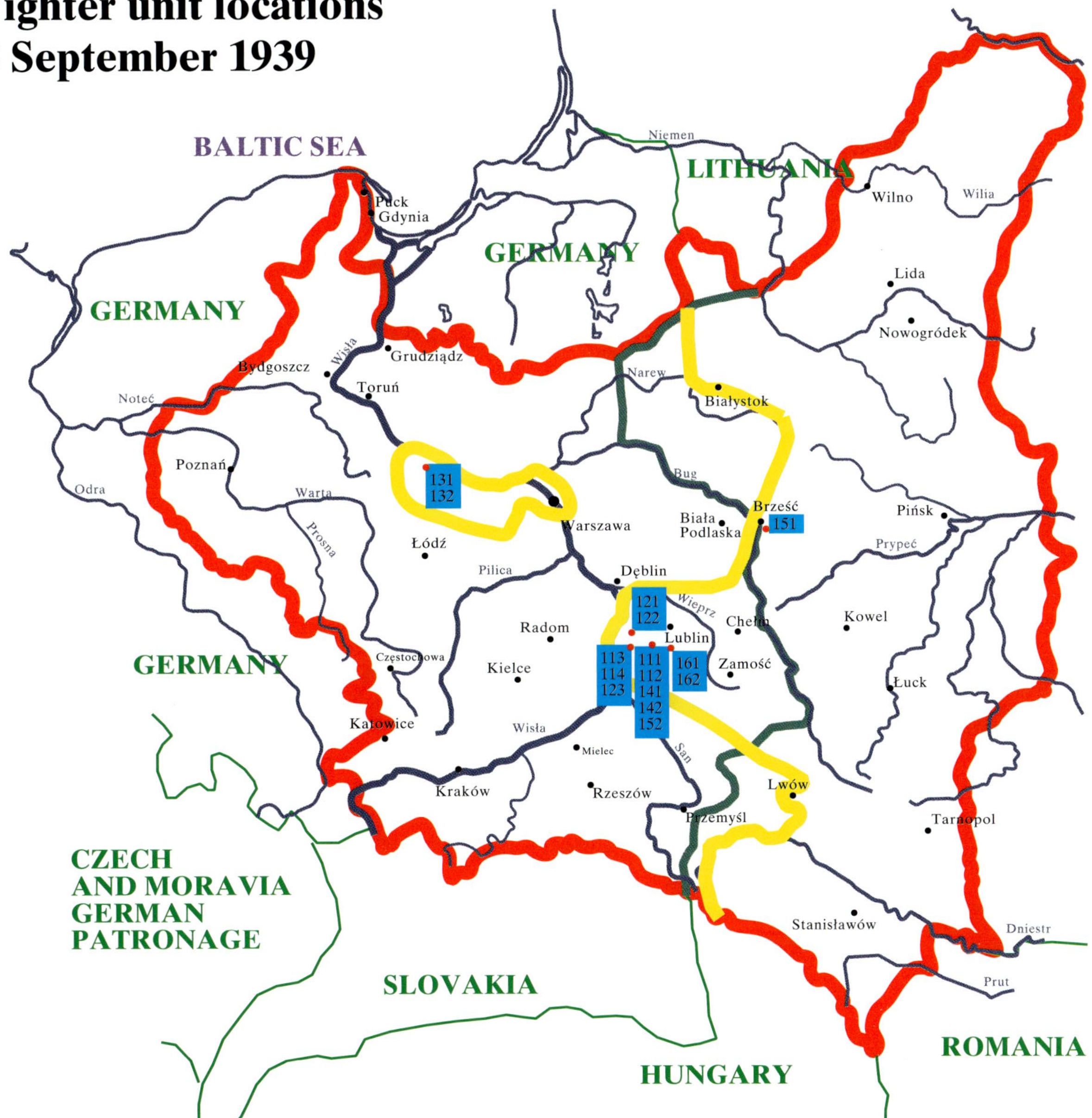

Eskadry myśliwskie (fighter units)	
111, 112, 141, 142, 152	Kierz
113, 114, 123	Bełżyce
121, 122	Kraczewice
131, 132	Krośniewice
151	Adamów
161, 162	Radawiec Duży

Fighter unit locations
15 September 1939

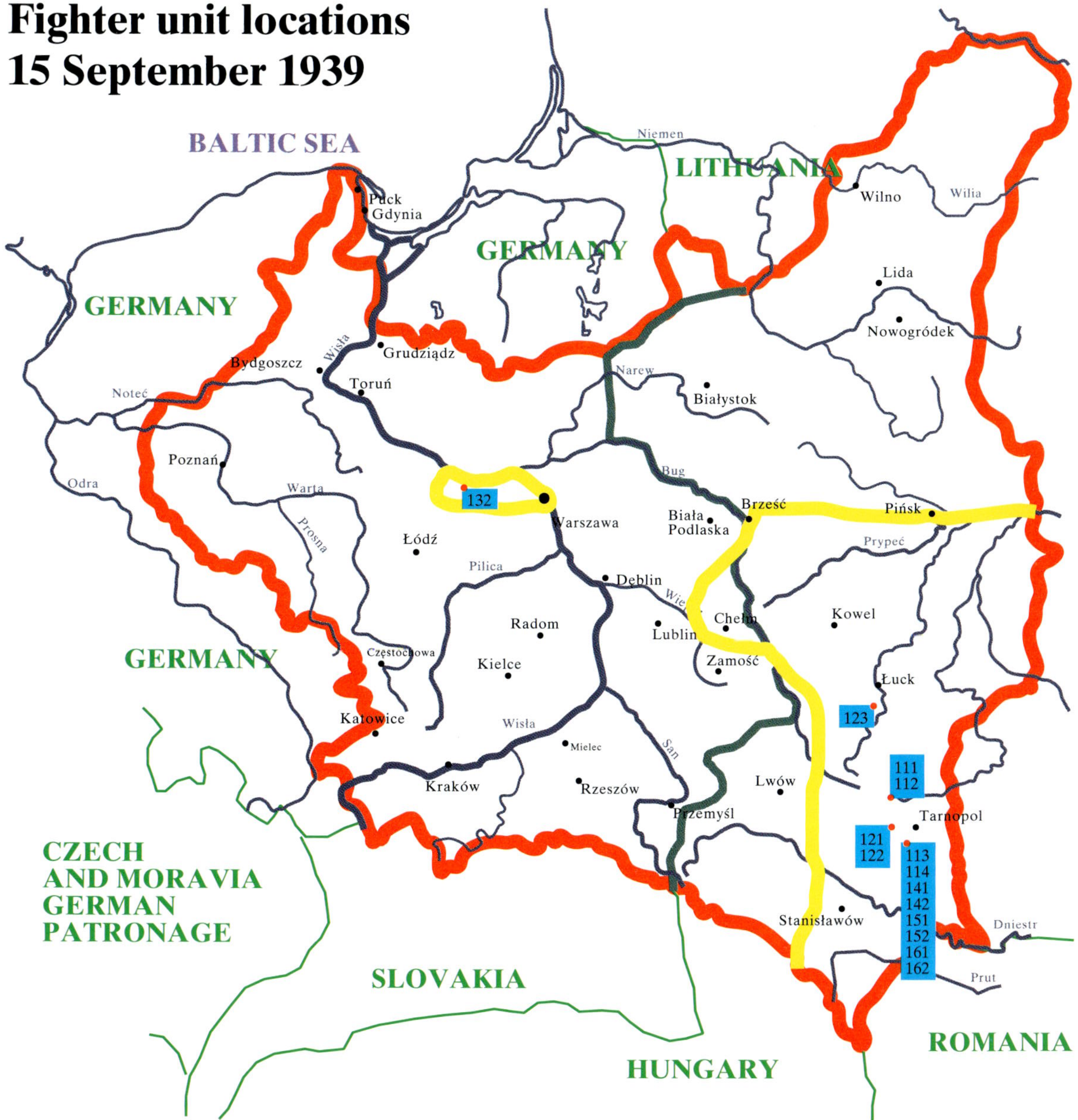

Eskadry myśliwskie (fighter units)	
111, 112	Denysów
113, 114, 141, 142, 151, 152, 161, 162	Liliatyn
123	Młynów
121, 122	Petlikowice
132	Luszyn

465: *A semi-inflated ex-French Caquot captive balloon and an ex-German Drachen type in a hangar, probably sometime in late 1919*

466: *A Caquot type observation balloon in a forest hide*

467: *The Vedette class airship* Lech *in flight*

Samodzielna Grupa Operacyjna 'Narew'. In most cases spotting units were not used in combat, with the exception of 5 Kompania of Armia 'Modlin'. The unit made 2 reconnaissance take-offs on 10 September 1939.

Barrage balloon companies were concentrated in the Warsaw area. They were reporting to the commander of Zgrupowania Balonów Zaporowych. Some 40-50 barrage tandems were put into position. The 1936 plan of barrage balloon use called for over 1,000 pairs to be used, unfortunately this failed to be achieved. The balloons were mainly set over bridges across the Vistula and in the PZL Okęcie area. They were used until about 7 September. Their number was too small, though, to have any significance in the defence of Warsaw from air attacks. Barrage balloon companies were equipped with Polish produced tandem pairs of WBS NN (upper) and WBS N (lower) balloons.

The sole patrol airship of the Polish Air Force has to be mentioned here. This was a French Zodiac VZ-11 airship of the Vedette class. During the First World War it was used by the French Army, patrolling the Mediterranean Sea as the *'Commandant Coutelle'*. Purchased in 1920 it received the name *'Lech'*. From 1921 it was used for airship pilot training. A total of 18 pilots and several dozen maintenance crews were trained. The airship finished its career in 1926.

1 bal. – balonowy – Balloon forces.

APPENDIXES

Aircraft manufactured at aircraft workshops in 1919–1923

Manufacturer/type	1919	1920	1921	1922	1923	total
Centralne Warsztaty Lotnicze Warsaw						
Hannover CL.II (series 18 – Słowik)	1 + 2					3
Hannover CL.II series E – modification		5				5
WZ-VIII		1				1
Warsztaty Lotnicze Lwów						
Hansa Brandenburg; CI type III Lwów	10					10
Warsztaty Lotnicze Krakow						
Oeffag DIII series 21 - modification	5	5				10
Oeffag DIII type K series 23 - modification			5	5		10
KW-2		10	10	10		30
KW-3					1	1
Warsztaty SL Ławica						
LVG CV series 9 - modification	10	10	10			10
Warsztaty Wentzel Ostrów Wielkopolski						
Type 1	1					1
Total	**29**	**31**	**25**	**15**	**1**	**101**

Production by E. Plage & T. Laśkiewicz factory

Role	Type	number	Notes	Role	Type	number	Notes
reconnaissance	Ansaldo A300	50		accompanying	Lublin R-XIII D	95	
fighter	Ansaldo Balilla	70		accompanying	Lublin R-XIII Dr	11	rally
reconnaissance	Potez XV A2	100		accompanying	Lublin R-XIII F	7	
reconnaissance	Potex XXV A2	100		accompanying	Lublin R-XIV/XIII	15	
bomber	Fokker FVII/3m	33		accompanying	Lublin R-XIV bis	70	
reconnaissance	Lublin R-VIII	4	3 converted to naval version	accompanying	Lublin R-XIII bis/hydro	3	for naval aviation
accompanying	Lublin R-X	5		accompanying	Lublin R-XIII ter/hydro	10	for naval aviation
accompanying	Lublin R-XIII B	50		accompanying	Lublin R-XIII G/hydro	6	
accompanying	Lublin R-XIII C	50		accompanying	Lublin R-XIII G	12	

Production by Lubelska Wytwornia Samolotow

Role	Type	production years	number	notes
reconnaissance	Potez XXV with Jupiter engine		46	(not including the aircraft converted to Jupiter engines)
accompanying	Lublin R-XIII F		25	
bomber	LWS-6 *Żubr*		15	
accompanying	RWD-14 *Czapla*	1938-1939	65	
accompanying	LSW-3 *Mewa*	1939	30	100 completed by the outbreak of war

Production by Wytwórnia Samolót

Role	Type	number	Role	Type	number
training	Hanriot HD-14	144	training	Bartel BM 4a	22
training	Hanriot HD-19	55	conversion training	Bartel BM 5a, 5b	40
medical	Hanriot HD-28s	16	conversion training	Bartel BM 5c	20

Production by Podlaska Wytwórnia Samolótow

Role	Type	number	Notes	Role	Type	number	Notes
reconnaissance	Potez XVA2	35	400 hp Lorraine-Dietrich engine	fighter	PWS-10	80	
reconnaissance	Potez XXVII A2	155	400 hp Lorraine-Dietrich engine	conversion training	PWS-14	20	
reconnaissance	Potex XXV A2	150	450 hp Lorraine-Dietrich engine	conversion training	PWS-16 bis	20	
fighter	PWS-A (Avia BH33)	50		conversion training	PWS-18 (Avro Tutor)	40	
training	Bartel BM 4h	50	licence of Wytwornia 'Samolot'	conversion training	PWS-26 bis	300	
training	RWD-8	500	licence of DWL	auxiliary	PWS-24	5	
liaison	PWS-5	5		auxiliary	PWS-24 bis	5	

Production by Państwowe Zakłady Lotnicze-Wytwórnia Platowców (WP) Nr 1 (1931–1939)

Role	Type	number	Notes	Role	Type	number	Notes
fighter	Spad 61 C1	30	French licence	liaison	PZL Ł-2	20	
fighter	Wibault 70 C1	25	French licence	accompanying	PZL-5	10	

Production by Państwowe Zakłady Lotnicze-Wytwórnia Platowców (PZL-WP) Nr 1 (1931–1939)

Role	Type	Year	Recipient	Number	Notes
fighter	PZL P.7a	1932/33	Poland	150	
fighter	PZL P.11b	1933/34	Rumania	50	
fighter	PZL P.11a	1934	Poland	30	
fighter	PZL P.11c	1935	Poland	175	
fighter	PZL P.24a	1936	Turkey	14	
fighter	PZL P.24a	1937	Greece	5	
fighter	PZL P.24b	1937	Bulgaria	14	
fighter	PZL P.24c	1936/37	Turkey	25	
fighter	PZL P.24c	1936/37	Bulgaria	20	
fighter	PZL P.24e	1936	Romania	5	
fighter	PZL P.24f	1938	Bulgaria	25	
fighter	PZL P.24f	1938	Greece	6	
fighter	PZL P.24a	1936	Turkey	20	parts and materials for assembly in Turkey
line	PZL P.23A *Karaś*	1935	Poland	40	
line	PZL P.23A *Karaś*	1936/38	Poland	210	
line	PZL P.43	1938	Bulgaria	12	
line	PZL P.43A	1938/39	Bulgaria	42	6 retained in Poland in September 1939
bomber	PZL P.37A *Łoś*	1938	Poland	30	
bomber	PZL P.37B *Łoś*	1938	Poland	50	
bomber	PZL P.37B *Łoś*	1939	Poland	14	
bomber	PZL P.37B *Łoś*	1939	Poland	10	of these 6 made at Wytwórnia Platowców Nr 2 in Mielec

Series production of engines by Polskie Zakłady Skoda

Engine type	production years	Power	Number	use
Lorraine-Dietrich 12 Ed	1927	400	100	Potez XV, XXVII
Lorraine-Dietrich 12 Eb	1927-1929	450	500	Potez XXV, Spad 61, PWS-10
Wright J5 Whirlwind	1929-1931	220	400	R-XIII, R-X, PWS-12, PWS-14, PWS-16, PWS-26, BM 5d, PWS-16bis
Bristol Jupiter VIIF	1931-1932	485	300	PZL P.7a
Bristol Mercury IV S2	1932	500	50	PZL P.11a
Bristol Mercury V S2	1932-1933	645	300	PZL P.11c
Bristol Mercury VI S2	1933-1934	645		PZL P.11c

Series production of engines by Państwowe Zakłady Lotnicze – Wytwórnia Silnikow (PZL-WS)

Engine type	production years	Power	Number	Use
Skoda G. 1620 Mors A	1934-1935	350	50	Lublin R-XIII F
Bristol Pegasus II	1935	590	50	PZL P.23A
Bristol Pegasus VIII	1935-1936	680	300	LWS *Żubr*, PZL P.23B
Bristol Pegasus XX	1936-1937	925	300	PZL P.37B
PZL-G. 1620 Mors B	1937-1938	450	100	LWS *Czapla* (RWD-14)
Bristol Mercury VIII	1938	840	150	PZL P.50 *Jastrząb*

Total number of series produced engines in 1926-1939

Production years	Number of engines	Number of types	Factory	Production years	Number of engines	Number of types	Factory
1927-1931	1000	3	Pol. Zakłady Skoda	1934-1939	700	2	PZInż.
1931-1935	650	4	Pol. Zakłady Skoda	1934-1939	300	1	Avia
1935-1939	900	6	PZL WS				

Bombs used by the Polish Air Force 1918-1939

country of origin	type and model	length (mm)	weight (kg)	notes
Germany (captured)	fragmentation 'air mouse' Nr 2	150	1,025	only cassette-launched
Germany (captured)	fragmentation 12.5 PuW	750	12.550	
Germany (captured)	fragmentation 75 kg PuW	1700	75.050	
Germany (captured)	high explosive 50 kg PuW	1700	50	
Germany (captured)	high explosive 100 kg PuW	1830	100	
Germany (captured)	high explosive 300 kg PuW	2750	3000	
Germany (captured)	ignition 'elektron' 1 kg	352	0.968	
Germany (captured)	ignition 5 kg PuW	758	5	
Germany (captured)	ignition 10 kg PuW	840	10.2	
Germany (captured)	training PuW	750	10.1	
France	fragmentation 10 kg PA	563	9.4	cast iron
France	high explosive 50 kg DT	1340	56	hammered steel
France	high explosive 100 kg	1500	115	hammered steel
France	illumination VM no.3	1090	13.5	
Poland	fragmentation 'mouse' 1 kg T wz. 34	360	approx 0.8	only cassette-launched
Poland	fragmentation 12 kg wz. 27	692	12	
Poland	fragmentation 12 FS wz. 35	645	12	
Poland	high explosive wz. 29	1158	50	
Poland	high explosive 50 kg T wz. 32	no data	no data	
Poland	high explosive 100 kg T wz. 31	1400	100	
Poland	ignition 'mouse' wz. 32	180	0.22	only cassette-launched
Poland	ignition 12 kg wz. 38	705	12	
Poland	smoke 10 kg wz. 34	no data	no data	
Poland	smoke 50 kg wz. 34			
Poland	training 6 kg	600	6.2	concrete
Poland	training 7 kg wz. 31	no data	no data	concrete
Poland	illumination 12 kg wz. 35	720	12	

Specification of machine guns and cannon purchased or produced in Poland after 1928

Origin	Type, name, model	Calibre (mm)	Overall length (mm)	Weight (kg)	Feed
France	observer's machine gun Lewis Mk 23	7.7	1,140	8.5	drum magazine for 97 rounds
Britain	observer's machine gun Vickers Mk F	7.9	1,050	11,5	drum magazine for 97 rounds
Poland	observer's machine gun wz. 37 ŇpupÓ	7.9	1,080	7,0	drum magazine for 91 rounds
France	pilot's machine gun Vickers wz. 09	7.7	1,110	14,5	sackcloth belt for 250 rounds
Britain	pilot's machine gun Vickers wz.08/19	7.9	no data	no data	metal belt (links)
Britain	pilot's machine gun Vickers wz. E.	7.9	no data	no data	metal belt (links)
Poland	pilot's machine gun wz. 33	7.9	1,000	11,5	metal belt (links)
Poland	pilot's machine gun wz. 36	7.9			metal belt (links)
Poland	cannon wz. 38 D	20	1,897	38,5	drum magazine for 60 rounds or metal belt (links)

Aeronautical guns captured, purchased or produced in Poland (numbers)

Type, model, calibre	Number in the Polish Air Force
observer's machine gun Parabellum wz. 14, cal. 7, 9	40
observer's machine gun Schwarzlose wz. 07/12, cal. 8 mm.	45
observer's machine gun Lewis Mk 15, cal. 7, 7 mm	600
observer's machine gun Vickers Mk F, cal. 7, 9 mm	907
pilot's machine gun Maxim wz. 08, cal. 7, 9 mm	3
pilot's machine gun Maxim wz. 10 Rus. cal. 7,62 mm	1
pilot's machine gun Maxim wz. 08/15 cal. 7, 9 mm	approximately 120
pilot's machine gun Schwarzlose wz. 07/12 cal. 8 mm	65
pilot's machine gun Vickers Mk 09, cal. 7, 7 mm	approximately 670
pilot's machine gun Vickers Mk 09/18, cal. 7, 7 and 7, 9 mm	approximately 780
pilot's machine gun Vickers Mk E, cal. 7, 9 mm	approximately 300
machine gun Lewis, wz. 15, cal. 7, 7 mm	12
machine gun Vickers, wz. 09, cal. 7, 7 mm	10
machine gun Schwarzlose, wz. 09, cal. 8 mm	2
machine gun Colt, wz. 14, cal. 7, 7 mm	9
pilot's machine gun wz. 33, cal. 7, 9 mm	472
pilot's machine gun wz. 33A, cal. 7, 9 mm	200
pilot's machine gun wz. 36, cal. 7, 9 mm	469
observer's machine gun wz. 47, 'pup', cal. 7, 9	339

Armament of fighter aircraft produced in Poland, by types

Type	Gun armament	feed number of rounds rate of fire (shots per min.)	gunsight	camera gun	bomb weight	bomb racks	flare dispenser	fire power (kg/s)
Ansaldo A-1 Balilla	2 m.g. Vickers wz. 09, 7, 7 mm	metal belt 2 x 300 500	Chretien					0.195
SPAD 61 C1	2 m.g. Vickers wz. 09, 7, 7	metal belt 2 x 500 850	Chretien Collbert	K-28			French pistol cal. 35 mm, 10 rounds	0.363
PWS-A	2 m.g. Vickers wz. 09/18, 7, 9	metal belt 2 x 500 850	Chretien	K-28			French pistol cal. 35 mm, 10 rounds	0.363
PWS-10	2 m.g. Vickers wz. 09/18, 7, 9	metal belt 2 x 500 850	Chretien Collbert	K-28			French pistol cal. 35 mm, 10 rounds	0.363
PZL P.7a	2 m.g. Vickers wz. E, 7, 9	metal belt 2 x 700 1000	bead and ring, Skoda	K-28			French pistol cal. 35 mm, 12 rounds	0.427
PZL P.11c	2 mg. wz. 33, 7, 9	metal belt 2 x 700 1100	bead and ring JS-2	K-28	35	2x12SW	Perkun wz. 36 pistol cal. 35 mm,, 12 rounds	0.469
PZL P.11c	4 m.g. wz. 33, 7, 9	metal belt 2 x 700, 2 x 400 1100	bead and ring JS-2	K-28	25	2x12SW	Perkun wz. 36 pistol cal. 35 mm, 12 rounds	0.934
PZL P.24a (exports only)	2 m.g. wz 33, 7, 9 2 Oerklikon FF cannon, 20	metal belt 2 x 600 1100 drum magas. 2x45 (90) 530	bead and ring JS-2	Wiliamson	50	SW	Perkun wz. 36 pistol cal. 35 mm, 12 rounds	2.660

Reconnaissance and bomber aircraft produced in Poland (selected)

Type	Fixed gun armament	feed number of rounds rate of fire (shots (per min.)	Movable gun armament gunsight, rotatable mount	feed number of rounds rate of fire (shots per min.)	Bombs weight	Racks	bomb sights	flares	flare dispenser
Ansaldo A-300-2	2 m.g. Vickers wz. 09, 7. 7	metal belt 2 x 200 500	2 m.g. Lewis, wz. 15, 7, 7 Reile-Scult	drum mag. 4x97 600	144	SW	STAe		
Potez XV A-2	1 m.g. Vickers wz. 09, 7. 7	metal belt 1 x 300 500	2 m.g. Lewis wz. 15, 7, 7 Reile-Scoult Scarff	drum mag. 10x97 600	125	Cassette and GPU	STAe		
Potez XXVII A-2	1 m.g. Vickers wz. 09, 7, 7	metal belt 1 x 300 500	2 m.g. Lewis wz. 23, 7. 7 Reile-Scoult Scarff	drum mag. 10x97 600	225	Cassette and GPU	STAe		
Potez XXV B-2	1 m.g. Vickers wz. 09/18, 7. 7	metal belt 1 x 500 850	2 m.g. Vickers wz. F, 7. 9 Norman T07 and Vickers	drum mag. 10x97 650	500	Cassette Michelin and GPU, SW, ZK	STAe	2 Holt flares	French pistol, cal. 35, 10 rounds
Potex XXV Jupiter	1 m.g. Vickers, wz. E, 7. 9	metal belt 1 x 500 1000	2 m.g. Vickers wz. F, 7. 9 Norman Vickers	drum mag. 10x97 650	500	Cassette Michelin and GPU, SW, ZK	STAe	2 Holt flares	French pistol, cal. 35, 10 rounds
Lublin R. VIII	1 m.g. Vickers wz. 09/18, 7. 9	metal belt 1 x 300 850	2 m.g. Vickers wz. F, 7. 9 Norman Vickers	drum mag. 10x97 650	300	GPU, SW	STAe		French pistol, cal. 35, 10 rounds
PZL P.23B *Karaś*	1 m.g. wz. 33, 7. 9	metal belt 1 x 500 1100	2 m.g. Vickers wz. F, 7. 9 Norman PZL hydraulic PZL	drum mag. 10x97 650	700	PZL wz. 37	RH-32	w race wz. 36	Perkun wz. 36 pistol cal 35, 12 rounds
Fokker F.VIIB 3m.	1 m.g. Vickers wz. 09,18, 7. 9	metal belt 1 x 500 850	3 m.g. Vickers, wz. F, 7. 9 TO0	drum mag. 15x97 650	1000	SW, Alcan	STAe lub OPL Kolberg	2 Holt flares	French pistol, cal. 35, 10 rounds
PZL P.37B *Łoś*	–	–	3 m.g. wz. 37, 7. 9 Fk-38 semi-rotatable mounts	drum mag. 18x97 1100	3580	PZL 20x100 wz. 37	TH-32 lub Goertz	Ð	Perkun wz. 36 pistol cal. 35, 12 rounds

Polish military aircraft (numbers) 1918–1924

Type	Captured	Built in Poland	Purchases abroad and gifts					Unknown origin	Total
			Britain	Austria	France	Germany	Italy		
AEG C-IV	91								91
AEG J-I	2								2
AEG N-1	3								3
AGO C-II	1					1			2
Albatros C-I	48					1			49
Albatros C-III	15								15
Albatros C-VII	27								27
Albatros C-X	32								32
Albatros C-XII	24								24
Albatros C-XV						18			18
Albatros J-I	10								10
Anatra Decan	3								3
Anatra Anasal (DS)	8								8
Ansaldo A-300-2		79					1		80
Ansaldo A-300-3							16		16
Ansaldo A-300-4							12		12
Aviatik C-II	1								1
Aviatik C-III	8								8
Avro 504K	1								1
Brandenburg C-I	22								22
Brandenburg C-I (Lwów)		14							14
Brandenburg (Krakow)		15 (30)?							15
Breguet XIV	2				156				158
Bristol F.2B Fighter			107						107
DFW C-II	1								1
DFW C-IV	3								3
DFW C-V	35					28			63
de Havilland DH-9			20						20
Farman F-10	10								10
Halberstadt CL-II	16								16
Halberstadt C-V	12								12
Halberstadt CL-IV	3								3
Hannover CL-II	24	3							27
Hannover Cl-V	1								1
Libied XII	1								1
Lloyd C-IV	7								7
Lloyd C-V	6								6
LVG C II	14								14
LVG C V	91					30		30	151
LVG C VI	12					3			15
Morane Saulnier MS-30	5								5
Oeffag C-I series 51	4								4
Oeffag C-II series 52	15								15
RE-8	1								1
Rumpler C-I	84								84
Rumpler C-IV	36					2			38
Rumpler C-V	1								1
Rumpler C-VII	3					7			10
Rumpler C-VIII	6								6
Sablatnik C-I	2								2
Salmson IIA2	1				52				53
SEA IV C2					1				1
SPAD A2	1								1
Sopwith 1 1/2 Strutter	3								3
SVA-10							86		86
SVA-5							3		3
SVA-9							1		1
Voisin III	6								6
Albatros D-II	1								1

Polish military aircraft (numbers) 1918–1924 *(continued)*

Type	Captured	Built in Poland	Purchases abroad and gifts: Britain	Austria	France	Germany	Italy	Unknown origin	Total
Albatros D-III	24					2			26
Albatros D-V	8					2			10
Ansaldo Balilla	69						37		69
Fokker D-VII	5				20	25			50
Fokker E-V	17								17
Martinsyde F-4 Buzzard			1						1
Nieuport 11C1 Bebe	2								2
Nieuport 16C1	1								1
Nieuport 17C1	7								7
Nieuport 17 bis C1	2								2
Nieuport 21E1	5								5
Nieuport 23C1	14								14
Nieuport 24C1	1								1
Nieuport 24 bis C1	5								5
Nieuport (unknown type)	4								4
Oeffag D-III		10		38		2			48
Pfalz D-XII						2			2
SE.5a			2						2
Sopwith F-1 Camel	1		1						2
Sopwith 5F-1 Dolphin			10						10
SPAD VIIC1	? unknown number				33				33 (?)
SPAD XIIIC1					40				40
RBVZ Ilya Muromets	1								1
Friedrichshafen G-III	2					1			3
Gotha G-III	5								5
Albatros B-I	5								5
Albatros B-II	88							28	116
Bleriot September	2	4			5				11
Brandenburg B-I	40								40
Caudron G-III E2					51				51
Etrich IV Taube	2					3			3
Farman II, IV, VII						2			2
Lohner 'C' B-II	1								1
LVG B-II/B-III	4								4
Morane Saulnier MS-29R1 Rouleur					5				5
Morane Saulnier MS-30E1					21				21
Nieuport 8 D2					21				21
Nieuport 80E2					15				15
Nieuport 83E1					22				22

Made in Poland (and/or used by Polish Air Force) after 1921

Type	Number foreign	made in Poland	used by the PAF	Period of use, including reserve and civil aviation
A-1 Balilla	35	70	105	1920–1927
SP-1		1		1926 (tests)
SPAD-51 C1	50		50	1926–1930
SPAD-61 C1	250	30	280	1925–1932
PWS-1		1		1927 (tests)
PWS-A	1	50	1	1929–1935
Wibault 70C1		25	25	1930–1937
PWS-10M1		2		1930 (tests)
PWS-10		80	80	1931–1939
PWS-15		1		1930 (tests)
PZL P.1		2		1929–1930 (tests)
PZL P.6		2		1930–1931 (tests)
PZL P.7		2		1931 (tests)
PZL P.7a		149	149	1932–1939
PZL P.8/9		2		1931–1932 (tests)
PZL P.11		3		1931–1932 (tests)
PZL P.11a		30	30	1934–1939
PZL P.11b		50	–	
PZL P.11c		175	175	1935–1939
PZL P.24		3	1	1933–34 (tests), 1 w 1939
PZL P.24a	20	19		
PZL P.24b		14		
PZL P.24c	20	46		
PZL P.24e	40	6		
PZL P.24f	60	51		
PZL P.24g		6		
PZL P.38 *Wilk*		2		1938–1939 (tests)
PZL P.50 *Jastrząb*		2		1939 (tests)
PZL P.11c *Kobuz*		1		1939 (tests)
Ansaldo A-300	30	50	80	1920–1925
Potez XV	110	135	245	1924–1935
Potez XXVII	20	155	175	1925–1937
Potez XXV	16	300	316	1927–1939
Breguet XIX	253		253	1925–1939
WZ-X		4	4	1926–1935
Lublin R. VIII		6	6	1928–1932
Amiot 123BN3	2		2	1928–1929
PWS-19B2		1		
PZL P.23 *Karaś*		3		1934–1935 (tests)
PZL P.23A *Karaś*		40	40	1936–1939
PZL P.23B *Karaś*		210	210	1936–1939
PZL P.42		1	1	1936–1939 (tests)
PZL P.43		12		
PZL P.43A		42	6	1939
PZL P.46 *Sum*		2		1938–1939 (tests)
F-68 Goliath	32		32	1926–1935
Fokker FVII B/3m		31	23	1930–1939
Fokker FVII A/1m	6		3	1938–1939
PZL P.30B *Żubr*		1		1936 (tests)
LWS-4 *Żubr*		15	15	1938–1939
LWS-6 *Żubr*		1	1	1938–1939 (tests)
PZL P.37 *Łoś*		2		1936–1939 (tests)
PZL P.37A *Łoś*		30	30	1938–1939
PZL P.37B *Łoś*		94	45	1939
PWS-5T2		7	7	1929–1935
PZL Ł-2		20	20	1929–1935
Lublin R-X		7	7	1929–1935
PWS-6		1	1	1930 (tests)
Lublin R-XIII A/B		51	51	1932–1939

Made in Poland (and/or used by Polish Air Force) after 1921 *(continued)*

Type	Number foreign	Number made in Poland	Number used by the PAF	Period of use, including reserve and civil aviation
Lublin R-XIII C		48	48	1933–1939
Lublin R-XIII D		95	95	1933–1939
Lublin R-XIII E		1		1934 (tests)
Lublin R-XIII F		58	58	1934–1939
RWD-14		4		1935–1936 (tests)
LWS-14 *Czapla*		65	65	1937–1939
LWS-3 *Mewa*		20	2	1938–1939
Hanriot HD-14	70		70	1924–1934
Hanriot HD-28		220	220	1925–1939
Hanriot HD-19	1	55	56	1924–1937
MS AR-35EP2	70		70	1925–1939
Bartel BM-2		1		1927 (tests)
Bartel BM-4		75	75	1928–1939
Bartel BM-5		60	60	1929–1939
Bartel BM-6		1		1930 (tests)
DH-60G	3		3	1928–1935
PWS-11SM		2		1929–1930 (tests)
PWS-12SM		2		1930–1931 (tests)
Lublin R-XIV		15	15	1930–1939
RWD-8 PWS		500	350	1934–1939
PWS-14		20	20	1933–1939
PWS-16		20	20	1933–1939
PWS-16bis		21	21	1934–1939
PWS-18	1	40	41	1937–1939
PWS-26		310	310	1934–1939
PWS-33 *Wyżeł*		2		1938–1939 (tests)
PWS-35 *Ogar*		2		1938–1939 (tests)
Breguet XIVT	1		1	1926–1927
HD-14S	2		2	1925–1935
HD-28S		16	16	1927–1935
Lublin R. XIVb		6	6	1932–1939
RWD-13S		3	3	1937–1937
Cierva	1			1934–1927 (?)
Aircraft ordered in 1939: 120 MS.406s 10 Hawker Hurricane Is 1 Supermarine Spitfire I 100 Fairey Battles				

468: *Ultimately 320 examples of the PWS-26 were built (Kopański)*

Aircraft of the naval aviation 1920–23

	Type of aircraft	Entry into service	quantity	Notes
1	Friedrichshafen FF 33H	1920	1	Ex-German, repaired by Polish technicians at Puck
2	Fokker D VII (land-based)	1920	1	Ex-German, repaired by Polish technicians at Puck
3	Friedrichshafen FF 33E	1920	1	No. 8 purchased in Gdańsk
4	Friedrichshafen FF 33L	1920	1	No. 9 purchased in Gdańsk
5	Friedrichshafen FF 49b	1920	1	No. 1 purchased in Gdańsk
6	Lubeck Travemünde F 4	1920	1	No. 7 purchased in Gdańsk
7	Sablatnik SF 5	1920	1	No. ? purchased in Gdańsk
8	Albatros B II (land-based)	1920	1	No. 4 transferred from Oficerska Szkoła Obserwatorów Lotniczych at Toruń
9	Albatros B II (land-based)	1921	2	
10	Hansa Brandenburg; NW	1921	1	No. 6
11	DFW C IV (land-based)	1921	2	
12	Albatros D V (land-based)	1921	1	No. 5
13	Nieuport Macchi M 9	1921	7 + 3	Nos. 2-1 to 2-9 assembled in 1922–23
14	FBA S 4 (S 180)	1921	9 + 4	Struck off charge prior to assembly due to technical condition

Aircraft of the naval aviation 1924–39

	Type of aircraft	Entry into service	quantity	Notes
1	Lioré et Olivier LeO H-13B	XI 1924	4	Assembled in March 1925, nos. 1-1 to 1-4
2	Schreck FBA-17 HE2	1926–27	6	Nos. 4-1 to 4-6
3	Schreck FBA-17 MHT2	1926–27	12	Nos. 5-1 to 5-10 + two civil ones 'LOPP' and 'Lubliniak'
4	Latham 43 HB3	1926–27	8	Nos. 3-1 to 3-8
5	CAMS-30E	1926–27	4	Nos. 2-1 to 2-4 (after the Macchi M-9s struck off charge)
6	Lioré et Olivier LeO H-135B3	1926–27	7	Nos. 6-1 to 6-7
7	WWS Bartel BM-300*	1930	5	Nos 56-68 to 56-72
8	Hanriot HD-14E2	About 1928	1	No. 30-32 on wheeled undercarriage
9	Hanriot HD-28S	About 1928	1	No. 30-14S on wheeled undercarriage
10	Morane Saulnier MS-35AR/EP2	About 1928	1	No. 50-46 on wheeled undercarriage
11	Lublin R-XIII hydro	1931	1	Prototype no. 54-15 on floats
12	Lublin R-VIII bis/ter/hydro 1	1932	3	Nos. 801-803
13	Lublin R-XIII bis/hydro	1932	3	Nos. 701-703
14	Lublin R-XIII ter/hydro	1934	10	Nos. 704-713
15	Lublin R-XII G/hydro	1934	6	Nos. 714-719
16	Lublin R-XIII G	1934	1	No. 720 on wheeled undercarriage
17	Lublin R-XX	1934	1	No. 806
18	RWD 17W	1938	1 + 5	Prototype SP-BPW, batch of 5. Failed to arrive at MDLot
19	CRDA CANT Z-506 Airone	1939	1	First of the batch of 6 aircraft
20	Nikol A-2	1939	1	Built at MDLot workshops as the future amphibian for the ORP 'Gryf'
21	RWD 13	1939	2	Civil RWD 13s, SP-ATB and SP-BML, impressed into the Pluton Łącznikowy

* BM-300 was a naval version for Polish Navy of Bartel BM-5c

Number of Eskadras equipped with individual types of aircraft

Fighter	1923	1924	1925	1926	1927	1928	1929	1930	1931	1932	1933	1934	1935	1936	1937	1938	1939
Ansaldo A-1	4	4	4														
Spad 51			1	2	2	2	2										
Spad 61			1	6	6	6	6	4	3								
Wibault 72								2	2	2							
PWS-A								2	2	2	1	1					
PWS-10									1	4	4	4					
PZL P.7											3	7	11	6	3	3	3
PZL P.11													2	7	10	12	12
Br XIX/P.XXV								1	1	1	1						
Total Fighters	4	4	6	8	8	8	8	9	9	9	9	12	13	13	13	15	15
Line	**1923**	**1924**	**1925**	**1926**	**1927**	**1928**	**1929**	**1930**	**1931**	**1932**	**1933**	**1934**	**1935**	**1936**	**1937**	**1938**	**1939**
Bristol F.2	3	3															
Breguet XIV	3	3	1														
Ansaldo A-300	3	3	3														
Potez XV		2	16	17	13	5	2										
Breguet XX				1	2	2	2	4	6	7	7	7	7	5	2		
Potez XXVII					3	11	12	9	2								
Potez XXV							1	4	9	10	10	10	10	10	2		
PZL P.23														2	13	17	12
Total Line	9	11	20	18	18	18	17	17	17	17	17	17	17	17	17	17	12
Spotting/Accompanying	**1923**	**1924**	**1925**	**1926**	**1927**	**1928**	**1929**	**1930**	**1931**	**1932**	**1933**	**1934**	**1935**	**1936**	**1937**	**1938**	**1939**
PZL Ł.2								1	2	2							
Lublin R.XIII										1	4	7	8	8	8	18	7
RWD-14																	5
Total Spotting								1	2	3	4	7	8	8	8	18	12
Bomber	**1923**	**1924**	**1925**	**1926**	**1927**	**1928**	**1929**	**1930**	**1931**	**1932**	**1933**	**1934**	**1935**	**1936**	**1937**	**1938**	**1939**
Fokker F.VII							1	2	3	3	3	3	3	3	3		
PZL P.37																3	4
Total Bomber							1	2	3	3	3	3	3	3	3	3	4
Naval	**1923**	**1924**	**1925**	**1926**	**1927**	**1928**	**1929**	**1930**	**1931**	**1932**	**1933**	**1934**	**1935**	**1936**	**1937**	**1938**	**1939**
Macchi M-9	1	1	1														
LeO H. 13/35				1	1	1	1	1	1	1	1						
Latham 43					1	1	1	1	1	1	1	1					
Lublin R. XIII ter												1	2	2	2	1	1
Total Naval	1	1	1	1	2	2	2	2	2	2	2	2	2	2	2	1	1

Losses of flying personnel in flying accidents 1921–1st September 1939

Years	Pilots	Observers	Gunners	Technicians	Total	Years	Pilots	Observers	Gunners	Technicians	Total
1921	11	2	–	4	17	1931	26	8	1	–	35
1922	7	–	1	1	9	1932	15	3	1	–	19
1923	16	7	–	4	27	1933	19	10	–	3	32
1924	13	3	–	3	19	1934	19	3	–	2	24
1925	12	4	–	1	17	1935	19	4	–	2	25
1926	11	4	–	3	18	1936	15	3	3	3	24
1927	12	–	–	–	12	1937	26	4	2	5	37
1928	18	6	–	3	27	1938	32	13	7	6	58
1929	22	4	–	1	27	to 1 Sept 1939	33	12	5	2	52
1930	14	4	–	5	23	**TOTAL**					**502**

Unit code letters (radio call code)

Unit	Code letter
1 Pułk Lotniczy	N
2 Pułk Lotniczy	K
3 Pułk Lotniczy	P
4 Pułk Lotniczy	T
5 Pułk Lotniczy	L
6 Pułk Lotniczy	S
CWL-1 (Deblin)	D
CWL-1 (Radom)	R
Szkoła Strzelania i Bombardowania	U
Centrum Wyszkolenia Podoficerów Lotnictwa CWL-2	M.
Centralna Eskadra Treningowa	Z

Supreme Commanders of the Polish Air Force

Commander	From	To
gen. bryg. pil. Hipolit Łossowski Szef Sekcji Żeglugi Napowietrznej Ministerstwa Spraw Wojskowych	Dec. 1918	July 1919
gen. bryg. pil. Gustaw Macewicz Szef Departamentu IV Żeglugi Powietrznej Ministerstwa Spraw Wojskowych	Aug. 1919	Dec. 1922
gen. broni. pil. Francois-Leon Leveque Szef Departamentu IV Żeglugi Powietrznej Ministerstwa Spraw Wojskowych	Jan. 1923	June 1924
gen. bryg. pil. Włodzimierz Zagórski Szef Departamentu Lotnictwa Ministerstwa Spraw Wojskowych	July 1924	Mar. 1926
gen. bryg. pil. Inż. Ludomił Rayski Szef Departamentu Aeronautyki Ministerstwa Spraw Wojskowych	May 1926	Mar. 1939
gen. bryg. pil. Inż. Ludomił Rayski Dowódca Lotnictwa	Aug. 1936	Mar. 1939
gen. bryg. pil. Wladyslaw Kalkus Dowódca Lotnictwa	Mar. 1939	Sep. 1939

Foreign flyers in Polish service

French

Ppłk. de Vergnette*	*Kpt.* Bollon	*Por.* Buisson
Mjr. Tetu*	*Kpt.* Bonneton	*Por.* Hotte
Mjr. Chapelet*	*Kpt.* Vincent	*Por.* Elave
Mjr. de Maisonneuve*	*Kpt.* Pacaquet	*Por.* Birkel
Mjr. Mesonait	*Kpt.* Trouver	*Por.* Gibbon
Mjr. Nardin*	*Kpt.* Lavidalie	*Por.* Lacome
Kpt. Eclancher*	*Kpt.* Sollier	*Por.* Pollak
Kpt. Hugon*	*Kpt.* Parteaux	*Por.* Geille
Kpt. Lemaitre*	*Kpt.* Delattre	*Por.* Haegelen
Kpt. Bellisant*	*Kpt.* Terrasson	*Por.* Goraguer
Por. de Gavardie*	*Kpt.* Mennier	*Ppor.* Schurk
Por. Lapeyrotte*	*Kpt.* Bovidier	*Ppor.* Bulteau
Por. Lienemann*	*Kpt.* Peron	*Ppor.* Cabella
Mjr. Rocheford	*Kpt.* Lete	*Ppor.* Cottier
Mjr. Mauger de Varennes	*Kpt.* Avil	*Ppor.* Simoni
Mjr. de Bernis	*Por.* Henin	*Ppor.* Vachet
Mjr. de Chivre	*Por.* Teppe	*Ppor.* Darmaillac
Kpt. Ollivain		

British

Kpt. Tanqueray** | *Kpt.* Stehling** | *Por.* Woodhouse**

Belgian

Ppor. Robert Vanderauvera***

Italian

Ppor. Veniero de Piza*** | *Ppor.* Virgilio Mastrelli***

American

Pplk. Cedric E. Faunt le Roy****	*Por.* Thomas H. Garlick****
Pplk. Merian C. Cooper****	*Por.* Edmund P. Graves****
Mjr. George M. Crawford****	*Por.* I. Inglis Maitland****
Kpt. Arthur H. Kelley****	*Por.* Kenneth M. Murray****
Kpt. T.V. Mc Callum****	*Por.* E. H. Noble****
Kpt. Edward C. Corsi****	*Por.* H. C. Rorison****
Por. Elliot W. Chess****	*Por.* K. O. Shrewsbury****
Por. Carl H. Clarc****	*Por.* John C. Speak****
Por. Earl F. Evans****	

* French Military Mission in Poland
** 1st Reconnaissance Squadron
*** 6th Reconnaissance Squadron
**** 7th Fighter Squadron

Designations of Polish aircraft

Designations 1919–25

Type of aircraft	Serial prefix
Fokker E-V	00
Albatros D-III, Oeffag D-III	0
Rumpler C-I	1
Albatros II	3
Albatros C-X	4
AEG CIV	5
DFW CV	7
Hannover Roland DL, II, CLII	8
LVG CV	9
Breguet XIV	10
SPAD VII C1	15
Ansaldo Balilla	16
Albatros BII	17
CWL CLII (prototype of the Polish version)	18
Bristol F.2B Fighter	20
MS-30	21
Fokker DVII	22
SPAD XII C1	24
DH-9	26

Designations 1925–39

Type of aircraft	Serial prefix	Type of aircraft	Serial prefix
SPAD 61 C1	1	HD-14, H-28	30
SPAD 51 C1	2	HD-19, H-19	32
Wibault 70 C1	3	Bartel BM-4H	33
PWS-A	4	RWD-8	34
PWS-10	5	MS-35	50
PZL P.7a	6	Bartel BM-5	53
PZL P.11a	7	Lublin R-XIV	54
PZL P.11c	8	PWS-12 (PWS-14)	57
		PWS-16	59
Breguet XIV	10	PWS-18	80
Potez XV	40	PWS-26	81
Potez XXVII	41		
Potez XXV	42	Breguet XIV T Bis	S. 10
PZL P.23 *Karaś*	44	Lublin R-XVI Bis	11
Breguet XIX	60	RWD-13S	12
		H-28S	30. _S
Fokker F-VII	70		
LWS-4 *Żubr*	71		
PZL P.37 *Łoś*	72		
PWS-5	51		
Lublin R-X	52		
PZL Ł-2	55		
Lublin R-XIII A-D	56		
Lublin R-XIII F	58		

Achievements of the Polish aviation development

	Designer	use	Notes
Puławski wing	Zygmunt Puławski	P.1 to P.24 series of fighters	copied in foreign aircraft
scissor undercarriage	Zygmunt Puławski	P.1 to P.24 series of fighters	used in post-war designs
sandwich skin project	Piotr Tulicz of Wytwórnia 'Samolot'	(not used)	project from 1926, sandwich skin has been popularly used on many aircraft after the war
wing torsion box	Franciszek Misztal	PZL 19, P.23, P.37	also used on Tu-2
Rudlicki V-tail	Jerzy Rudlicki	tests including a Hanriot H-28	project of 1920, used in many aircraft after the war
vertical tail lowered in flight	Jerzy Teisseyre and Augustyn Zadaniewski	tests on Lublin R-XIII aircraft	tests in 1932–1934
Wing high-lift devices on RWD aircraft	DWL company	RWD-6, RWD-9 aircraft	virtually one of the first series produced STOL aircraft (International Challenge de Tourisme competition winners)
Twin-wheels	Piotr Kubicki	PZL P.37 Los	excellent operation of the undercarriage on rough terrain

Organisation of Polish Air Force Schools by year

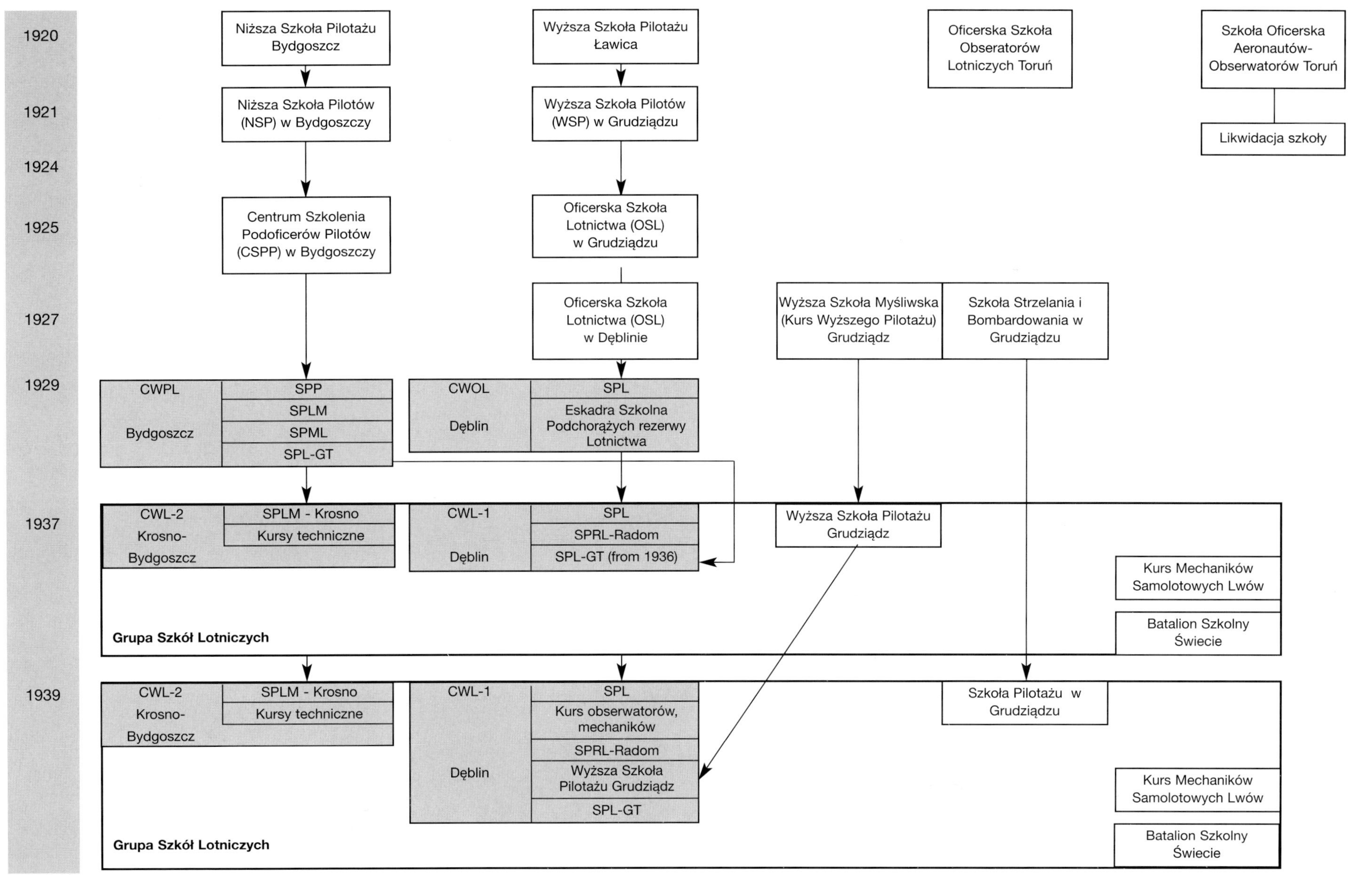

BIBLIOGRAPHY

CAW Archives in Rembertów
Polish Institute and Sikorski Museum Archives in London
Polish Aviation Museum Archives in Krakow.

Belcarz B. – *Samolot szkolno akrobacyjny PWS-26 (training-acrobatic aircraft PWS-26)*, MON Warsaw 1988.
Chwałczyk T., Glass A. – *Samoloty PWS (PWS Aircraft)*, WKŁ Warsaw 1980
Cieslak K., Gawrych W., Glass A. – *Samoloty mysliwskie wrzesnia 1939 (Fighter Aircraft of September 1939)*, NOT SIGMA Wasaw 1987
Cumft O., Kujawa H.K. – *Księ ga lotników polskich poległych, zmarłych zaginionych 1939–1946 (Book of Polish Airmen 1939–1946)*, MON 1989
Cynk J. B. – *History of The Polish Air Force 1918–1968*. Osprey Publishing 1972.
Cynk J. B. – *Samolot bombowy PZL P.37 Łoś (PZL P.37 Łoś Bomber Aircraft)*, WKŁ Warsaw 1990
Cynk J. B. – *Siły lotnicze Polski i Niemiec (Air Forces of Poland and Germany)*, WKŁ Warsaw 1989
Cynk J. B. –*The Polish Air Force at War*, Schiffer Military History Atglen 1998
Falkowski J. –*Z wiatrem w twarz (With the Wind in My Face)*, MON Warsaw 1990
Glass A. – *Polskie konstrukcje lotnicze 1893–1939 (Polish Aircraft Designs 1893–1939)*, WKŁ Warsaw 1977
Glass A., Kopański T., Makowski T. – *PZL P.11c pt. 1 and 2*, AJ-Press 1997
Gretzyngier R., Matusiak W. – *Polish Aces of World War 2*, Osprey Publishing London 1998
Kędzierski J. – *Z kabiny obserwatowa (From the Observer's Cockpit)*, MON 1980
Koniarek J. – *Polish Air Force 1939–1945*, Squadron Signal Carrollton, Texas 1994
Kopański T. – *16 (39-a) Eskadra Wywiadowcza 1919–1920*, WIH 1994
Kopański T., Sikora, – *PZL P.23 Karaś*, AJ-Press
Kowalski T. J. – *Godło i barwa w lotnictwie polskim 1918–1939 (Polish Air Force Emblems and Colours 1918–1939)*, WKŁ Warsaw 1981
Krolikierwicz T. – *Polski samolot i barwa (Polish Aircraft and Colour)*, MON Warsaw 1990
Kurowski A. – *Lotnictwo polskie w 1939 roku (Polish Air Force in 1939)*, MON Warsaw 1962
Kurowski A. – *Lotnicy w bitwie nad Bzurą (Airmen in the Battle on Bzura)*, RSW Ruch Warsaw 1975
Luranc Z. – *Samolo myśliwski PZL P-8 (Skrzydla w miniaturze nr 8)* AVIA PRESS *(PZL P-8 Fighter Aircraft)*, AVIA PRESS Gdansk 1992
Michulec R., – *Elita Luftwaffe (Elite of Luftwaffe)*, Armagedon Gdynia 1999
Morgała A. – *Polskie samoloty wojskowe 1918–1939 (Polish Military Aircraft 1918–1939)*, MON Warsaw 1972
Morgała A. – *Polskie samoloty wojskowe 1939–1945 (Polish Military Aircraft 1939–1945)*, MON Warsaw 1976
Morgała A. – *Samoloty w polskim lotnictwie morskim*, WKŁ *(Aircraft of the Polish Naval Aviation)*, WKŁ Warsaw 1985
Morgała A. – *Samoloty wojskowe w Polsce 1918–1924 (Military Aircraft in Poland 1918–1924)* Bellona-Lampart Warsaw 1997
Olejko A. – *Morski Dywizjon Lotniczy*, Ajaks Pruszków 1992
Olejko A. – *Polski Cant* (Polish Cant), Karnak Tarnobrzeg 1998
Olejko A. – *Rzeczna Eskadra Lotnicza Flotylli Pińskiej*, Ajaks Pruszków 1994
Pawlak J. – *Brygada Pościgowa – alarm! (Pursuit brigade – Scramble!)*, MON Warsaw 1977
Pawlak J. – *Polskie eskadry w latach 1918–1939 (Polish Eskadras in 1918–1939)*, WKŁ Warsaw 1989
Pawlak J. – *Polskie eskadry w Wojnie Obronnej 1939 (Polish Eskadras in the Defence War 1939)*, WKŁ Warsaw 1982
Pawlak J. – *Polskie eskadry w wojnie obronnej (Polish Eskadras in the Defence War)*, WKŁ Warsaw 1991
Pawlak J. – *Pamieci lotników polskich 1918–1945 (To memory of Polish airman 1918–1945)*, Bellona Warszawa 1998
Pawlak J., Nowakowski W. – *Brygada Bombowa – kurs bojowy! (Bomber Brigade – Combat Course!)* MON Warsaw 1983
Prauss S. P. – *Z Zakopanego na Stag Lane (From Zakopane to Stag Lane)*, Ossolimeum Wroclaw 1996
Rolski T. H. – *Uwaga, wszystkie samoloty! (Attention, All Aircraft!)*, PAX Warsaw 1974
Skalski S. – *Czarne krzyże nad Polską (Black Crosses over Poland)*, MON Warsaw 1975
Slawinski K. – *Rozpoznać wroga z północy (Reconnoitre the Enemy from the North)*, MON Warsaw 1979
Steyer W. – *Samotny półwysep (Lone Peninsula)*, Wydawnictwo Poznańskie Poznań 1983
Colletive – *Lotnicy września (September Airmen)*, Nasza Ksiegarnia Warsaw 1972
Zbiorowa pod redakcją M. Romeyki – *Ku czci poległych lotników*. Ksiega pamiątkowa, Warszawa 1933

Magazines

Aeroplan
Air Enthusiast
Lotnictwo
Militaria
Skrzydlata Polska
Wojskowy Przegląd Historyczny